Lin MacDonald

LINCO PRODUCTIONS LTD.
1846 S.E. MARINE DRIVE
VANCOUVER, B.C. V5P 2R8
PH: (604) 327-6401 FAX: (604) 327-8314

DESIGNER HOTELS

DESIGNER HOTELS

**Albrecht Bangert
and Otto Riewoldt**

The Vendome Press · New York

Copyright © 1993 Albrecht Bangert and Otto Riewoldt
Copyright © 1993 English translation Calmann & King

First published in the United States of America by
The Vendome Press, 515 Madison Avenue, New York, NY 10022.

Distributed in the United States of America and Canada by
Rizzoli International Publications, 300 Park Avenue South, New York, NY 10010.

All rights reserved. No part of this publication may be reproduced, stored in a retrieval system, or transmitted in any form or by any means without prior permission of the Publisher.

Library of Congress Cataloging-in-Publication Data
Bangert, Albrecht, 1944-
      Designer Hotels/by Albrecht Bangert and Otto Riewoldt.
      p.   cm.
      ISBN 0-86565-143-4
        1. Hotels, taverns, etc. 2. Architecture, Modern- - 20th century.
I. Riewoldt, Otto. II. Title.
NA7840.B36   1993   93-11121
728'. 5'09045- -dc20   CIP

This book was designed and produced by Calmann & King Ltd, London
Text design by Karen Stafford, D.Q.P, London
Translated from the German by Dr David McLintock
Research by Gudrun Thiel
Printed by Cayfosa in Barcelona

ACKNOWLEDGEMENTS

It would have been impossible to conduct this world-wide survey and present findings on the many-faceted development of hotel architecture and design without the energetic support of numerous hotel experts, architects, designers, photographers and journalists. The authors, Albrecht Bangert and Otto Riewoldt, and the project editor Gudrun Thiel, owe thanks to many colleagues and friends for their advice and support during the preparation of this ambitious project.

Special thanks are due to the photographer friends who generously placed their extensive material at our disposal: Richard Bryant, Santi Caleca, Bernd Limberger, Peter Moody Meyer, Deidi von Schaewen, Wolfgang Schwayer, Lisa Siegelmann.

We also owe thanks to all the designers and architects who readily gave us information about their projects, some not yet realized, above all to Arquitectonica, Miami; Elisabeth and Gottfried Böhm, Cologne; Branson Coates, London; Dieter Brell (Adieu New York), Wiesbaden; Coop Himmelblau, Vienna; Wolfgang Döring, Düsseldorf; Michael Graves, Princeton; Zaha M. Hadid, London; Hirsch/Bedner & Associates, Atlanta; Steven Holl, New York; OMA/Rem Koolhaas, Rotterdam; Murphy/Jahn, Chicago; Johanne and Gernot Nalbach, Berlin; Jean Nouvel and Emmanüel Cattani, Paris; Dirk Obliers, Selb; John C. Portman & Associates, Atlanta; Andrée Putman, Paris; Georg Ritschl, Berlin; Aldo Rossi, Milan; Ettore Sottsass and Johanna Grawunder, Milan; Siss AG, Geneva; Jan Wichers, Hamburg.

Thanks also go to the managers, colleagues, companies and agencies in the hotel business who helped with information and material, in particular: Wolfgang Berkenkamp (Wasserturm Hotel), Annette Biggs (Tophotels), Albert J. Kelly and Craig W. Parsons (Hyatt Hotels and Resorts), Sidney Leung (Island Shangri-La), Andreas Pflaum (Pflaums Posthotel), Silvia Pluschke (Maritim Hotels), Nicolas Rettie (The Halkin), Gabriele Rüdiger (Hyatt International), Claus Sendlinger (Travel Trends), Marriott Marquis/Atlanta, The Mirage/Las Vegas, Billie Strauss/Stuttgart.

We were consistently supported in our work by colleagues and friends Anne Brooks, London; Lynne Bryant, London; Barbette Havriliak, New York; Nicole Herzog, Madrid; Rita Werner, Paris. The international co-production and the English edition were handled by Sophie Collins, Joanne Lightfoot and Judy Rasmussen.

CONTENTS

Introduction   9

1 DESIGNER HOTELS   12

MORGANS HOTEL, NEW YORK, USA
INTERIOR DESIGN: ANDRÉE PUTMAN   14

WASSERTURM HOTEL, COLOGNE, GERMANY
ARCHITECTURE: KONRAD L. HEINRICH
INTERIOR DESIGN: ANDRÉE PUTMAN   20

LE LAC, KAWAGUCHIKO-CHO, JAPAN
INTERIOR DESIGN: ANDRÉE PUTMAN   26

LA VILLA, PARIS, FRANCE
INTERIOR DESIGN: MARIE-CHRISTINE DORNER   30

ART HOTEL SORAT, BERLIN, GERMANY
ARCHITECTURE: KLAUS EFFENBERGER
INTERIOR DESIGN: JOHANNE AND GERNOT NALBACH   34

PFLAUMS POSTHOTEL, PEGNITZ, GERMANY
INTERIOR DESIGN: DIRK OBLIERS   38

HAUTERIVE, BOULIAC, FRANCE
ARCHITECTURE/INTERIOR DESIGN: JEAN NOUVEL, EMMANÜEL CATTANI ET ASSOCIÉS   44

LES THERMES, DAX, FRANCE
ARCHITECTURE/INTERIOR DESIGN: JEAN NOUVEL, EMMANÜEL CATTANI ET ASSOCIÉS   48

LE CHEVAL BLANC, NÎMES, FRANCE
INTERIOR DESIGN: JEAN-MICHEL WILMOTTE   52

D-HOTEL, OSAKA, JAPAN
ARCHITECTURE/INTERIOR DESIGN: KIYOSHI SEY TAKEYAMA, AMORPHE ARCHITECTS   56

DREAMLAND HEIGHTS, SEASIDE, FLORIDA, USA
ARCHITECTURE/INTERIOR DESIGN: STEVEN HOLL   58

THE ROYALTON, NEW YORK, USA
INTERIOR DESIGN: PHILIPPE STARCK   62

THE PARAMOUNT, NEW YORK, USA
INTERIOR DESIGN: PHILIPPE STARCK   68

OTARU MARITTIMO, OTARU, JAPAN
INTERIOR DESIGN: BRANSON COATES ARCHITECTURE   72

THE TRITON, SAN FRANCISCO, USA
INTERIOR DESIGN: MICHAEL MOORE   76

KELLY'S HOTEL, BENSHEIM, GERMANY
INTERIOR DESIGN: ADIEU NEW YORK DESIGN, DIETER BRELL   80

IL PALAZZO, FUKUOKA, JAPAN
ARCHITECTURE: ALDO ROSSI/MORRIS ADJMI
INTERIOR DESIGN: SHIGERU UCHIDA, ALFREDO ARRIBAS, SHIRO KURAMATA, GAETANO PESCE, ALDO ROSSI/MORRIS ADJMI, ETTORE SOTTSASS   84

2 THE SALON HOTEL 92

LOS SEISES, SEVILLE, SPAIN
ARCHITECTURE/INTERIOR DESIGN: JORGE PENA MARTIN — 94

THE MONTALEMBERT, PARIS, FRANCE
INTERIOR DESIGN: CHRISTIAN LIAIGRE — 98

THE HALKIN, LONDON, UK
ARCHITECTURE/INTERIOR DESIGN: LABORATORIO ASSOCIATI, LORENZO CARMELLINI, ROCCO MAGNOLI — 104

COUR DES LOGES, LYON, FRANCE
ARCHITECTURE/INTERIOR DESIGN: YVES BOUCHARLAT, PIERRE VURPAS — 108

LA PERGOLESE, PARIS, FRANCE
INTERIOR DESIGN: RENA DUMAS — 112

THE HAVANA PALACE, BARCELONA, SPAIN
ARCHITECTURE/INTERIOR DESIGN: JOSEP JUANPERE MIRET, ANTONIO PUIG GUASCH — 116

THE IMPERIAL PALACE, ANNECY, FRANCE
ARCHITECTURE: SISS
INTERIOR DESIGN: ARC+ — 120

THE ROLANDSBURG, DÜSSELDORF, GERMANY
ARCHITECTURE/INTERIOR DESIGN: WOLFGANG DÖRING — 124

THE CLARIS, BARCELONA, SPAIN
ARCHITECTURE/INTERIOR DESIGN: MBM ARQUITECTES
J. MARTORELL, O. BOHIGAS, D. MACKAY, A. PUIGDOMENECH — 128

THE PORTMAN, SAN FRANCISCO, USA
ARCHITECTURE/INTERIOR DESIGN: JOHN PORTMAN & ASSOCIATES — 132

3 ARTIST HOTELS 136

THE FURKABLICK, FURKA PASS, SWITZERLAND
ARCHITECTURE (REBUILDING): REM KOOLHAAS/O.M.A. — 138

DER TEUFELHOF, BASEL, SWITZERLAND
ARCHITECTURE: HANS PÖSINGER
INTERIOR DESIGN: ARTISTS FROM SWITZERLAND, GERMANY AND FRANCE — 142

NEW SIRU, BRUSSELS, BELGIUM
INTERIOR DESIGN: ATELIER 20 — 146

SPADARI AL DUOMO, MILAN, ITALY
ARCHITECTURE: URBANO PIERINI
INTERIOR DESIGN: UGO LA PIETRA — 150

L'ATELIER SUL MARE, CASTEL DI TUSA, SICILY
INTERIOR DESIGN: MICHELLE CANCELLA, HIDETOSHI NAGASAWA, FABRIZIO PLESSI AND OTHERS — 154

4 THE ATRIUM HOTEL 158

ATLANTA MARRIOTT MARQUIS, ATLANTA, USA
ARCHITECTURE: JOHN PORTMAN & ASSOCIATES — 160

STERLING HOTEL HEATHROW, LONDON, UK
ARCHITECTURE: MANSER ASSOCIATES
INTERIOR DESIGN: MANSER ASSOCIATES/PETER GLYNN-SMITH ASSOCIATES — 164

THE ISLAND SHANGRI-LA, HONG KONG
ARCHITECTURE: WONG & OUYANG
INTERIOR DESIGN: LEESE ROBERTSON FREEMAN DESIGNERS — 168

HYATT REGENCY LA JOLLA, SAN DIEGO, USA
ARCHITECTURE/INTERIOR DESIGN: MICHAEL GRAVES — 172

MARITIM HOTEL, COLOGNE, GERMANY
ARCHITECTURE: GOTTFRIED BÖHM, KRAEMER, SIEVERTS & PARTNER, STEFAN SCHMITZ
INTERIOR DESIGN: REINHARDT + SANDER, FRANJO POOTH, ELISABETH BÖHM   176

HYATT REGENCY ROISSY, PARIS, FRANCE
ARCHITECTURE: MURPHY/JAHN ARCHITECTS, JEAN-MARIE CHARPENTIER
INTERIOR DESIGN: HIRSCH/BEDNER & ASSOCIATES   180

GRAND HOTEL ESPLANADE, BERLIN, GERMANY
ARCHITECTURE: JÜRGEN J. SAWADE
INTERIOR DESIGN: JOHANNE AND GERNOT NALBACH   182

GRAND HYATT HONG KONG, HONG KONG
ARCHITECTURE: NG CHUN MAN & ASSOCIATES
INTERIOR DESIGN: HIRSCH/BEDNER & ASSOCIATES   186

5 RESORTS AND FANTASY HOTELS   192

HYATT REGENCY WAIKOLOA, HAWAII, USA
ARCHITECTURE: LAWTON & UMEMURA ARCHITECTS
LANDSCAPING: TONGG, CLARKE & MECHLER, HOWARD FIELDS & ASSOCIATES
INTERIOR DESIGN: HIRSCH/BEDNER & ASSOCIATES   194

SHERATON MIRAGE, PORT DOUGLAS, AUSTRALIA
ARCHITECTURE: DESMOND BROOKS INTERNATIONAL, MEDIA FIVE
INTERIOR DESIGN: BARRY PETERS   200

THE MIRAGE, LAS VEGAS, USA
ARCHITECTURE: JOEL DAVID BERGMAN/ATLANDIA DESIGN
INTERIOR DESIGN: ROGER P. THOMAS/ATLANDIA DESIGN   204

THE DISNEY WORLD SWAN/DOLPHIN, ORLANDO, FLORIDA, USA
ARCHITECTURE/INTERIOR DESIGN: MICHAEL GRAVES   208

6 VISIONS AND PROJECTS   214

THE HELMSLEY CENTER, MIAMI, USA
ARCHITECTURE: ARQUITECTONICA   216

CONGRESS HOTEL, AGADIR, MOROCCO
ARCHITECTURE: REM KOOLHAAS/O. M. A.   218

INTERCITY HOTEL, BERLIN, GERMANY
ARCHITECTURE: GEORG RITSCHL   222

KEMPINSKI AIRPORT HOTEL, MUNICH, GERMANY
ARCHITECTURE: MURPHY/JAHN
INTERIOR DESIGN: JAN WICHERS   224

BILLIE STRAUSS, KIRCHHEIM, GERMANY
ARCHITECTURE/INTERIOR DESIGN: ZAHA HADID   226

SPREEHOTEL TREPTOW, BERLIN, GERMANY
ARCHITECTURE: GOTTFRIED BÖHM   230

THE OCEAN, CHIKURA, JAPAN
ARCHITECTURE: ALDO ROSSI/MORRIS ADJMI   232

CENTRAL COURT, KUALA LUMPUR, MALAYSIA
ARCHITECTURE: ETTORE SOTTSASS, JOHANNA GRAWUNDER   234

GARTENHOTEL ALTMANNSDORF, VIENNA, AUSTRIA
ARCHITECTURE: COOP HIMMELBLAU   238

ARCHITECTS AND DESIGNERS   240
PROJECT INFORMATION   246
PHOTOGRAPHIC CREDITS   255

WORLDS OF EXPERIENCE
THE NEW HOTELS OF THE LATE TWENTIETH CENTURY

THE CLOSING YEARS OF the twentieth century are witnessing the revival of an institution long frozen by standardization, convention and plushy classicism: the hotel is once again posing a challenge to the creativity of leading architects and designers. Courageous entrepreneurs and a few international luxury chains, seeing the quality of experience afforded by contemporary architecture and design as a marketing asset, are willing to stake their money on hotels. At the same time, with the boom in the global tourist industry, there is a demand for more and more striking attractions. It is no longer enough to offer far-away holiday destinations; the artificial dream world, an oasis of intriguing show effects and unprecedented comfort, is becoming a place of promise where the borderline between illusion and reality is blurred. The urge to create new forms and the craving for exaltation are two aspects of a trend that is once more making hotel building the paradigmatic task that it was in the *belle époque*. In this era of the grand hotel and the rapid expansion of the international hotel trade, hotels were theatres of life characterized by escapism and fantasy. Of the Raffles in Singapore, Somerset Maugham wrote: "It stands for all the fables of the exotic east." Yet the idea of setting off into the unknown was balanced by its opposite – arriving in the familiar. Marcel Proust, whose refuge was the Paris Ritz, said: "They don't hustle me, and I feel at home here."

Nowhere today does the spirit of the age manifest itself so clearly and with such rich variety as in the hotel, a traditional institution that has always dovetailed public functions and private needs. An intimate ambience in an unfamiliar place, a scene of adventure within reassuring confines – this is the aim of the new aesthetic that is challenging the dreary uniformity of the conventional hotel industry. The unique, the superlative and the deliberately provocative are the marketing tools of the nineties. The new hotels set out to provide their paying guests with new worlds of experience.

This book examines six aspects of these new departures. The first chapter discusses designer hotels in the narrow sense of hotels whose interiors carry a recognizable signature in both the consistency of their design and the obvious targeting of particular groups. Innovative hoteliers have started to respond to a phenomenon that has been discernible at a personal level for some time. Since the 1980s, product design – the design of everyday objects from furniture to household equipment – has become bound up with personal status symbols. Like fashion labels, watches and cars, other objects now convey the message: "Show me what you have around you and I'll know who you are." In both private and professional spheres, designer objects indicate that the owner belongs to a community of insiders whose taste is indisputable. The universal sign language of the "form gourmets" is constantly communicated and updated through the amplifiers of advertising and the media. In ever-widening circles, designers are attaining the status of fashion creators: more and more companies are hiring designers as couturiers for new products for the world wide "Alessi" generation.

This is the public targeted by designer hotels. The media effectiveness of the artistic signature of Philippe Starck, Andrée Putman or Aldo Rossi guarantees a response from the target group. To designers and architects, on the other hand, the task of giving shape to a hotel affords a chance to create a total work of art. A spectrum of ideas that might otherwise be realized piecemeal can be formulated in full as a comprehensive statement of principle. Ideally, architecture, interior design, product design, graphics and accessories are all supplied by the same hand. The narrative design strategy by which all interior details are invested with significance and symbolism turns the designer into a kind of author or stage designer, and turns the user, as it were, into a reader or actor. The first designer hotel, Andrée Putman's Morgans Hotel in New York, opened its doors in 1984. Now examples are to be found all over the world.

The second chapter introduces a related type – the salon hotel. As in the designer hotel, its interior architecture is in keeping with the style of the times, yet no longer as an end in itself, but as a means to create a new culture of taste. Avant-garde objects are used in the manner of quotations: they accentuate, but do not dominate, the spatial inventions. New buildings may relate to historic models without lapsing into pastiche; what attracts architects and designers is the reconquest of old fabrics. Salon hotels seek to create a new elegance from the past – one which is often restrained and never shrill, sometimes luxurious but never kitsch. What is new is the invention of spatial solutions, and the sure touch of the sensitive furnisher is required rather than the heavy hand of the sole provider who models everything himself. The guests are assumed to be an open-minded clientele who have money to spend but must not be overburdened with extravagant offerings. Modernity must be matched with discretion. What counts is the atmosphere, and the hackneyed set pieces of the uniform hotel trade are willingly jettisoned.

The art hotels described in the third chapter tell a different story. They give free rein to the intentions of individual modern artists. In such hotels, architecture and interior design have at most an ancillary function – to serve the guest and to serve art. Either the artistic performance varies from room to room – as at the Teufelhof in Basel and the New Siru in Brussels – or the interior is a base from which to view sculptures and artworks in the open air; this is true, for instance, of the Swiss Furkablick hotel. The hotel may function as a gallery for the exhibition of inhabitable artistic environments; it may also (or alternatively) be surrounded by contemporary artworks. This is a logical solution to the frequent demand that there should be no division between art and life. After the 1960s had made the trivial myths of everyday life into fit subjects for art, and the 1970s had seen a turning away from the museum approach, the 1980s made art into a kind of party game. Today the higher spheres of life are increasingly pervaded with works of art. Companies, private individuals and even public bodies seek to enhance their status by acquiring and promoting the most recent works. The art hotel is a particular product of the art boom, offering those who are devoted to art a chance to stay in surroundings where they can become part of the object of their passion. For the artists the hotel is a new field of activity and offers them a new means of displaying their work. However, their fantasies are sometimes required for only a brief spell: the exhibitions must change and old productions must give way to the new; nothing is preserved, for hotels, unlike museums, have no facilities for storing works of art.

The fourth chapter pays tribute to the signal achievements of one man, the American architect John Portman, and to the continuing effects of his pioneering designs. With the arrival of mass tourism after the Second World War, American hotel chains sought their corporate identity in the ubiquity and interchangeability of the hospitality they offered. A Hilton was always a Hilton – whether in London or Berlin; a Holiday Inn, no matter where, remained a calculable commodity. Hotel design and room layout were off the peg, until John Portman arrived on the scene. By setting a new and aesthetically ambitious standard for his client Jay A. Pritzker, this visionary from Atlanta broke up the previous interchangeability. In the 1960s Portman's designs for the Hyatt group – which had only recently arrived on the market – with their breathtaking glass-roofed atriums, sometimes thirty storeys high, made hotel architecture overwhelming once more. The Atlanta Marriott Marquis shows how superbly he can paraphrase his basic form.

The initial idea was to create a city turned inwards; to make the hotel into a closed-off urban space with a central piazza. The idea is still productive, as recent projects demonstrate. The latest European examples, however, do not stress the vertical dimension – which is specific to the United States – but explore horizontal solutions. Moreover, the Cologne Maritim and the Sterling Heathrow (Heathrow Hilton) are context-related: in the former the central, glass-roofed atrium suggests a market hall and a city arcade, in the latter a hangar and an aeronautical function. Vitally important to these usually large undertakings is the provision of conference and congress areas. It is not the transient holiday-maker or the short-stay business traveller who makes the simulated city profitable, but a rapid succession of organized functions, from specialist conferences to show events. Building expenses are accordingly concentrated on the public or semi-public areas. The grandiose architecture is seldom matched by the furnishing of the guest-rooms; the architectural gesture comes up against the compromises of interior design in which mainstream aesthetics carry the day. The claim to be oases of superlative luxury, offering an immense range of services and a variety of experiences, is realized by extraordinary new, large hotels in Hong Kong and the United States. Yet in view of the reluctance of companies and well-to-do private travellers to spread their money around after the Gulf War and the onset of the international recession, projects that were already on the drawing board have become rather like stranded luxury liners, evidence of the reckless consumerism of the 1980s. The big hotel concerns have cancelled most of these projects and now seek their salvation in down-pricing and marketing models for mass-produced, medium-priced hotels that hold out a prospect of better utilization and safer returns.

Perhaps even more characteristic of the high noon of five-star tourism are the resorts and fantasy hotels discussed in the fifth chapter. The period since the early 1980s has seen the creation of holiday paradises – gigantic complexes that offer the guest self-contained vacation refuges from Hawaii to Australia, from the Caribbean to southeast Asia. These multi-million-dollar investments seldom display any architectural inventiveness, but there are two exceptions – the Hyatt Regency Waikoloa in Hawaii and the Sheraton Mirage on the coast of Queensland, Australia. The most blatant experiments in extravagant fantasy are to be found in Las Vegas, the Eldorado of gaming and show business. The Mirage has set up in competition with the imperial glamour of "Caesar's Palace" and the chivalric kitsch of the huge Hotel Excalibur, and currently tops the bill as a major attraction.

Entertainment architecture – fiction in concrete form, a model world tailored for child-like identification – has long been the domain of the Disney concern in its various theme parks. What is new is the determination of Disney-boss Michael Eisner to engage notable architects for these entertainment projects. Michael Graves, the American protagonist of postmodernism, was at first condemned for collaborating with this amusement concern, but he has been followed by such illustrious colleagues as Frank Gehry, Arata Isozaki and Antoine Predock. Yet Graves's fun structures are still the ideal answer to the architectural ambitions of the Disney empire. This is true above all of the Dolphin and Swan Hotels, the gigantic twin project in Florida's Disneyworld. Here Graves evinced a lightness and a love of story-telling that is not matched in his later Hotel New York in the Euro-Disney complex near Paris. The fanciful world of the Dolphin and the Swan lies on the borderline between the stage-set and contemporary style. The design in which Mickey Mouse receives his guests, contextually appropriate and tinged with a playful irony, extends the canon on which the narrative trend of present-day architecture has been at work for some time, drawing on a classical fund of themes. In the world of the comic and the fairytale, postmodernism comes into its own: in these hotels it reveals more of its essential character, which stimulates both sentiment and resentment, than it could ever have done through extravagant architecture produced for companies or public bodies.

A survey of contemporary hotels would be incomplete if it were confined to projects already realized. Hence the last chapter, while not claiming to be exhaustive, brings together a representative selection of international projects that have not yet been built. Visions that have scarcely any prospect of realization, yet seem to point the way ahead by virtue of their boldness, co-exist with more pragmatic projects, some of which are already in the course of construction. The utopia schooled in the avant-garde of the 1920s and influenced by the virtual realities generated by computer-aided design proves to be the real point of reference for a new exoticism. Architecture and design become metaphors of a special kind, no longer referring back to the panorama of foreign styles and attributes from which the hotels of a hundred years ago were derived and which are now being revived in a number of exemplary restorations.

In recent years even the grand hotel has been reborn. The Langham in London, built in 1864, has become the Victorian flagship of Hilton International; the Paris Ritz is again resplendent having been superbly restored; and the St Regis in New York has been resurrected as the showpiece of ITT Sheraton. These three examples are representative of many others, which make it possible to study, almost in the original, the magic world of the palace hotels of yesteryear. "The private person, who in his office takes account of reality, demands of the interior that it should support him in his illusions. This gives rise to the phantasmagorias of the interior which represents his universe. In it he collects distant places and past ages. His drawing room is a box in the world theatre...." This is how, in his essay "Paris – Capital of the 19th Century", Walter Benjamin described the bourgeois attitude that with the coming of tourism – admittedly still for the privileged few – was transported from the box of the private drawing room to the stage of the grand hotel. The *belle époque* was the high point in this development when the grand hotel, with its historical and exotic décor, became a provisional palace.

Whereas in earlier centuries the church and the stately home had been the significant models for architecture, industrialization exalted another duo of splendid buildings: the great railway station and the hotel. In large cities and spa towns, at the seaside and in the mountains, the hotel was the guests' castle, a scene of social rituals. The formal language of these hotels, centred on courtly styles and eclectic mixtures of elements, proved relatively resistant to the sobering effects of art nouveau and remained almost totally aloof from the emergence of modernism. It was only the art deco of the 1920s and 1930s that had an enduring effect on the appearance of hotels. The recently renovated Dorchester in London is evidence of this period. The style remained popular in the countless small and medium-sized hotels in the art deco district of Miami Beach until the 1950s. Among the floating luxury hotels, the great ocean liners, it was the *Normandie* that provided exemplary documentation of the artistry and interior design of this period. As a result of the economic crisis, developments in hotel architecture that might have set new standards remained unrealized –

such as the projects of the Viennese architect Adolf Loos for the Semmering or the Promenade des Anglais in Nice. Frank Lloyd Wright had more luck in Japan, where he was able to build the Imperial Hotel in Tokyo between 1915 and 1922 – a significant parallel to the recent Japanese vogue for the Euro-American avant-garde.

The come-back of the grand hotel, which after the Second World War fell victim to neglect and often to the wrecker's ball, is accompanied by a wave of nostalgia that finds inspiration in historical models and sees interior design as an activity which involves revelling in time-honoured styles, antiques, replicas and décors. The new conservatism is international. One of the most successful new enterprises in the top levels of the hotel trade, the American Ritz Carlton Group, has made a plush-laden classicism its trademark. The refurbished or borrowed splendour of yesterday is an aspect of the recent hotel boom that is not illustrated in this volume. A new genre, however, which also takes its model from a revived middle-class salon culture, must be considered among recent approaches to design. It involves new interpretations, rather than imitations, of past grandeur. Architects in Spain especially seem to succeed in effortlessly combining a modern feeling for life with traditional values, as is demonstrated by the quality and stylishness of the Spanish examples included in this book. Features of the old grand hotels are not restored to serve as stage sets, but are translated into a new language of forms. An affinity with the present age is discerned in the *belle époque*, and this is taken up with a mastery that is modern in performance, but conservative in conviction. These splendid worlds of style, so modern in their staging, are competing to an increasing extent with the more wayward pure designer hotel, which bears the ambitious individual signature of the designer and inevitably appeals only to a design-conscious minority.

All hotels that are committed to up-to-date architecture and contemporary design – or even to more traditional design concepts – provide "experience architecture" and in their own ways win back a historical dimension that was present in the great hotels of the nineteenth century and the turn of the century. Our *fin de siècle* is not characterized by warmed-up historicism or an artistic reform movement like art nouveau, but by a plurality of styles and marketing strategies that have certain themes in common: travel, dreaming, the parallelism of public and private spheres of life, illusion and escape. As in Thomas Mann's novella *Death in Venice*, the hotel is again becoming a superbly designed stage for social ceremonies and a sentimental refuge in which a period and its culture are authentically reflected.

1
DESIGNER HOTELS

THE TREND FOR DESIGNING PUBLIC interiors in line with current styles spread to the hotel business at the turn of the decade. Following on from minor projects such as boutiques, bars and restaurants, hotels are now presenting a challenge to prominent designers and architects in the United States, Japan and Europe. As a rule, the decision to sponsor the construction of a total work of art – which ideally embraces architecture, interior design, product design, graphics and accessories – is taken by courageous individuals in the hotel business who are endowed with an unerring feel for the moods of a younger, successful international clientele, gourmets of form who wish to assert their own standards – in clothes, furniture and consumer habits – outside as well as inside their homes.

The forerunners of the new design-conscious generation of hoteliers were two American entrepreneurs, Ian Schrager and the late Steve Rubell. As early as 1984 they opened Morgans Hotel in New York, and five years later the Royalton. Their collaboration with the French star designers Andrée Putman and Philippe Starck set the pattern for many subsequent designer hotels. It was not long before the spectrum widened considerably, as later examples prove. Common to all these projects is a firm artistic thesis that goes beyond contemporary interior design. Designer hotels do not draw upon elements of avant-garde design simply as accents in space; rather, they themselves form the avant-garde. To check in at them is to check in with the trend; guests can expect surprises; they will encounter much that is unfamiliar, but which at the same time anticipates future needs and is a reaction to contemporary furniture design and styles of living.

The model of the designer hotel operates independently of star classifications: most are quite small, three-star hotels on city sites, but even four-star and five-star establishments successfully exploit the individualistic concept. Not even the rural idyll seems to inhibit experimentation, as is demonstrated by Jean Nouvel's Hauterive in Bouliac, France and Pflaums Posthotel in Pegnitz, Germany.

Above: Morgans Hotel at the end of Madison Avenue. In 1983 the successful New York entrepreneurs Steve Rubell and Ian Schrager commissioned the French interior architect Andrée Putman to set new design standards when renovating a run-down city hotel. Morgans was thus New York's first designer hotel.

Right: The strong point of the indirectly lit hall is its graphic spatial design.

MORGANS HOTEL
New York, USA, 1984

Interior Design: **Andrée Putman**

Steve Rubell and Ian Schrager, New York's most successful nightclub owners, famous for Studio 54 and the Palladium, were adept at turning run-down picture palaces into goldmines. When they commissioned their first hotel, they were alive to the wishes of a trend-orientated public with a taste for the theatrical. For the Palladium they had engaged the Japanese master architect Arata Isozaki, and they brought in another celebrity to remove the dust from a run-down hotel in Madison Avenue. With their proverbial flair, they entrusted the work of modernization to the Parisian interior architect Andrée Putman, with a remit to design something exceptional. What they had in mind was up-to-date metropolitan accommodation that would appeal to modern trend-conscious guests who abhor traditional, clichéd hotels.

Andrée Putman designed the whole layout of the new Morgans like a new edition of an imaginary classic. Chequerboard borders in graphic black and white line the soft, dark carpeting in the corridors, dimly illuminated by downlighters. The scene in the ground-floor reception area resembles a fusion of strict Viennese Secession and sultry art deco. Back-lit glass panels in sternly geometrical surrounds of patinated bronze exude the atmosphere of a revived cinema world. Andrée Putman's décor for Morgans recalls a stylized metropolis, but on a distinctly human scale.

The human dimension is evident in the proportions of the rooms, in which, as on a ship, every square centimetre is put to practical use. Each of the 112 hotel rooms has been agreeably thought out to suit the taste of a clientele drawn from show business and the media. Comfortable window niches with integrated sofas afford a welcome addition to the interiors. Designer carpets in subdued colours and classic modern furniture in chrome and wood generate an atmosphere of modern art deco which reaches a graphic climax in the chequered tiling of the bathrooms. Andrée Putman produces a sense of security in this hotel above all by psychological means, through her cultivated style. It was on the basis of this quality, which relies on aesthetics, that the Parisian designer inaugurated a new trend in hotel design. Morgans is the structural embodiment of Andrée Putman's thesis that modern design is not a matter for the spirit of the age, but for an inner attitude. Comfort and cultivated living originate in the mind and are not created by soft sofa cushions.

The bathrooms at Morgans are laid out in the chequerboard pattern characteristic of Andrée Putman's style.

Window niches in the guestrooms are shaped into comfortable seats. In her design Andrée Putman takes the view that even comfort is a visual matter.

Andrée Putman's style makes a hotel room into a place of unique character. The cultivated atmosphere creates a sense of pleasant security.

Chequered borders act as a leitmotif in the atmospherically lit corridors.

Left: The brick cylinder of the old water tower was carefully modified to serve as a hotel. **Right:** The hall with its historic spiral staircase in cast iron presents a fascinating labyrinth of perspectives.

WASSERTURM HOTEL
Cologne, Germany, 1990
Architecture: **Konrad L. Heinrich**
Interior Design: **Andrée Putman**

Transforming a functional building of the last century into a top-class hotel – this difficult task, unique in its way, was entrusted to Andrée Putman. The architectural requirements – restoring the historic fabric and modifying the façades and floor divisions – were met by Konrad L. Heinrich, a local architect. The water tower, the biggest of its kind in Europe when it was built in 1872, survived the bombing of the Second World War and, though seriously damaged, remained standing in the middle of the city, a brick-built fossil that had long since lost its function. As a listed building, the semi-ruin was protected against demolition, and among the many plans for its re-utilization was one that would have transformed it into a depository for funerary urns.

The entrepreneurial decision to convert this industrial monument into a five-star hotel was inspired by faith in the skill and stylistic flair of the *grande dame* of contemporary design, already famous for the Morgans hotel in New York (see page 14) and numerous other projects. Andrée Putman's sober hand, guided partly by models from the twenties, can be discerned throughout the interior, from the reception lobby, the bar and the 90 rooms and suites – some designed as maisonettes – to the restaurant, with its panoramic view over the cityscape of Cologne. The fabric – often the original raw brick – and the restrained salon elegance of the interior furnishings blend into a harmonious whole. Furniture, carpets and accessories are all specially designed. Recurrent motifs are the circle and the cylinder – the tower shape being echoed in armchairs, tables, wash basins and door mountings.

By contrast with the "non-colours" of other Putman interiors, the furniture is upholstered mainly in strong yellows and blues. Admirable economy is displayed in handling the difficult outlines of the guest-rooms, which are shaped like sections of a cake. For Andrée Putman the key element was the lighting: "Of all the disparate factors that contribute to the welcoming hospitality of a hotel, light is ultimately crucial if the desired harmony is to be achieved." The dramatic inset lighting – room-high, back-lit, frosted glass walls or narrow, free-standing illuminated panels, ingeniously compensates for the absence of exterior windows dictated by the form of the building.

Circles are a leitmotif of Andrée Putman's interior design. Back-lit glass walls compensate for the lack of daylight.

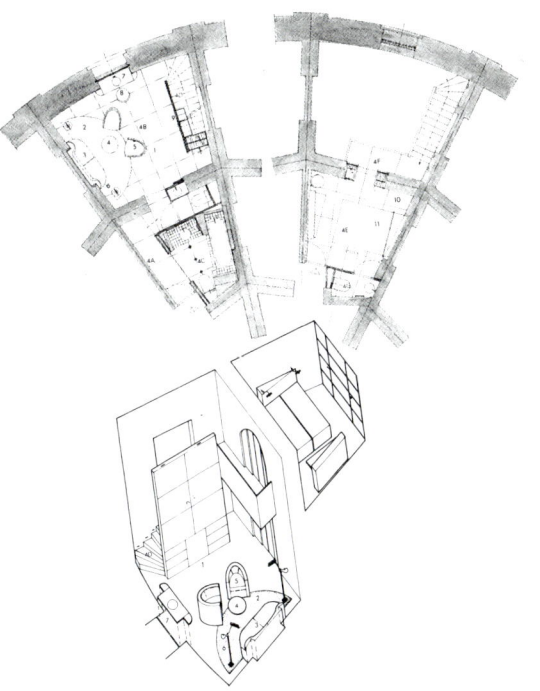

The Presidential suite of this five-star hotel adheres to the sober salon style of the project as a whole. A spiral staircase leads to the bedroom areas. The drawings show how optimal use was made of the floorspace in rooms shaped like sections of a cake.

Unadorned elegance and a restrained choice of colours characterize the bedrooms. On the left is one of the illuminated frosted glass panels.

A bar on the ground floor has a glass counter. The use of dark browns and ochre turns these ascetic surroundings into a discreet meeting place.

Right: Circles and squares are also found in details, such as this door mounting.

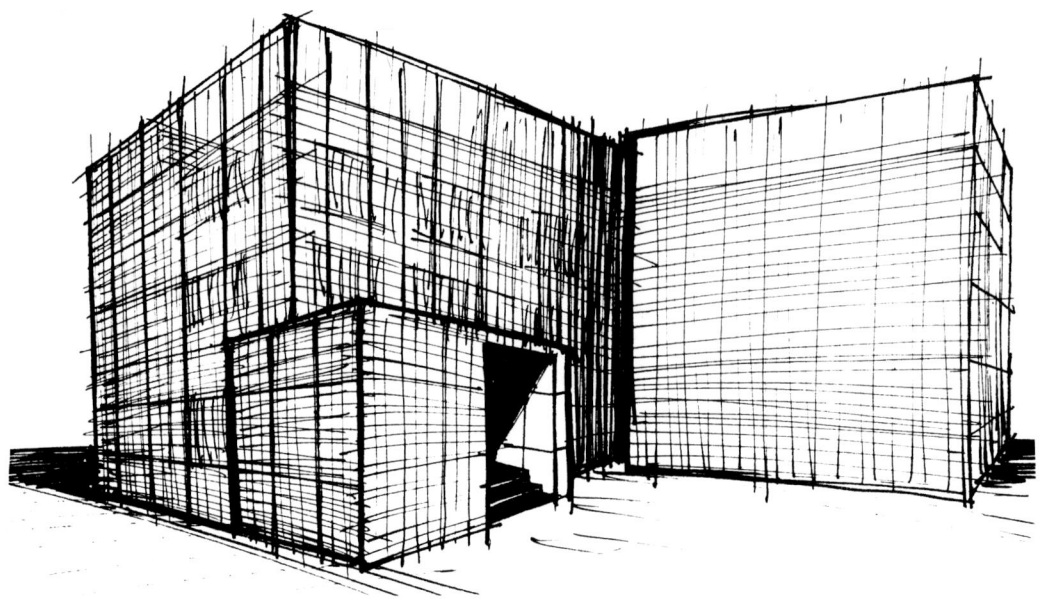

Above: View of Le Lac. Andrée Putman enclosed the old building with a metal scaffold, over which "Koolshade" netting was stretched.

Right: Metal panels placed on the glass entrance door allow daylight to enter through narrow slits, creating effective plays of light. The colour palette consists of unobtrusive natural tones.

LE LAC
Kawaguchiko-Cho, Japan, 1990
Interior Design: **Andrée Putman**

The past decade has seen a lively exchange between Japan and Europe, especially in the field of architecture, with Japanese investors inviting the most notable representatives of the European avant-garde to help their most expensive real estate reach the heights of architectural distinction. The engagement of internationally famous architects and designers appeared to secure world-wide appreciation for even the most extreme building projects.

One of the most élitist products of this cultural exchange is a hotel which, despite its small proportions, has caused a stir throughout the world. Andrée Putman was commissioned to redesign an existing hotel on Lake Kawaguchiko. This celebrated designer, whose fame had spread to Japan, was to transform a featureless building into an exquisite eight-room jewel of the highest distinction. She decided to employ extreme stylistic resources. She began by enclosing the existing building in a cubic frame of steel profiles, which she then covered with "Koolshade", a wire mesh imported from America. This produced a transparent aura that filters the natural light during the day, and casts interesting light patterns at night, when the building is illuminated.

The design of every room evinces a hitherto unknown refinement. In the rectangular rooms, between 35 and 40 square metres in area, the bathroom and main living space form a single flexible unit divided only by a folding partition. When this is opened, the sculpturally shaped double washbasin resembles an altar, dominating the wall in which the window is set. Body culture and lifestyle fuse into a sophisticated unity in the almost choreographically designed rooms of Le Lac. The restaurant too, like the project as a whole, offers a synthesis of European and traditional Japanese aesthetics. This small room, designed in an élitist mode that concentrates rigorously and convincingly on essentials, is furnished with French tubular steel chairs by Michel Dufet and has plain oak parquet flooring. In this most élitist of modern hotel projects Andrée Putman reduces ambience to the basic necessities and so makes one's stay into a challenging ritual.

Left and below: The interiors are designed like comfortable apartments. Despite their variable floor plans, living rooms and bathrooms are not separated.

Plan of the upper floor with guest-rooms.

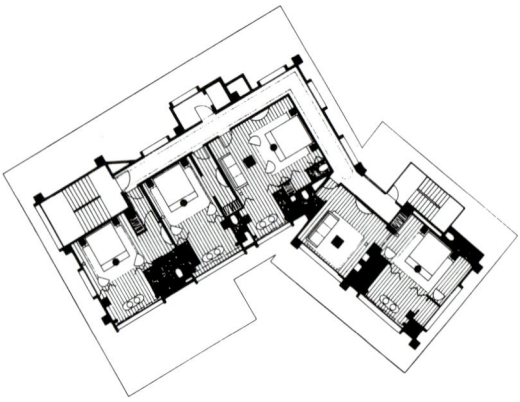

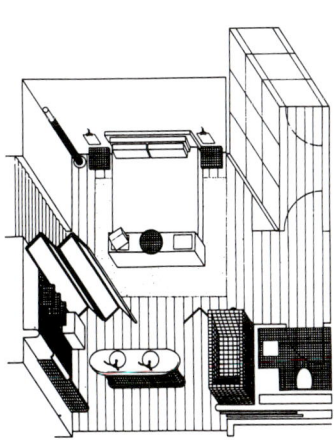

Isometric diagram of a guest-room, consisting of bedroom and bathroom areas.

The aesthetic of the bathrooms and lounges does not vary. Nor does the flooring, which is deliberately kept simple.

Left: Outwardly, the up-to-date design of La Villa is not discernible. For the interiors of the historic building, the architect Marie-Christine Dorner evolved a language of forms harking back to the fifties.

Right: Dorner also designed the furniture for La Villa. The overall composition was thus given an unmistakable signature, to be found in the smallest details.

LA VILLA
Paris, France, 1988
Interior Design: **Marie-Christine Dorner**

Three designers and their hotel projects have made contemporary French design internationally famous. Whereas Andrée Putman and Philippe Starck made their New York débuts with trend-setting city hotels, Marie-Christine Dorner, a young designer from Strasbourg, set new standards with a designer hotel realized in the Parisian quarter of Saint Germain. With this, her first work, she succeeded in doing justice both to the eighteenth-century building, with its intricate ground plan, and to the claims and visions of an entirely independent design concept. La Villa is genuinely representative of Saint Germain, yet is at the same time one of the most rigorous manifestos of contemporary French design. Dorner's world of forms and colours conveys an impression of vivacity and youthfulness that imbues the old hotel with new wit and sparkle.

Before planning the interior of La Villa, Dorner spent a year in Japan where she had great success as a designer of furniture and interiors, but her furniture designs and spatial compositions for the Parisian hotel are totally French. In this she belongs to the great line of *artistes décorateurs* who approach interior design with emotion, taste and – for all their modernity – a firm sense of tradition, and who see their task as a contribution to French culture. The dialogue with French culture begins with the design of the breakfast tables, whose tops hang on a patinated metal "arm" reminiscent of one of Max Ernst's surrealist sculptures.

Art and a feeling for life are ingeniously blended in other details of the appointments. The banisters leading down from the breakfast room to the basement – where in true left-bank style there is a jazz club – are made up of freely composed lines and resemble the kind of abstract metal sculpture which one would expect to see in a museum rather than a hotel. In the guestrooms the door mountings are shaped like eccentric metal ornaments. They too can be seen as a free development of an art deco style. Decorative art and a sense of style are also combined in the ceiling lights; shaped like elliptical clouds, they are reminiscent of fifties mobiles. Their built-in spotlights illuminate the irregular angles of the small rooms. The asymmetric furniture with pointed legs, and the curved, bold but comfortable chairs and upholstered beds might very well date from the era of the kidney-shaped table.

Such echoes of the period after the war, when Saint Germain was the intellectual hub of Paris, and existentialists such as Jean-Paul Sartre and the singer Juliette Greco set the tone of the quarter, create the lyrical ambience for which La Villa is often praised and which contributes to the hotel's atmosphere and credibility. For in spite of its revolutionary forms and striking colours, La Villa is not an alien presence: indeed, it has already become an authentic part of the Saint Germain of today. It suits the business policy of the hotel's owners to preserve La Villa's refinement as a unique commodity. Dorner's furniture, unlike Philippe Starck's from the Royalton, has not been reproduced – though it is just as strong and popular and has become a symbol of fashionable living – and this reinforces the uniqueness of La Villa.

Marie-Christine Dorner evolved a range of colours reminiscent of the fifties which gives each room an individual character.

The most effective detail in La Villa is the banister leading from the breakfast bar to the jazz club.

Floor plan showing the entrance, bar, breakfast area and stairs to the jazz club.

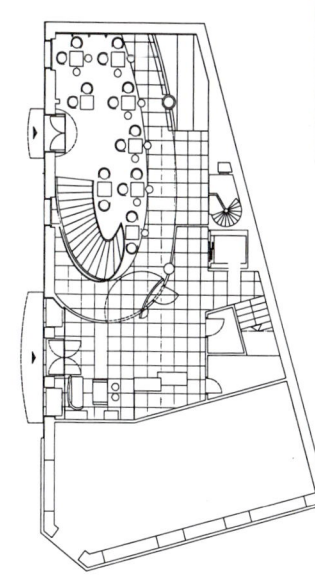

Left: Even before they enter the hotel, guests are prepared for the unusual interior design by the dominant turquoise and red colour scheme.

Right: The sculpture in the foyer is by the Fluxus artist Wolf Vostell, whose works are found in all parts of the hotel.

ART HOTEL SORAT
Berlin, Germany, 1990
Architecture: **Klaus Effenberger**

Interior Design: **Johanne and Gernot Nalbach**

Johanne and Gernot Nalbach, two Austrian architects living in Berlin and noted for the interior design of the Grand Hotel Esplanade (see page 182), conceived the small, medium-priced Art Hotel Sorat around the work of Wolf Vostell, a contemporary artist and protagonist of the Fluxus movement. His sculptures are to be seen high up on the façade and in the foyer, and the 75 guest-rooms are decorated with his graphics. This hotel is not a neutral, museum-like shell, like "art hotels" in the narrow sense of the term: far from creating or dictating the use of space, art is respectfully integrated into a self-assured architectural plan.

Despite a limited budget and the functional requirements of a middle-class hotel, the interior architects sought to achieve an overall design that would generate, down to the smallest details, an individual aesthetic in the choice of materials, forms and colours. "Paradox, curiosity, restraint" – these are the terms in which Nalbach & Nalbach define their approach. Their aim is the interplay of atmosphere, possible fields of association and the emotions of the users, which results in flexible solutions rather than the repetition of a fixed stylistic vocabulary: "At first a spatial concept was evolved, and this then determined the form and the detail." A recurrent motif in the Art Hotel Sorat is the wave: gold-coloured corrugated metal incorporated into the ceilings leads to the breakfast-room; in the guest-rooms, wave-shaped wall mountings link various fittings; in the bistro, the tables can be endlessly realigned, wave-edge to wave-edge. The dominant colours are bold red and turquoise-green. In addition to their own designs, the Nalbachs have introduced furniture and carpets by other designers, ranging from classical modern to post-modern – from Eileen Gray to Philippe Starck and Javier Mariscal. The Nalbachs' frame of reference is the contemporary cultural horizon, a heterogeneous fund on which they draw freely. The appointments and shapes of the rooms are standardized, serially produced but unique – until the first 75 units are supplemented by 75 more in an extension.

The whole concept developed for Berlin is due to be repeated shortly, as the client and the architects are planning other "art hotels" in what was formerly East Berlin, Leipzig and Frankfurt an der Oder – again as a homage to a particular artist and his work.

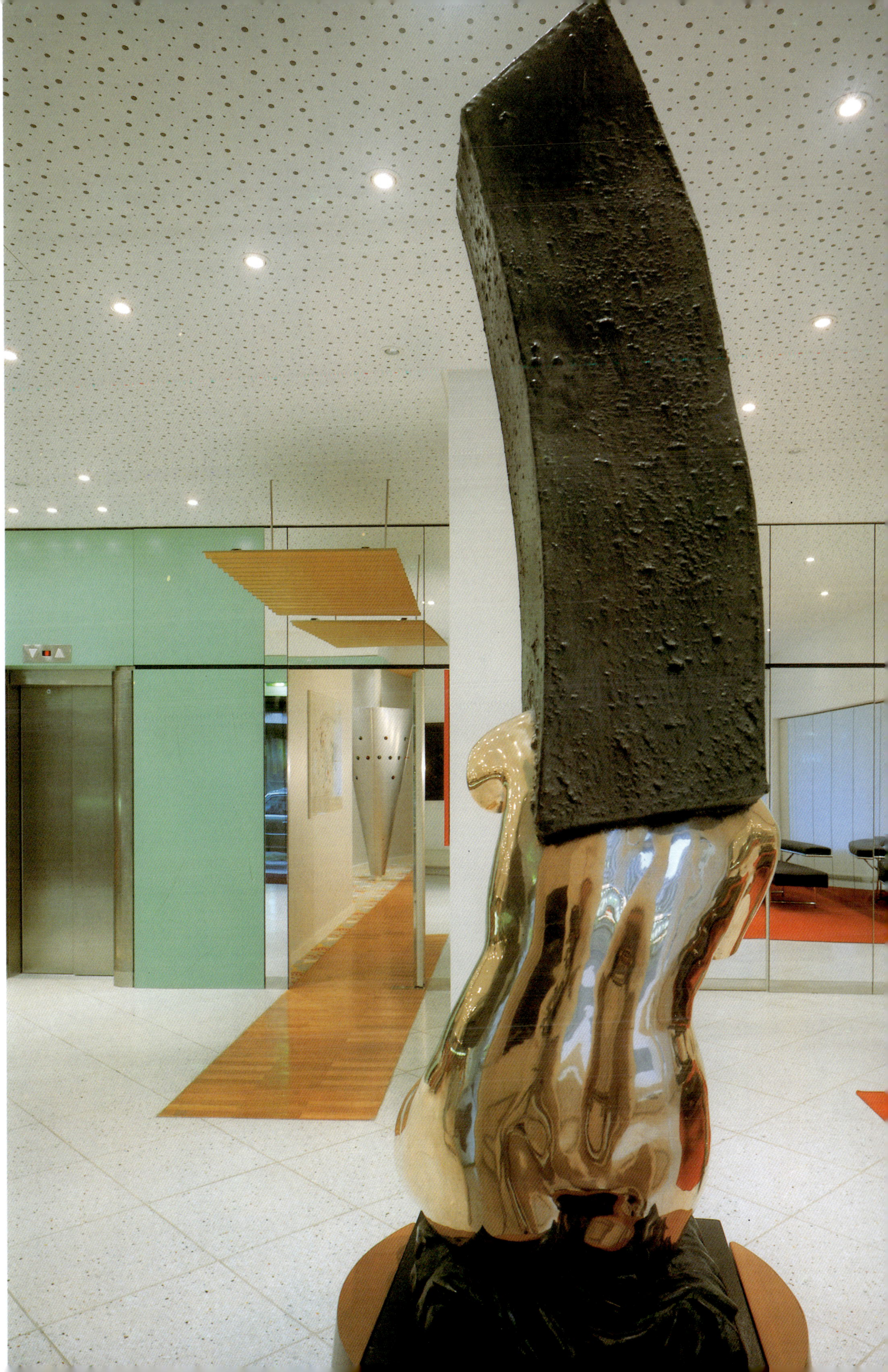

The reception is also a bar – with bar stools by the Spanish designer Javier Mariscal.

The furnishing of the guest-rooms is reduced to the basic necessities; furniture is fitted to the walls to save space.

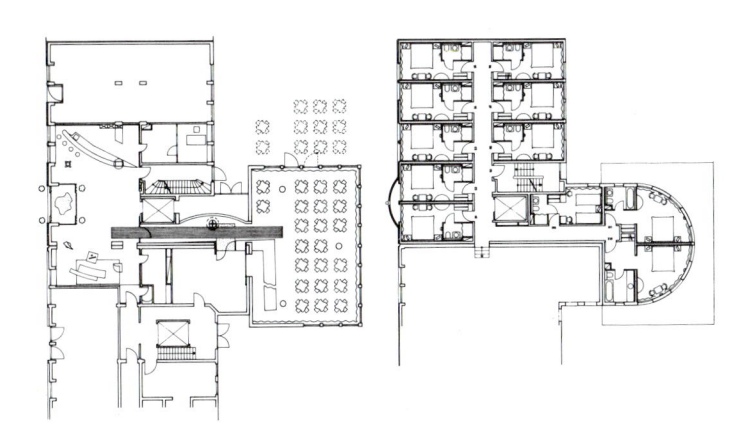

Above: Plans of the lobby and breakfast-room (left) and one of the upper floors with guest-rooms (right).

Right: Metal cones used as newspaper stands are one of the details designed by Johanne and Gernot Nalbach.

37

Left: The interior of this historic inn in the German provinces has been transformed by contemporary design.

Right: The colourfully designed entrance hall acts as the prelude to an adventure landscape of contemporary interior design.

PFLAUMS POSTHOTEL
Pegnitz, Germany, 1989-92
Interior Design: **Dirk Obliers**

Pflaums Posthotel in Pegnitz is a handsome, half-timbered inn, over three hundred years old. The tradition of the great Franconian staging posts, when mail and travellers were carried overland by coach, seems to live on here. Inside the building, however, the romance has not remained intact since 1989, when the designer Dirk Obliers set about transforming parts of the hotel, one after another, into an assemblage of contemporary stylistic elements. The inspiration comes from subjects and characters in the operatic world of Richard Wagner (the festival town of Bayreuth is, after all, close by). The new suites have names like "Venus in Blue", "Klingsor's Magic Garden" or "Parsifal". The fitness centre is named after Jacques Offenbach's "Orpheus in the Underworld", and the indoor golf course has been christened "Orpheus Plays Golf".

Obliers once worked as artistic executive for Rosenthal, the china firm, where he was responsible for the architecture of the sales studios. He does not aim at a uniform design gesture. His decorative style, reminiscent of theatre sets, is a mix of contemporary forms and modern materials, with no attempt at historicizing. The substance of the original building has been broken down into free spatial compositions. The interior architecture contains some surprising – and successful – functional combinations: of bedroom and bathroom furnishings and fittings, for instance, in the form of a generously proportioned jacuzzi placed next to a double bed. Special attention is paid to the lighting. In his choice of furniture Obliers relies on well-known names and makes, but places the pieces, like design icons, in settings devised by himself.

The courage that the owners, Andreas and Hermann Pflaum, showed in mounting such a spectacle in the provinces has paid off handsomely. Their Janus-headed establishment, which looks nostalgically backwards without losing sight of current fashion, has become a meeting place for celebrities. During the Wagner season, international opera stars are among the regular guests, and international concerns invite visiting VIPs to stay here. The Pflaum brothers treat this adventure in design as work in progress, surrendering their family heirloom bit by bit to the inventiveness of Dirk Obliers. The "Parsifal" suite, opened in the summer of 1992, with its martially constructed, multi media "sleep cave", a resting place for star-warriors of the third millennium, provides the guest with music and scenes from the operas, including the "Ride of the Valkyries", on laser disc.

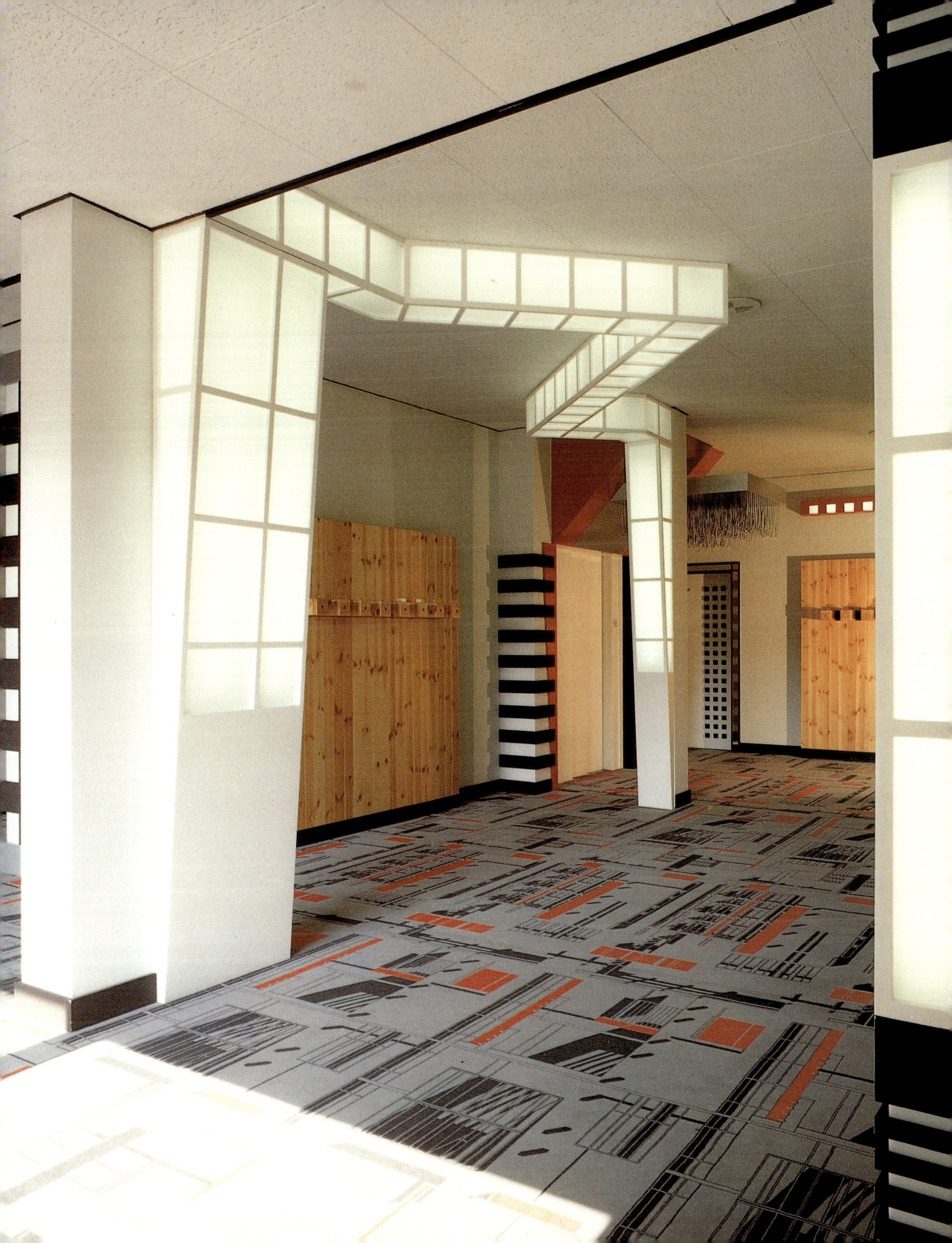

The indoor golf course in the basement of Pflaums Posthotel (also shown in the drawing, right), with its light effects and contrasting metal and stone, is called "Orpheus Plays Golf".

40

Golf-Fangnetz

Golfabschlag

The luxury suite "Klingsor's Magic Garden" offers an original combination of art deco features and contemporary design.

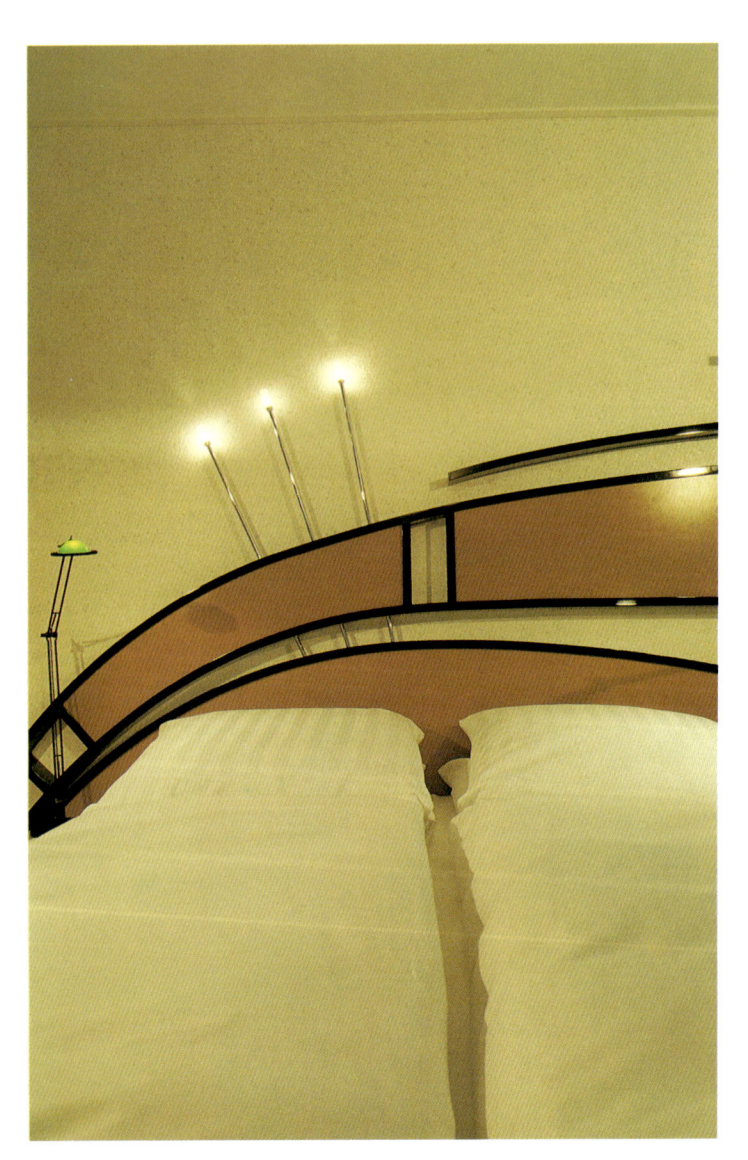

Each of the suites designed by Dirk Obliers relates to a Wagner opera: the Parsifal Suite has a bed with a light firmament and multimedia entertainment electronics.

Left: Above a newly planted vineyard near the historic village of Bouliac, Jean Nouvel built the four houses of the Hauterive hotel.

Right: Rust-red grilles over the façade afford protection against the sun and can be raised by an electromechanical device.

HAUTERIVE
Bouliac, France, 1989
Architecture/Interior Design: **Jean Nouvel, Emmanŭel Cattani et Associés**

When Jean-Marie Amat, the celebrated chef, was planning a small hotel as an annexe to his gourmet restaurant Saint James, which is housed in a classicist village building, his choice of designer was at first puzzling. He commissioned Jean Nouvel, the technology-obsessed architect of the Institut du Monde Arabe in Paris, to provide the appropriate ambience for his gourmet guests. Below the church tower of Bouliac, on a hill that affords a view across the Gironde valley out beyond Bordeaux, is a sight that is no longer common: four simple structures covered by a rusty latticework skin and standing in a newly laid-out vineyard; three are gabled and one apparently incomplete, having a roofless top storey. This surprising phenomenon is in keeping with local tradition, however, the ultimate model being the old tobacco barns of the region.

The external simplicity of the Hauterive hotel does not lack ingenuity, for the latticework hanging over the façades can be raised by an electrical mechanism to shield the windows from the sun. At night the glass surfaces of the interiors seem to shine through a mysterious grid. The guest is confronted by an architecture that operates with extreme contrasts. The dark exterior of the buildings contrasts with interiors drenched in light. "My luxury is space" – this statement by the architect is realized here. The new restaurant, the bistro and the hotel rooms radiate a severe and all-pervasive asceticism. The unusual outlines and the minimalism of the materials and fittings – polished concrete, smooth plasterwork, bleached birchwood, metal, glass, white fabrics – make the 18 guest-rooms into examples of an abstract, almost monastic architecture, but the effect is never depressing.

Some of the bathrooms are separated from the bedrooms only by a sheet of glass. Some of the beds stand on unusually high bases, so that from them one can survey the ever-present landscape. Every room has a view – which explains the absence of interior decoration: the panorama of the world outside is the dominant picture that fills the rooms. Nouvel designed all the interior furnishings; the characteristic chairs, reduced to the frames and upholstered surfaces, have since been reproduced and are available on the market.

Beside the large projects on which the architect is engaged, these rusty houses at Bouliac represent a fairly small commission, but their consistent, concentrated aesthetic allows us to see Nouvel's principles and methods as though through a magnifying glass. Here he could experiment without having to compromise, and Jean-Marie Amat's gourmet tourists involuntarily supplied him with a public on which to experiment.

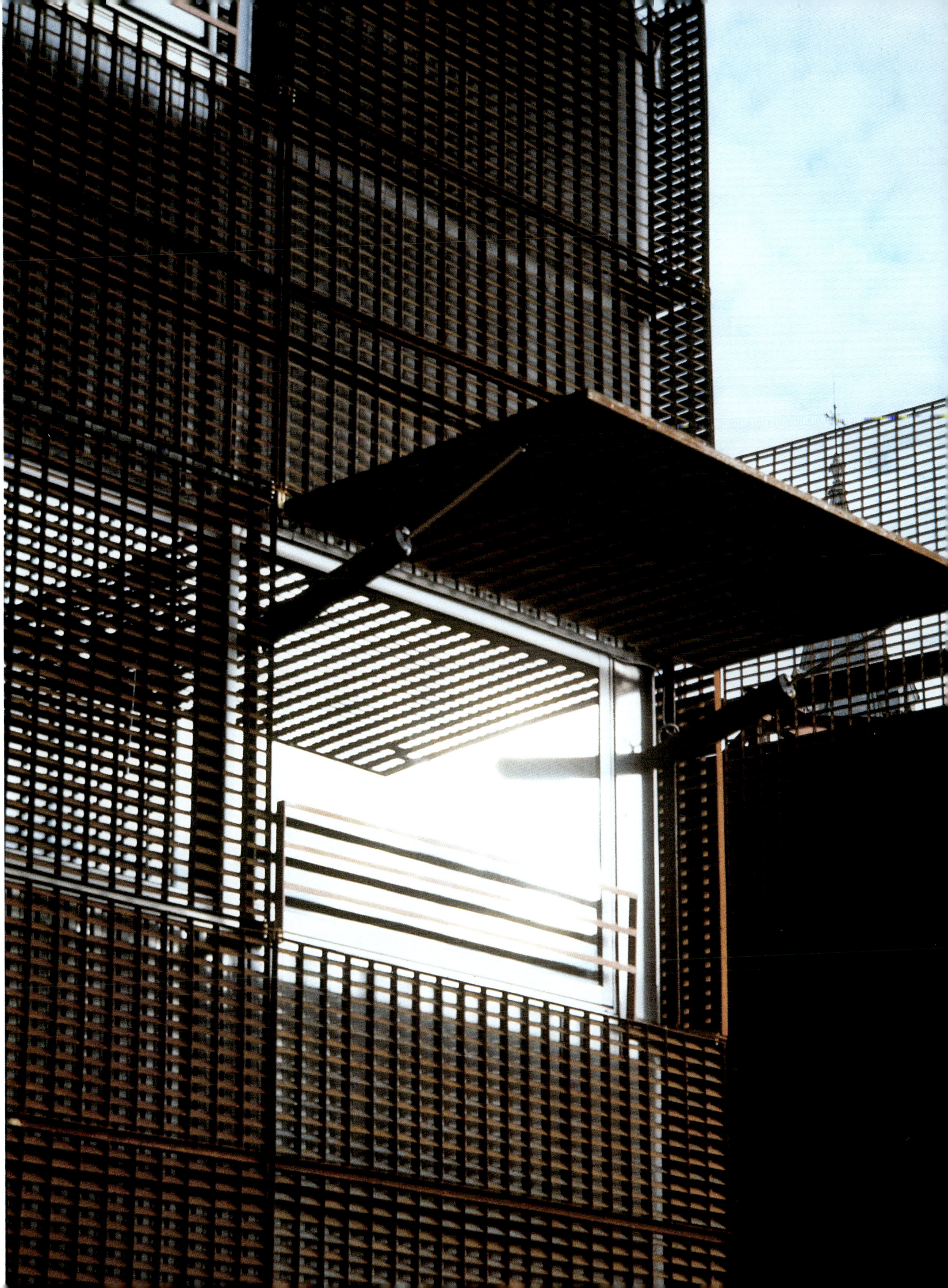

Right: In the new restaurant, as in the rooms (above), no compromise was allowed to impair the overall design concept, and the culinary delights on offer are counterpointed by an austere aesthetic.

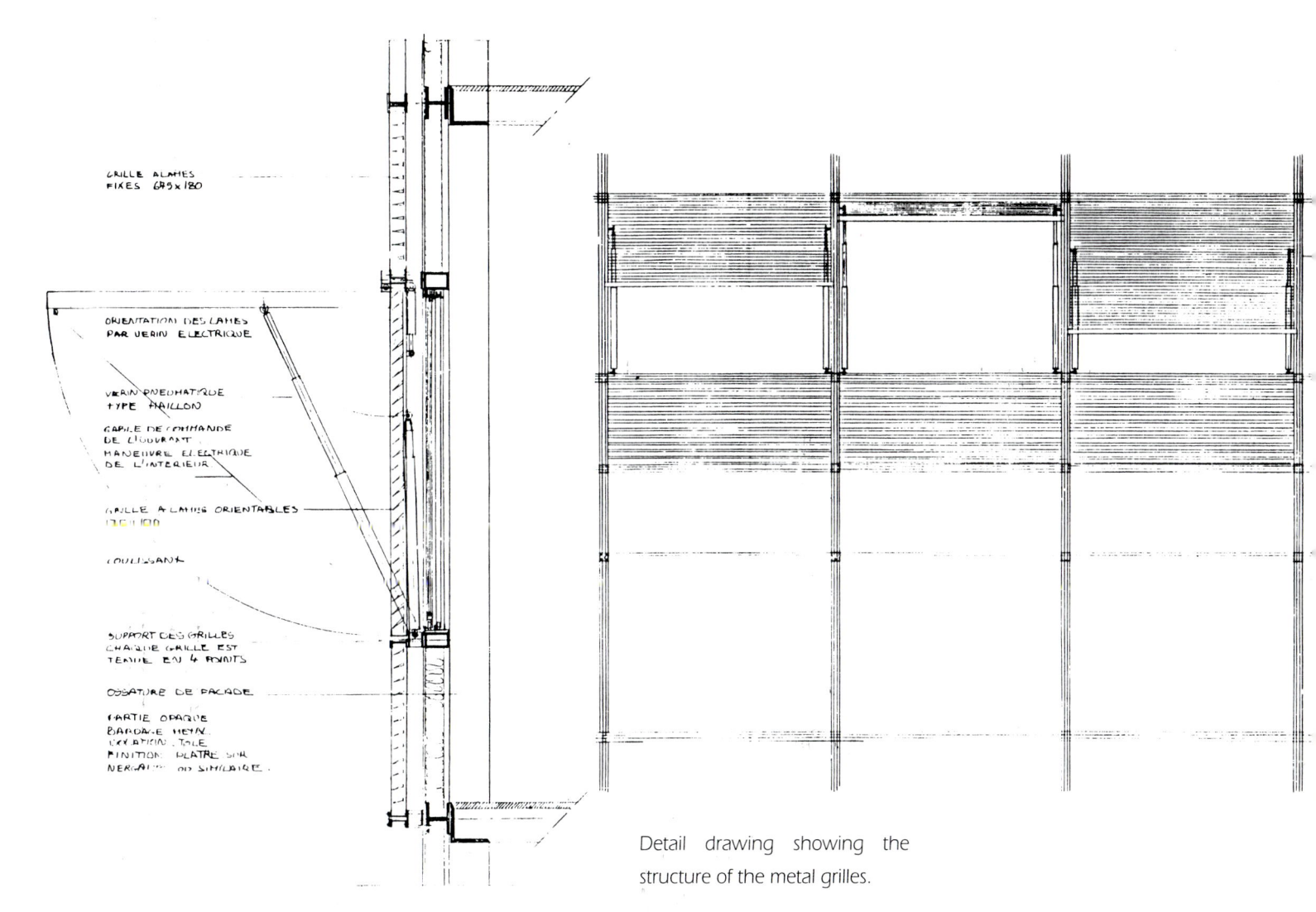

Detail drawing showing the structure of the metal grilles.

Above: The pattern of shadows cast by the metal grilles forms the only decoration on the walls of the rooms. The decorative French glass is part of the hotel owner's collection.

47

Left: The model of Les Thermes shows the building as if it were hovering over a transparent base.

Right: A view of the bath-hall. Thermal cure facilities are an integral part of the project.

LES THERMES
Dax, France, 1992

Architecture/Interior Design: **Jean Nouvel, Emmanŭel Cattani et Associés**

Dax is a spa near Biarritz, not far from the Atlantic coast. Here it was planned to build a new three-star hotel with thermal baths. Since the project was to occupy a central site, next to the traditional hotel Splendid and the casino in the Cours Verdun, it was of outstanding importance within the urban context. A competition was held, and the prize went to the Paris office of Jean Nouvel and Emmanŭel Cattani. It was their second such triumph, after the bigger spa hotel Santé Beauté in Vichy, which has not yet been realized.

Nouvel's design for Dax follows the building lines of the adjacent Splendid. The ground plan, with its slightly reduced narrow side stretching down to the River Ardour, leaves room for a garden and so makes the area between the two hotels into a small park with palm trees. The main structure is characterized by the contrast, typical of Nouvel, between massiveness and filigree transparency. The loosely defined limits of the structural volume are marked by the vertical, rhythmically arranged metal struts, illuminated at night by white and coloured lights. French- or Italian-style wooden shutters are used for protection against the sun. The narrow entrance lobby, open to the roof, is at the centre of the new building; here the greenery outside is echoed by palms and other plants. The ground floor and first floor of the hotel are reserved for the thermal areas. The 90 single and double rooms are reached by way of long covered corridors. The glass corridor on the top floor is roofed by a wooden grid construction that resembles the window-shutters and projects outwards.

The clients, the Compagnie Thermale de Dax, were attracted not only by Nouvel's striking architectural language, but by his obvious understanding of the therapeutic function of the "gentle medicine" practised in Dax. Experience with projects designed for people of modest means – the social housing project Nemausus 1 in Nîmes, for instance – may have helped the architect in solving this particular building task. The hotel eschews luxury; simple furnishing and the generous use of space combine to produce an ascetic work of art that does not overwhelm the recuperating guest with its stylistic authority, but serves the overall therapeutic purpose.

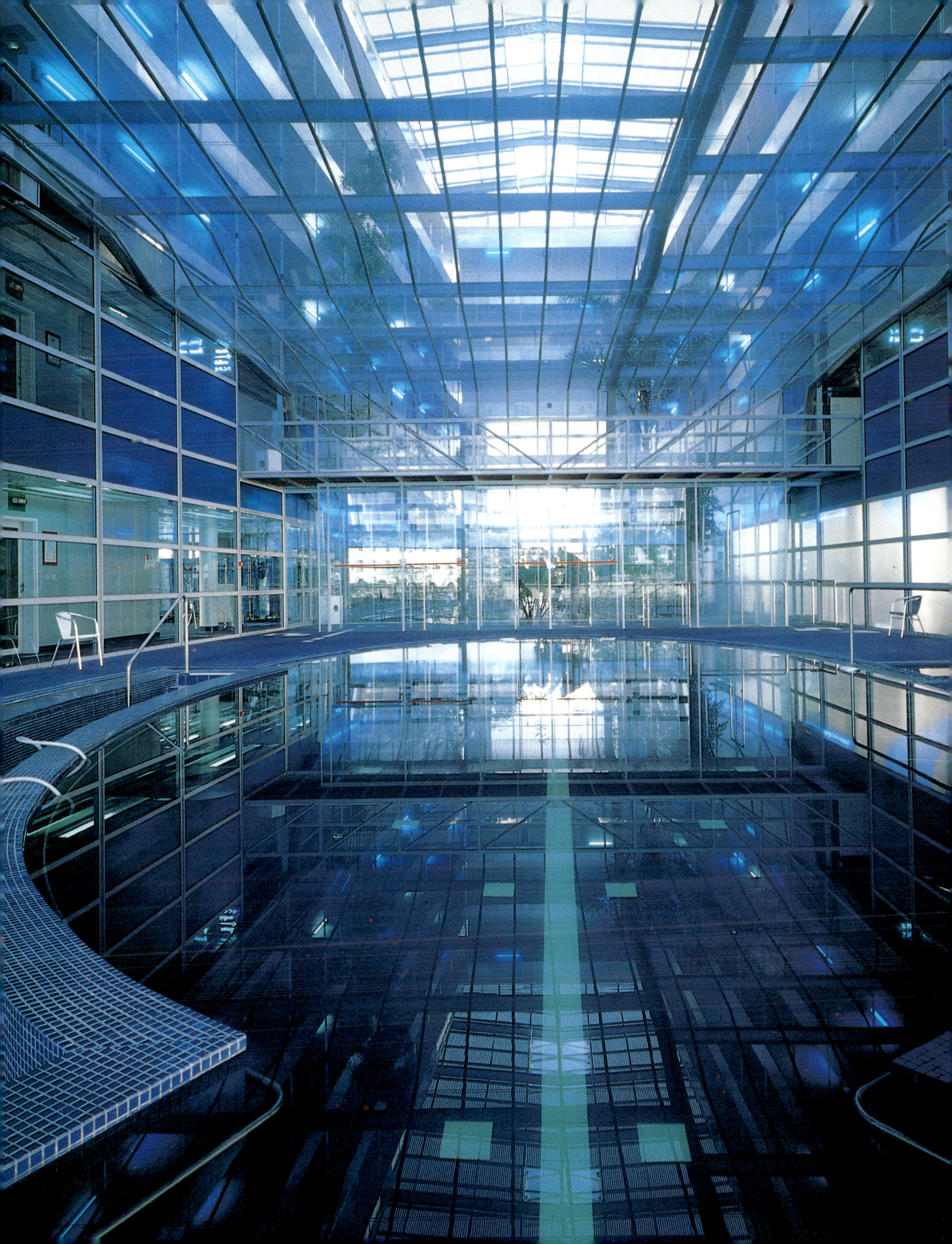

The façades of the accommodation floors are glazed to room height and provided with wooden window shutters for protection against sunlight. The projecting construction on the roof continues the vertical grid structure horizontally.

The interiors of the guest-rooms were also designed by Nouvel. They meet the requirements both of an inexpensive spa hotel and of contemporary aesthetic standards.

LE CHEVAL BLANC
Nîmes, France, 1991
Interior Design: **Jean-Michel Wilmotte**

In his rebuilding of a hotel in Nîmes, the French architect Jean-Michel Wilmotte combines the expressiveness of the ancient fabric with modern design by using the simplest materials – glass, wood and metal. Light, wood and masonry determine the modern look of the guestrooms. The effect of the light can be modified by sliding wooden walls.

When Le Cheval Blanc at Nîmes in the south of France was redesigned, the biggest challenge was posed by the site. The former inn stands directly opposite the Roman arena and is itself a property that bears the mark of many centuries, but has been repeatedly rebuilt. The French architect Jean-Michel Wilmotte, who was responsible, with the American architect I. M. Pei, for the interior design of the underworld beneath the glass pyramid of the new Louvre, is well-known for his skill in dealing with ultra-modern architecture and old historic structures. He was commissioned by a company of which the French night-club queen Régine is a member to convert this historic building into a four-star hotel with conference rooms.

Behind the additions of more recent times, the vaults of a medieval monastery were discovered. Wilmotte carefully exposed them and incorporated them into his new concept. This supplied the programme for the new building. With his graphic, high-tech-oriented avant-garde architecture, Wilmotte sought to create a dialogue with the historic pile. Anything dramatic that was discovered was exploited. He exposed the staircase, which was set in the building like a barrel, and built in concrete girders to increase the dramatic spatial effect with the help of openings and bullet-proof glass floors.

The Cheval Blanc has 19 rooms and 7 maisonette suites on the upper floors, a "Restaurant Gastronomique" run by the chef Thierry Marx, a bistro, wine-bar and two conference rooms. It is thus an ideal venue for business meetings.

Aesthetically, the rooms too are consummate achievements of interior architecture. In the rooms and maisonette suites, which vary in outline, a spartan aesthetic switches suddenly to a superb handling of materials and forms. Luxurious monastic cells of natural wood and smooth white plaster produce the highest degree of refinement. In order to bring in the southern French light, if required, as an atmospheric element in these clearly articulated rooms, Wilmotte fitted sliding chestnut shutters. His design for the hotel is a splendid demonstration of how modern avant-garde architecture and an ancient structure can be perfectly harmonized, interacting in such a way that each enhances the dramatic effect of the other.

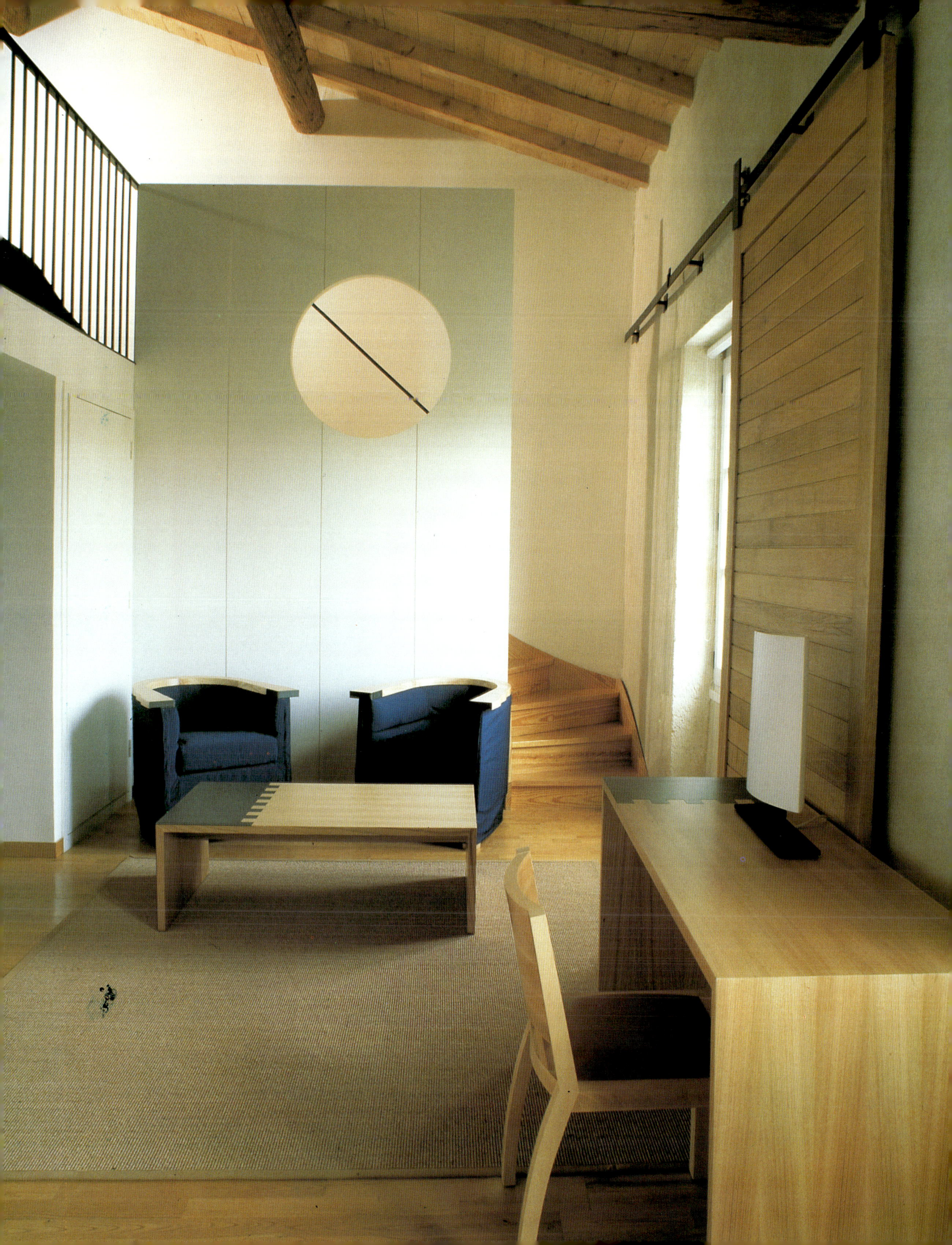

The austerity of the interior appointments is reminiscent of the Japanese aesthetic, and their clarity enhances the effect of the ambitious architectural concept.

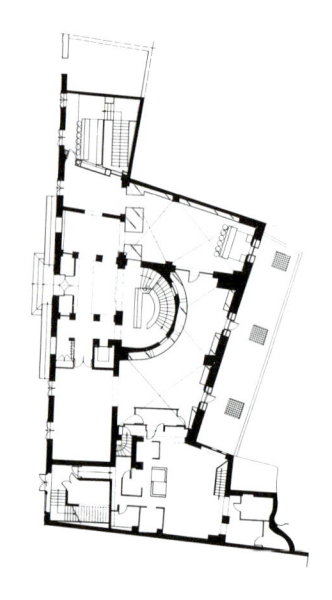

Ground-floor plan.

Second-floor plan with conference rooms.

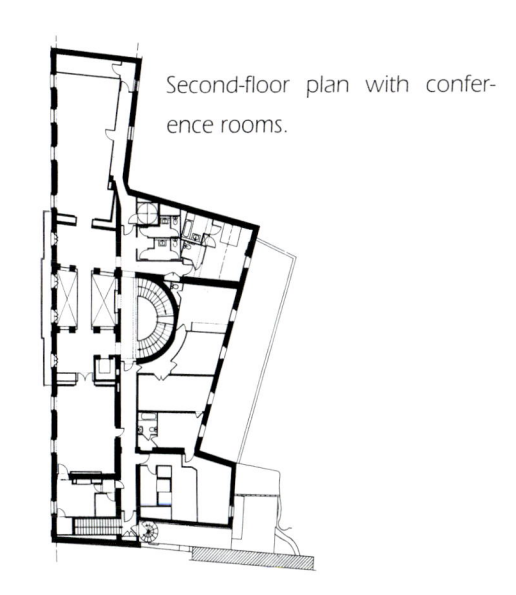

Upper-floor plan showing guestrooms.

Glass ceilings between the floors increase the monumental effect of the semi-rotunda incorporated into the building. Filigree metalwork underlines the graphic effect.

55

The concrete façade of this graceful high-rise building arches up forbiddingly like a shield. Nothing indicates the presence of the hotel, which is entered through the basement.

D-HOTEL
Osaka, Japan, 1989

Architecture/Interior Design:

**Kiyoshi Sey Takeyama,
Amorphe Architects**

The Japanese aesthetic of concrete has been consistently employed in almost all branches of architecture – even in church buildings by Tadao Ando and in residential structures ranging from the apartment block to the family house, the obligatory five-finger exercise for any Japanese avant-garde architect. In the 1980s the fashion designer Rei Kawakubo based her boutique empire Comme des Garçons on an austere aesthetic sensitized solely to the grey tones of concrete, which she used as an effective background against which to display her black and coloured creations to advantage. In the interior architecture of the eighties, concrete became the fashion, synonymous with an uncompromising avant-garde style.

This attitude of mind also produced a hotel building that can scarcely be surpassed in its ideological severity. The graceful nine-storey structure is in Dotonbori, Osaka's amusement district, among countless night-clubs, busy restaurants, yakitori bars and pachinko parlours. The site is extremely narrow and, with its 206 square metres, so small as to be conceivable only in Japan. Here the avant-garde architect Kiyoshi Sey Takeyama, 34 years old at the time, built this diminutive skyscraper, its concrete façade modishly curved towards the river front. At ground level there is only a gallery-type shopping arcade. Anyone wishing to enter the hotel has to walk down to the basement, where he is received by a passage with concealed lighting that could not have been designed more plainly or sparely for a monastery. Here, there is only a fire door at the front, the reception desk in the middle, and between them two lifts to the hotel rooms, which are arranged in pairs round the lift-shaft on each of the upper floors.

In each of the twelve hotel apartments the only natural light enters through a square window opposite the entrance door and through two facing windows in the open bathroom adjoining the bedroom. The guest is confronted with an architecture that is radically different from that of the usual western-style Japanese hotel. The absence of any neon sign and the concealed entrance corridor in the basement make the hotel, in the architect's opinion, into a place that guarantees utter peace and seclusion. In his D-Hotel Kiyoshi Sey Takeyama set out to create the exact opposite of the western-style designer hotel, in which interaction among the guests – seeing and being seen – is one of the most important features of hotel life and vital to the success of the establishment.

Under the extremely narrow site of the hotel is an access corridor with a reception and two lift-shafts.

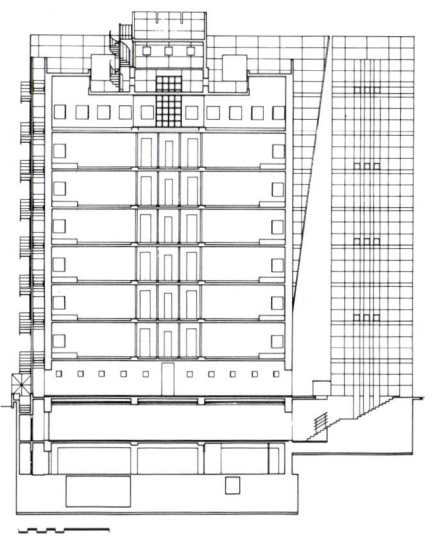

Section

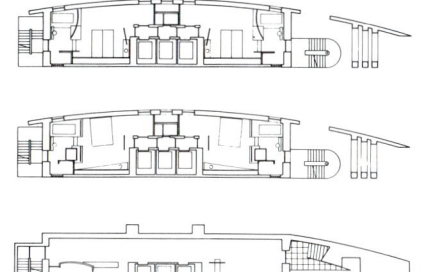

Upper-floor plans showing two guest-rooms.

Floor plan at entrance level.

The bathroom and hotel apartment form one unit. The plainness of the hotel's exterior is matched by that of its interior.

In the dune landscape of Florida's new coastal resort, Seaside, stands its biggest building so far. The hotel's guest apartments are grouped together to form a roof landscape.

DREAMLAND HEIGHTS
Seaside, Florida, USA, 1989
Architecture/Interior Design: **Steven Holl**

The Arcady of backward-looking neo-classicist postmodernism is Seaside, a holiday home project in Florida, 80 miles east of Pensacola on the Gulf of Mexico. Here the developer Robert Davis felt he had a mission to demonstrate, by means of a traditional small-town structure and pastel-coloured wooden houses, that a revival of yesterday's idyll still held out the promise of a better quality of life today. It was all the more surprising, then, that Steven Holl, a New York modernist, should have been the architect invited to plan Seaside's largest building to date, a complex comprising restaurants, shops, a conference hall and a two-storey hotel.

Holl adhered to the precise stipulations regarding land use without forfeiting his aesthetic principles. Dreamland Heights, appositely described by the architect as a "hybrid building", presents a rigorously structured aspect to the central square of Seaside: colonnades two storeys high with a barrel roof of grey metal. Only a few metal bars, protruding irregularly above the roof, indicate that things are less orderly on the rear side. Here, on a wide base, stand three separate blocks of maisonettes, beach architecture seemingly thrown together at random and surmounted by strange punk scaffolds.

For the local community, with its fondness for mini-temples, columns and architraves, Holl's subversive scheme meant a degree of readjustment. Yet the heresy was legitimized by the credo of the client, Robert Davis: "The project is a step into a new world, but fits in with the overall plan of our traditionally structured town. Within this existing framework we go for individual solutions, and we always want to leave room for surprise." The architect himself was attracted by the context, dominated as it was by values and theorems from the past. He dedicated the eight hotel apartments of Dreamland Heights, with their shared roof piazza, to a "company of strangers", differing in temperament and admiring unknown heroes. The five western units are intended for extravagant personalities, "late risers and sunset-worshippers", the three eastern units for "melancholy natures". Each of these has its patron saint: "Tragic Poet", "Musician", "Mathematician". The symbolism is partly reflected in the interiors: the Poet's house is entered by an interlocking double door; the interior staircase of the Musician's house adheres to the black and white of a keyboard. Yet the symbolism is not overdone: in general Holl demonstrates his repertoire of simple materials and surprising divisions of space.

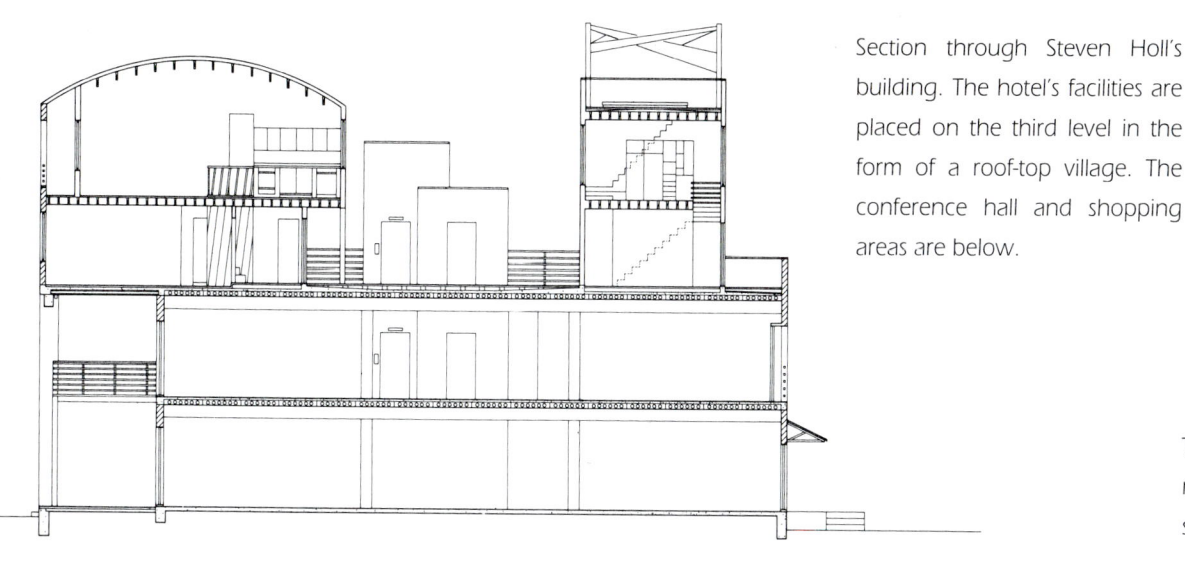

Section through Steven Holl's building. The hotel's facilities are placed on the third level in the form of a roof-top village. The conference hall and shopping areas are below.

The roof area between the hotel maisonettes takes the form of a semi-public piazza.

Steven Holl's interiors offer austere holiday architecture. **Left:** Stairs in the Mathematician's house. **Right:** A spiral staircase in one of the hotel apartments.

61

Left: The classicist façade of the Royalton, built in 1898. Neon signs were deliberately avoided.

Right: In the long foyer the wall lamps, with the archaic look typical of Starck's design, become surreal signposts.

THE ROYALTON
New York, USA, 1988
Interior Design: **Philippe Starck**

In the middle of Manhattan, between Broadway and Fifth Avenue, is the Royalton, the first New York hotel designed by Philippe Starck. It is a key work not only for the artistic biography of this internationally famous French designer, but also for the designer hotel of the new *fin de siècle*. Following individual commissions for cafés, shops and restaurants, the Royalton marked the beginning of Starck's experimentation with large, differentiated spatial creations. Frequently disparaged as a master of allegedly short-winded ideas, he at once demonstrated that his at times irritating inventiveness could be marshalled and disciplined into a coherent design. Starck is thus in line with a genuine French tradition that combines current fashion, luxury, decoration and functionality in exemplary interior appointments.

For the total renovation of this aging, run-down city hotel, Starck chose an overtly theatrical medium: "The customer wanted a hotel with a certain luxury, but not of the usual sort. At the same time it had to convey a very intimate atmosphere, such as is found in a city palace rather than a hotel. A place of discreet luxury, elegant but not commonplace." Visitors and guests entering the lobby find themselves on a catwalk – actors on a stage, strolling across the lobby area below. The theatricality continues into the 168 rooms and suites, where the furniture and fittings are endowed with a symbolic, fetishist character; resistant to instant decoding, they are nevertheless, within the scheme of Starck's formal inventions, semantic signals for those who are initiated into his special community of taste.

Yet the bizarre theatrical elements are never dysfunctional. In the normal rooms, for instance, the design of the interiors, the furniture and the bathrooms is almost ascetic. Starck's concern was "primarily to serve the traveller. And the traveller is by definition someone remote from his familiar shell – which is always depressing. His first impression on entering his room must therefore be one of security. Hence the bed is the centre of the room, partly boxed in as in a ship's cabin." The original fireplaces were deliberately retained, though with new surrounds, to suggest traditional comfort.

The strategy of the show staged at the Royalton follows the pattern of subtle entertainment. The long central hotel lobby, illuminated mainly by uplighters, interrupts everyday reality by separating the noisy street outside from the curious interior and affording a transition to the private, unobtrusive atmosphere of the rooms. The benevolent spirits of the house – everywhere present on the carpets designed by Brigitte Starck – escort guests wherever they go.

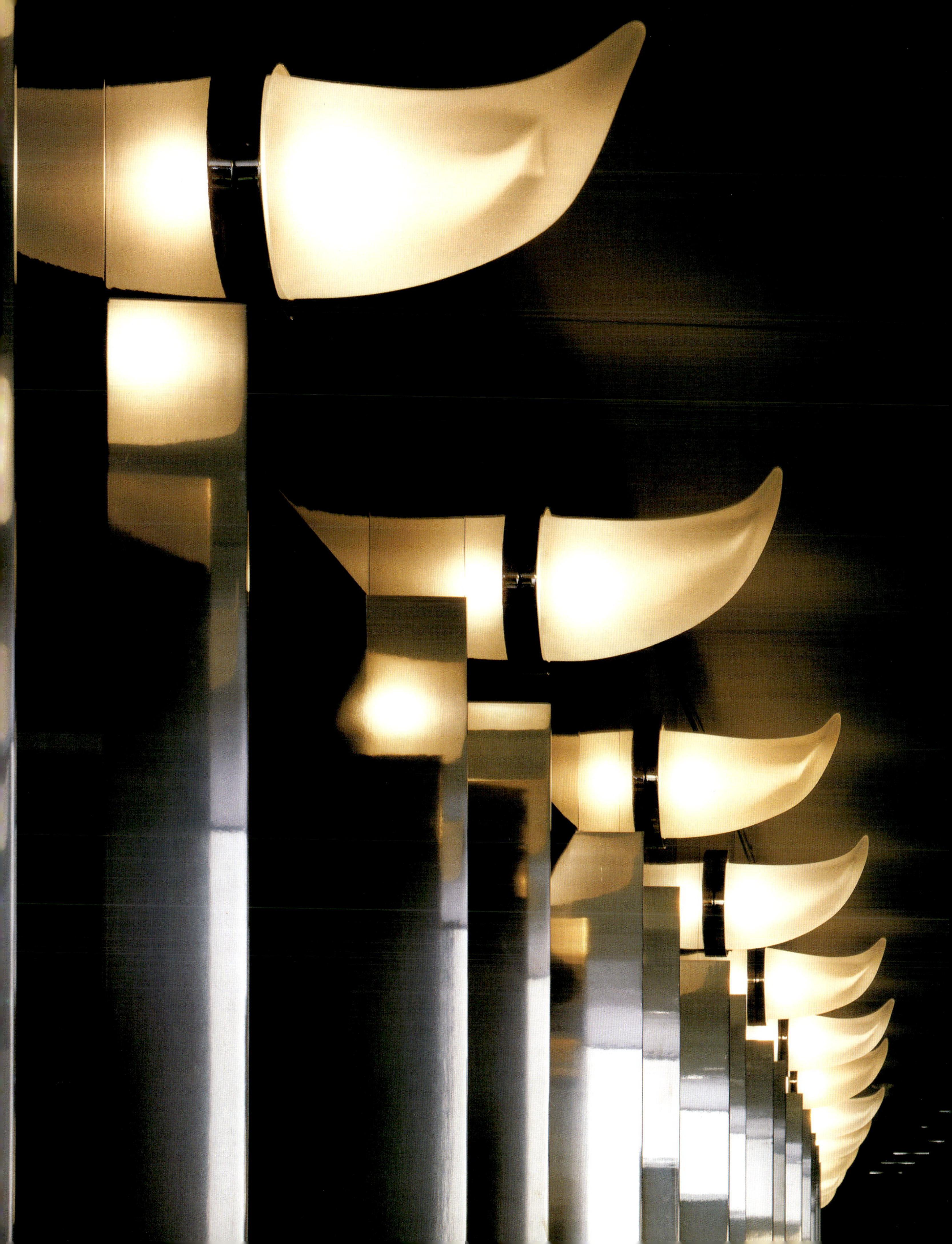

Furniture in a penthouse suite. Most of the pieces were designed for the hotel and only later came on to the international market as the "Royalton" collection.

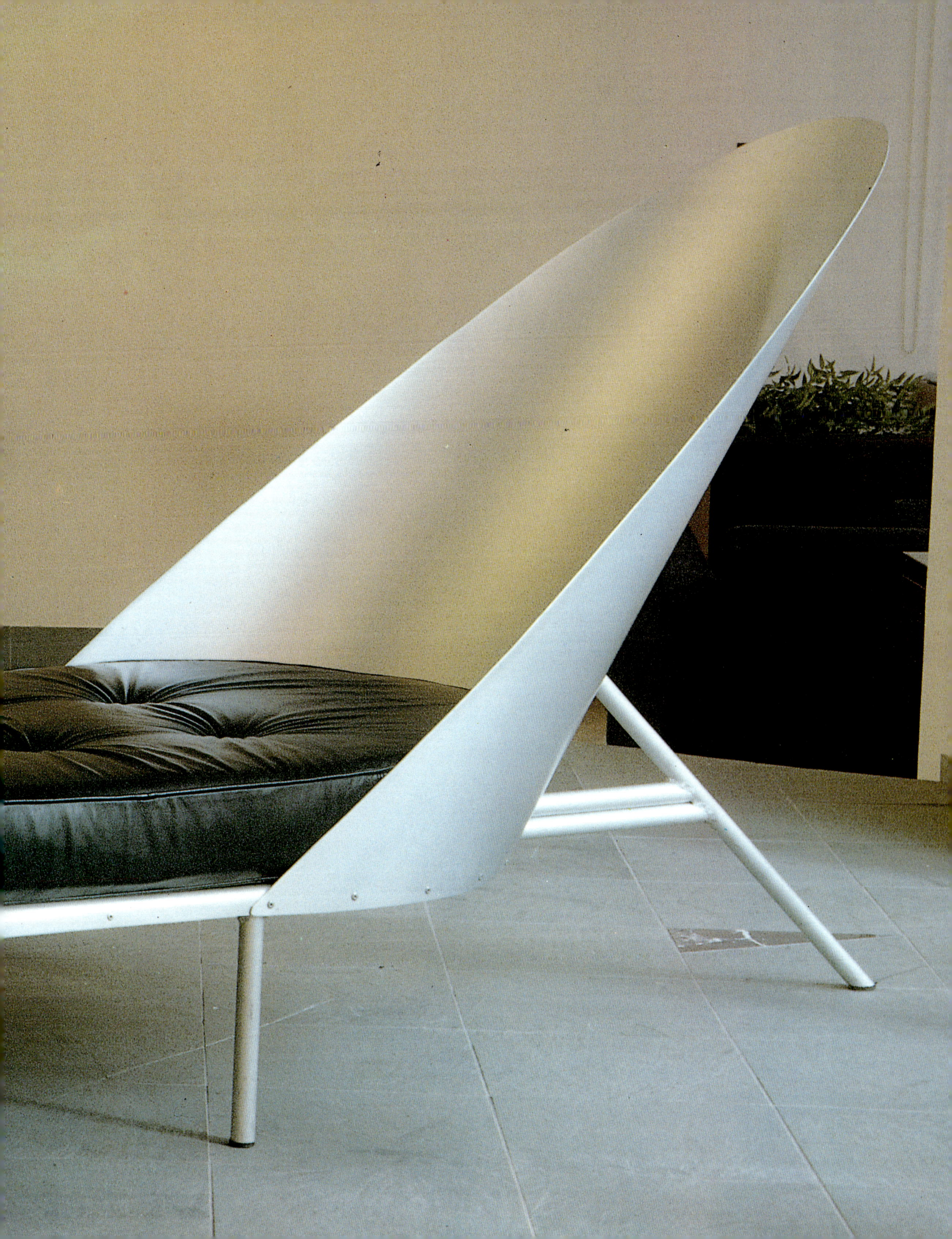

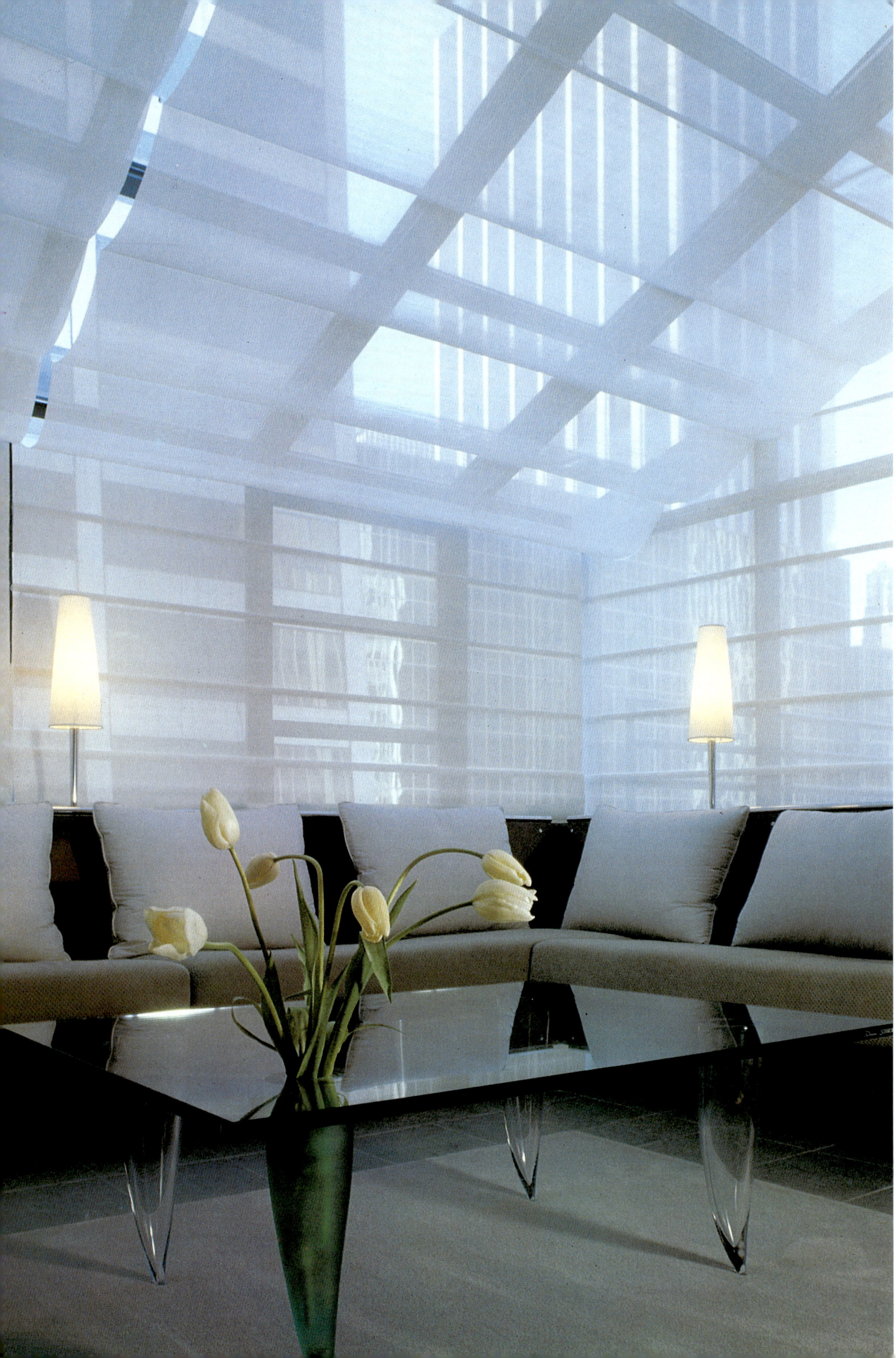

Left: While the interior appointments on most floors fit in with the old fabric, the penthouse suites on the top floor offer new architectural solutions. **Below:** In the junior suites the old fireplaces were left in place but given new stone surrounds.

Left: In the foyer area on the ground floor are the Round Bar and (below) a reading desk with current art catalogues and magazines.

67

Left: The Paramount is entered through a granite-clad passage.
Right: The lobby is dominated by a theatrically tapering staircase which leads up to the restaurant gallery, and a collection of upholstered seats arranged on the chequerboard-patterned floor.

THE PARAMOUNT
New York, USA, 1990
Interior Design: **Philippe Starck**

Philippe Starck's second commission to redesign an old, run-down New York hotel had different aims and dimensions from those of the high-class, medium-sized Royalton (see page 62). Close to Times Square, the Paramount was envisaged as a trendy budget hotel for a young international public drawn from the advertising and media scene, and of course for (design-orientated) tourists. The client was again Ian Schrager, New York's most innovative hotelier who, describing his association with Starck, commented that "his projects mark the birth of a new phase in contemporary aesthetic thinking, for his design will change the way we live and work". The Parisian in New York was not inhibited by the restricted budget, but put on a fresh piece of hotel theatre in the building, which was built in 1927. He himself claimed that in designing the Paramount he was creating "democratic *haute couture*". Instead of a five-finger exercise of his talents, he delivered a virtuoso performance. Central to the experience of the hotel is the hall, two storeys high, from which a staircase leads up to the surrounding restaurant gallery, widening out towards the top to create a teasing perspective. The slightly tilted rear wall of this "stairway to heaven" meets the ceiling at an acute angle and is covered with platinum leaf. In the square lobby there is an eclectic mixture of furniture and fittings – even old-world black telephones – which deliberately recalls the old-fashioned groups of miscellaneous upholstered furniture commonly found in aging hotels. In Starck's case they represent all stages in the history of modern design – from Marco Zanuso, Franco Albini and Jean-Michel Frank to Carlos Riart, Jasper Morrison and Marc Newson. The guests are greeted in poetic fashion: set in the middle of each of the square, grey, marble-inlaid stones lining the walls of the entrance corridor is a red rose.

Over 600 rooms (among them only a handful of suites) are distributed among 20 floors. The very narrow ground plan of the standard guest-rooms called for extreme economy in redesigning the building. Starck's choice of an upholstered copy of Vermeer's *Lacemaker* in a lavish gold frame (with a museum light) as an oversized headpiece for each of the beds is just one of many minor strokes of genius. The television set disappears in a slim, movable cabinet; through a "magic eye" cut into the doors the screen glimmers when the set is switched on. The lifts are lit in dark colours ranging from sinful red to nocturnal blue. In the similarly underlit corridors, illuminated displays inform guests about the state of the weather.

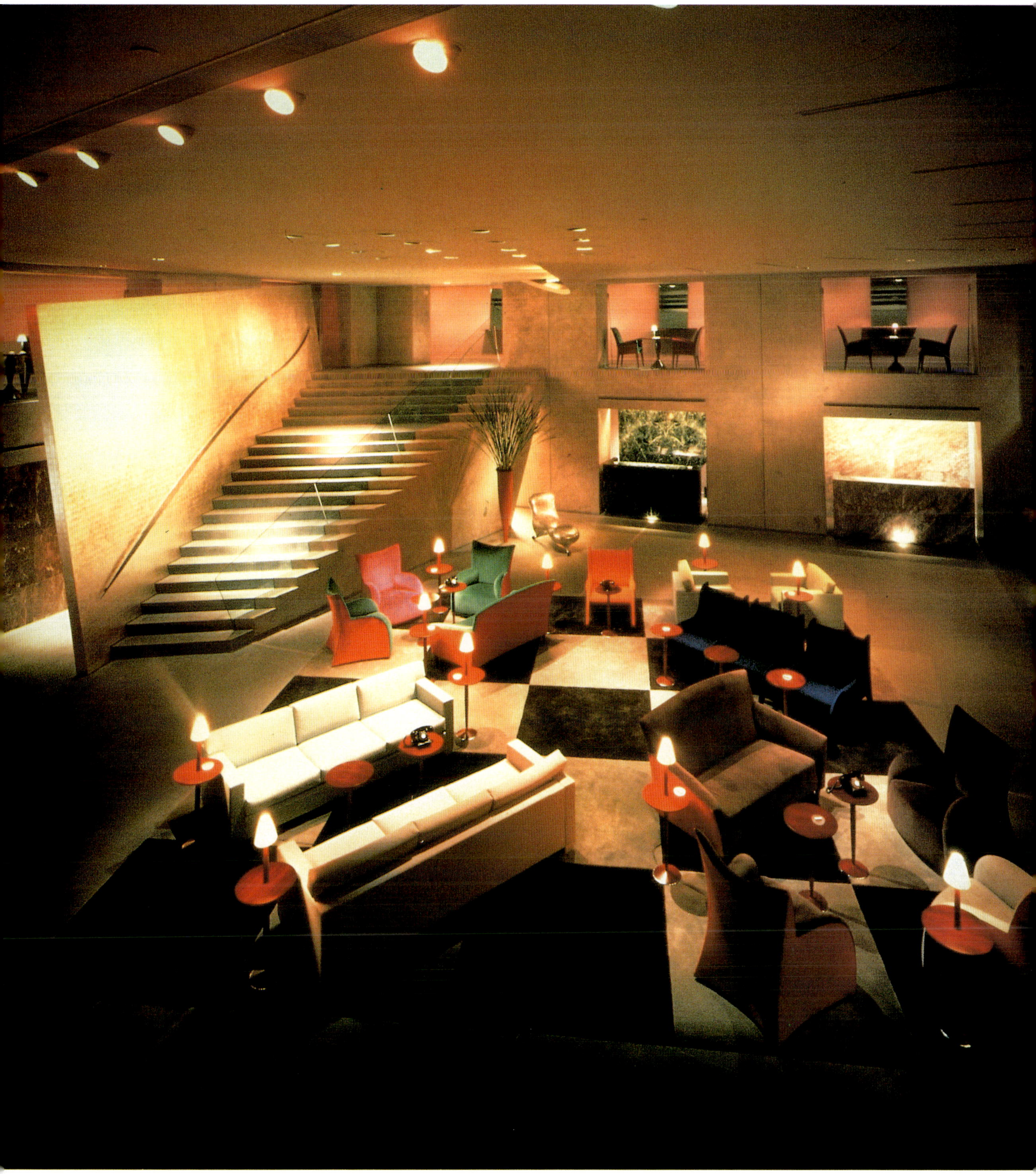

Right: Ground plan of the mezzanine.

Below: The lobby and mezzanine emphasize the old principle of seeing and being seen. The atmospheric upholstered furniture and small table lamps suggest the mood of an aging American hotel lobby.

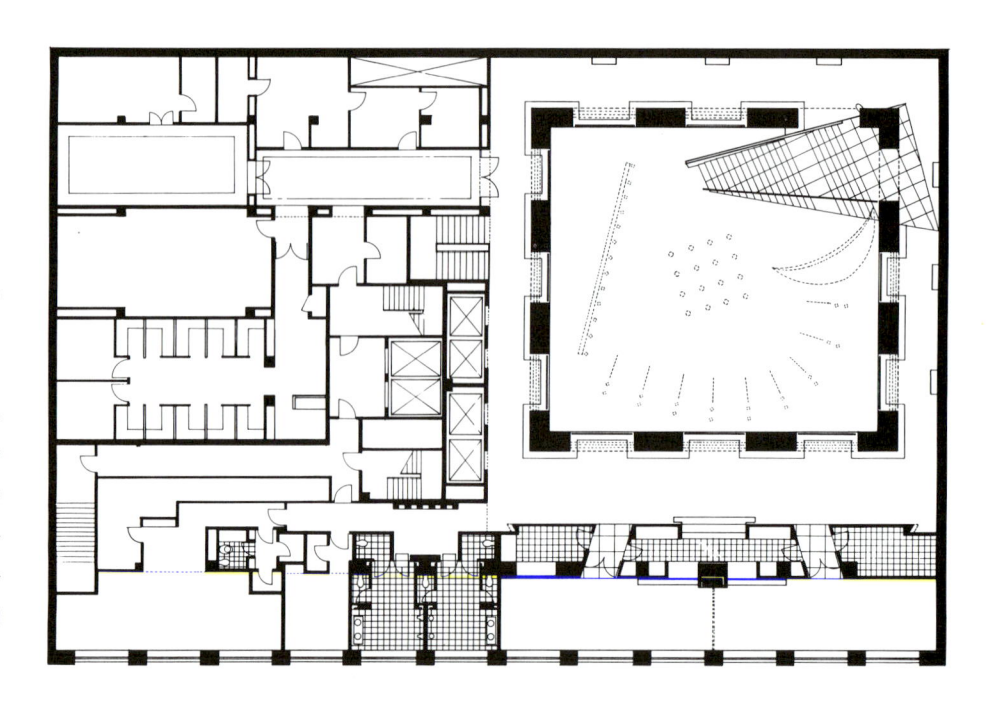

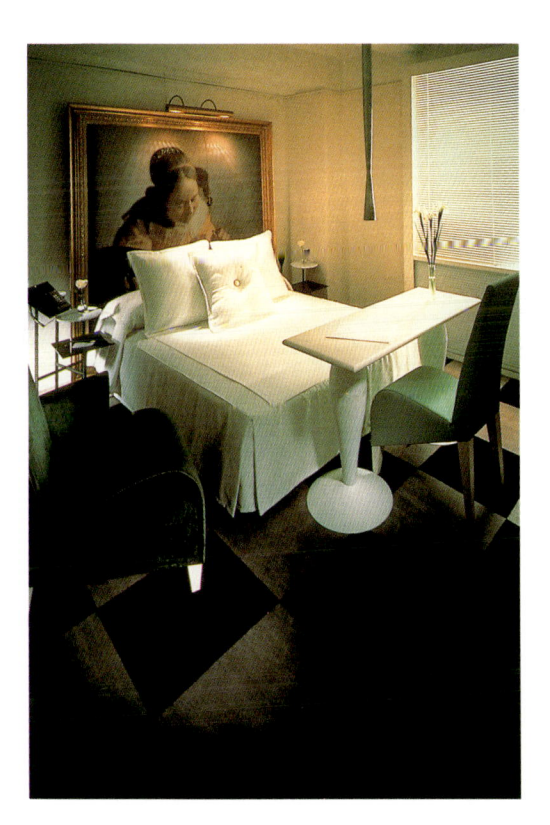

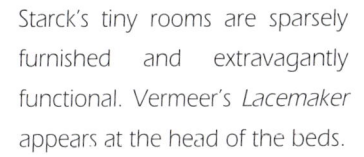

Starck's tiny rooms are sparsely furnished and extravagantly functional. Vermeer's *Lacemaker* appears at the head of the beds.

The bathrooms were not completely redesigned. Only the conical wash basin with its mirror and a few accessories are unmistakably by Starck.

In front of the stairs in the lobby the eye is caught by a couch covered with aluminium plate. Designed by the Australian Marc Newson, it is more an artistic sculpture than a practical item of furniture.

The Hotel Marittimo occupies an old bank building in the Japanese city of Otaru.

OTARU MARITTIMO
Otaru, Japan, 1989
Interior Design: **Branson Coates Architecture**

The great days of sea travel, which shaped the golden age of the northern Japanese seaport of Otaru, came to an end after the Second World War. Sewing machines and fountain pens from Europe and America are no longer unloaded at the docks, and the chic ocean liners no longer leave the quayside. Yet the docks, warehouses and splendid bank buildings of Otaru's boom years are today a picturesque historical set and an object of speculation for the tourist trade. It was this new branch of industry that the Japanese investment firm Jasmac had in mind when it engaged British architects Branson Coates to transform an art deco bank building into a sensational tourist hotel. The hiring of foreign architects was above all an aesthetic speculation. Branson Coates had already made a shocking début in Japan with a tasteless but nerve-tingling catastrophe scenario. The architects had crashed one wing of a bomber, together with engines and landing-flaps, into the façade of the "Parco", a Tokyo department store, and installed a coffee bar underneath it.

For the Marittimo project they were expected to come up with something equally unusual. They designed 25 rooms as picturesque pirate dreams, showpieces which were intended to arouse emotion and bring home Otaru's great past to the tourist.

As in a ballad, 25 seaports in faraway lands and far-off days are evoked in the hotel rooms – old Bombay, romantic Naples, optimistic New York, mysterious Alexandria, classical St Petersburg – with the help of original props, picture carpets and bizarre designer furniture. The vanished world of sea travel, long sunk beneath the waves, is a leitmotif that pervades the whole hotel. The lobby recalls the office of a shipping company. On the first floor the Star Bar, with its imaginary planetarium, offers a glimpse of the galaxies. Next to it a bizarre "Shipping Museum" entices the guest with curiosities from all over the world. Even the World Fish restaurant in the two-storey hall of the former bank, with its classical stucco columns, is more like a set for a kitsch pirate film than a twentieth-century hotel. Yet it is this eccentric display of a world one would not expect to find in a modern hotel that accounts for the charm and success of this collage of nautical antiques, designer furniture, first-edition carpets and decorative set pieces. Branson Coates' morbid yet highly subtle adventure design has turned a historic bank building into a total work of art with great entertainment value.

In what was the main hall there is now a theatrically appointed fish restaurant. As in the decoration of the rooms, an attempt is made to blur the borderline between illusion and reality.

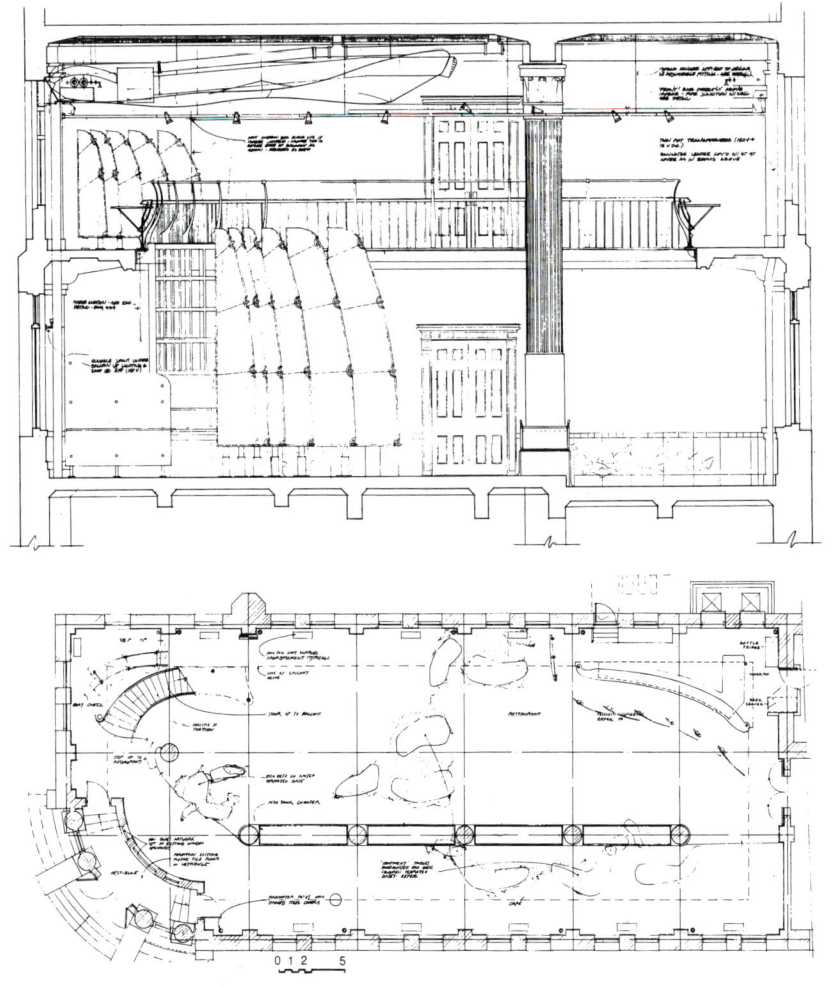

73

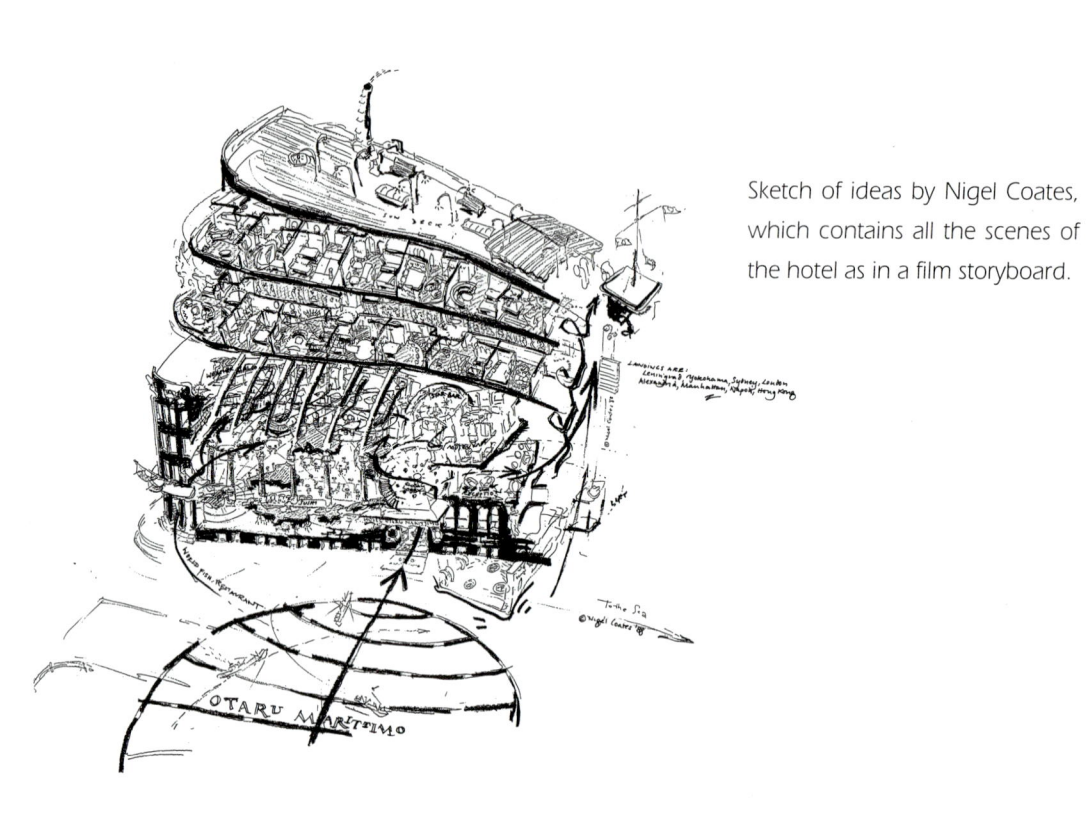

Sketch of ideas by Nigel Coates, which contains all the scenes of the hotel as in a film storyboard.

The rooms are dedicated to famous international ports and partly furnished with original props. Each room thus evokes a different world of experience: Bombay (far left), Alexandria (left), London (above left) and Manhattan (above right). Each of the upholstered chairs designed by Nigel Coates is covered differently, and the Irish-made carpets are inspired by the different seaports.

Left: The lobby of the Triton can be seen from outside, like a window display. **Right:** Guests are greeted by inverted columns.

THE TRITON
San Francisco, USA, 1991
Interior Design: **Michael Moore**

The Triton, a mythical creature of antiquity, half human and half marine animal, supplies the programme for the interior appointment of the San Francisco hotel of that name. Guests are transported at once into an atmospheric world of fantasy by the charming hotel scenery, which recalls the cheerful mythology of ancient times. Michael Moore, formerly a decorator for Macy's, collaborated with local artists to produce this pastel-coloured west-coast Elysium, which represents a new genre of hotel décor. Although there was no plan to produce a designer hotel, the Triton has had this special status conferred on it by the public and the press.

Unlike the designer hotels of New York, which exploit ideas imported from Europe, the Triton draws upon the expressive vitality of local artists, who, under Michael Moore's direction, have created scenery that is at once inspired and eccentric. Behind this successful project lies the experience of Bill Krimton, a west-coast hotel impressario who has revitalized nearly a dozen old hotels. For the Triton he and a finance consortium bought the Beverly Plaza, an aging hotel in a popular city location adjoining Chinatown, and turned it into a showpiece with a distinctly west-coast orientation.

All seriousness is dispelled at the entrance by the "Laughing Columns" – inverted, golden columns, designed by the artist Arlene Elisabeth. These inverted symbols of classical order set the tenor of the whole of the 140-room hotel, and guests are drawn into its spirit. Elsewhere in the interior décor the familiar is parodied in ways that are relaxing, exciting or entertaining. It is a far cry from the solemnity of New York's designer hotels, for here the dusky, pastel-coloured murals invite smiles. The upholstered seating, reminiscent of oriental smoking rooms and arranged in the manner of a Victorian drawing room, balances between kitsch and the art of interior furnishing. The high point of the deliberately overdone design is reached with the bizarre "dervish chairs" in the entrance area with their backrests shaped like night-caps. Bill Krimton appositely describes his medium-sized establishments as "boutique hotels", and he attracts far more bookings for these publicity-laden individual ventures than the average hotel in San Francisco.

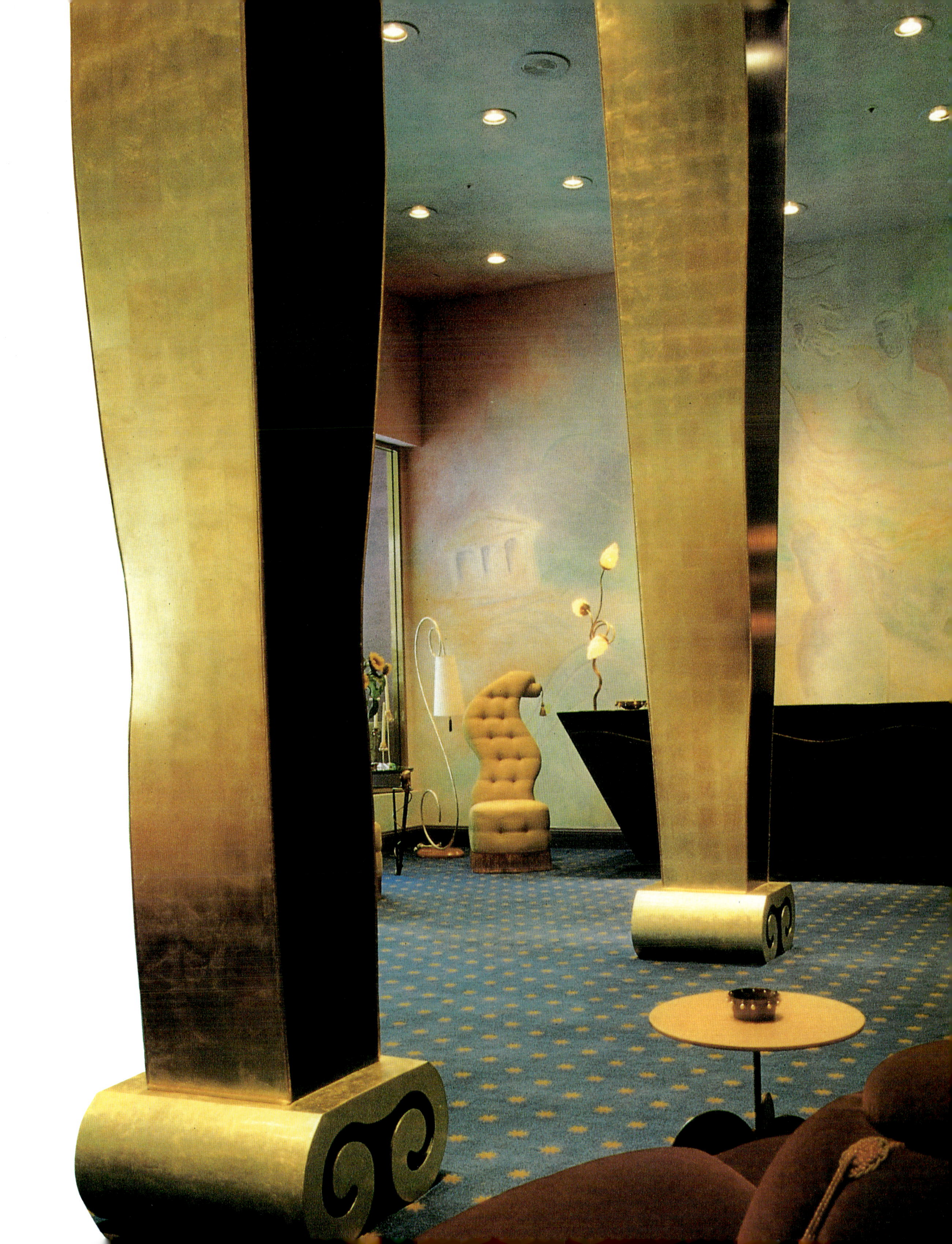

In the lobby, dervish chairs by Goodman & Charlton are the prelude to the fanciful world of the salon.

Right: The atmosphere in the Triton is lavish without being plushy. Traditional forms in pastel shades and gold tones, are arranged in a bold, modern manner and create an imaginative fairytale world.

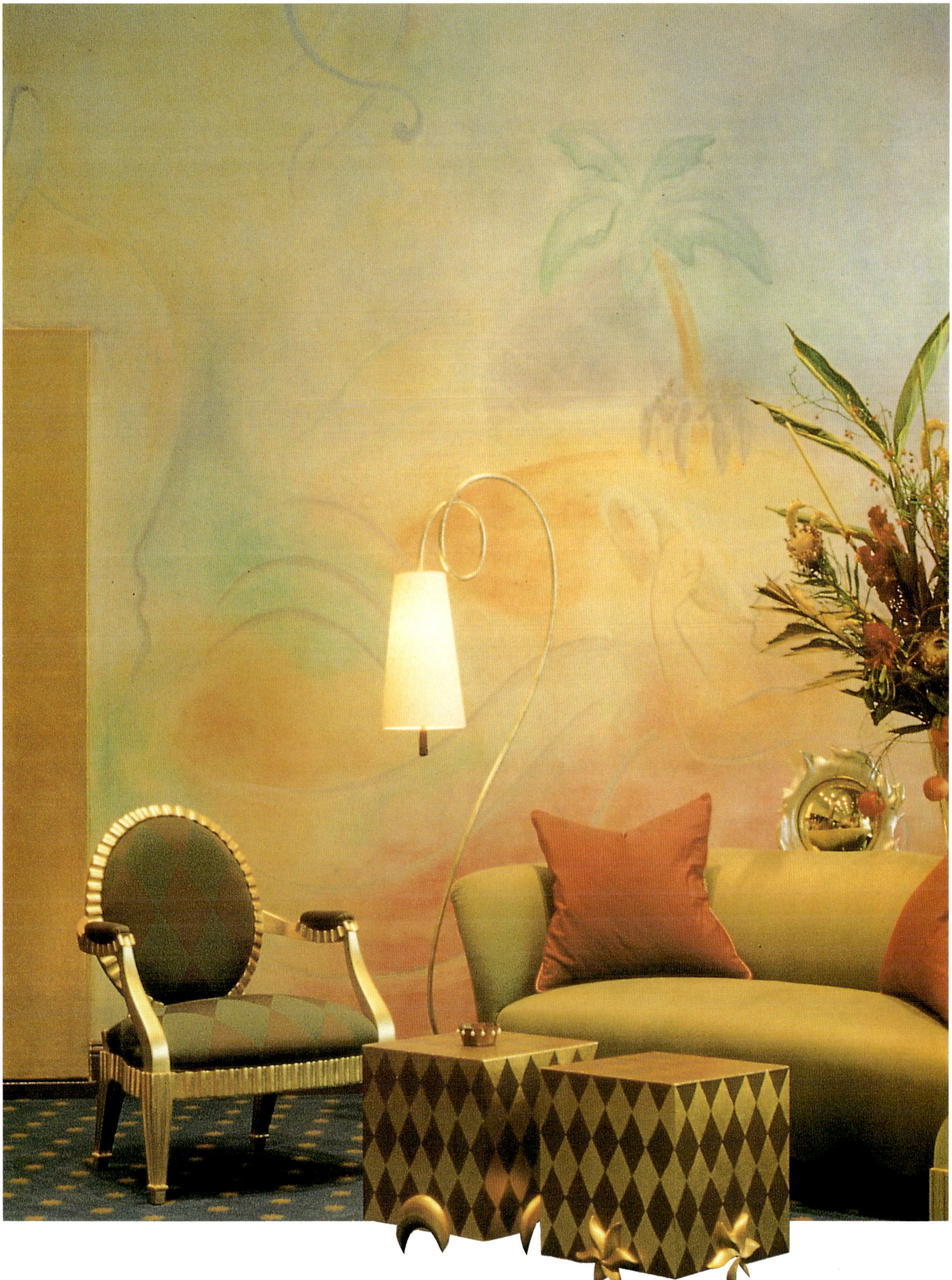

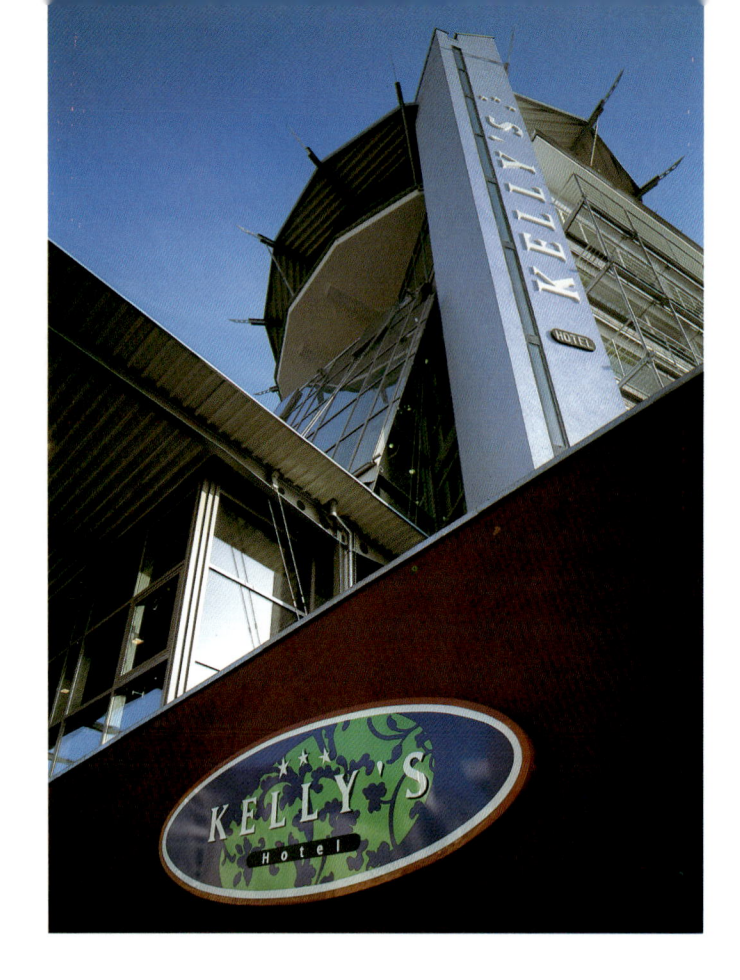

Left: The hotel's steel façade hides a colourful world of pop art and fifties style.

Right: For the corridors the architects invented a striking scheme of colour and light.

KELLY'S HOTEL
Bensheim, Germany, 1992
Interior Design: **Adieu New York Design, Dieter Brell**

The clients who commissioned the first designer hotels were mostly individuals responding to an inner conviction. In the progressive nineties they have been succeeded by a generation of younger entrepreneurs who have transformed the individual case into a marketing strategy that can be generalized. Among them are the initiators of Kelly's Hotel in the little German town of Bensheim. This idyllic spot on the Bergstrasse, a route that skirts the Odenwald and is lined by castles and stately homes, is close to the busy industrial and commercial centres of Mannheim and Frankfurt, but also to the romantic city of Heidelberg. Here, of all places, it was planned to build the prototype of a trendy three-star hotel, soon to be copied in Berlin and Budapest: "In future Kelly's Hotels will appeal to those who have grown up with Mickey Mouse, MTV, Tekkno or sushi bars. And this generation is increasingly moving into decision-making positions and will have a crucial say in shaping the values and standards of the next decade."

This entrepreneurial credo relies on an obvious change in the travelling habits of businessmen. Only five per cent stay in four- or five-star hotels; the rest, thanks to shrinking budgets, have to settle for medium-priced accommodation. The younger clientele is splendidly entertained in this first Kelly's Hotel. Adieu New York, a team of newcomers from Wiesbaden, makes no attempt at great feats of design, but delights in its imitative role, parodying the gravitas and artistic pretensions of its models, revelling in borrowings from pop art and cartoons.

There is nothing of any real value in the 122 rooms, but nearly everything is entertaining. The persiflage of the wide world is deliberate; fictive souvenirs from non-existent sister-hotels in Lhasa or Dar es Salaam are on sale at the reception, while a row of clocks behind the desk records the time of day in five continents. The service, on the other hand, has to be professional; this includes the provision of conference rooms and communication facilities of the requisite technical standard. The packaging may be playful, but the basic needs of the targeted business clientele are treated seriously. In the furnishing no attempt has been made to introduce designer icons – primarily to avoid expense, but also to establish an ideology: everywhere guests must feel that they are moving in a thoroughly familiar and entertaining ambience, yet the impression created by every interior and item of the décor must be highly individual and contribute to the unique brand image of Kelly's.

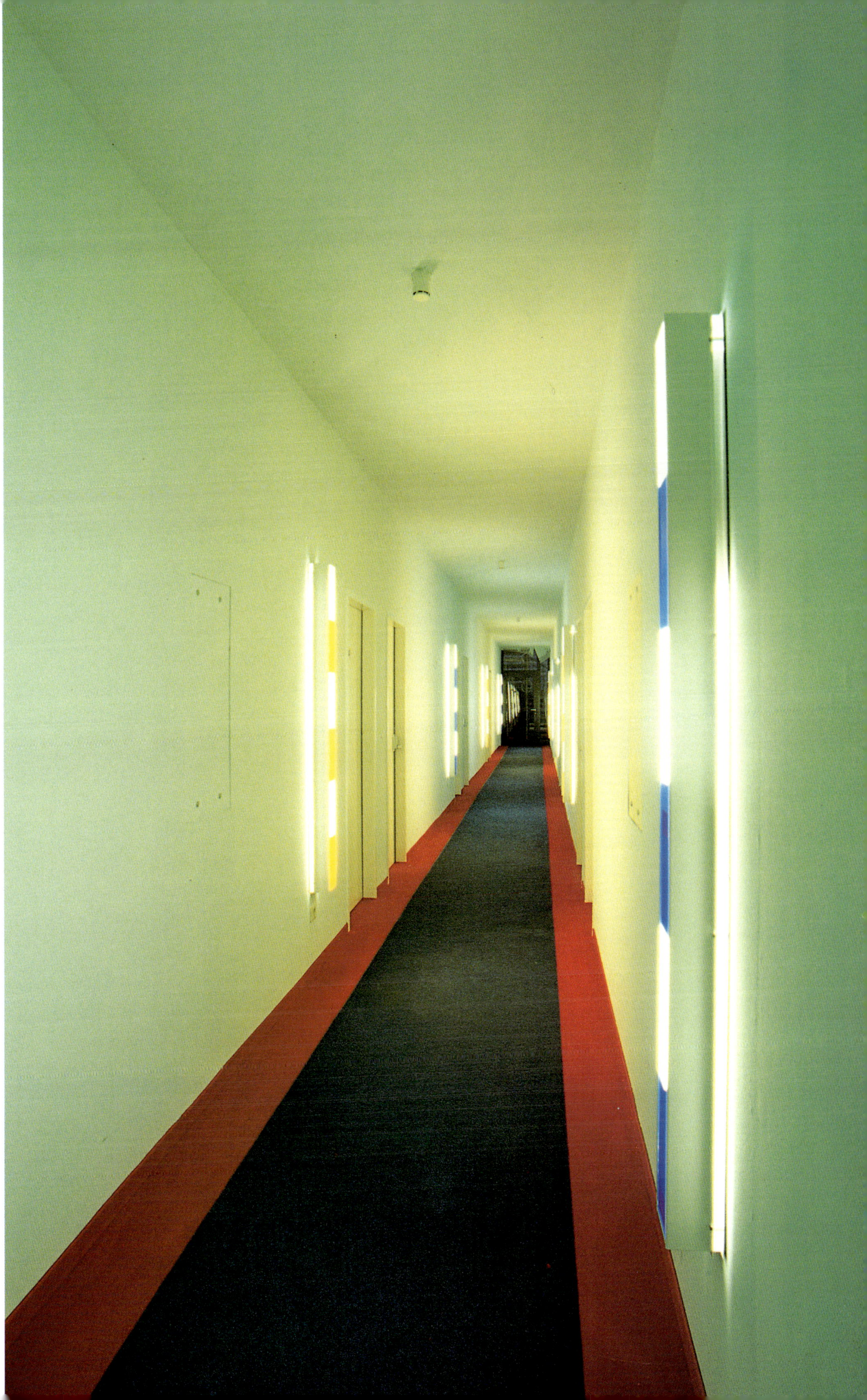

Behind a glazed steel façade is the entrance area with reception desk, lobby and adjacent bar-restaurant.

82

Two examples of the guestrooms. Using decorative shapes, colours and materials, the German design group Adieu New York created an entertaining and popular hotel.

83

Left: The hotel's windowless façade with travertine columns is flanked by two long side structures housing four designer bars.
Right: View from the main building to a brick-built side wing.

IL PALAZZO
Fukuoka, Japan, 1989

Architecture: **Aldo Rossi/Morris Adjmi**
Interior Design: **Shigeru Uchida, Alfredo Arribas, Shiro Kuramata, Gaetano Pesce, Aldo Rossi/Morris Adjmi, Ettore Sottsass**

During the years of the unbridled property boom, Japan became a playground for the European avant-garde in architecture and design. The publicity value of commissioning designs from star designers was used to counterbalance the horrendous land prices. The most brilliant monument to this marketing strategy was erected in the provincial city of Fukuoka. Mitsuhiro Kuzuwa, a seasoned speculator and entrepreneur who heads the Jasmac concern, had bought up a whole area of the city in order to revive it commercially through new construction projects, including numerous entertainment enterprises. The first landmark was to be the hotel project Il Palazzo, which is a collage of prominent European and Japanese design styles.

The Italian rationalist Aldo Rossi and his partner Morris Adjmi designed the architectural shell, a massive, central structure with an imposing windowless façade of travertine columns and green copper transverse girders, flanked by two long side structures. Shigeru Uchida was responsible for the interior architecture of the lobby, the restaurant and the 62 rooms. In the public areas he adopted Rossi's strategy, which relies on colourful materials, by using Chinese quince veneer and green onyx terrazzo; even the design of the furniture is strikingly monumental. The guestrooms, divided among five floors, are largely western in style, with Far Eastern accents, but the top floor has suites in the traditional Japanese style.

Four bars and an underground nightclub area supply the peripheral entertainment, which is in fact the motive force behind the whole project. Aldo Rossi's bar, El Dorado, contains a back-lit replica of the hotel façade. Ettore Sottsass and his collaborators Marco Zanini and Mike Ryan, created the Zibibbo bar, a miniature "town" beneath Egyptian stars. Gaetano Pesce's El Liston bar is a cavern full of strange forms and bewildering colours. And Shiro Kuramata's Oblomova, a bright, transparent zone, demonstrates the transient nature of bars everywhere – as settings for drinks or stop-off points for brief encounters. In his Barna Crossing, Alfredo Arribas created a nocturnal world with optical and technical refinements: a disco, a bar-restaurant and clubs occupying 1,500 square metres of floorspace.

The additive principle – the unedited assembly of different design exhibits – has one unifying strand: Rossi's rigid architectural design, which combines with the cool splendour of Uchida's interiors to provide the artistic framework within which the other soloists perform. Viewed in this way, Il Palazzo may be said to be an architectural compilation, a portfolio compiled to illustrate the spirit of the times.

IL PALAZZO

The monumental architecture of Aldo Rossi is reflected in Shigeru Uchida's interior design. In the entrance area and first-floor bar Uchida uses an impresssive combination of red-stained quince and onyx terrazzo.

The Zibibbo bar by Ettore Sottsass, Marco Zanini and Mike Ryan is conceived as a southern village under a starry sky.

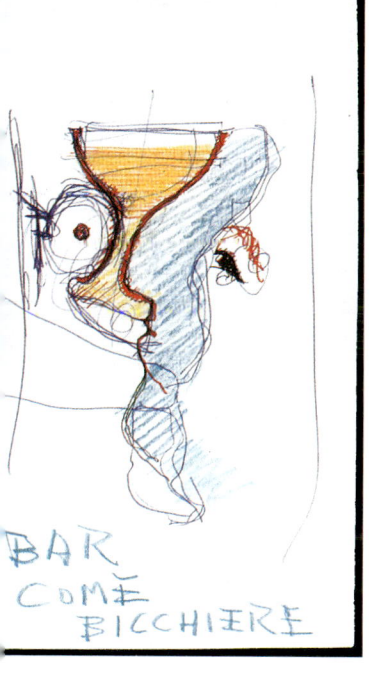

Below: A model for Gaetano Pesce's El Liston bar. The Italian designer developed the form of the bar counter from a drawing (left) that shows the profile of a drinker and the contour of a wine glass.

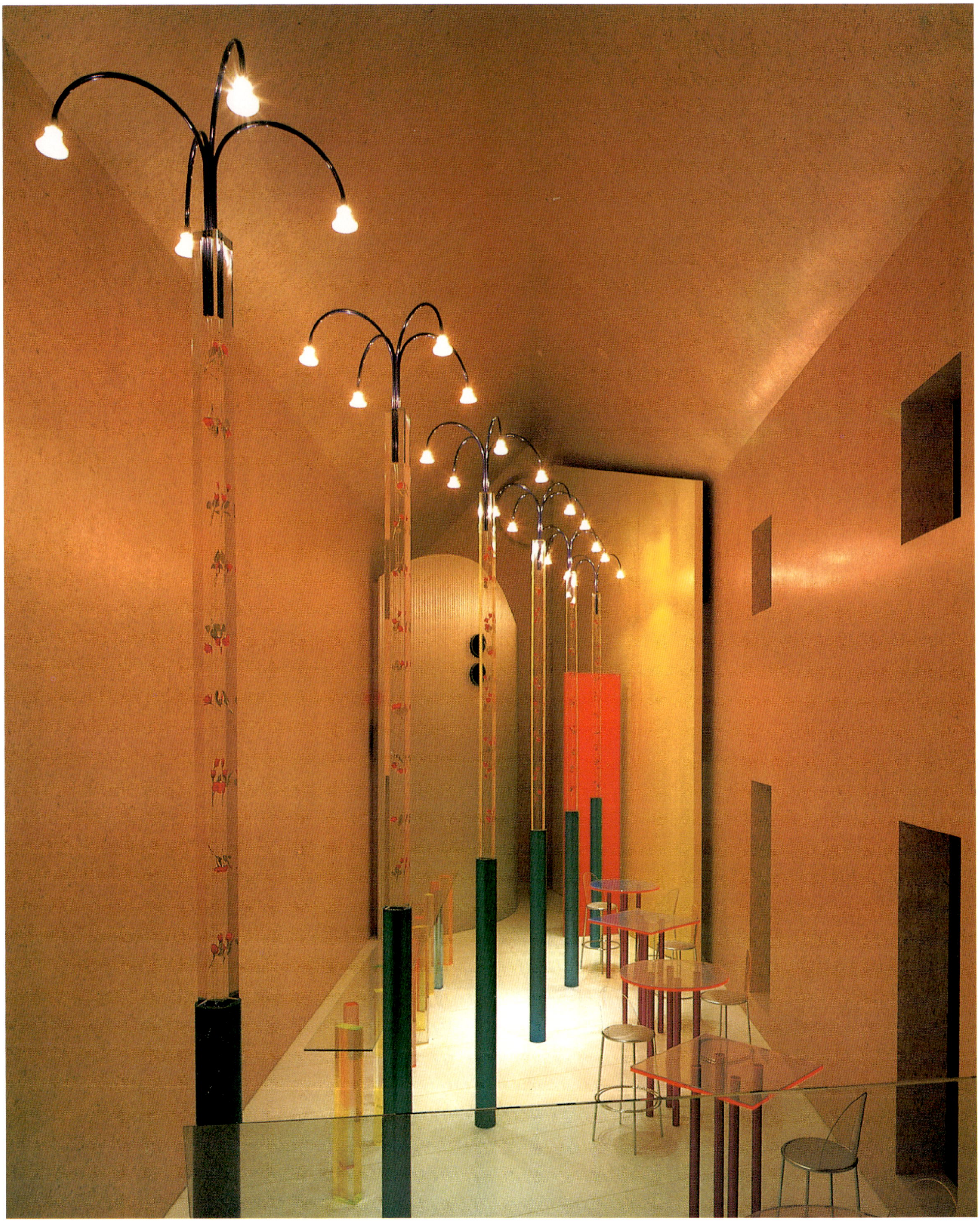

Right: The ground floor of Il Palazzo is devoted to nightlife. In the main building, flanked by the four designer bars, is a nightclub designed by Alfredo Arribas.

Below: A plexiglass model of the Oblomova bar by Shiro Kuramata. In this project the Japanese designer sought to make music visible through colour. **Left:** Kuramata's style might be described as poetic minimalism.

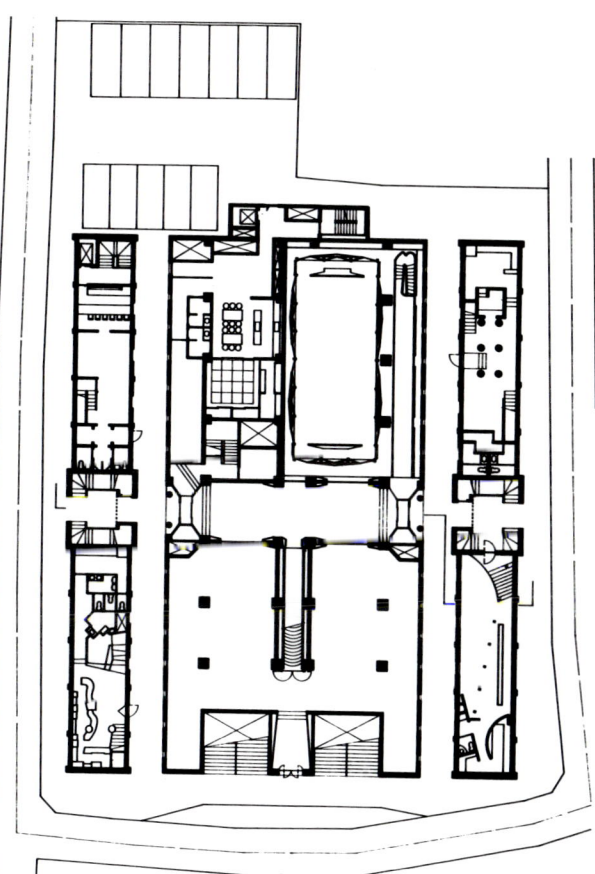

Below: View of a Japanese-style guest-room designed by Shigeru Uchida, in the middle part of the building.

Right: The standing clock "Dear Morris" by Shigeru Uchida lends an architectonic accent to the hotel corridors.

A western-style suite designed by Uchida.

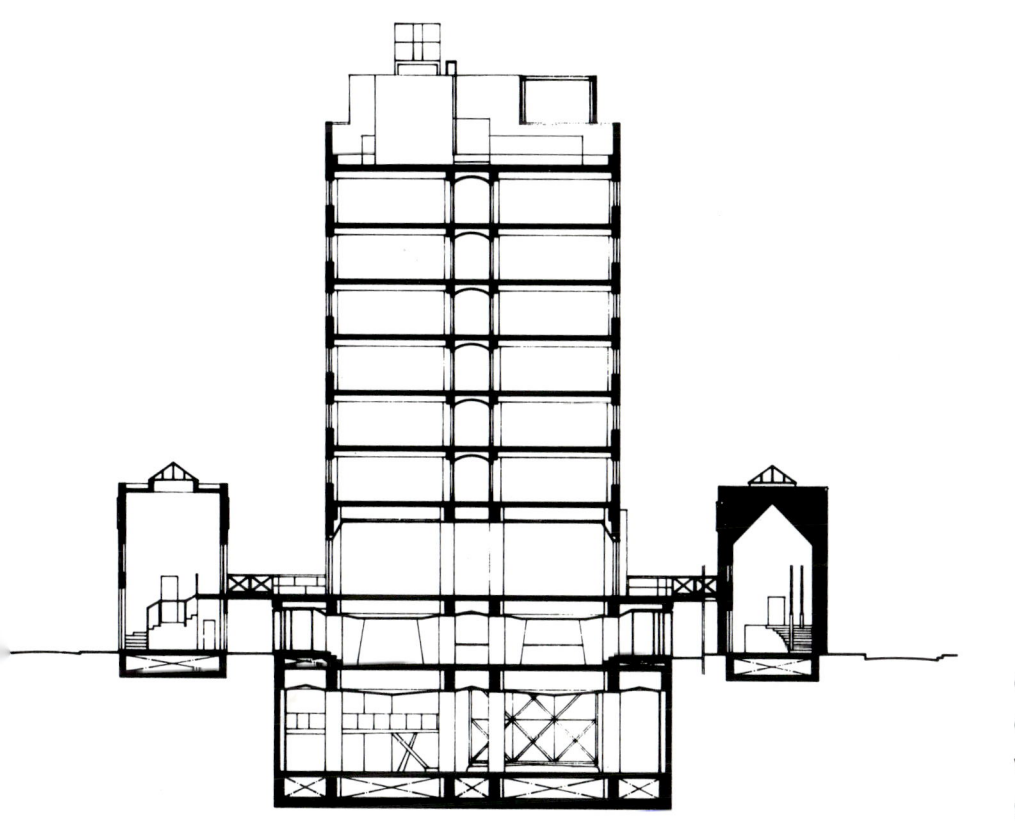

Cross-section showing the night-club in the basement, the bar wings and the section with guest-rooms.

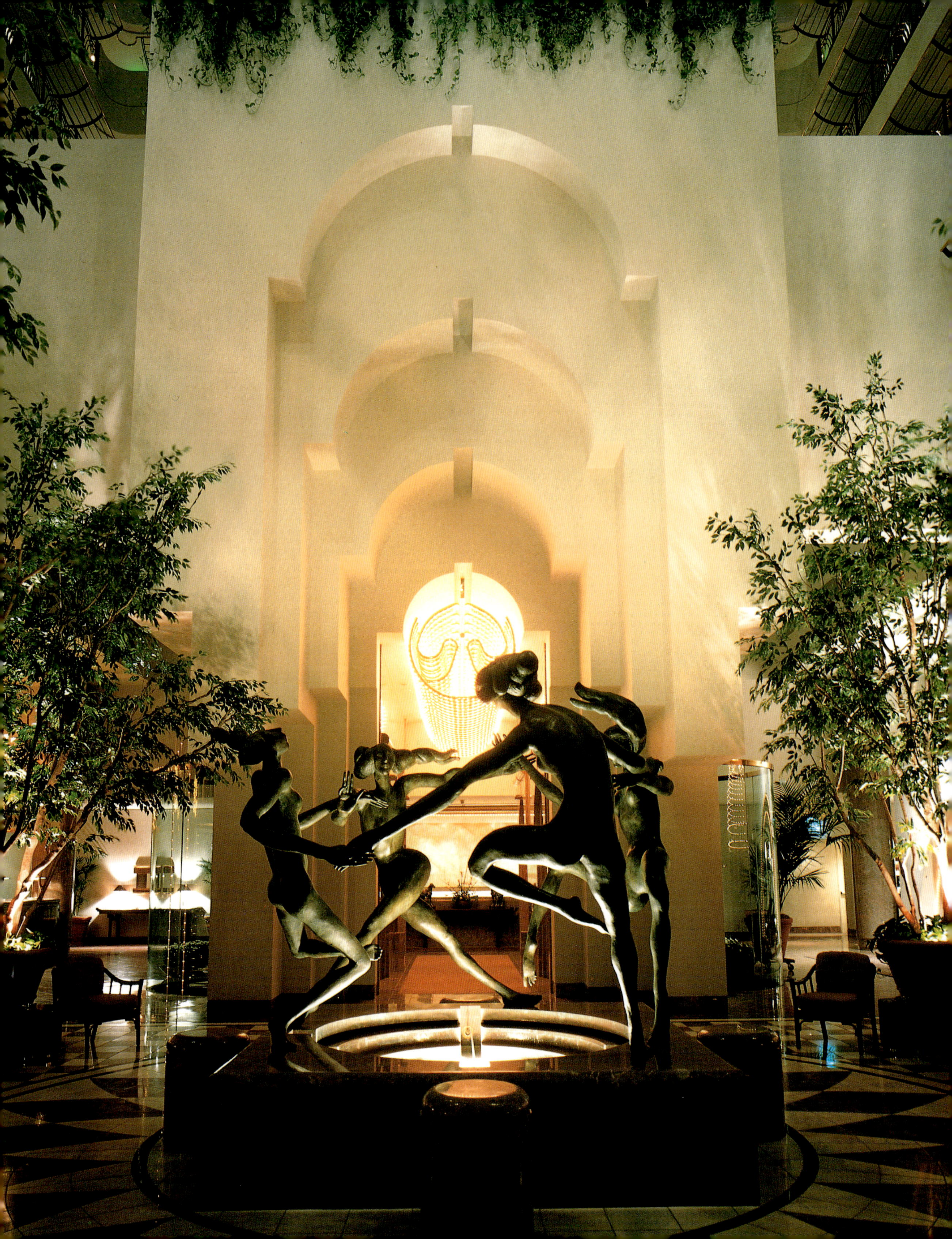

2
THE SALON HOTEL

THE IDEA OF THE HOTEL as a theatre of gracious living is going through a revival that harks back to the great days of the *belle époque* and art deco. This trend reflects the spirit of the times and has quite clearly been taken into account by contemporary hotels that have discovered an affinity with the lifestyle of the *belle époque* and are once more celebrating its superb synthesis of all the arts in the salon-like design of their foyers and public areas and the stylish appointment of their rooms. The upper-middle-class salon – modern in gesture, conservative in attitude and staged with consummate virtuosity and style – has reappeared in the interior design of ambitious hotels, most notably in Paris, where the *belle époque* has been revived in two redesigned city hotels, the Montalembert and the Pergolese. These highly successful reconstructions show how the proverbial "coolness" of modern design can be skilfully blended with the atmospheric and so form part of a convincing stylistic composition that is in tune with the times, but is above all friendly and welcoming.

Style also plays a vital role in a new type of business hotel, a prototype of which Asian investors have had built in London by Italian specialists. The Halkin, the most expensive hotel per square metre in the metropolis, marries state-of-the-art electronics with classicism in the contemporary mode to add a final polish to the businessman's performance. In this type of hotel, with its deliberately moderate proportions, the original function of style has been rediscovered – that is, an instrument of power, a perfectionist device that confers superior status. Paris has thus experienced the joyous reunion of old and new arts, and London the calculated synthesis of service and scenario. Meanwhile, Spain has been producing ambitious hotels that pay due heed to the current taste for salon culture.

John Portman, the visionary architect whose hotels of the 1960s and 1970s foretold the shape of things to come, started a new trend in the late 1980s with his own hotel, The Portman in San Francisco, by giving expression to the retrospective charm of the new cult of luxury and style. The move away from the public atrium towards the more private luxury of the salon and the club signals a withdrawal into a world of style that is at once grand and intimate.

The new salon style, realized in the form of an intimate hotel environment, has become both a symbol and an attribute of a world of luxury that caters to a status- and form-conscious public, who understand turnout and dress – from shoe to tie, from watch to fountain pen – as a functioning system of semiotics. They now expect to find this system fittingly reflected in the stylish décor of exclusive hotels.

Left: The garden patio of the hotel Los Seises in the palace of the archbishop of Seville.

Right: The old and the ultramodern are effectively contrasted in the salon-bar. The architect Pena Martin integrated archaeological fragments discovered during the rebuilding into his modern composition.

LOS SEISES
Seville, Spain, 1992
Architecture/Interior Design: **Jorge Pena Martin**

Probably no other hotel project in the world displays such a range of styles and periods as Los Seises, which has recently opened in Seville. Here is a genuine meeting of archaeology and modern design that makes it possible to experience the different periods and styles. The Andalusian architect Jorge Pena Martin, a specialist in the restoration of ancient structural fabrics, leaves old and modern intact and simply confronts the typical means of expression of the various eras. Old mosaics from the Roman baths are found beside ultramodern steel architecture, arches with chiselled capitals beside soft designer upholstery, old choirstalls beside modern wall-lights with finely designed reflectors.

The activities connected with the world exhibition in Seville in 1992 had prompted the church authorities to make a building complex situated in the archbishop's palace, in the historic centre of Seville, temporarily available for the construction of a comfortable hotel. The ecclesiastical origin of the project is betrayed only by its name, "Los Seises," which is also the name of a dance performed at Corpus Christi.

During the reconstruction work the neglected gardens and buildings yielded a fund of archaeological treasures. The archaeologists discovered the remains of walls belonging to the Roman baths that were situated here in the second century, during the reign of the Emperor Hadrian, as well as frescoes, mosaics, capitalled columns and ancient floors. Pena Martin, already distinguished for his earlier work, which included the conversion of the monastery of San Juan de Aznalfarache into a style-conscious hotel, proceeded in stages, working with the archaeologists and integrating whatever they unearthed into his modern concept. Glass elements in filigree metal profiles were chosen for a long wing of the building, to produce a gallery-like salon to which an arched colonnade and a chequered floor lend the atmosphere of an ancient house. The architect also introduced theatricality as an effective stylistic element when he cut open a vault in an old seventeenth-century kitchen to create a fascinating round ceiling light through which the upper floors of the surrounding parts of the building can be viewed.

Colour too is superbly exploited as a stylistic means. "For the people of Seville colour expresses cultivation," says the architect. "White is regarded here only as a symbol of poverty." The whole building therefore adheres to a scale of earthy colours.

Not only aesthetics but comfort played a decisive role in the conversion of the old monastery buildings. A swimming pool was built on the roof terrace, with a view over the roofs of Seville and towards the nearby cathedral; here too, as in the whole complex, ancient and the modern are skilfully blended. However, this conversion into a stylish, comfortable hotel is only a temporary measure, as the church intends to close Los Seises and use its 43 rooms as retirement accommodation for the clergy.

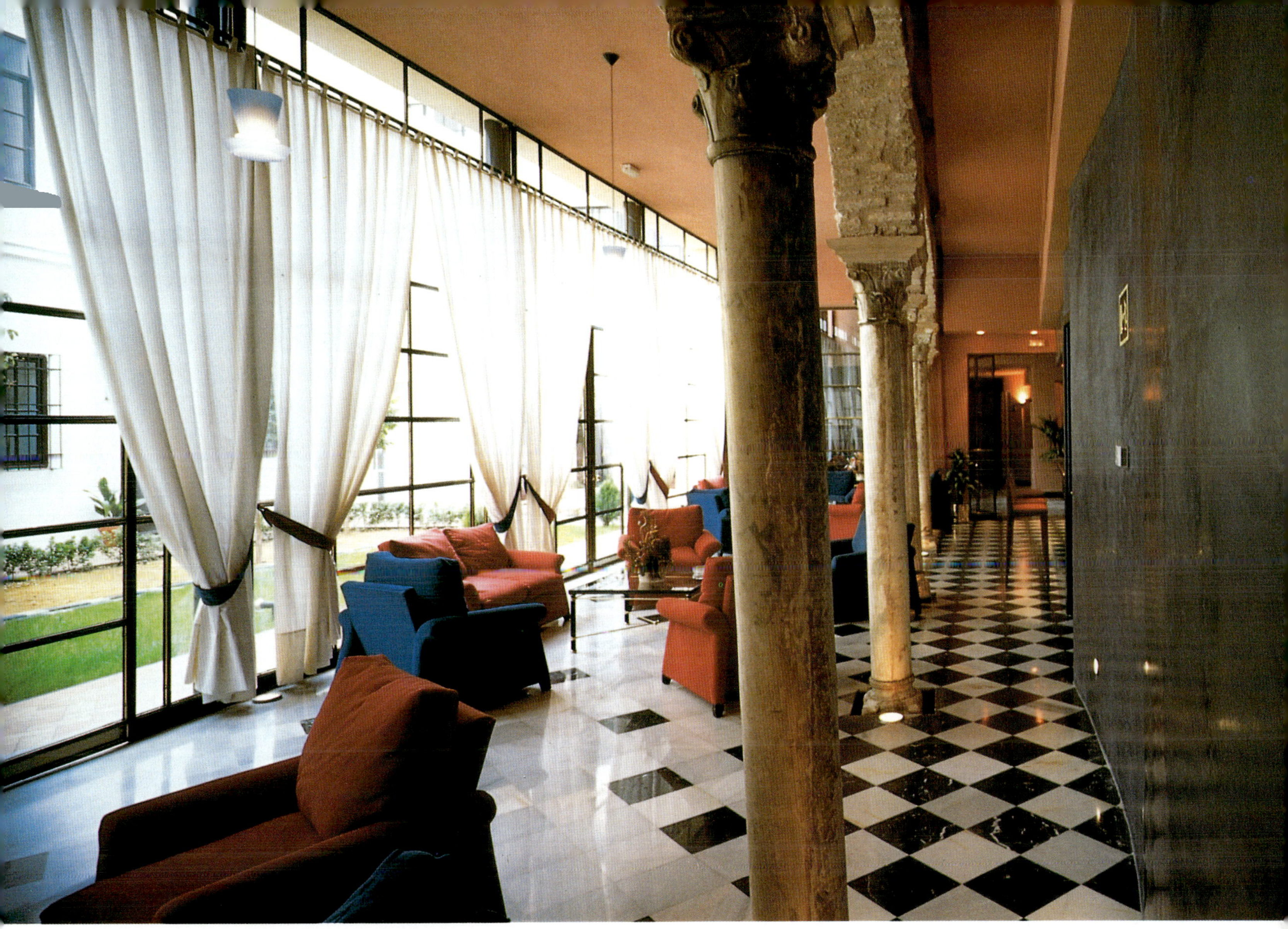

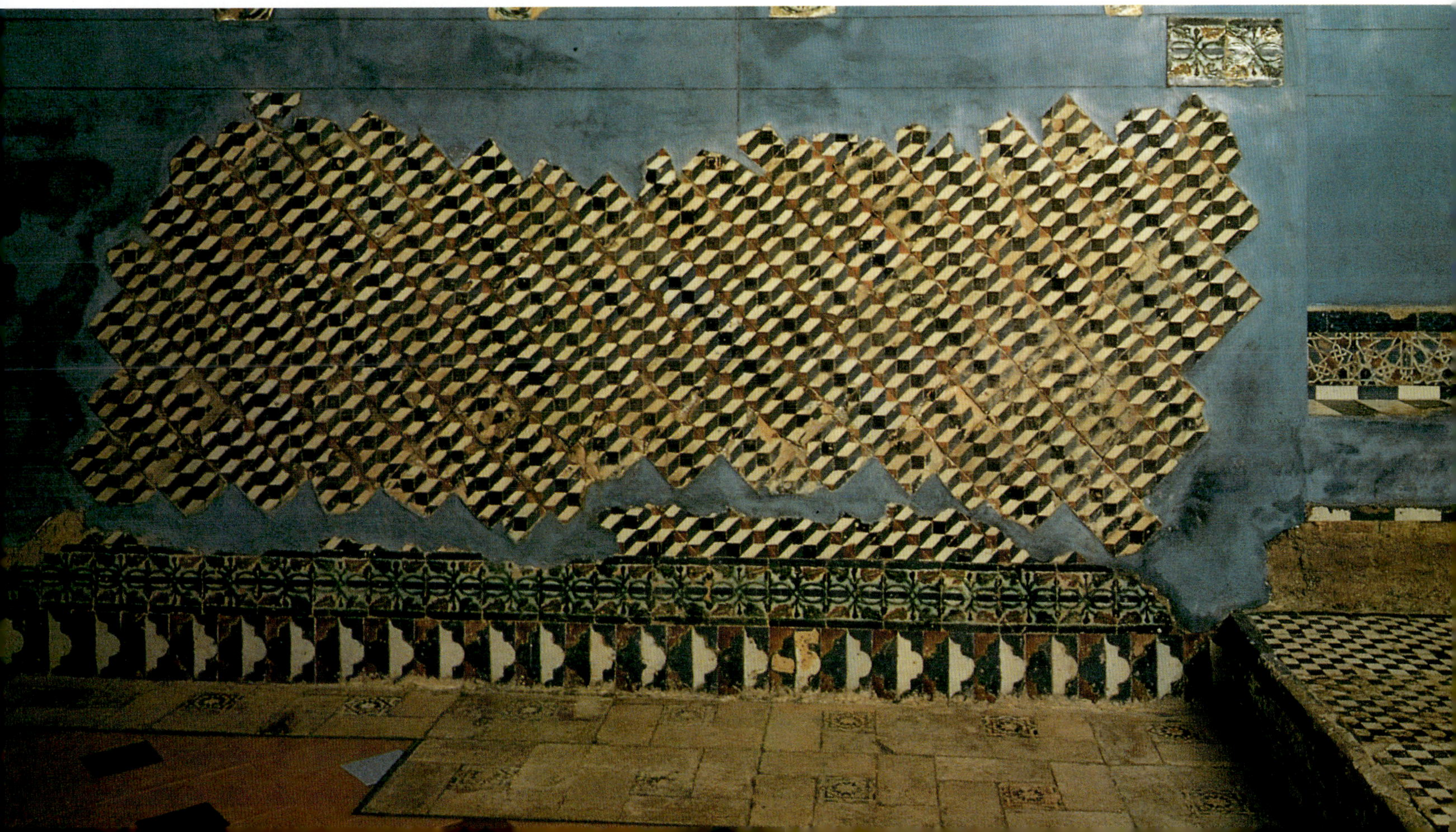

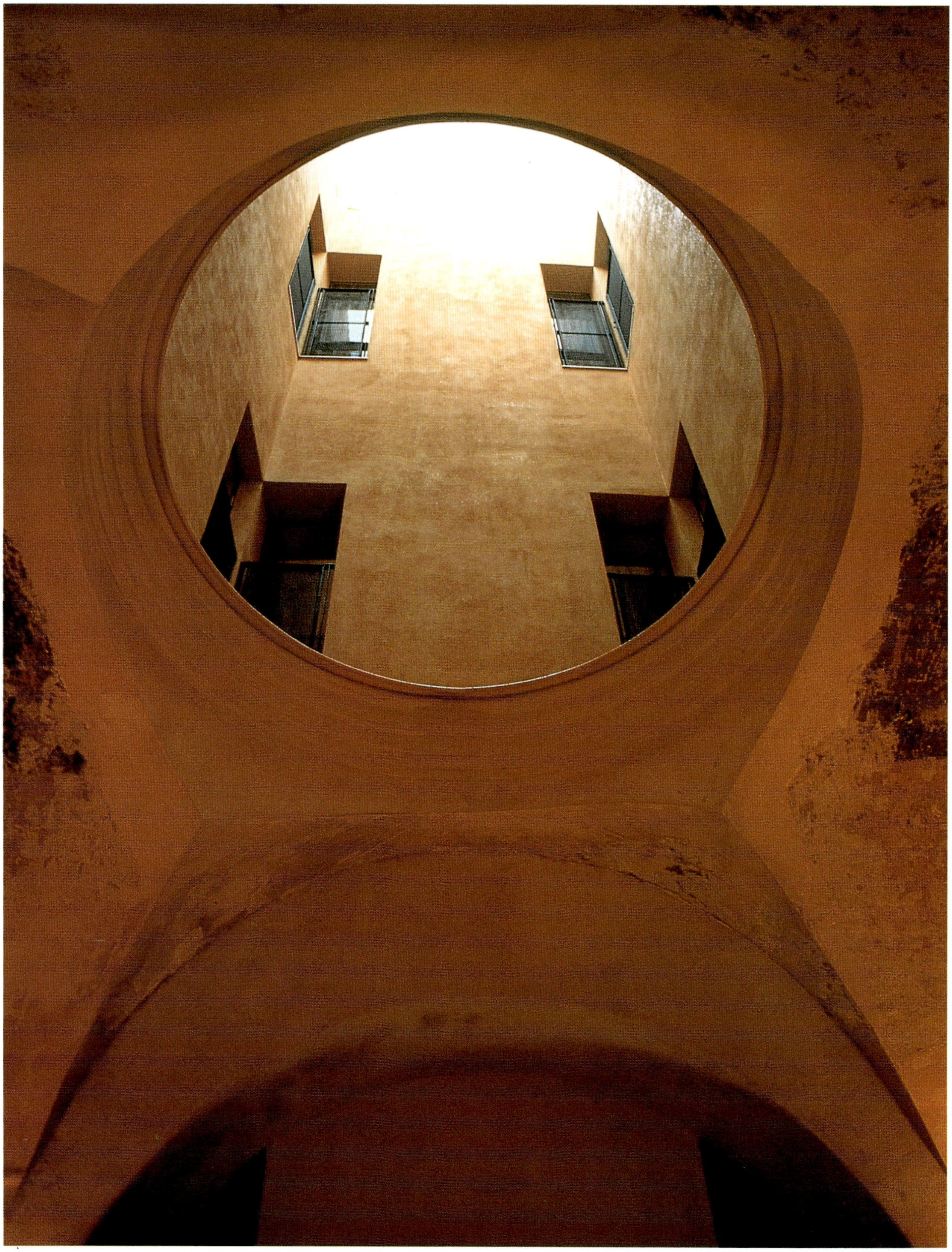

Left: The ceiling arch of the old kitchen was turned into a ceiling light.

Above: On the roof of the 17th-century building is a swimming pool with a view of the cathedral and the Giralda.

Right: In the Salon Deza the ecclesiastical past of the hotel is still present and becomes a decorative motif.

THE MONTALEMBERT
Paris, France, 1990
Interior Design: **Christian Liaigre**

Left: Above the hotel's entrance the architect Christian Liaigre placed a modern but stylized canopy of metal and glass.
Right: The entrance area is in bright natural colours which contrast with the dark frames of the wall openings and windows.

Instead of comfortable anonymity, a hotel may convey the lyrical mood of a particular quarter, especially if it is located, like the Montalembert, in Saint Germain, the artists' quarter of Paris. This striking environment, beloved of tourists, supplied the design motifs for the successful conversion of a faceless twenties building into a four-star hotel of unequivocally Parisian character. The new owner, Grace Léo-Andrieu, speaks of a "hôtel de charme" – a term commonly used by French estate agents to describe stylish old buildings.

The building, dating from 1926, belongs to no particular tradition, but its environment represents the genuine culture of Saint Germain and determines the character of the stylish new Montalembert, a four-storey hotel named after the street in which it stands. This highly acclaimed project revives a lost world for tourists and allows them to experience the feel of the quarter – which admittedly has been artificially intensified. No one staying at the hotel can doubt that they are right in the middle of Saint Germain.

Christian Liaigre designed this highly professional *mise-en-scène*. A cosy chimney corner with an "authentic" library – a tribute to the many local publishing houses – contributes to a sense of well-being. For enthusiastic visitors to Paris there are enticing bridal beds with striped counterpanes and stacked pillows, some authentic and dating from the age of Louis Philippe. There is a certain modernity in the combination of dark door and window frames with cream-coloured walls, ceilings and floors. Christian Liaigre's renovation concept does not replace the old by the new, but tends rather in the opposite direction: he enriches the structural fabric, mutilated and disfigured by his predecessors, with emotional and atmospheric additions. The old is restored and reinterpreted, and used to revive a lost age. In addition to "genuine" props such as exotic sculptures and photographs, Liaigre – who trained as a furniture designer – features his own work. The lifestyle of the *belle époque* is echoed in lamps designed by Eric Schmitt, and bronze monsters shaped like jelly-fish and starfish, seemingly lifted from the pages of Jules Verne, pervade the atmospheric landscape of the Montalembert in the form of door handles and hanging lamps.

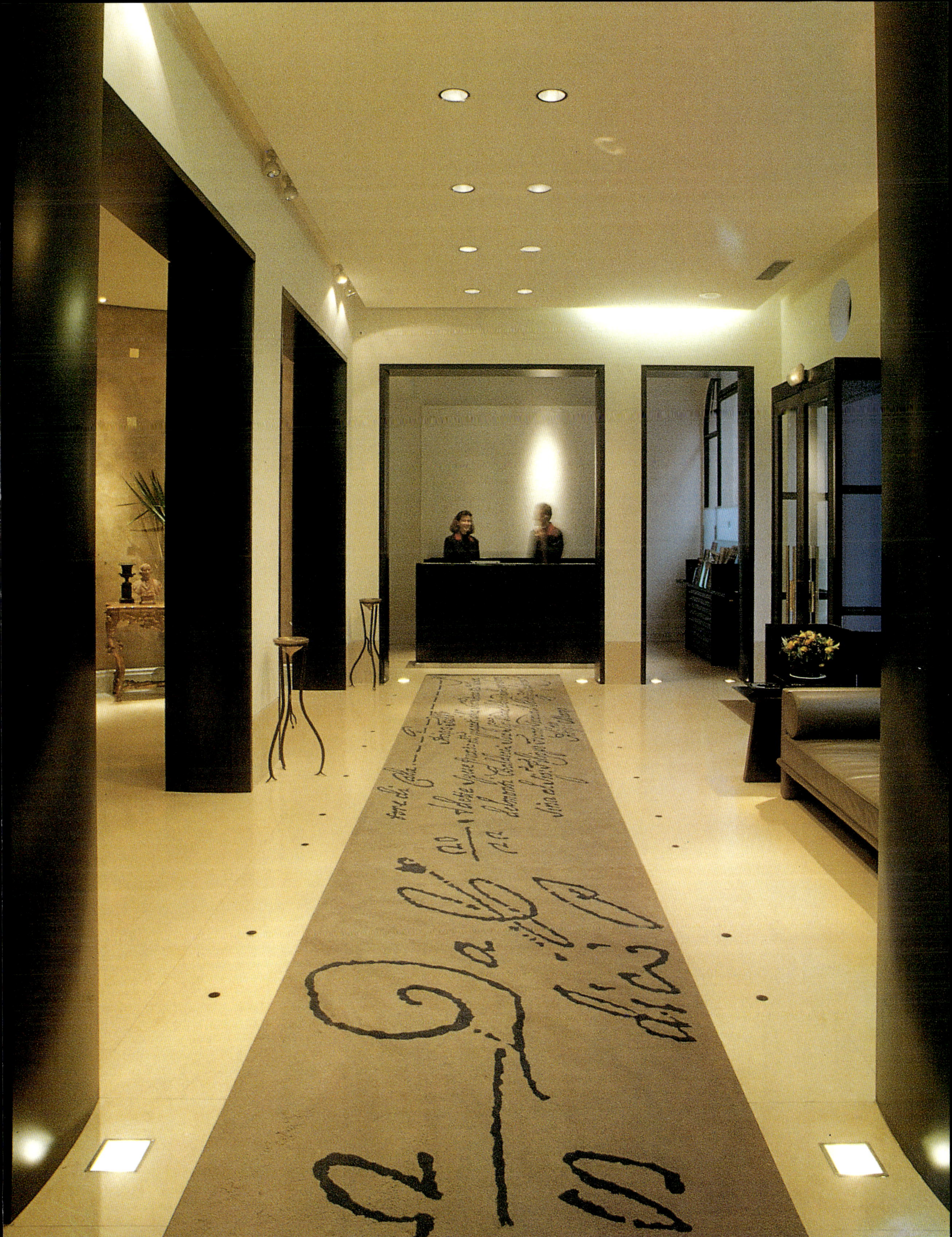

The bronze lights by Eric Schmitt combine the formal language of art nouveau with contemporary aesthetics.

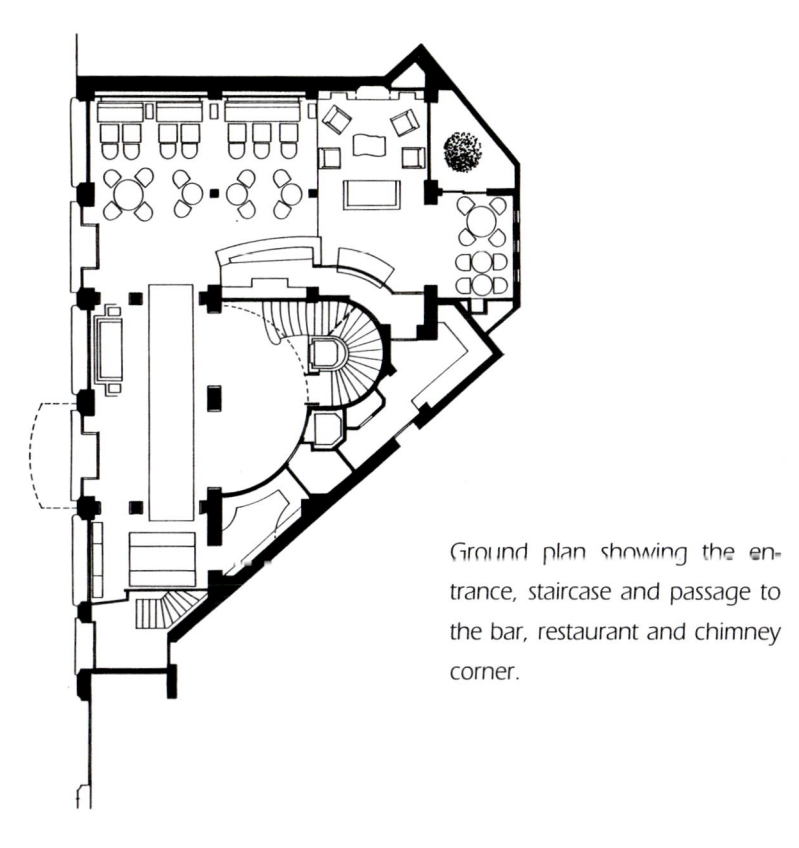

Ground plan showing the entrance, staircase and passage to the bar, restaurant and chimney corner.

Rough cast bronze fittings take up the art nouveau aesthetic of the building. Where it has survived, Liaigre retains the old fabric and accentuates it by modern stylistic means, thus creating an ambience that is at once atmospheric and up-to-date.

101

Left: The bathrooms offer modern comfort in the style of the twenties and thirties.

Above right: The chimney corner on the ground floor is one of the hotel's great attractions. Here, too, through the use of natural materials and traditional forms, Liaigre is able to create a salon atmosphere that is not in the least stuffy. A glass-roofed inner courtyard ensures natural light during the day.

Right: The design of the rooms is simple but effective, with a timeless quality.

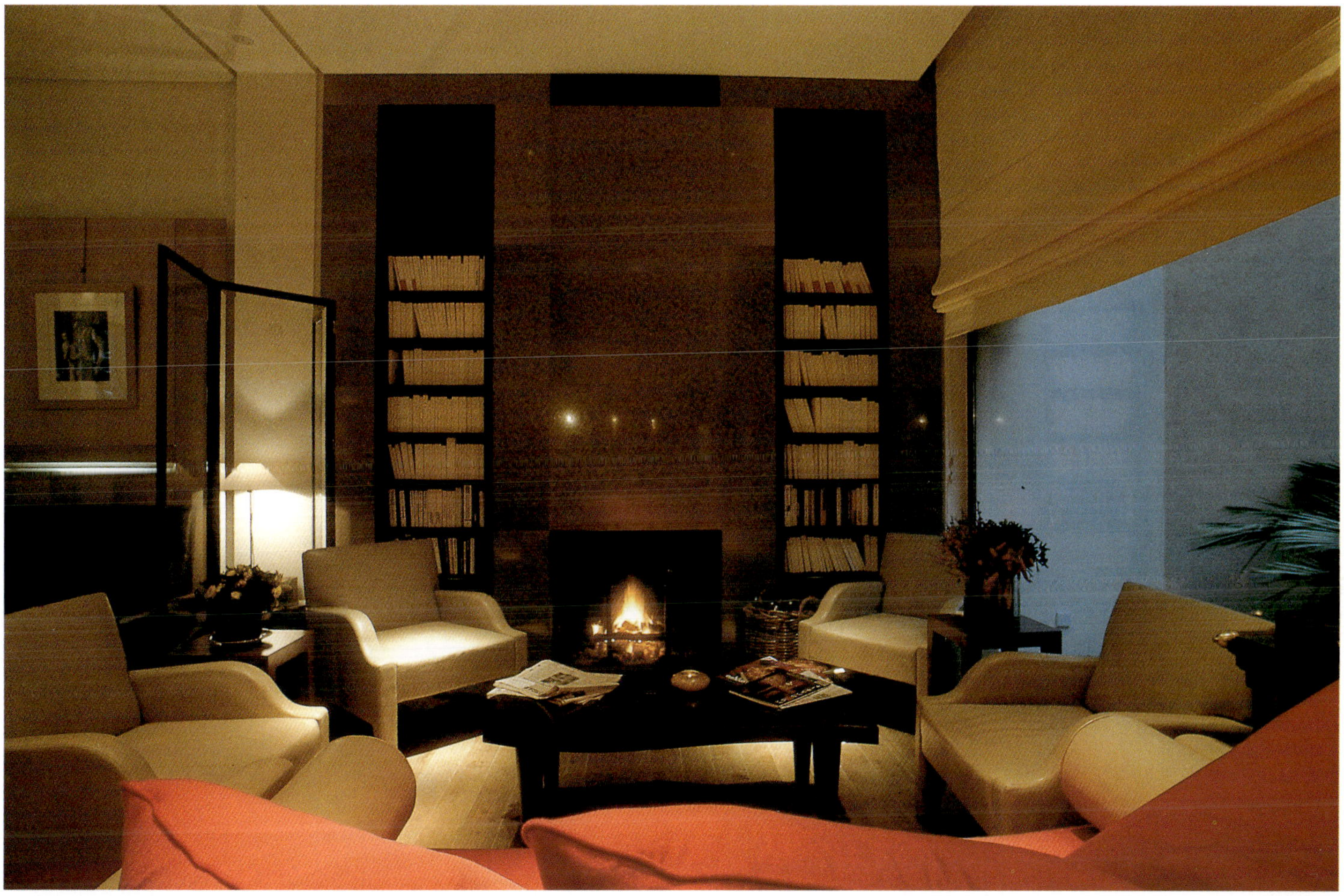

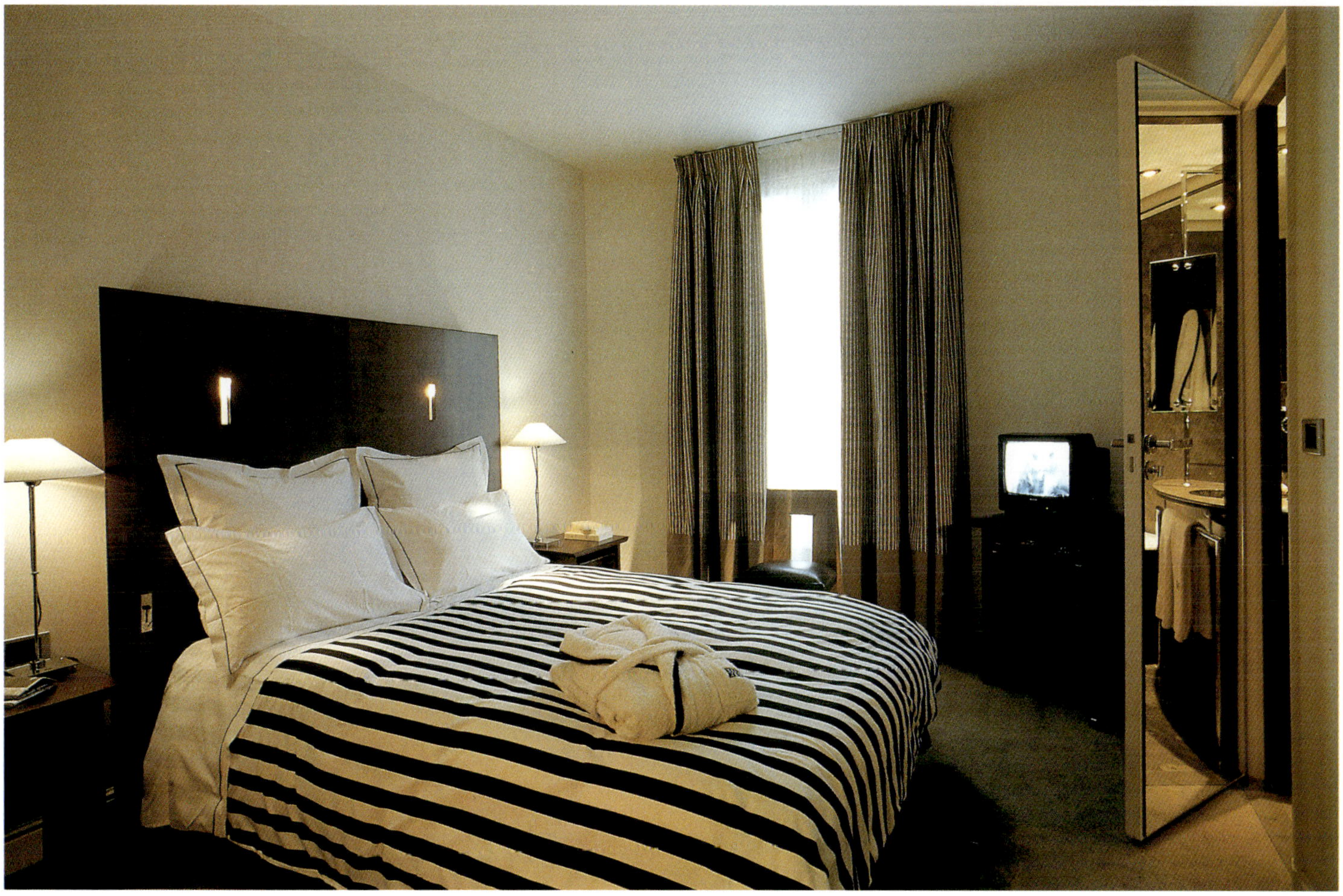

Left: This newly built hotel fits in with the traditional appearance of London's Belgravia. **Right:** Archaeological sculptures create an élitist atmosphere in the guest lounge.

THE HALKIN
London, UK, 1991

Architecture/Interior Design:

Laboratorio Associati, Lorenzo Carmellini, Rocco Magnoli

As a hotel of superlatives – not in size, but in perfection of style, execution and function – the Halkin was to set new standards in the hotel trade and to guarantee up-to-date flexibility: as a business hotel it was to be a pleasant place to live and a functional place in which to work. This hotel project, the most ambitious and expensive in central London, was commissioned by a Singapore tycoon. What Mr Ong Beng Seng and his wife had in mind was the business hotel of the nineties, unsurpassed in catering to the needs of top businessmen. To perform this ambitious task they brought in seasoned professionals from Italy. The architectural image of their perfectionist hotel was entrusted to the house architects of Gianni Versace, the Milanese fashion designer. On the basis of Versace projects in Paris and London, this Milanese office is reputed to be absolutely confident at handling a neo-classicist architectural language geared to prestige and perfection. This kind of architecture, more intent on high-flown self-advertisement than on innovation, was to supply the framework for the new business hotel. Given an almost unlimited budget and a remit to set new standards of hotel service, a new type of business hotel emerged.

At the Halkin the business traveller not only has stylish surroundings, but also one of the best temporary addresses in London. The outwardly discreet building is situated in a quiet street in Belgravia, London's diplomatic quarter. The perfectly appointed 41-room hotel is more like the town house of a Georgian aristocrat than a grand hotel. The Italians' architectural style, both inside and outside the hotel, is an interpretation of the conservatively classical mood of Belgravia. Their use of superbly worked traditional materials is proof of their perfectionism. Marble floors, wood, leather, silk and polished stucco walls create the high standards of luxury and comfort one would expect to find on a royal yacht. The marble floor of the lobby is inlaid with sterling silver. Classical busts and traditional upholstery set the tone of the reception area – a foretaste of what is in store elsewhere.

As a business hotel the Halkin offers not just style, but superbly organized service. It can therefore, if necessary, serve as a temporary office. "Office en suite" is part of the programme, which includes secretarial services, fax facilities and two telephone lines with conference loudspeakers in every room. On request, a meeting room for six to twenty people can be booked.

The rooms and suites are designed rather like elegant cabins. Here too – as in the great days of art deco – marble, wood and leather predominate but go hand in hand with modern hotel technology and electronics. The Halkin is run on the principle that it should be possible to do business in London without ever leaving the hotel. To round off this claim there is also a gourmet restaurant, for which the Milanese chef Gualtiero Marchesi was engaged as guarantor of top-quality fare.

With the Halkin, Lorenzo Carmellini and Rocco Magnoli have inaugurated a new "executive business style", a skilful amalgam of stylish representation and technological infrastructure that points the way forward for hotel design in the nineties.

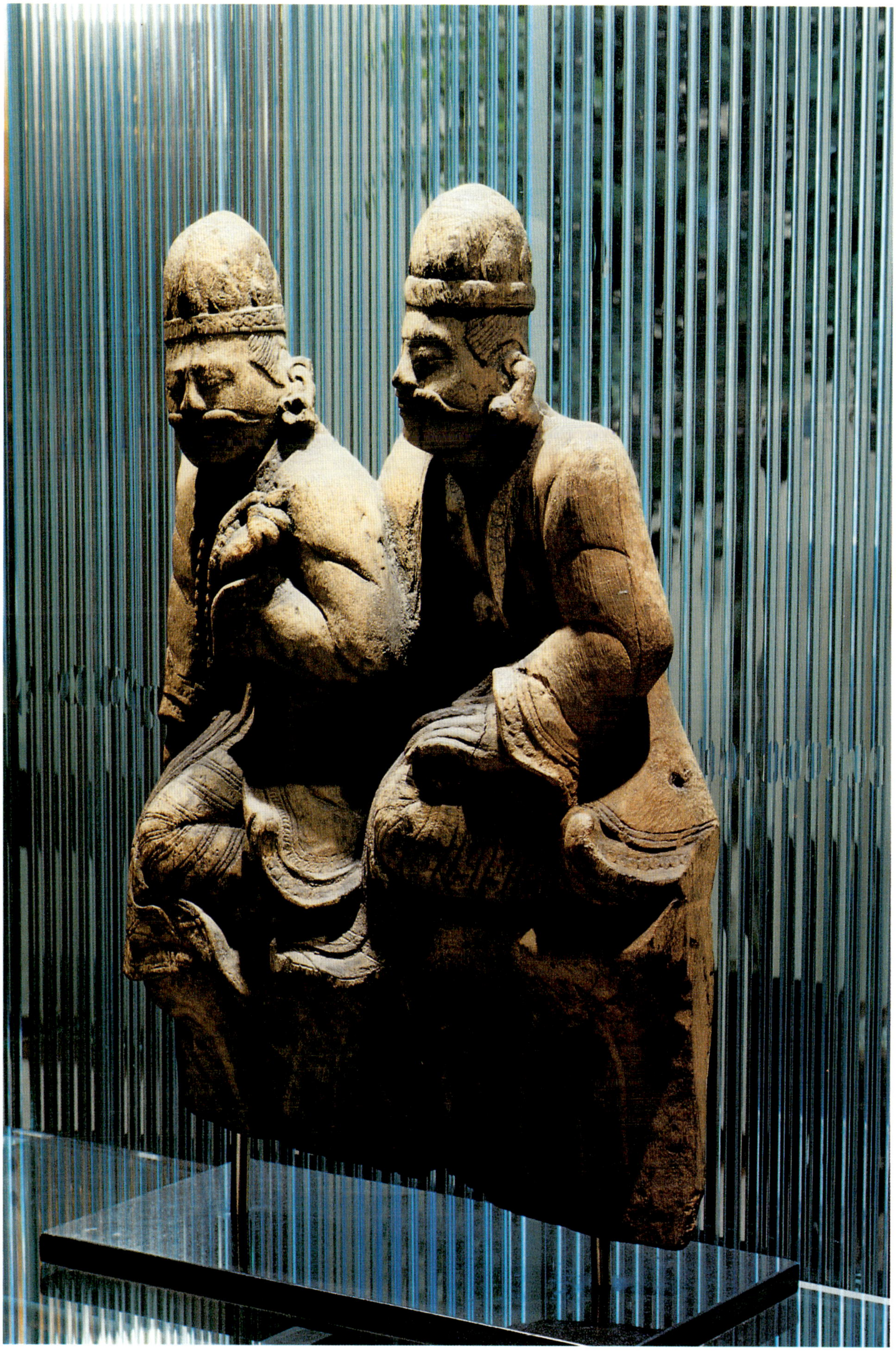

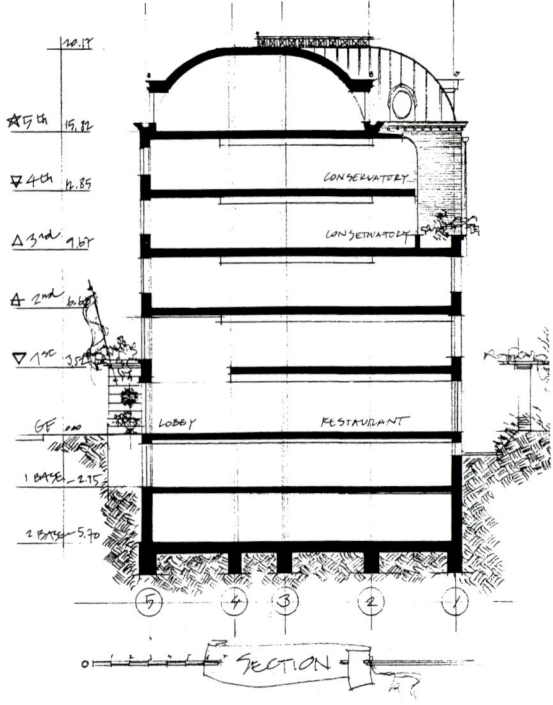

Cross-section of the building.

Above: The hotel corridors have been generously designed so that the doors are hardly visible. **Right and far right:** The spacious suites on the upper floors are very precisely designed in terms of materials and composition. **Above right:** The attic rooms have vaulted ceilings or are designed as glazed conservatories leading to a roof terrace. Fine sculptures underline the quality of the rooms.

106

107

Left: A trompe-l'oeil painting on the blind wall represents the construction of the new hotel, showing the inner courtyard that has been made into the foyer.

Right: The historic galleries running round the glass-roofed inner courtyard provide access to the accommodation levels.

COUR DES LOGES
Lyon, France, 1987

Architecture/Interior Design:

Yves Boucharlat, Pierre Vurpas

When the Renaissance quarter of the old city of Lyon was redeveloped, one of the main projects was the Cour des Loges. Four old houses standing close to one another in the rue du Boeuf were preserved in their historic fabric, but at the same time converted into an unusual four-star hotel, whose 63 rooms and suites are now grouped round a courtyard surrounded by gallery arcades and covered by a glass roof. The site is of historical importance, having been a temporary residence of the Duke of Burgundy in the 14th century. Respect for the cultural monument was matched by the courage to give expression to contemporary taste. The Lyon architects Yves Boucharlat and Pierre Vurpas refused to introduce a spurious romanticism into the venerable walls: what remained of the original patina was carefully restored, but for the rest the designers realized a consistent individual vision of modern hospitality.

The inner courtyard became the hotel lobby, up-to-date in design, but not excessively so. From here one can reach the various lounges, the bar and the restaurant. Angular and spiral staircases lead to the guest quarters, which are ingeniously implanted in the different houses, chiefly in the form of maisonettes. It is more convenient to use the lifts, which are discreetly integrated into the medieval labyrinth. In the rooms the new fixtures are easy to recognize: colourfully varnished dividing walls, eminently functional wooden steps with metal handrails, simple oak floors, contemporary carpet designs, useful furniture and functional grey bathrooms. Regional echoes are to be found, if at all, in the decorative fabrics. Individual items of furniture are supplied by well-known firms and designers. The accommodation units are variously furnished, but each has a dominant colour – blue, green, turquoise, pink, grey or orange. Room sizes vary between 25 and 60 square metres.

An essential feature of the design concept is the presence of original works of contemporary art in all the rooms and public areas. Next to the hotel is the Athisma Gallery, which regularly supplies new works for different parts of the hotel; these can be purchased by the guests. Not only art-lovers, but wine-lovers too, receive special attention. The Cour des Loges stocks the best vintages in its vaults and runs its own connoisseur club, which provides expert advice and, on request, the use of private safes, where regular guests can deposit their fine wines. More mundane pleasures can be enjoyed in "Les Thermes des Loges", which comprises an indoor swimming pool, a sauna and a fitness centre. Among the incidental touches devised by the architects are the small, flower-bordered sun terraces on the roofs between the buildings, which recall the traditional atmosphere of the old city.

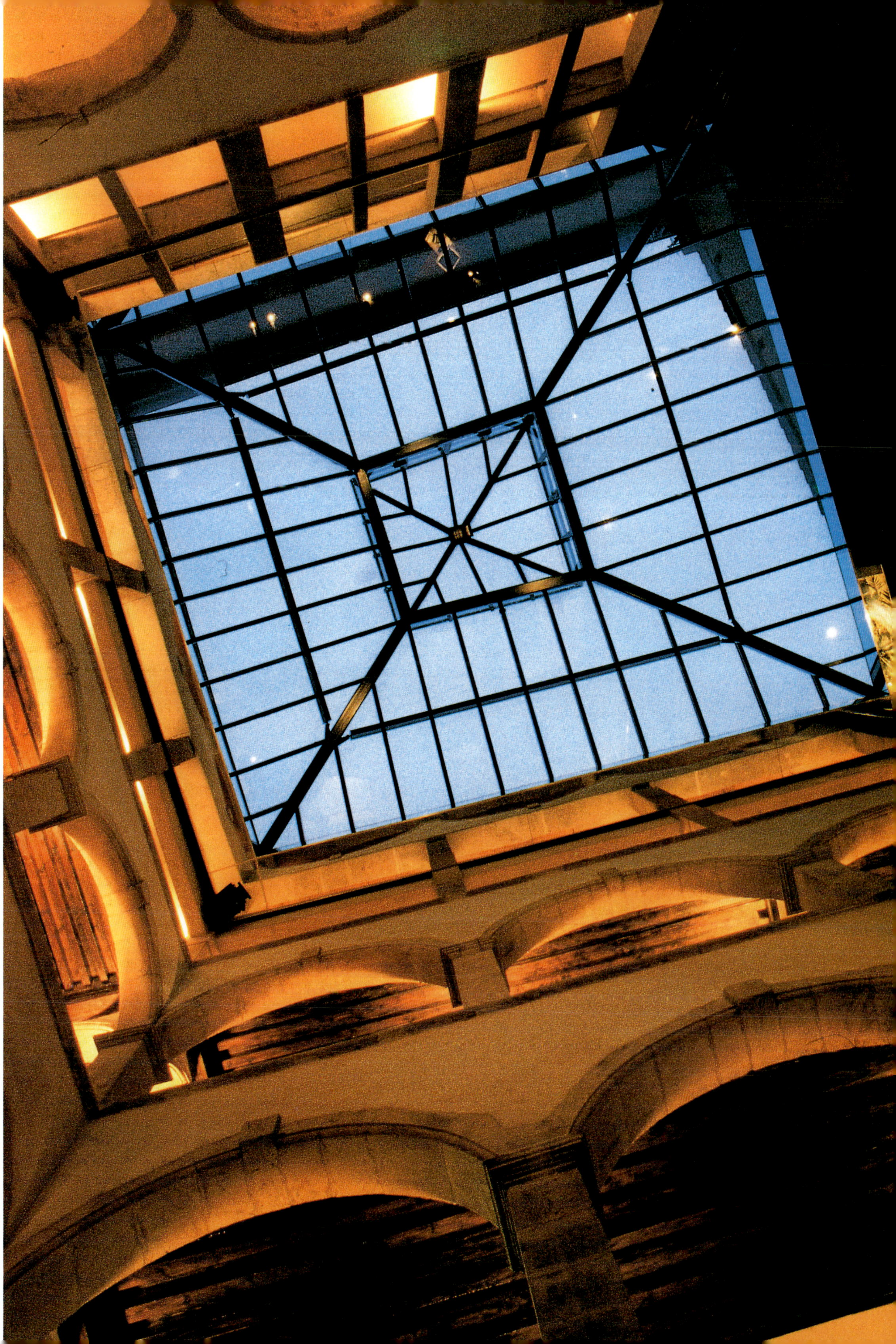

The guest-rooms are economically furnished with Italian designs and make no concessions to nostalgia.

Right: The conversion of the historic building resulted in completely new architectural divisions. Many guest units are on different levels and the functional areas are handled in an unconventional manner.

111

Redefining a typical Parisian hotel: the entrance to the hotel in the Rue Pergolese.

LA PERGOLESE
Paris, France, 1991
Interior Design: **Rena Dumas**

The typical small Parisian hotel, named after the street in which it stands, was the model adopted for the newly designed La Pergolese, but it was to be interpreted in a novel and contemporary manner, with no attempt at nostalgia. The interior architect, Rena Dumas, who also tends the image of the Hermès boutiques throughout the world (her husband heads this luxury concern), accepted the commission. In this three-star hotel she showed that aesthetic quality does not depend on the size of the budget. The old sandstone building, constructed at the end of the 19th century not far from the Arc de Triomphe, was completely redesigned. The client, Edith Vidalenc – who owns other hotels, including the Étoile Maillot in Paris – wanted an "atypical building for the guest, which avoided the beaten track, but combined modernity with charm".

The blue door under the art nouveau canopy at the entrance prepares one for the surprises in store in the interior, which is bright and trend-conscious but elegant. An elective affinity between Rena Dumas' own spatial ideas and designs, and those of prominent contemporaries or models informs the whole interior. In the lobby one sits in groups of armchairs and sofas by the De Stijl veteran Gerrit Rietveld and on chairs by Antonio Citterio. On the walls hang specially commissioned works by Hilton McConnico – graphic compositions of plants and grasses. The tables in the breakfast restaurant were designed by Philippe Starck. Chrome washstands by Andrée Putman are integrated into the bathrooms. The interior architect skilfully incorporates all these elements into her own inventions.

The 40 rooms – including one suite – follow a colour scale of five tones: blue, yellow, apricot, red and green. The furnishing hardly varies, the bed ensemble, the occasional table and the dressing table being made of ash and the tall bar/TV unit of mahogany. The bathrooms are lined with white Thassos marble, and the bathroom area of the suite is divided off by glass blocks under a sloping roof. The size of the rooms is very restricted, yet they do not seem cramped, in the first place because they all have plenty of natural light, but also because the architect employs a successful trick: all the furniture in the guest-rooms is very low, corresponding to the windows, which start low down and rise high. This creates an atmosphere in which any sense of claustrophobia is avoided.

The lobby with artworks by Hilton McConnico and leather armchairs by Antonio Citterio.

Room furnishings designed by Rena Dumas. **Left:** A bar/television cupboard with a built-on desk surface. **Below:** An ashwood bedhead.

Below: Great care was put into the detail of the bathrooms, with washstands by Andrée Putman.
Right: The entrance to a room has elegant door mountings by Rena Dumas.

Left: The entrance of the Havana Palace, a nineteenth-century apartment block converted into a 150-room hotel.

Right: The kidney-shaped atrium with glazed floor galleries.

THE HAVANA PALACE
Barcelona, Spain, 1991

Architecture/Interior Design:

Josep Juanpere Miret, Antonio Puig Guasch

In Ensanche, one of the superior residential areas of the Catalan capital, the architects Josep Juanpere Miret and Antonio Puig have transformed an upper-middle-class apartment block, built in 1872, into a 150-room hotel, whose interior no longer betrays any affinity to the historical fabric. The façade of this imposing corner building is a listed structure and has been perfectly restored, but outward appearance is deceptive, for on entering the Havana Palace one moves into a different age. After the interior had been gutted, the eight floors were arranged around a new central area, open to the glass roof; although not especially high, the steeply soaring, kidney-shaped lightwell is quite breathtaking, and there is a vertiginous downward view from the highest of the glass-encased galleries. The round tables disposed about the lobby, each with four chairs, recall the red and black flower-like shapes common in pop art.

The restrained luxury of the interior, designed exclusively by the architects, has an undeniable affinity with present drawing-room trends in Spanish furniture design. Many of the formal inventions might have been lifted from the repertoire of Carlos Riart or Oscar Tusquets Blanca. The use of maritime models is obvious – the traveller as passenger, surrounded by the solidity that once characterized the great ocean liners. In this redefinition of an intimate top-class hotel, the analogy is not far-fetched, Barcelona being a seaport that played host to the world during the Olympic Games of 1992.

This investment project was prompted by the prospect of the games, but the design by which it was realized will certainly long outlast the event. A cosmopolitan clientele no longer insists on being presented with the same old clichés that are to be found in the big international hotels, but is oriented rather to smaller and more exclusive establishments, where the various regional virtues of modern design are concentrated in an ideal setting. The superb craftsmanship and design of the Havana Palace make it one of the best examples of this type. With no undue pretension to originality, it is an obvious and unostentatious refuge for the five-star globetrotter.

As well as a superb restaurant called "Grand Place", the hotel offers a piano bar called "La Copula" and four function rooms that can accommodate up to 200 people. In the lobby and the guestrooms one is struck by the costly mahogany panelling. The furniture and fittings too are largely of mahogany. The bedheads are covered in heavy monochrome art deco fabric.

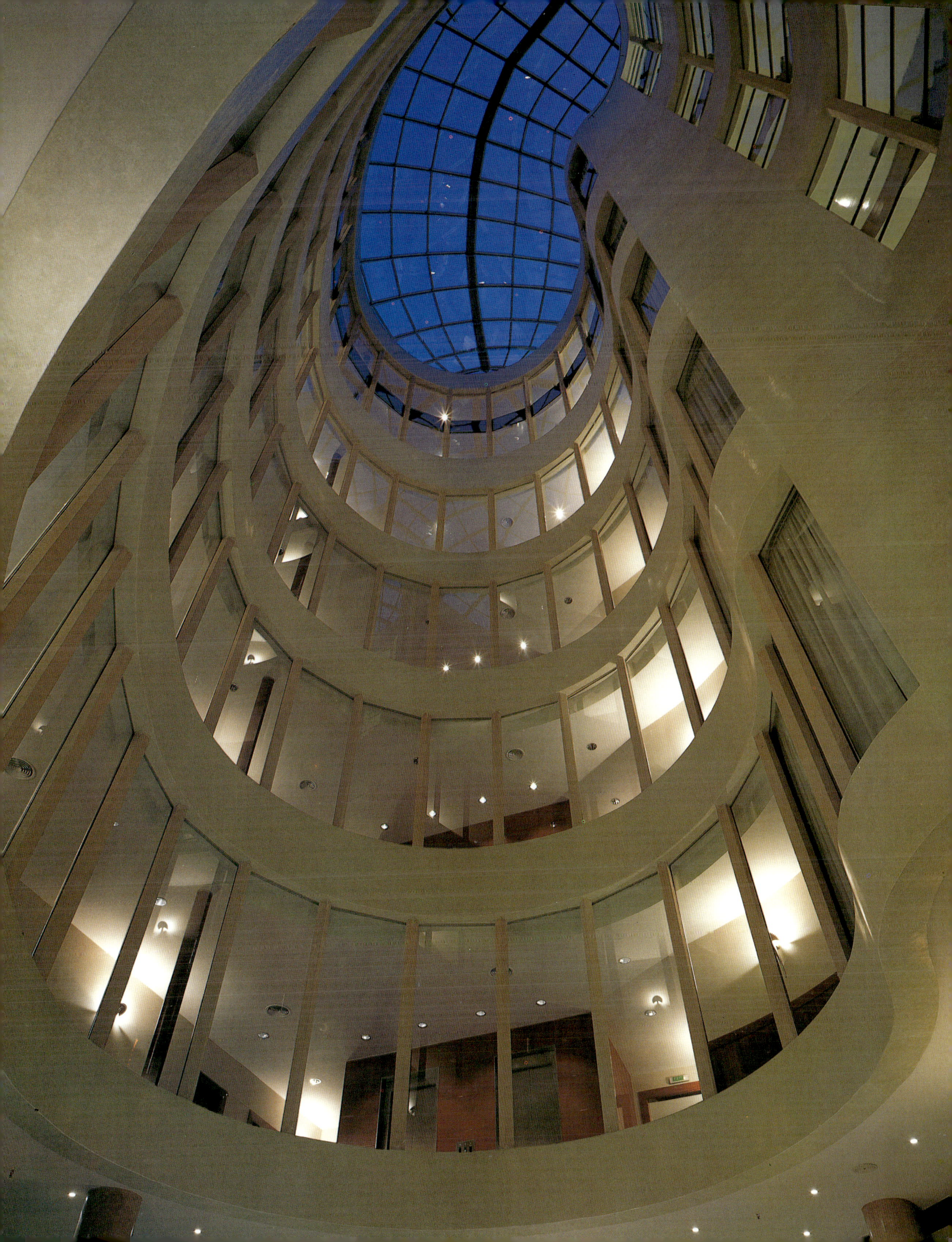

The cabin style of the nineties: the furnishing of the rooms suggests a theme of transatlantic travel. The old clock on the front of the building still works and resembles an enormous porthole.

Above: The various corridors off which the rooms open lead to the curved galleries reached by a double lift. **Left:** In the lobby with its bar and piano, blue armchairs are grouped in a flower pattern around tables of reddish wood.

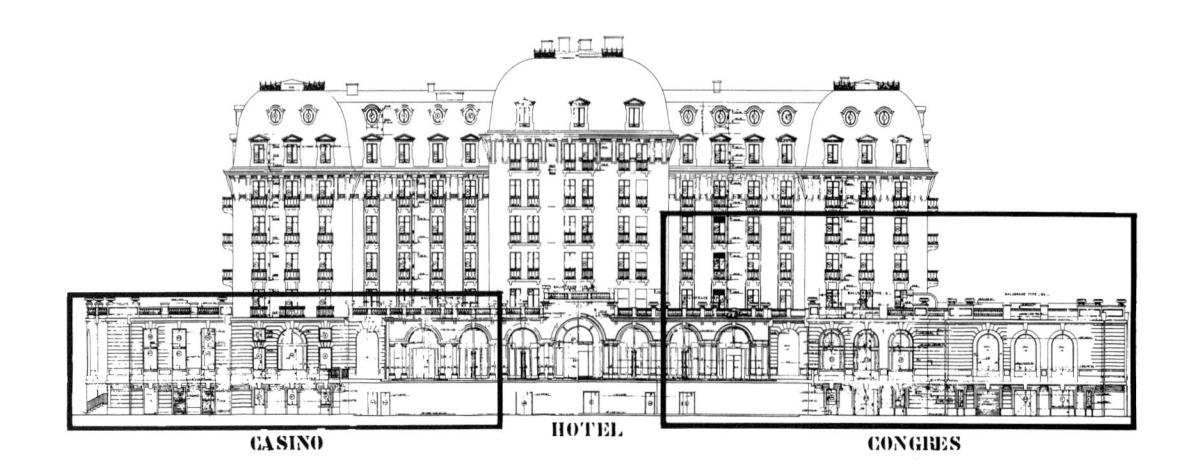

THE IMPERIAL PALACE

Annecy, France, 1991

Architecture: **SISS**

Interior Design: **Arc +**

Above: The old palace hotel, having been gutted, acquired two new functional areas: the casino and the congress centre.

Right: The restored Imperial Palace. The hotel has occupied a classic setting on the Lac d'Annecy since 1913.

From the outside, the Imperial Palace appears to be a faithful reconstruction of a venerable grand hotel, but in fact it is an almost wholly new structure; the original building had long stood empty, ravaged by time and gutted by disastrous fires, so that only the outer walls were standing when it was decided to bring it back to life. Had the councillors of Annecy, a small town 40 kilometres from Geneva, not been so confident in the future of their lakeside hotel, the site would have long since been taken over by an expensive and soulless apartment block. Instead, the French municipality acquired the whole plot, turned the surroundings into a public park and waited for the right investor.

The waiting ended when the German Hopf Group (which also owns the Wasserturm Hotel in Cologne, see pages 20–25) took an interest in the property. In 1913 the building costs had amounted to the then considerable sum of one million gold francs; now 320 million francs were needed to turn the Imperial Palace into a five-star hotel, linked to a conference centre (financed by the municipality) and a casino. It was fortunately decided not to hark back to a remote, long-vanished tradition, but to rethink the concept of the exclusive grand hotel in a landscaped environment. What one experiences in these historic walls is not an oppressive, overloaded imitation of bygone greatness, but an unforced and entirely contemporary grandeur.

The interior architecture and furnishing were entrusted to the local team Arc + of Annecy, who brought impressive assurance and unobtrusive elegance not only to the designing of the public areas and the 98 rooms and suites, but also to the more down-to-earth planning of the conference accommodation, which comprises a number of distinctive, carefully furnished rooms and halls. These accommodate up to 500 participants, who in daylight can enjoy a view of the lake. The new casino, with the inevitable gaming machines, is one of Europe's most modern, with an adjacent restaurant and jazz club. The hotel's top-class restaurant is called "La Voile", a name that supplies the theme for the décor: the sections of the window in this spacious room are divided by white sails, like the side-hangings of a baroque stage. The interiors of the guest-rooms adhere to a single colour – restful tones of light and dark green. Wood and stone are used sparingly, and no attempt is made at spectacular effects. The lighting employs simple archetypal forms combined with state-of-the-art technology – downlighters, uplighters and ceiling floods.

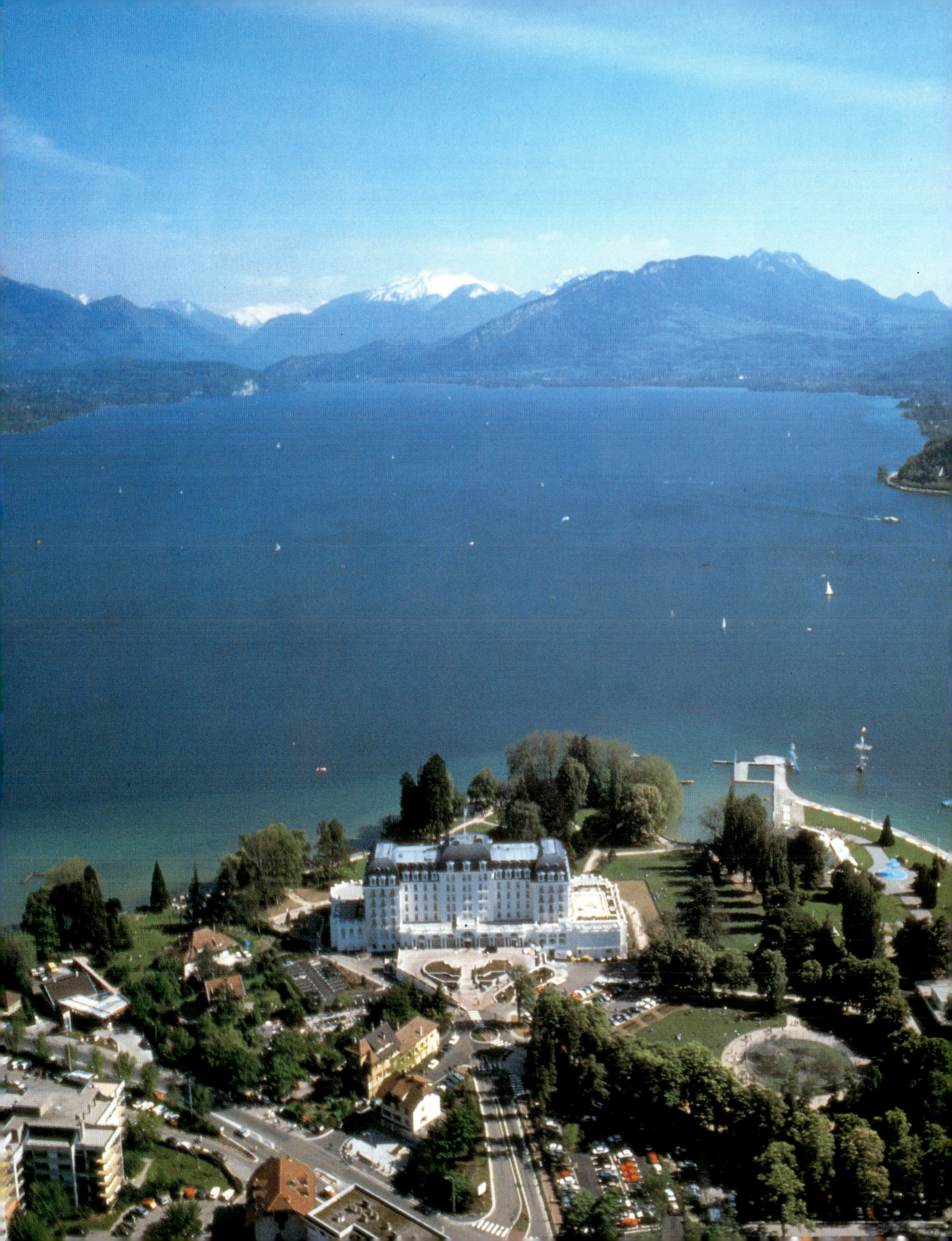

Above: Conferences are one of the Imperial Palace's main sources of income. The conference centre contains a total of 15 banqueting and conference rooms.

Right: Classical in the contemporary mode: a guest-room created by the interior design team Arc +.

The unostentatious reception area: stone tiles, stucco and light-coloured wood are the principal materials.

123

INNENRAUMPERSPEKTIVE FOYER

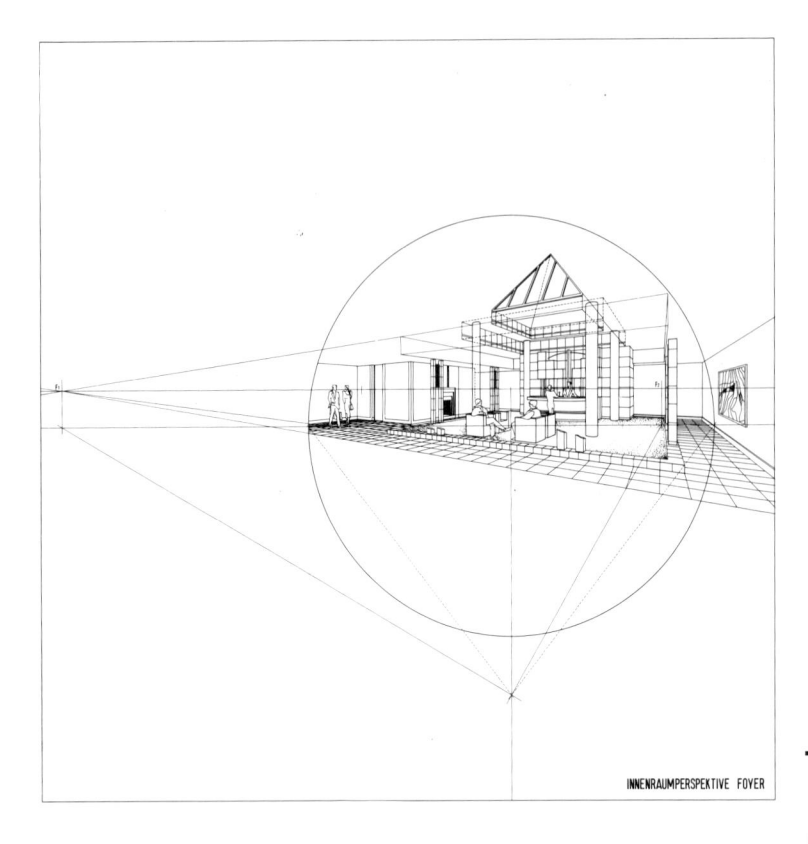

Left: The Rolandsburg hotel, situated in a rural conservation area, moves stylistically between Bauhaus, rationalism and neo-classicism. The design is determined by geometrical figures such as the circle, the cylinder, the cube and the pyramid.
Right: The bar area with its glass light well.

THE ROLANDSBURG
Düsseldorf, Germany, 1988
Architecture/Interior Design: **Wolfgang Döring**

Outside Düsseldorf, the capital of the lower Rhineland, lies Grafenberg Forest, a nature reserve and an important recreation area for the city. Hence the new hotel that was planned here, called the Rolandsburg after a long-vanished fortress, had to meet numerous requirements in order to ensure that it would fit in with its surroundings. To design this small, exclusive hotel, the client commissioned Wolfgang Döring, an architect who had made his name through a number of striking projects in the tradition of the Bauhaus, rationalism and neo-classicism. He had a rare chance to design not only the building, but the whole of the internal architecture – right down to the lighting appliances.

The design is dominated by archetypical geometric forms such as the cylinder, the circle, the cube and the pyramid. The complex consists of two structures: the square building to the front, which has a glass atrium with a pyramidal roof at its centre, and the round building next to it, surmounted by a ball set on the apex of the chimney stack. There is trelliswork for climbing plants, which provide whole sections of the building with greenery.

The Rolandsburg, with its 59 rooms, large restaurant, conference rooms, summer terrace and indoor swimming pool, is like a solitaire that fits harmoniously into its natural setting – an effect due in large measure to architectural echoes of the traditional stately villa. From the very first sight, the absence of a basement or any reference to a central axis indicates the hospitable public function of the building. The hotel is only a few minutes' drive from the city, yet at the same time discreet and secluded; it is thus an ideal temporary residence for the clientele at which it is targeted – salesmen accompanied by partners, who wish to spend their time conferring and relaxing. The atrium, with its bar and open fireplace, illustrates the principle that governs the interior planning of the Rolandsburg: a tastefully assured composition based on symmetry and a synthesis of classical modern furniture, mainly black, and bright colours. Sparing use is made of marble and other materials that might suggest opulence. Yet the impression conveyed by the décor throughout the hotel is distinguished, and the distinction resides in the restraint.

In the guest-rooms, grey and Bordeaux-red bird's-eye maple predominates. The bathrooms are white-tiled with a black frieze. In the pool and fitness areas, turquoise tiles contrast with the dominant brilliant white. Even at night the ancient woods surrounding the hotel become a panorama in which the gigantic, flood-lit trees seem like phantoms gently swaying in the breeze.

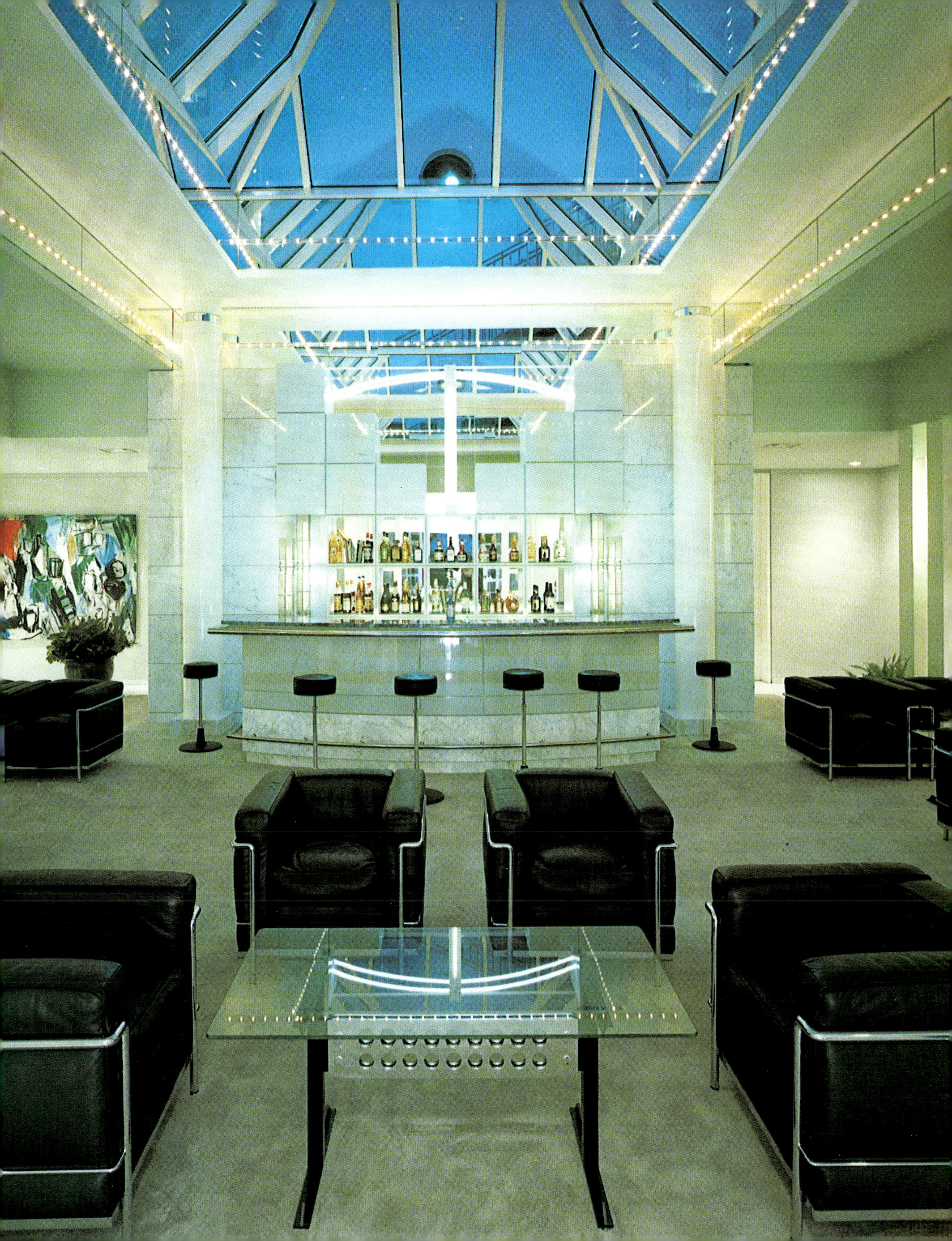

Right and below: Drawings showing a suite and a double room.

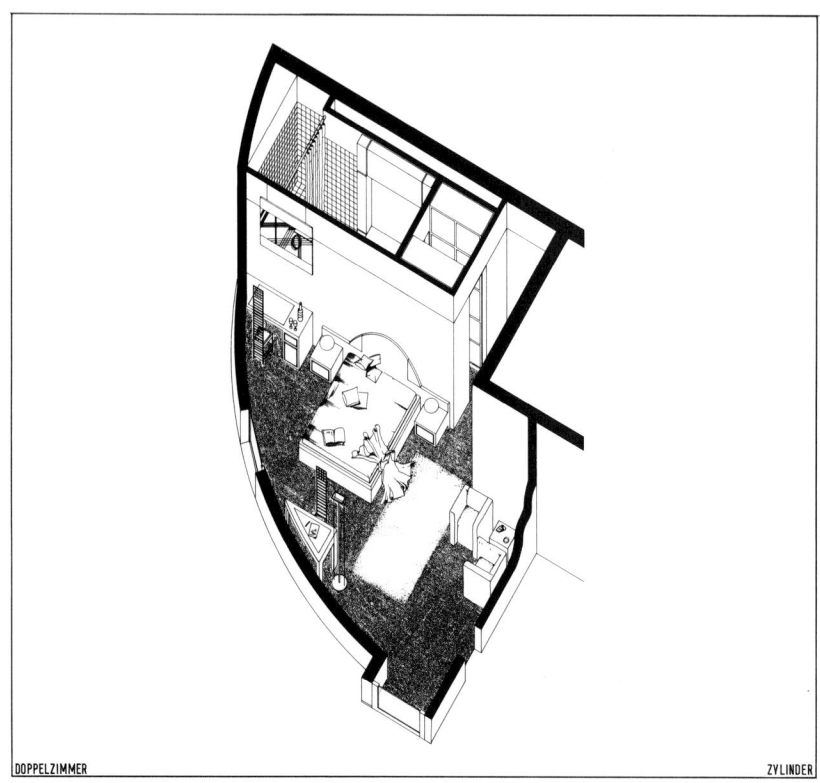

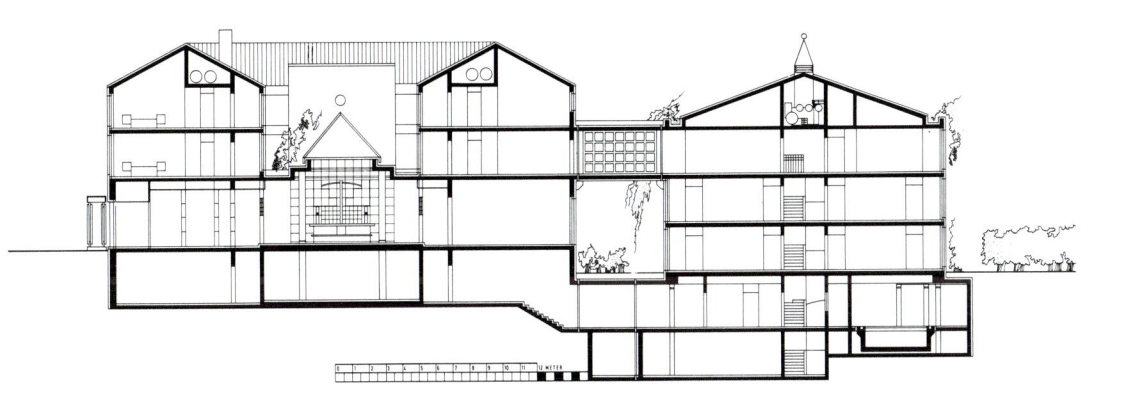

Cross-section of the building.

Right: The indoor swimming pool speaks the same clear geometrical language as the design of the hotel as a whole, which is reminiscent of traditional villa architecture.

Left: In the Claris the building tradition of the 19th century is combined with ultramodern Spanish architecture and design culture to produce an impressive total work of art. **Right:** An atrium with a concrete-encased staircase, lifts and access corridors was incorporated into the building.

THE CLARIS
Barcelona, Spain, 1991

Architecture/Interior Design:

MBM Arquitectes J. Martorell, O. Bohigas, D. Mackay, A. Puigdomenech

Seldom has an ancient structural fabric been so successfully transformed as in one of Barcelona's most recent hotel projects. A three-storey building dating from Barcelona's *belle époque* used to stand on the site of the new Claris, called after the street of the same name. Both the client and building regulations insisted on the preservation of the façade, which was constructed in 1892. The celebrated architects, who belong to the "Escuela de Barcelona", left the façade on the corner site intact, adding only a modern portal. Inside the building they created an access patio that is nothing short of an architectural masterpiece. It consists on one side of an oval stair-tower in exposed concrete, with port-hole-type windows and a diagonally placed lift-shaft. Pergola-type levels leading to the guest-rooms run around these tower-like elements. This access system forms a surprising contrast to the traditional façade. It enabled the architects to avoid dark hotel corridors and gives the building a modern character.

No less skilful is the use of materials: stone, metal, glass and wood are handled with a mastery that is both craftsman-like and traditional. In the style of the interior appointments, too, the architects are able to combine the classical and the modern with such subtlety that no incongruities arise. Traditional furniture is faultlessly combined with modern Spanish designer pieces. The stone floors throughout the building are covered with over a hundred kilims which create a pleasantly modern effect.

The *pièce de résistance* is undoubtedly the lobby, which is designed as a private museum displaying outstanding works of Egyptian art. In addition to the 124 rooms there are two restaurants and a roof-top swimming pool.

Despite its comfortable modern appointments, the Hotel Claris still retains the atmosphere of a palace. For all its show, its modern stylistic culture never seems ostentatious and is able to blend objectivity with an aura of atmosphere and culture. The Claris eschews all plush-laden classicism and theatricality: what we find here is modern art deco with a healthy rational component, in keeping with the recognized architectural credo of the MBM Studio of Barcelona.

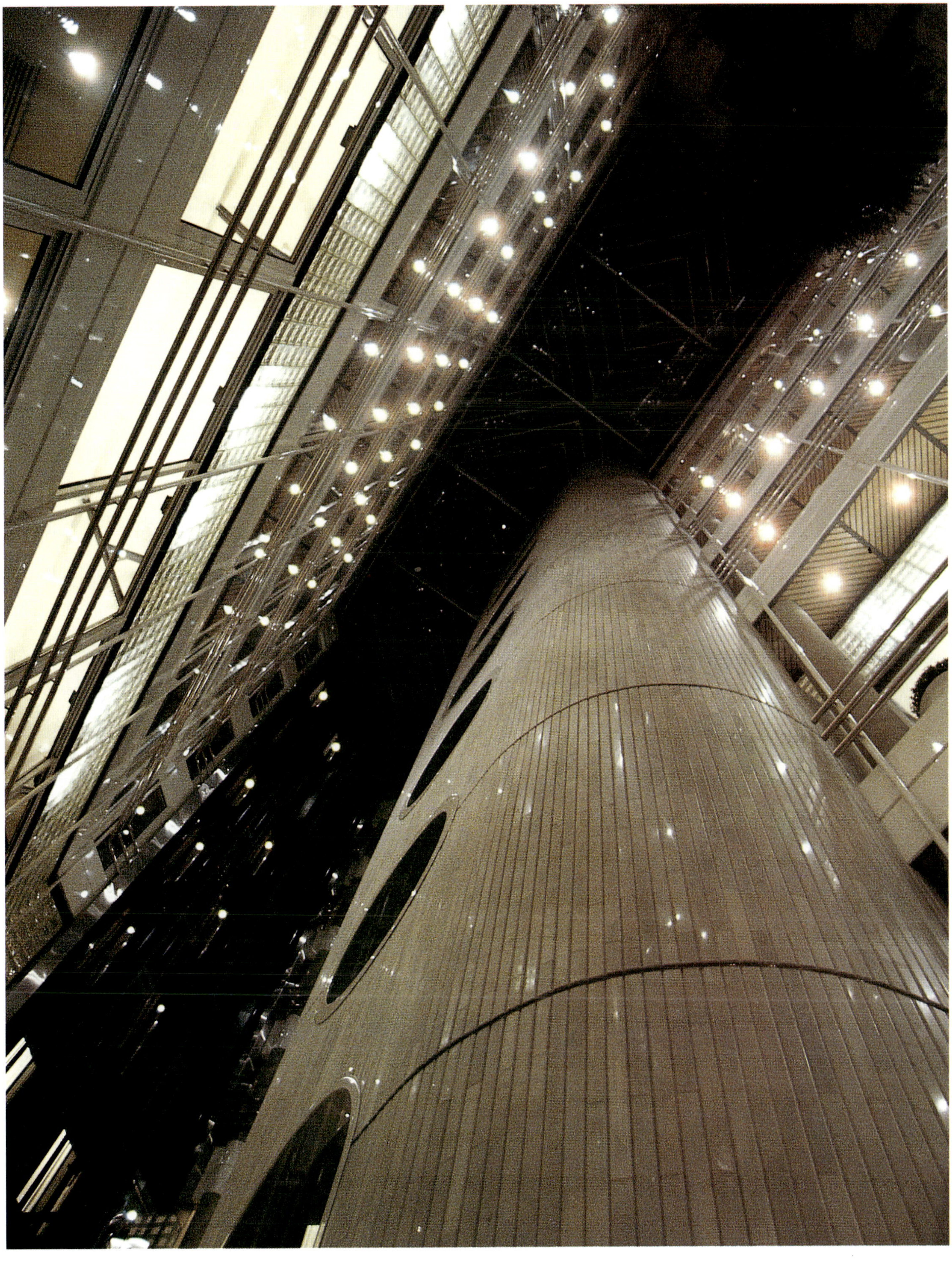

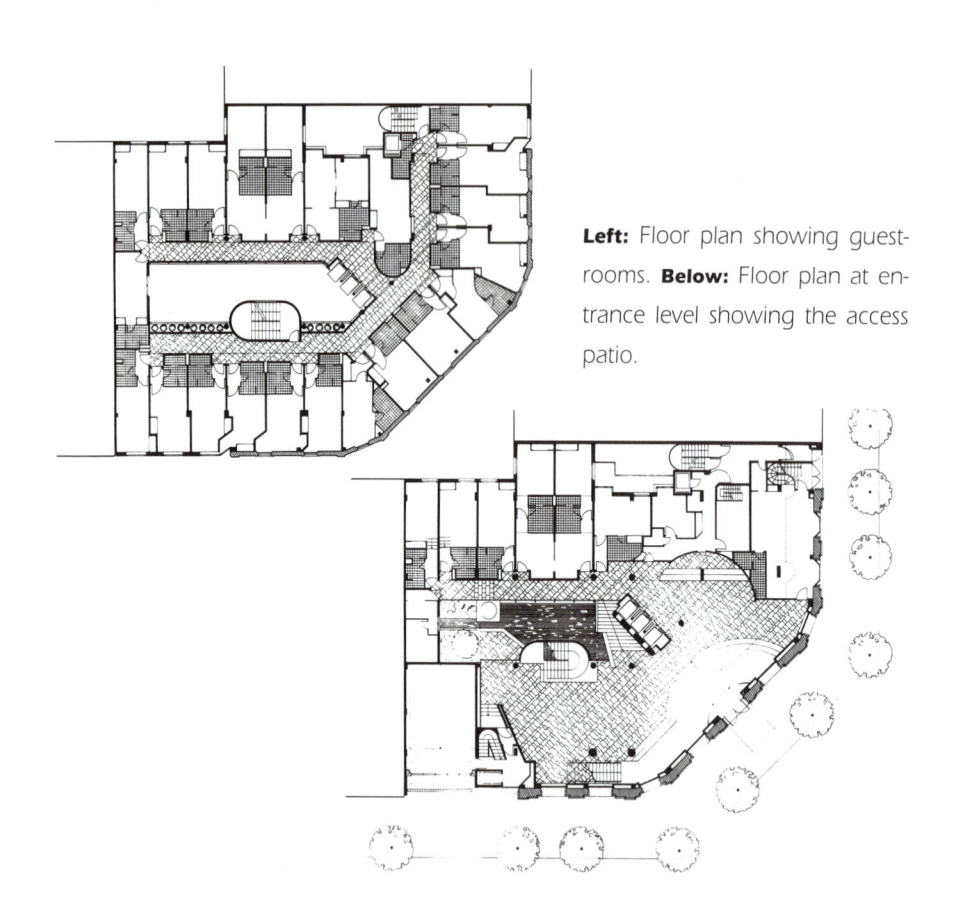

Left: Floor plan showing guestrooms. **Below:** Floor plan at entrance level showing the access patio.

Below: The exhibition of Egyptian antiquities in the lounge underlines the cultivated ambience of the hotel.

Above: The toilets – made of brass and marble with indirectly lit ceilings – are no less ambitious in their design than the architecture of the building as a whole.

Right: The rooms at the Claris bear witness to the high standards of Spanish interior architecture. The superb handling of contrasting materials and shades of colour produces an atmosphere that does justice to Barcelona with its Catalan culture and design tradition.

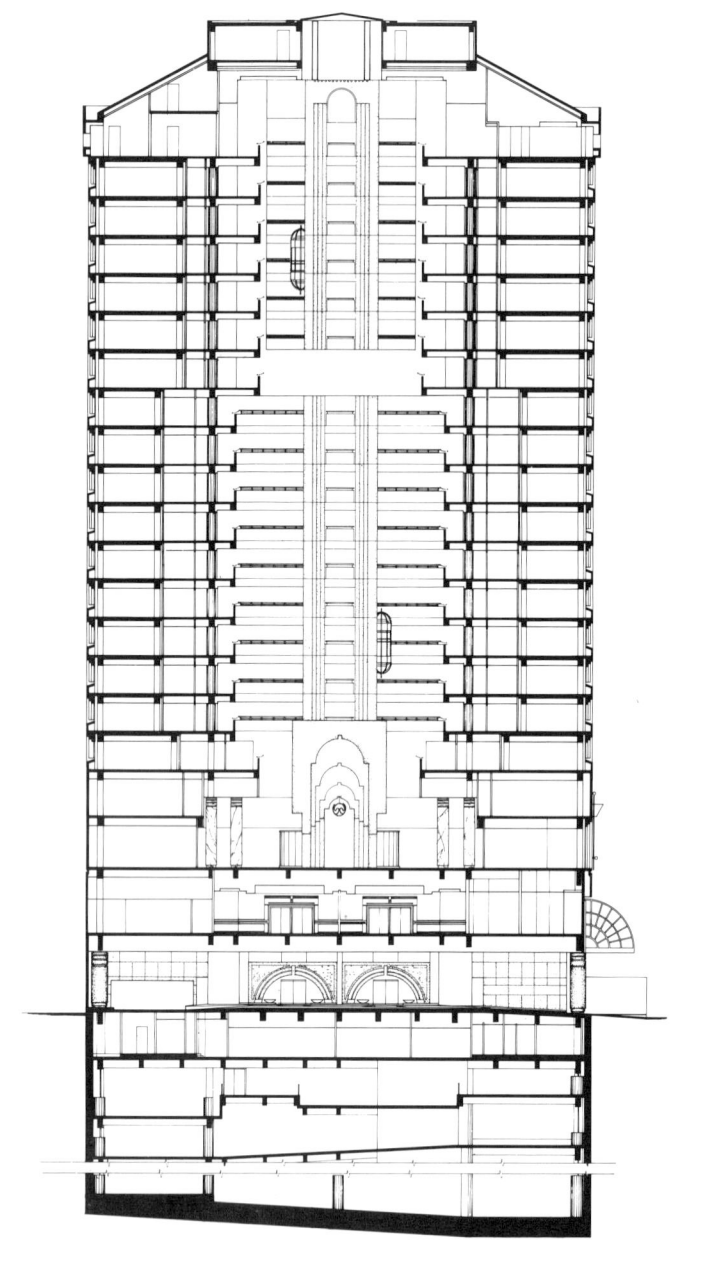

Left: A section of the hotel, a small project by Portman's standards.

Right: The lobby was designed in the style of the art deco revival and features *Joie de Vivre*, a bronze sculpture by Elbert Weinberg.

THE PORTMAN
San Francisco, USA, 1987

Architecture/Interior Design:

John Portman & Associates

As an architect who creates spectacular hotel buildings, John Portman has been much sought after since the late sixties (see pages 10, 160). With this project in San Francisco, he and his Asian partners took the risk of switching from the role of designer to that of entrepreneur. The Portman was to inaugurate his own chain of medium-sized luxury hotels. He took as his models the discreet, comfortable, opulently furnished hotels of the turn of the century, such as the Gritti in Venice or the Connaught in London. This backward look determines the external aspect of the architecture. With the Portman he abandons the dynamic organization of geometric volumes, his hallmark hitherto, and paraphrases the historical repertoire, bringing in numerous arches, external ornamentation in brick and prefabricated concrete, and glass canopies.

The interior décor underlines the stylistic revision. Though Portman does not abandon the roof-high atrium with gleaming glass lift cabins, what was previously a roofed public space has been transformed into something splendidly private. This is the architect's way of acknowledging the changing spirit of the times in America and celebrating its arrival in the money-struck, show-struck Reagan era. Monumental arches, floors with marble inlays and Persian carpets, groups of heavy leather seats, plants in wide terracotta pots, muted colours and restrained lighting are in tune with the grand architectonic gesture. Portman stated his objective: "The interior of the hotel should present an ideal of luxury and personal comfort. The blend of materials, furniture and art follows the principles of a private salon or club, not those of a commercial hotel."

At the Portman one looks in vain for the usual gastronomic variety: one top-class restaurant is available to the guests 24 hours a day. The 21-storey building contains 348 rooms and suites. The furnishing does not seem extravagant compared with that of other top-class hotels; the colour schemes are not oppressive, and the generous use of silk, costly woods and marble appears altogether fitting. Portman skilfully balances nostalgic kitsch and contemporary taste. The top floor is reserved for the Presidential suite and another suite adjacent to it, a grand conference room and "The Club" – a sociable, intimately furnished meeting place for hotel guests, with a double fireplace, a bar, a small buffet and a sun terrace situated high above the streets of San Francisco.

133

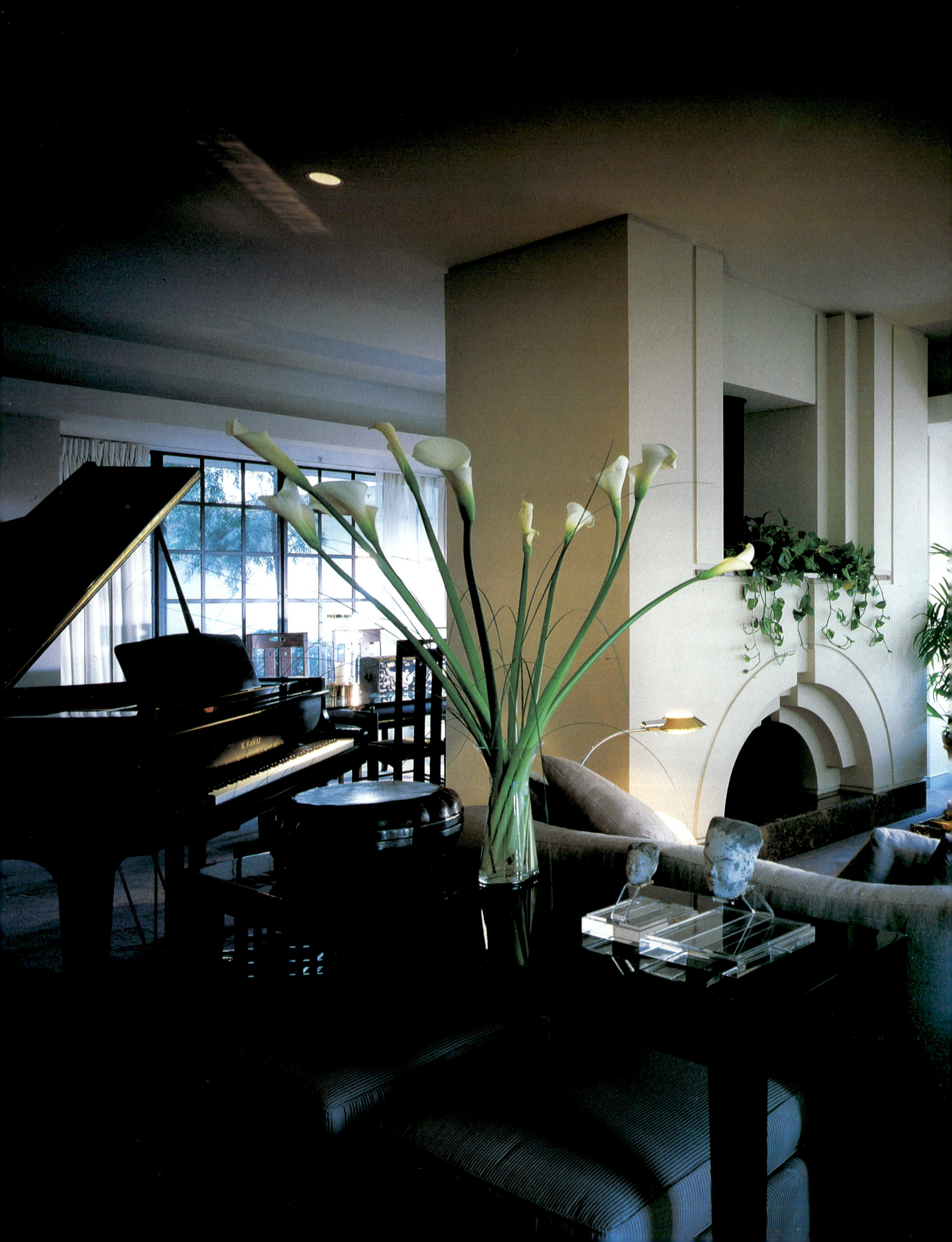

Below: Plan of the hotel at roof-top level showing suites, a lounge and a boardroom.

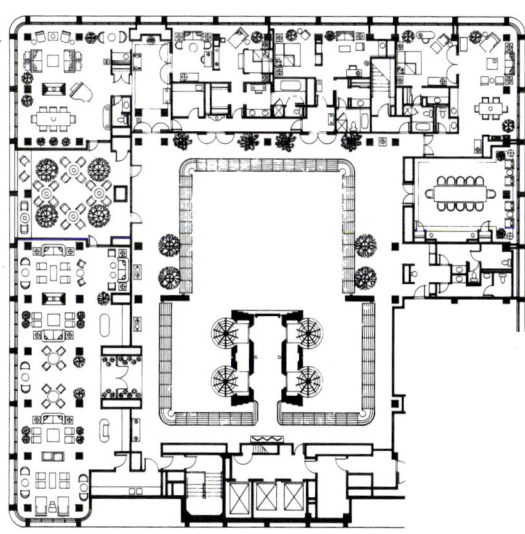

Left: In the Presidential suite on the 21st floor, a massive double fireplace divides the living and dining areas.

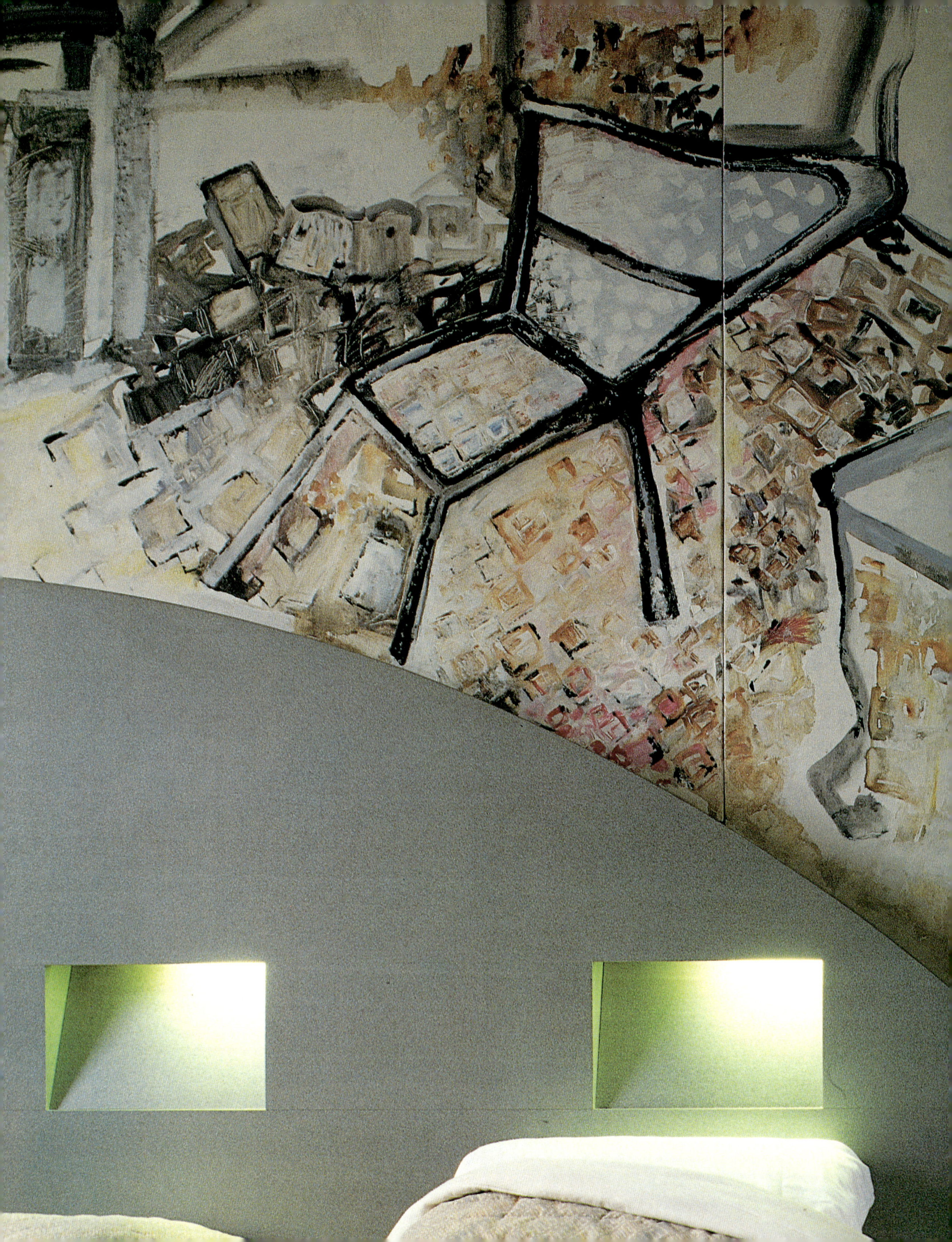

3
ARTIST HOTELS

IN THE 50-ROOM SICILIAN HOTEL L'Atelier sul Mare a Japanese artist declared a hotel room an art room and accordingly designed it as an authentic work of art. When the moon is full, its light streams through the window of the room and catches a brass-covered surface – a moon-altar standing where one would expect to find a bed. Such a symbiosis is far from exceptional today: there are extraordinary instances of hotels becoming scenes of superb artistic displays. These experiments are nearly always set up by outsiders to the hotel business, for example, art collectors or gallery owners. As a rule, idealistic hotel owners invite artists to design one room each. Thus, in the New Siru in Brussels, an important collection of modern Belgian art was assembled in 101 rooms; in Basel, in one of the most intimate artist hotels, Der Teufelhof, a mere eight rooms were given over for a period of two years to installations created by artists.

That the artist hotel can even tempt commercial investors is proved by the fact that in San Francisco a shrewd businessman commissioned local artists to convert the aging Beverly Plaza into a mythological playground full of wit and poetry; renamed the Triton, it became a great public attraction.

The most striking instance of a hotel generating a heroic sense of art has been provided by a Swiss gallery owner. At an altitude of over 6,000 feet, where Romantics used to marvel at the great glaciers and mountain massifs, the Furkablick hotel puts on an exhibition of the latest works of conceptual art every summer when the snow has receded.

Art fanatics have always dreamt up bold combinations of the hotel world and the art world, but have now found they have soulmates in a new breed of no less passionate art tourists. With art and culture currently enjoying an unprecedented popularity, the subjective world of the artist hotel is appreciated as never before. Meanwhile, the unexpected acclaim accorded to this extravagant and thought-provoking hotel type has given new heart and a new impetus to a business that is staking more and more of its resources on the provision of novel experiences.

Left: The old Alpine hotel Furkablick with its new metal entrance designed by Rem Koolhaas. Guests enter through the side of the metal structure.

Right: Daniel Buren provided the house with striped window shutters.

THE FURKABLICK
Furka Pass, Switzerland, 1991

Architecture (rebuilding):

Rem Koolhaas/O.M.A.

Where nineteenth-century Alpine couriers and travellers sat shivering in the parlour, and where Goethe put up in 1779 on his way to Italy, the modern traveller is promised both early Victorian style and avant-garde. For three months in the summer the former staging post on the Furka Pass in Switzerland is the focus for unusual artistic activities. Marc Hostettler, a gallery owner from Neuenburg, purchased this angular, sparsely appointed monument to the heroic pioneering age of Alpine tourism. In this hotel building, which stands defiant near the top of the pass at an altitude of over 6,000 feet, he runs two businesses. On a specially built sun terrace and in a practical and newly furnished restaurant he caters to the needs of modern tourists who are just passing through, while reserving the historically furnished guest-rooms for participants in workshops and seminars associated with the international FurkArt project, which he inaugurated in 1983. The dusty, weather-worn building would never have become an international attraction were it not for the fact that world-famous artists visit this Alpine wilderness year after year in order to expose their works to the landscape.

The hotelier owes the architectural up-grading of the hotel to an architect of world class. With a few assured strokes Rem Koolhaas transformed the building into a composition in which the old and the ultramodern are brought together in a tense and striking confrontation. Koolhaas added the free-standing steel terrace to this curious building, constructed a funnel-shaped metal entrance on the west face for the tourist part of the hotel, and designed the restaurant as a minimalist work of art. Such restraint not only preserved, but underlined the defiant aspect of the old building.

Not only the Furkablick itself, but the grandiose mountain landscape is involved in the artistic endeavour. The French artist Daniel Buren provided the hotel with striped window shutters; Richard Long put "wind arrows" on the gable of an adjacent building; Per Kirkeby set up a stone stele in the landscape; Panamarenko constructed a rucksack aeroplane for the airy heights; and Ian Hamilton Finlay contributed a stone with the signature of Ferdinand Hodler, the Swiss landscape painter who worked here.

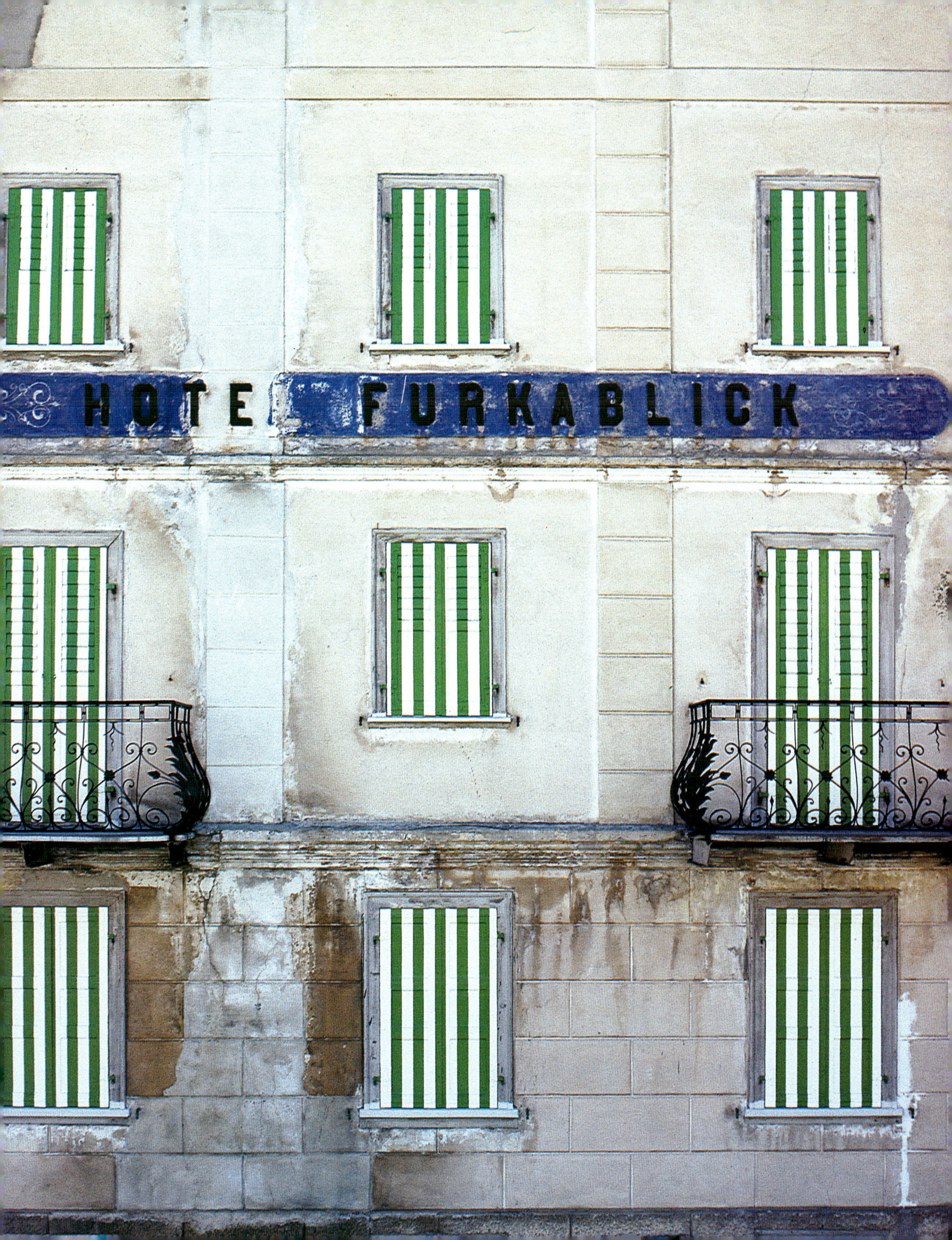
HOTE FURKABLICK

The construction of the porch.

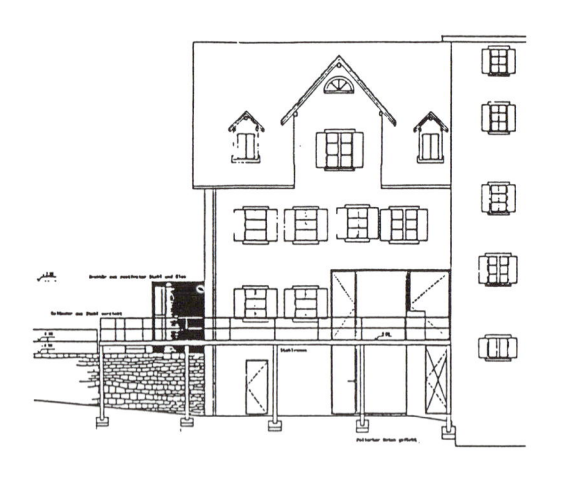

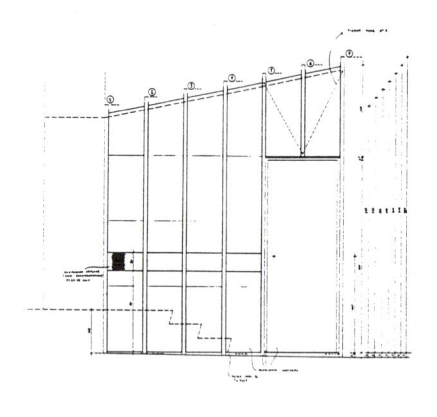

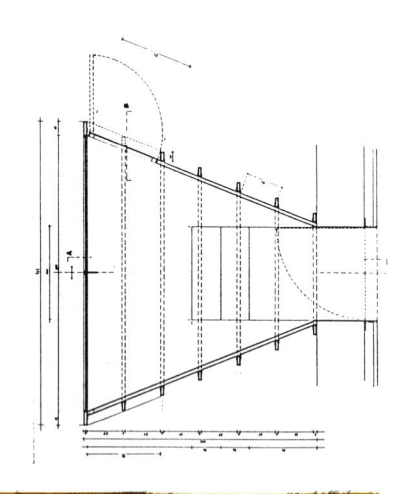

Left: In the restaurant area, which is fronted by a sun terrace, Rem Koolhaas cut a large graphic opening in the old structural fabric. **Above:** The old dining room now serves as a lounge for conferences.

The guest-rooms have been left in their original condition. Once occupied by Alpine tourists, they now attract art-lovers.

Internationally celebrated artists place signs in the landscape, making the region a focus of the art scene.

Above: On the top floor and in the attics of the Teufelhof, artists who would otherwise exhibit only in galleries and museums can each design one of the eight guest-rooms. Their designs will remain in place for two years. **Right:** The attic room with the book ceiling was designed by the German artist Hubertus Gojowczyk.

DER TEUFELHOF
Basel, Switzerland, 1989

Architecture: **Hans Pösinger**

Interior Design: **Artists from Switzerland, Germany and France**

To publicize the hotel room as an ideal place in which to promote art involves a good deal of idealism and passion. The link between the promotion of art and gastronomy nearly always rests on a personal love of art and a passion for communicating artistic values. It is usually gallery owners who suddenly move sideways into the catering business. The case of Monica and Dominique Thommy-Kneschaurek is different. This art-loving couple, who have established a highly successful art hotel in Basel, come from the world of the theatre. In their art hotel they have succeeded over the years in combining various cultural activities under one roof. The building is steeped in history and contains many objects of interest.

The layers of culture at the Teufelhof begin at the foundations and end in the extended attics. In the basement rooms one can marvel at the prehistoric town walls of Basel, dating from Celtic times. Above the "Archaeological Cellar" there is one of the two theatres. On the ground floor are a café-bar, a wine bar and another theatre; in the *bel étage* there is a gourmet restaurant seating 50, and finally, on the top floor and in the attic, the hotel's eight artists' rooms.

At first the owners subsidized their own theatre and café from the takings of the restaurant, which was so successful that they were finally encouraged to branch out and add a hotel. For one month, eight artists can occupy the rooms they are hired to design. Each receives a fixed fee of 8,000 Swiss francs and retains ownership of his or her work, which after two years is replaced by that of a successor. The première took place in 1989, and two years later a second group of artists took over. During the two-year period the artists have the opportunity of showing other works at separate exhibitions in the theatre and the wine bar.

The idea of the artist hotel is prompted by the wish to make art something to be "lived with". The guest's stay appears to offer an ideal opportunity for this kind of art promotion: the hotel room proves an unexpectedly congenial place in which to become acquainted with the world of art.

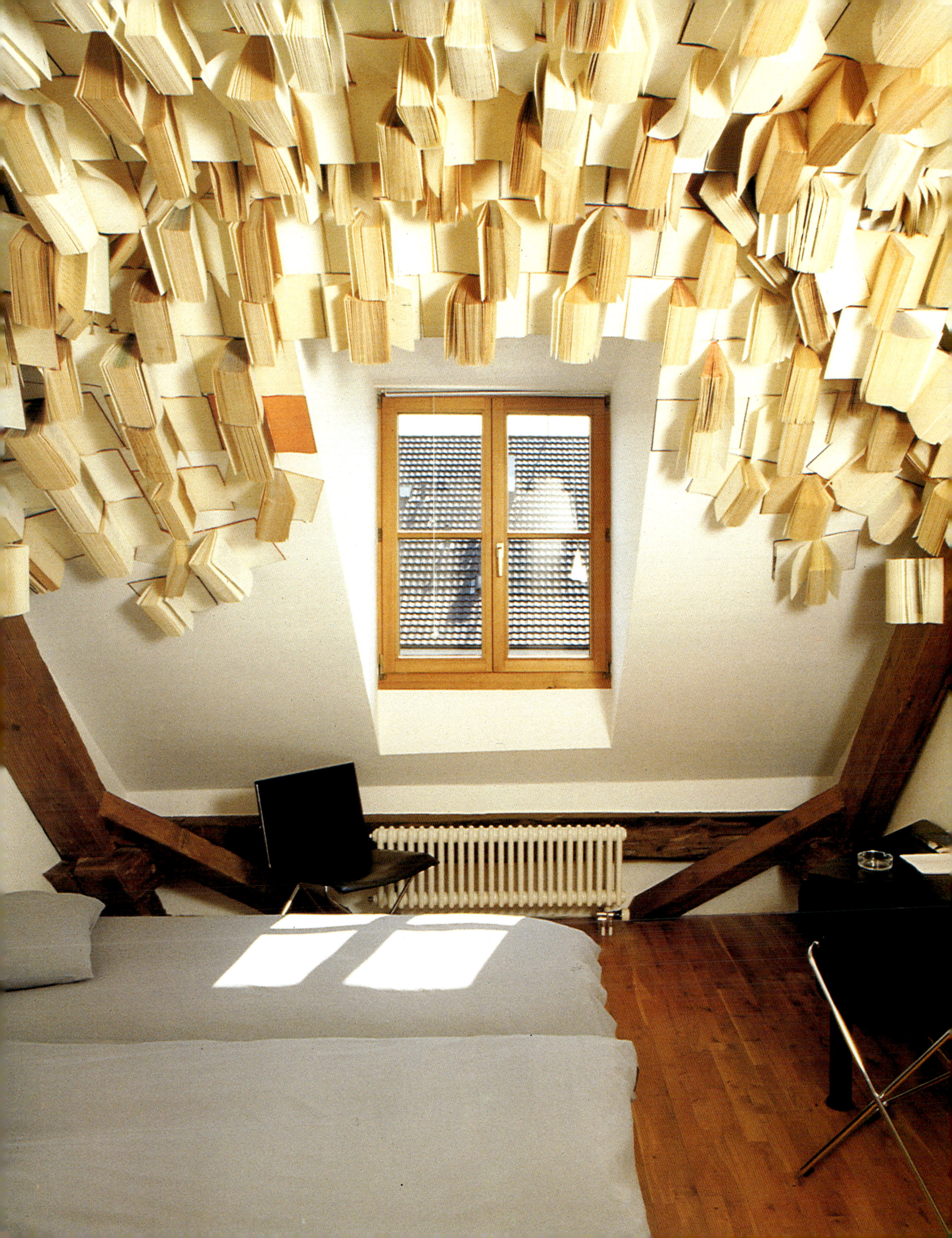

All the artist rooms at the Teufelhof lay claim to being inhabitable works of art. This applies to the video installations of the Swiss artist Guido Nussbaum (above), the abstract graphics of the German artist Hubertus von der Goltz (top right) and the "morphograms" thrown on the wall by Klaus Schmidt, also German (bottom right).

145

NEW SIRU
Brussels, Belgium, 1989
Interior Design: **Atelier 20**

Above: In 1932 the Belgian real estate firm Siru built a tower-like building on a corner site in the Place Rogier for the World Exhibition in Brussels. Today the New Siru contains 101 rooms designed by artists. **Right:** The Belgian painter César Bailleaux designed the brightly coloured room 308, which he calls "A traveller's dream".

Wedged between modern high-rise buildings of glass and concrete in the Place Rogier in Brussels is a whimsical relic from the age of art deco. In 1932 for the World Exhibition in Brussels the Belgian real estate firm Siru built an angular city fortress with an oriental-type corner tower in the then respectable quarter near the North Station. Even today this art deco palace has lost nothing of its curious aura, a synthesis of progress and nostalgia. The building has always been a hotel, and in its day it was considered ultramodern – it was the first hotel to have room telephones. The no less unconventional museum hotel New Siru has now been opened within it. The internal appointments of this curiosity are the joint work of 130 Belgian designers and artists.

The hotelier Jacques Hollander and his wife Galila had 101 rooms and 7 hotel corridors decorated with works by modern Belgian artists. The initiators of the project are private collectors who believe that art only becomes exciting and alive when it is not confined in a museum. The artists were able to live in the hotel for a time to gain inspiration. The experiment was successful and became a media spectacle – over 400 newspaper articles ensured the fame of the Brussels museum hotel. Apart from the media public, businessmen and Eurocrats book into this four-star hotel at moderate prices. Rooms can be chosen from photographs at the reception. Originality is vital as a marketing instrument for the hotel's success, since the area near the North Station no longer counts as one of the most desirable in Brussels. All the same, thanks to inventive marketing, the New Siru, as a mixture of gallery and hotel, gets more bookings than the surrounding concrete blocks. The restaurant is also distinguished by its individuality and imaginativeness. It is called "Le Couvert" because the hotelier uses it to show off his impressive collection of cutlery.

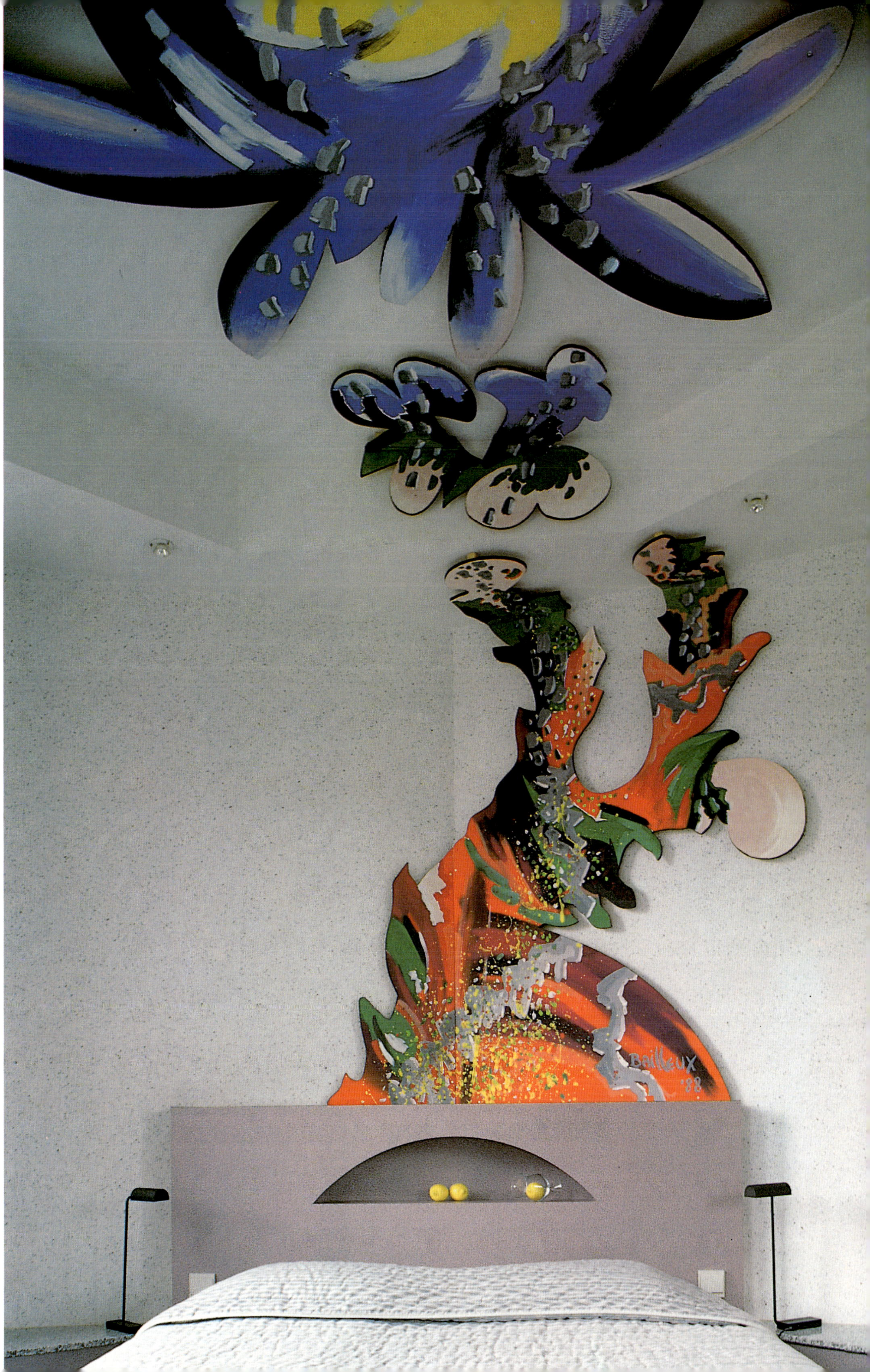
BAILLEUX
'88

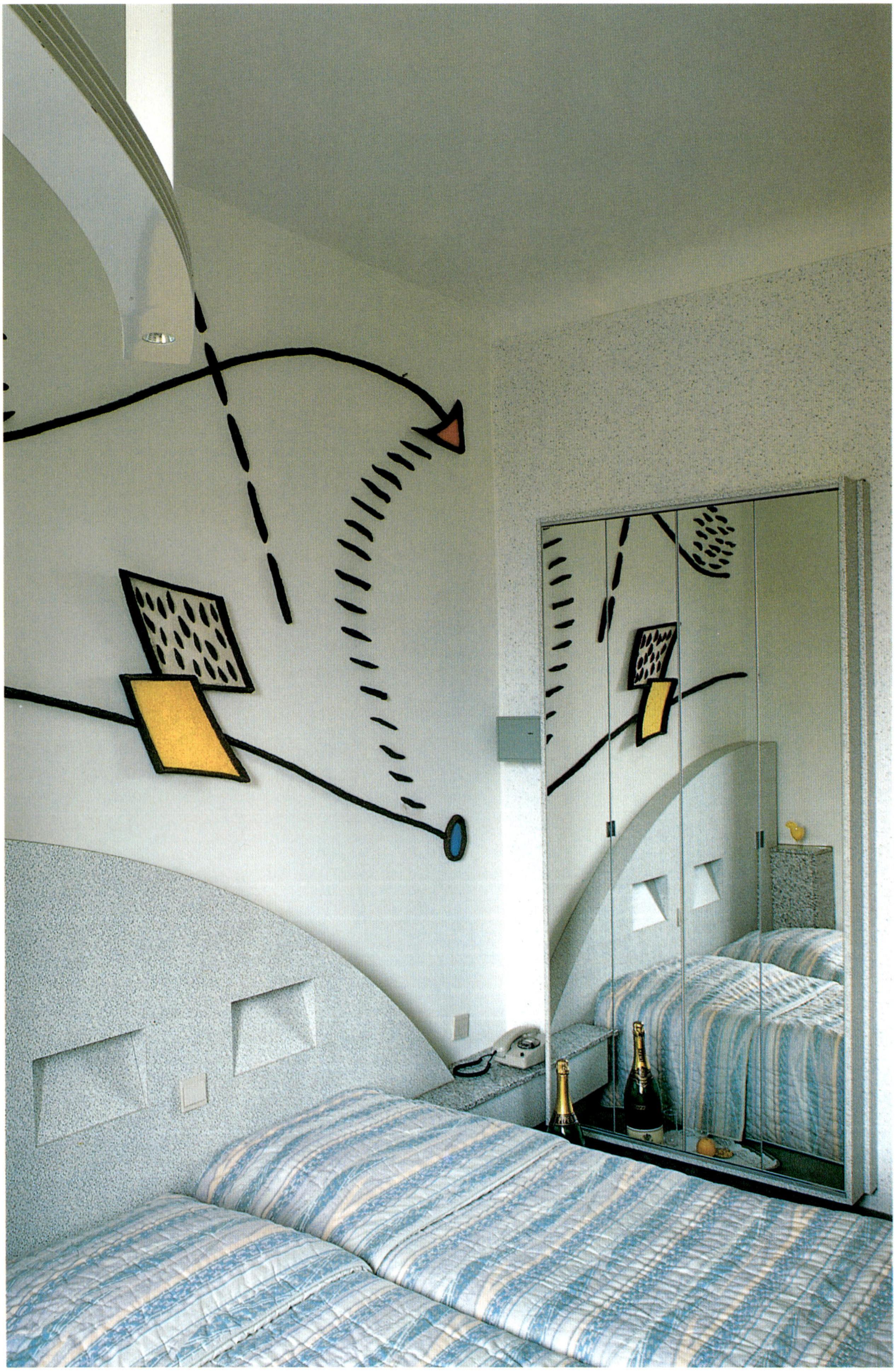

The rooms in the New Siru represent one of the largest collections of contemporary Belgian art. **Far left:** *Mirrored Reflections* by Luc Coeckenberg. **Left:** Installation with pebbles by William Sweetlove. **Below left:** Murals by Francis Tordeur. **Below:** *Marilyn Monroe* by Adelin Guyot.

149

SPADARI AL DUOMO
Milan, Italy, 1991

Architecture: **Urbano Pierini**

Interior Design: **Ugo la Pietra**

The old philanthropist's dream of uniting art and life has been publicized for more than a decade by the Italian artist-designer Ugo la Pietra. In his exhibitions entitled "Abitare con l'arte" ("living with art"), regularly mounted at furniture fairs in Verona and Milan, he has given striking proof of how arts and crafts can be combined with private and public living, even in the late twentieth century. La Pietra's theory of life and art has been applied consistently by Marida Martegani, a Milanese hotelier, to the ambitious reconstruction of her hotel in central Milan. At the new Spadari guests can now experience "Abitare con l'arte" in room after room. For the successful realization of this idea the owner took its dedicated protagonist on to her staff to advise on internal architecture and appointments. The whole hotel, starting with the furniture, was to be governed by the theme of "living with art". There is no modern factory-made furniture in the rooms – only hand-made pieces, which provide an exceptionally apt context for the Milanese avant-garde art displayed there.

The combination of arts and crafts generates an intimate atmosphere quite unlike that of a public gallery. Yet in its basic structure the Spadari remains a traditional Milanese hotel, whose only practical function is to provide overnight accommodation. In a busy city like Milan nothing else is required. When the 8-storey building with its 38 rooms was converted into a four-star hotel, the main consideration was how to widen this function. It was decided to use the interior décor to remind temporary guests that they were in Italy. This aim could be achieved through the integration of Italian art into all the public areas from the breakfast restaurant to the individual rooms. The hotel occupies a prime city site next to the cathedral, and after rebuilding it acquired a curious character, in spite of retaining all its conventional outlines.

At the Spadari art goes beyond the leitmotif of Ugo la Pietra's hand-crafted furniture, and performs a role that further determines the quality of the hotel. An attractive fireplace by Italy's top sculptor Gio Pomodoro catches the eye of guests as they enter the hotel. The breakfast room immediately to the right has become a gallery for Italian ceramics and a showpiece in its own right, with pastel-coloured frescoes by Valentino Hago. Large pictures by Milanese *avant-gardistes* on the walls of the rooms combine with cultivated furnishings to create an atmosphere in which big-city tourists feel they are living with their own art collection, renting not just the room but the art too.

Ground-floor plan showing the entrance, breakfast room and waiting area.

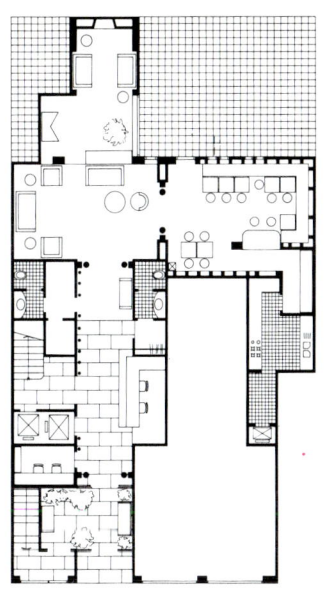

Upper-floor plan showing the conventional arrangement of the rooms.

Left: The façade of the Spadari follows the sober, rational style of most Milanese hotels. **Below:** Inside, however, the guest is greeted by stylishly ordered fantasy. In a waiting area opposite the entrance, the sculptor Gio Pomodoro has created a huge fireplace decoration.

151

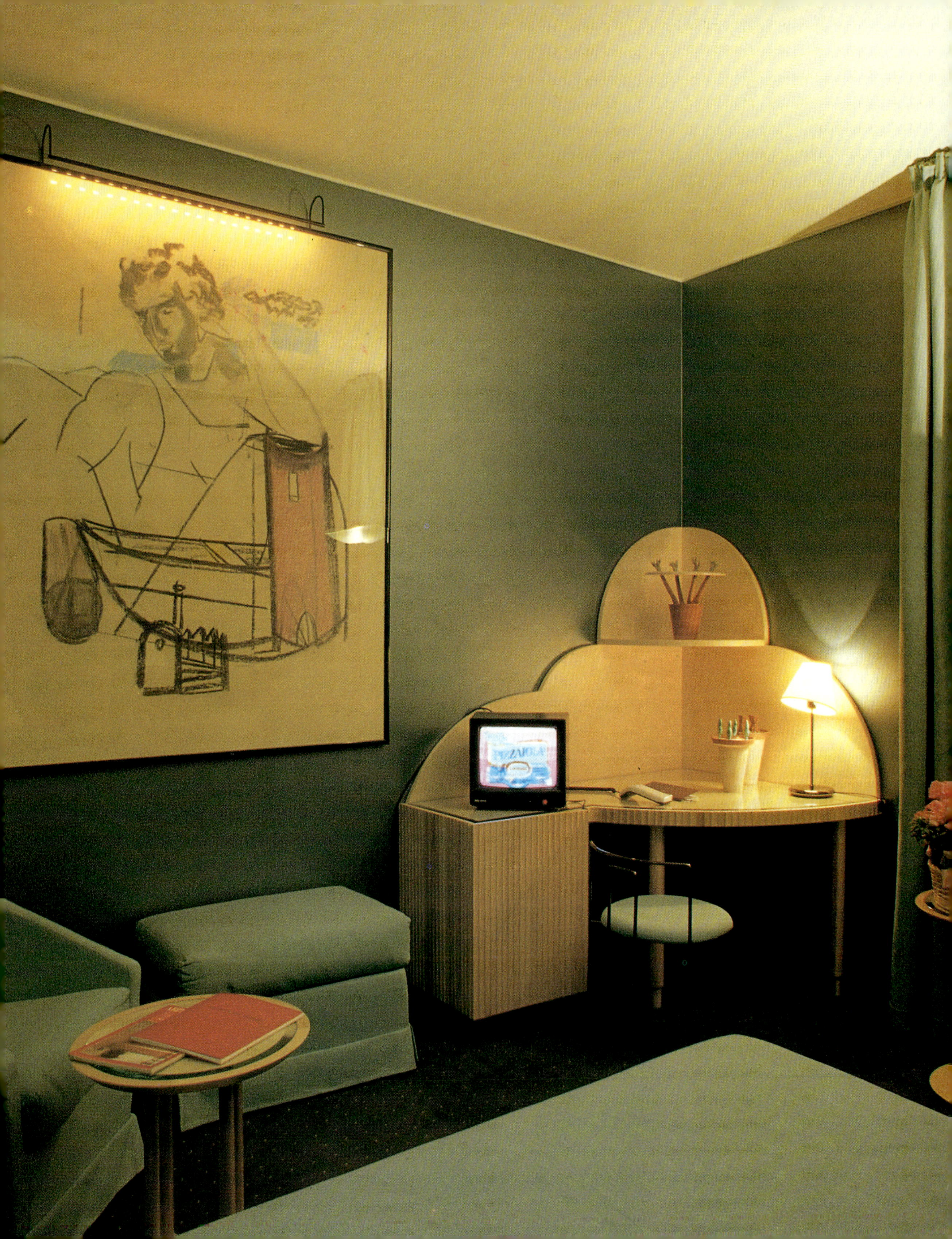

The furniture in the rooms is by the Italian architect Ugo la Pietra; the paintings are by leading representatives of the Milanese avant-garde. The rooms are individually decorated with new art and new Italian crafts.

L'ATELIER SUL MARE
Castel di Tusa, Sicily, 1989

Interior Design: **Michelle Cancella,**

Hidetoshi Nagasawa,

Fabrizio Plessi and others

Above: The hotel L'Atelier sul Mare, on the north coast of Sicily, is owned by hotelier and builder Antonio Presti who commissioned notable international artists to transform the guest-rooms into works of art. **Right:** Nest of Man is the name given by the Italian sculptor Paola Icaro to his walled-castle bed.

Castel di Tusa would be a small, insignificant Sicilian fishing village with the remains of a castle, a handful of houses, a garage, a few bars and three hotels, were it not for its great concrete sculptures. These huge works of art have turned a river valley on the north coast of Sicily into an open-air museum. This was at any rate the dream of the building contractor Antonio Presti. The monuments he produced to designs by notable Italian artists made headlines in the world press when the Sicilian authorities wanted to demolish *Ariadne's Labyrinth*, a land sculpture by Italo Manfredini that was the size of a village square, the imposing, blue *Monument for a Poet*, one of the last works of the Italian pop artist Tano Festas, and an 18-metre-high concrete monument by Pietro Consagra that resembles a head.

The objection to the open-air sculpture park was that no building permission had been given for it. The art enthusiast Presti therefore moved indoors and is now concentrating on an artistic expansion of his 50-room hotel L'Atelier sul Mare. As a counterpoint to open-air art, he is making the building into an artist's studio and wants in due course to have one room after another designed by well-known artists. Art in this context is not to be decorative, but experiential. The first artist involved came from Japan. Hidetoshi Nagasawa has already created a room dedicated to the Sicilian full moon. This moon-room has no light switches or artificial lighting. Only when the moon is full does the artist's installation become an intoxicating work of art. Then the moonlight, entering through the window, shines on a bed made of brass and sets it aglow.

No less sensitive is the work of the Italian artist Fabrizio Plessi. This world-famous electronic art magician has contributed a windowless room. Instead of a sea view, the guest experiences the world outside on video. Other installations now in preparation include a striped room by Daniel Buren and a stone room conceived by the Spanish sculptor Eduardo Chillida. Although the region is extremely remote, this successful symbiosis of art, local cuisine and public relations seems to spell success for an enterprise underpinned by enthusiasm.

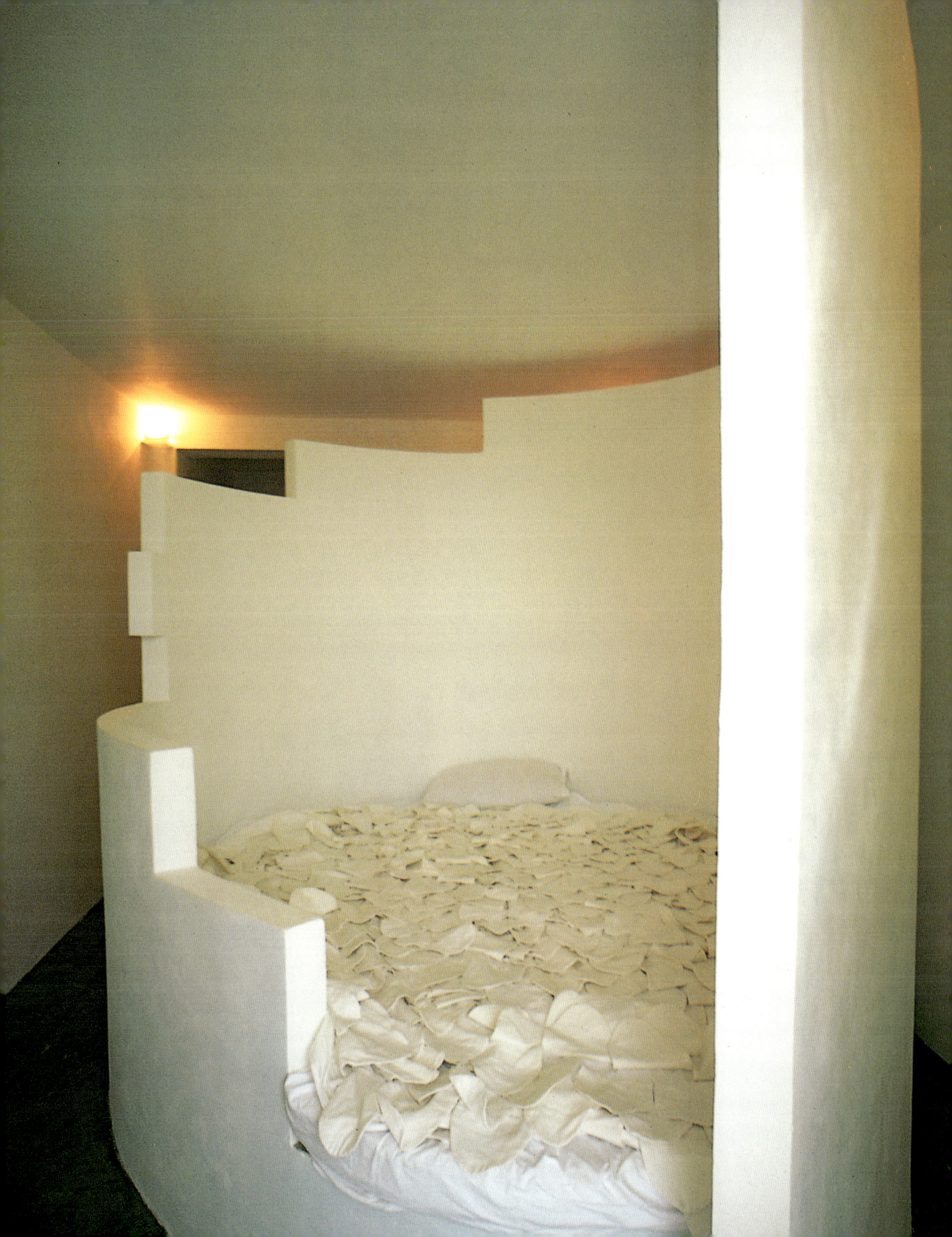

Top: Plan showing the artworks constructed by Presti in a river valley. **Above:** *Ariadne's Labyrinth* is the name given by Italo Manfredini to his monumental concrete labyrinth. **Right:** The sculpture *Matter could not exist there* by Pietro Consagra is 18 metres high.

Left: The room with Paolo Icaro's stone bed looks out over the Mediterranean, as does the room designed by the Japanese artist Hidetoshi Nagasawa (below left). Nagasawa installed a brass cube in the room which represents a bed and is intended to gleam in the moonlight. The only light comes from a candle and the moon.

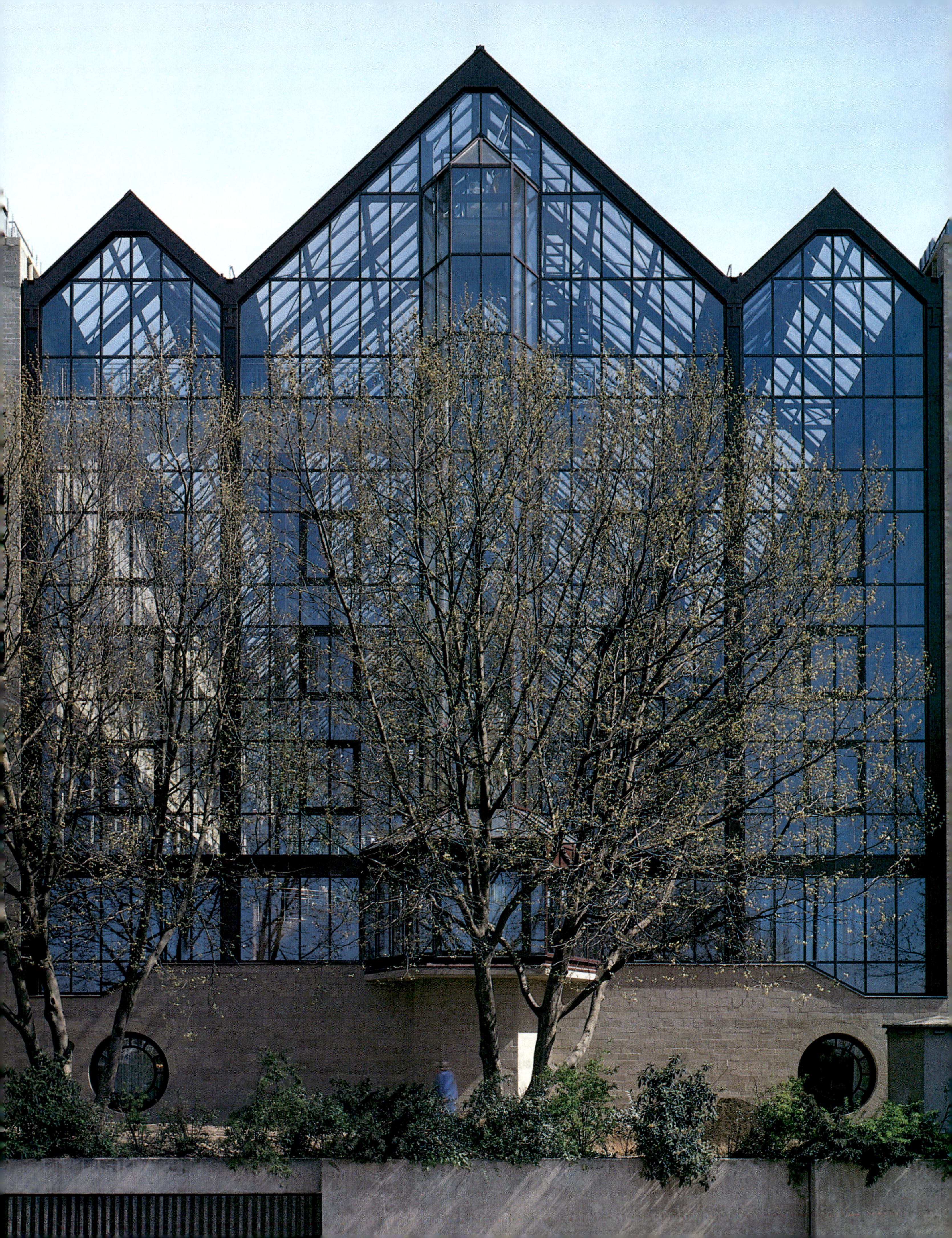

4
THE ATRIUM HOTEL

THE REVOLUTION IN HOTEL ARCHITECTURE initiated by the skyscraper atriums of the American architect John Portman continues to produce lasting results. Portman hit upon the notion – paradigmatically realized in his designs for the Hyatt Group – of the city turned inwards. The urban blight increasingly afflicting the centre of almost every big American city triggered the then revolutionary idea of turning the hotel interior into an urban piazza, a public place that could offer everything – shops, restaurants, leisure facilities – and yet shut out the insecure world beyond it: the street-life, the traffic, the day-to-day crime and social problems. The atrium lobby is surrounded by gallery floors or marginal structures in which the guest-rooms are located.

New hotels such as the Maritim in Cologne, the Heathrow Hilton and the Hyatt Regency Roissy at Charles de Gaulle Airport in Paris paraphrase the Portman principle by interposing an enormous glass hall between accommodation wings. In the last two cases the atrium model has been shifted to the urban periphery. The atriums in these hotels are deliberate reminders of the girder constructions familiar from aircraft hangars. The blocking off of the world outside is due mainly to the need for noise insulation: the sky and the aircraft are still present to the mind.

In the matter of design, some of the new atrium hotels present the same dilemma as their predecessors: the grand architectonic gesture is at variance with the interior design, which often represents a compromise. Behind the doors of the guest-rooms and in the restaurants and congress areas the ambience tends towards the conventional; the grandiose spatial creations peter out in the mainstream of tedious ready-made solutions. Just how far – and how variously – some of the city simulations have diverged in style from the initial pattern is clearly demonstrated by recent examples from Hong Kong, where the reflecting exteriors of the huge skyscrapers conceal an art deco revival (the Grand Hyatt Hong Kong) or the monumentality of *la belle époque* (the Island Shangri-La). Only Michael Graves' postmodern palace hotel in San Diego, the Hyatt Regency La Jolla, reveals everything about its Technicolor-classical Roman character – what you see is what you get, and in abundance.

Left: The Atlanta Marriott Marquis, the third Portman hotel in the Peachtree district, has 53 floors and over 1,700 rooms.

Right: The atrium rises to a dizzy height of over 48 storeys: the textile sculpture of the artist Daniel Graffin ends over the Grandstand piano bar.

ATLANTA MARRIOTT MARQUIS
Atlanta, USA, 1985
Architecture: **John Portman & Associates**

For first-hand experience of John Portman's outstanding significance for the hotel architecture of recent decades one need only go to Atlanta. There, in the Peachtree Center, one can see three landmarks of the architect's career in close proximity. It was in 1967, with the Hyatt Regency Atlanta, that the success story of the skyscraper-dwarfing hotel atrium began. With the 73-floor glass cylinder of the Westin Peachtree Plaza Portman realized the concept of the atrium as an interior "town", with the vertical structure shooting up from it. In the Atlanta Marriott Marquis, completed in 1985, he built up the outer sculptural shell into an expressive crescendo of perspectives by means of twisting, protruding and receding floor galleries. The exterior parabola of the 53-floor hotel matches the Chinese puzzle provided by its interior, but it also recalls the cube and the cylinder of the two earlier hotel buildings.

Once again the architect proved to be adept at meeting all the requirements of the type of hotel that he inaugurated with his earlier projects and that has since been copied world-wide: the central, functional, luxurious El Dorado in a city context, designed for large conferences, run by an international chain and frequented by thousands of visitors and guests. The functional areas of the building are clearly separated vertically. On the level below the atrium lobby are the reception area, the ballroom, the congress centre and the conference rooms. At atrium level there are five restaurants, as well as shops, lounges and swimming pools; the atrium also serves as a public space – a town turned inwards. Above it are 46 floors of guest-rooms. "The vertical organization very effectively divides the generally accessible areas of the hotel from the more private ones", explains John Portman.

The interior design is modest in relation to the imposing architecture. The rooms are furnished in accordance with the usual superior, unostentatious and easily maintained standard of the Marriott Group and so meet the expectations of businessmen and conference guests, which are determined by this kind of uniform design. At the Atlanta Marriott Marquis, then, as in Portman's Marina Square in Singapore, it was left to the artist Daniel Graffin to give the architecture an individual accent that would add to the imposing character of the building. In the atrium his installation of fabric strips sweeps down from above, gathering in a red cloud above the balcony of the Grandstand piano bar.

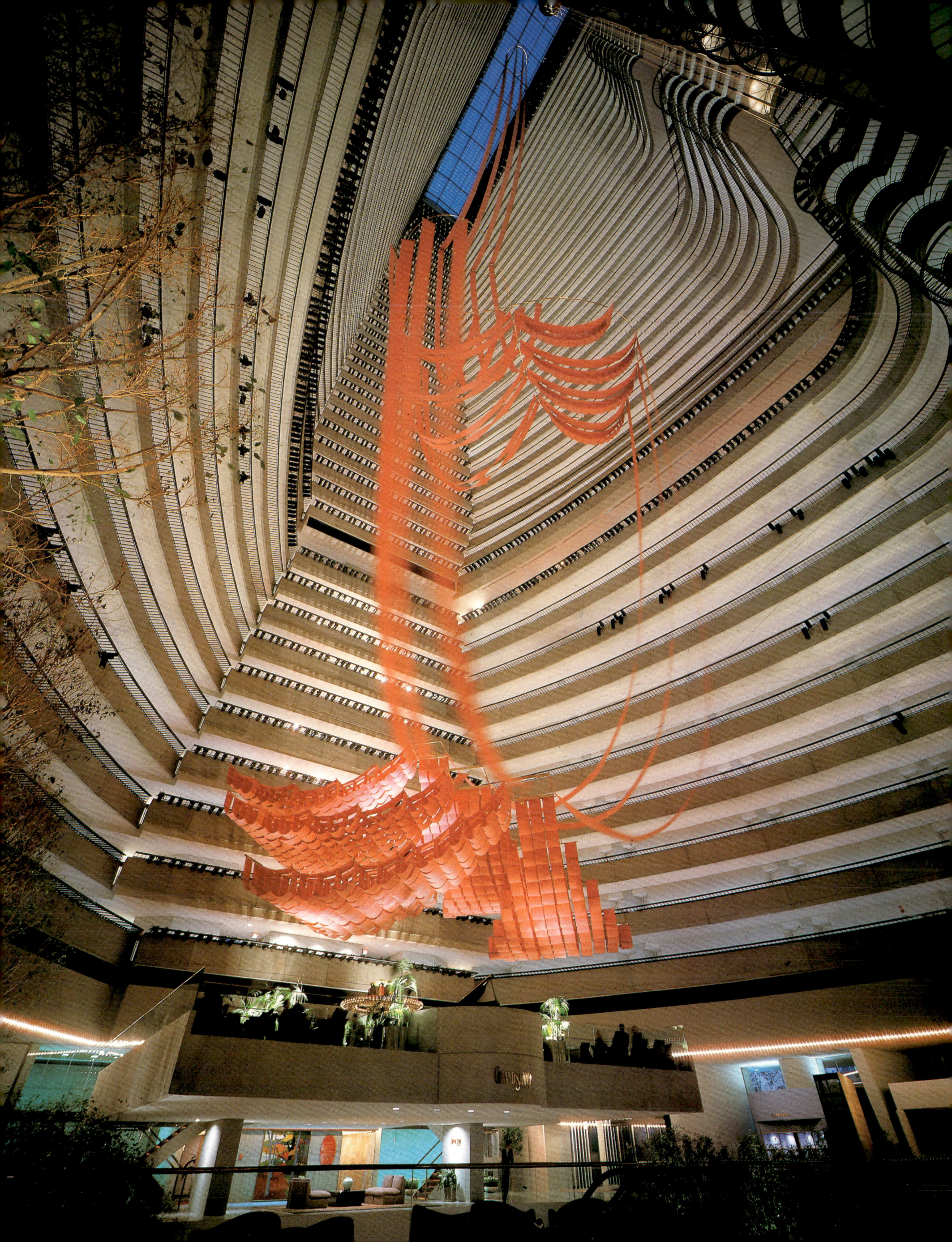

The glass lift cabins in the atrium move between the floors as if pulled by cords – one of John Portman's inventions that has been added to the repertoire of international top-class hotels.

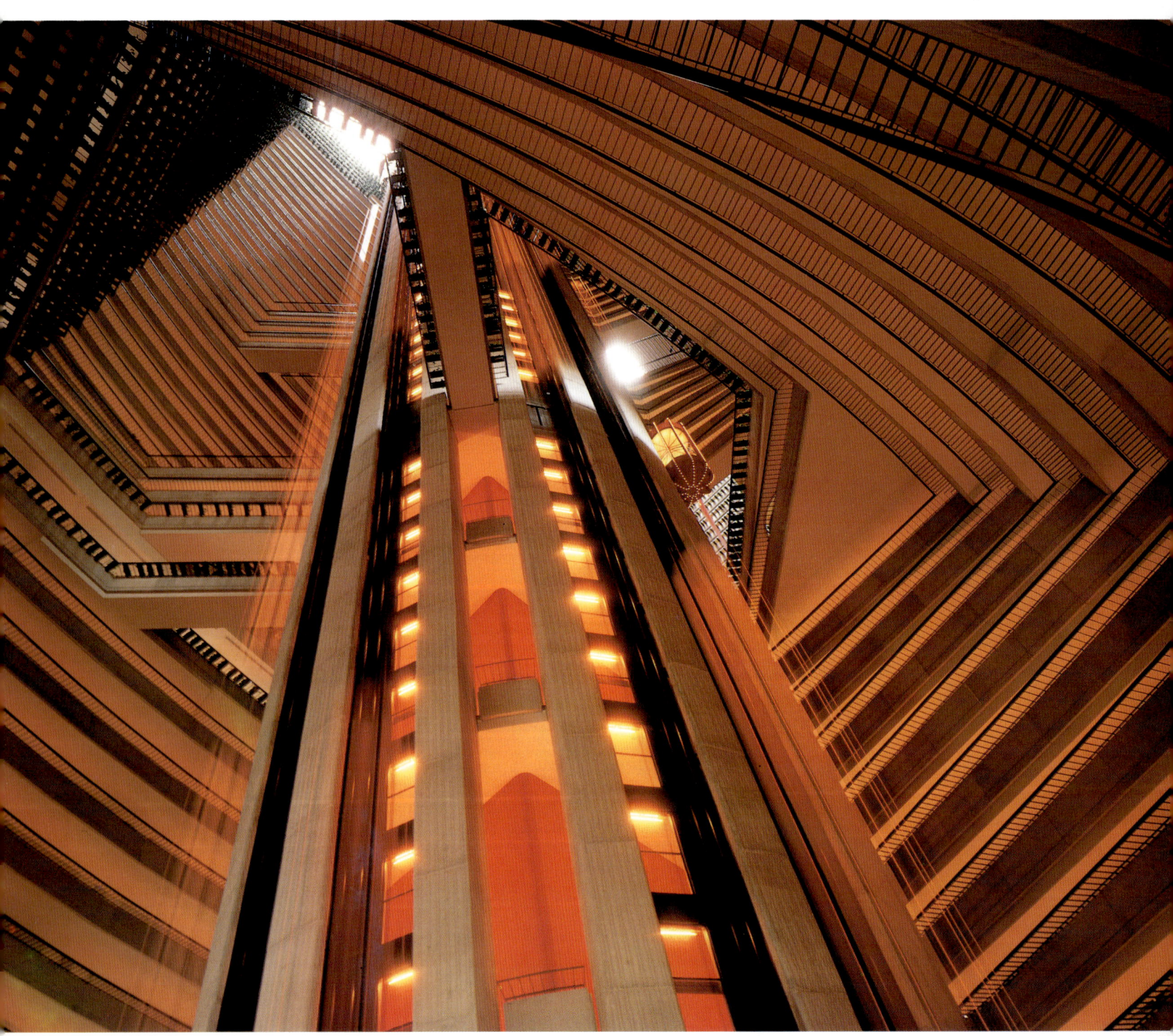

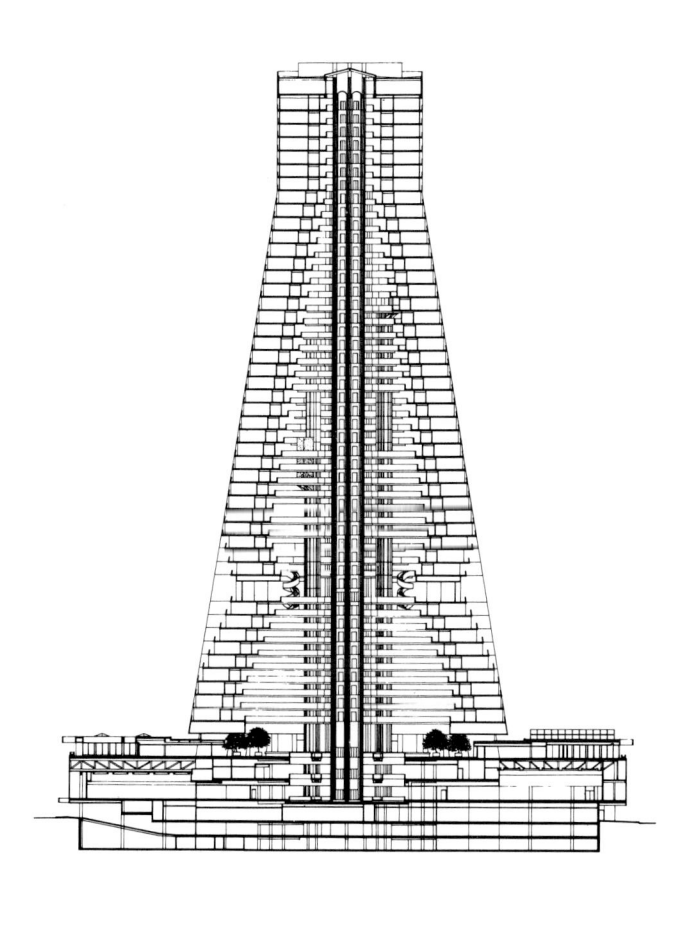

Large-scale functionality, expressively designed: the drawings show (left) a section of the hotel tower which tapers towards the top; and ground plans of the two lobby floors (bottom left) and a typical accommodation floor (below).

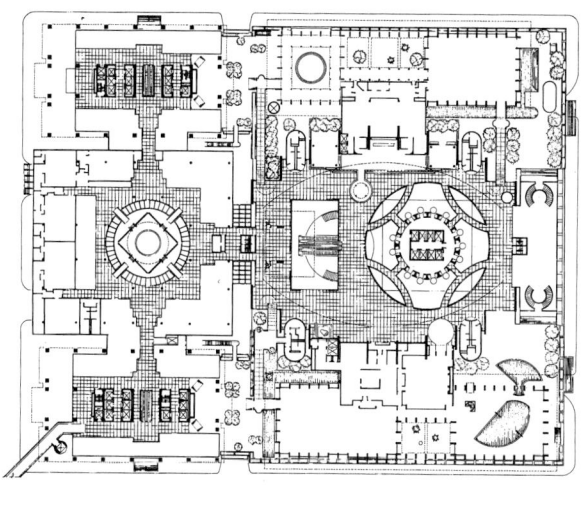

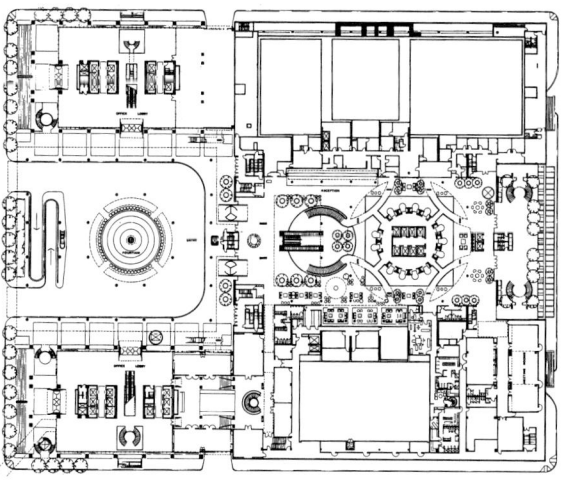

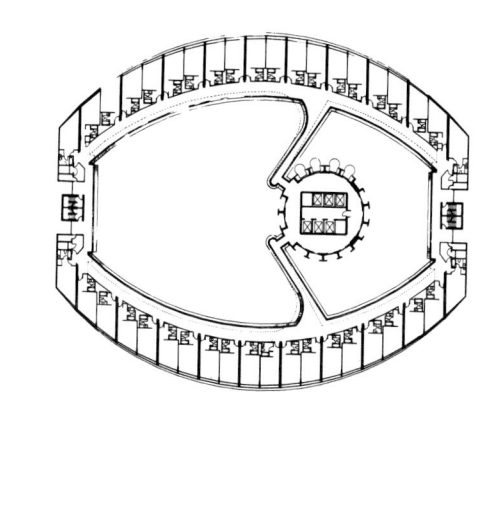

Left: A hangar for guests: the Sterling Hotel (now the Heathrow Hilton) at Heathrow Airport, London.

Right: Five storeys high, 30 metres wide and 90 metres long, the metal and glass ceiling structure spans the atrium. Allan Jones's sculpture *The Dancers* stands on a stepped pedestal.

STERLING HOTEL HEATHROW
London, UK, 1990

Architecture: **Manser Associates**

Interior Design: **Manser Associates, Peter Glynn-Smith Associates**

While airport projects are becoming a favourite medium for the display of extreme high-tech architecture, airport hotels still lead a shadowy aesthetic existence. Dotted seemingly at random in gaps around the runways, they are usually makeshift solutions or off-the-peg products from a particular hotel chain. Not so in London: the constantly expanding Heathrow Airport has admittedly spawned a dreary mass of faceless, nondescript buildings, but the Sterling Hotel (which became the Heathrow Hilton in May 1992) mirrors the high-tech appearance of the airport terminal.

The architects, Manser Associates, resolved upon a large form reminiscent of a modern hangar, and adapted stylistic features from the English high-tech school of Foster, Rogers and Grimshaw. The ground plan of the hotel, located next to Terminal 4, is a parallelogram. The two long sides are taken up by the main blocks, housing the guest-rooms and conference rooms. The narrow sides are transparent surfaces reaching up to the roof and measuring 30 x 20 metres; they are double-glazed, with an inner gap of 2.8 metres to provide the necessary but expensive sound-insulation.

The free atrium area in the middle measures a handsome 90 x 30 metres, is five storeys high and could comfortably accommodate Concorde. Here the eye is caught by Allan Jones's sculpture *The Dancers*. The glass fronts face east and west, and in the atrium the incidence of the light at different times of day produces changing abstract patterns that replicate the supporting elements of the construction.

The utilization concept for this four-star hotel proceeded from the premise that guests checking in for a night's stopover should expect more than just bed and breakfast. Three restaurants, a bar, shops, a health club and a swimming pool were incorporated into it, as well as spacious and flexible conference areas. The 397 rooms are reached by walkways that cross the atrium at each floor level, branching off from the glass lift-tower. In the two accommodation blocks the rooms open off both sides of the corridor, so that some have a view of the airport, while others overlook the lively scene in the atrium. The interior appointments are somewhat at odds with the hotel's architectural clarity. Despite the ambitious nature of the project, the norms of standardized hospitality once more assert themselves in the layout and furnishing of the rooms. The efficient grid of the guest-rooms even made it possible to install prefabricated bathrooms, made in Denmark, that had merely to be plumbed into the hotel's sanitation system.

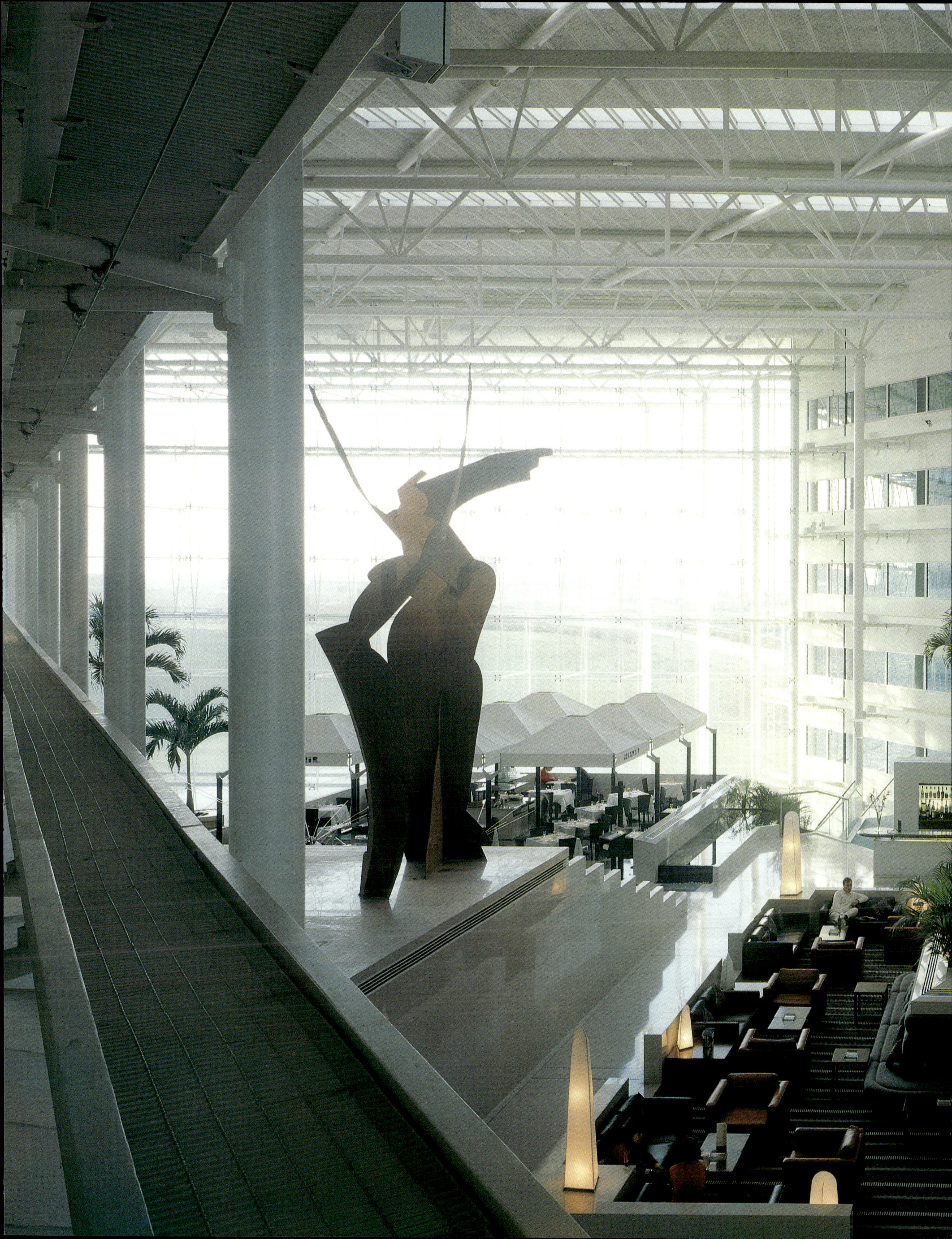

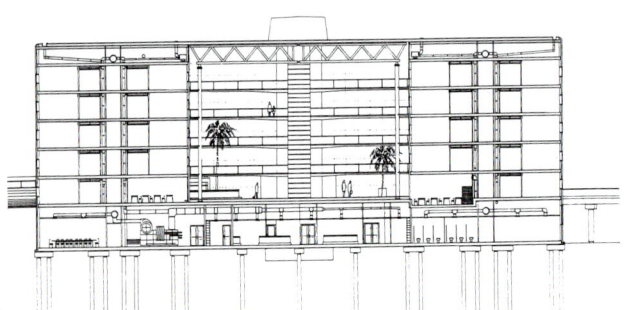

Cross-section

Above: Sound-absorbing transparency. The proximity of the runways meant that the double-glazed front of the atrium had to satisfy special requirements for sound insulation.

166

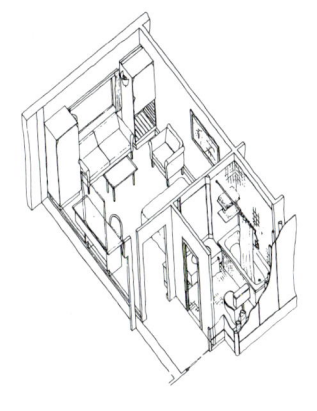

Top: From the swimming pool below the foyer level there is a panoramic view of planes taking off and landing.

Left: The Windsor Room restaurant with its view of the atrium
Above: The layout of the guestrooms is largely standardized. They include prefabricated bathrooms.

167

Left: With its 56 floors, this is Hong Kong's highest hotel tower to date. The Island Shangri-La is 235 metres high and has 565 rooms.

Right: The atrium contains yet another superlative: the largest silk painting in the world, created by 40 artists from the Peking Institute of Arts and Crafts.

THE ISLAND SHANGRI-LA
Hong Kong, 1991
Architecture: **Wong & Ouyang**

Interior Design: **Leese Robertson Freeman Designers**

Shangri-La International is one of the expanding top-category hotel groups in the Asian and Pacific area, and the Island Shangri-La was its second project in Hong Kong. By contrast with the Kowloon Shangri-La, which contains more rooms but has aged somewhat since its opening in 1981, the new hotel was intended to be an ideal embodiment of the group's philosophy: "Our hotels are meant to be warm, inviting places, full of peace, quiet and comfort." The lavish interior architecture of this 565-room luxury hotel offers an eclectic mixture of period styles, both European and Far Eastern. It bears no relation to the ultra-modern exterior, which adds yet another boldly shaped skyscraper to the Hong Kong skyline: a curtain façade in the form of an ellipse constructed of glass and polished natural stone. It is the tallest hotel tower in the city: 235 metres high and containing 56 storeys. The guest-rooms occupy the 39th to the 55th floor. On the 56th floor are the "Petrus" restaurant and the "Cyrano" cocktail lounge, both affording grandiose views.

In preparation for the planning stage, the president of Shangri-La sent Paul Leese, the interior architect – already engaged to design the Shangri-Las in Peking, Bangkok, Penang and Jakarta – on a two-week trip to Paris to cull ideas from classic hotels such as Le Crillon, the Ritz and the Bristol. Their influence is obvious when one views the product of Leese's studies, though this is not a faithful copy but a highly individual adaptation. Parts of the large lobby, for instance, are covered with a kind of 18th-century Parisian stone façade in beige-coloured Italian Svero marble. From the high ceiling hang gigantic chandeliers made in the Bakalovits workshop in Vienna. A tribute is paid to regional culture in the form of the largest silk painting in the world – 250 separate pictures that form a tableau measuring 51 x 14 metres; entitled *Great Motherland of China*, it was created by 40 artists from the Peking Institute of Arts and Crafts. How one puts on a show of grandeur, without concealing the fully glazed façade that rises to the height of two storeys on the inside, is demonstrated by the library on the 39th floor, with its ceiling fresco and marble columns.

Ten restaurants and bars are available to the guests at the Island Shangri-La. Other facilities include a ballroom, conference rooms, a heated swimming pool, a health club and numerous shops. No expense was spared in the rooms (standard floor-space: 44 square metres) and suites, whose spacious bathrooms gleam with Spanish and Portuguese marble.

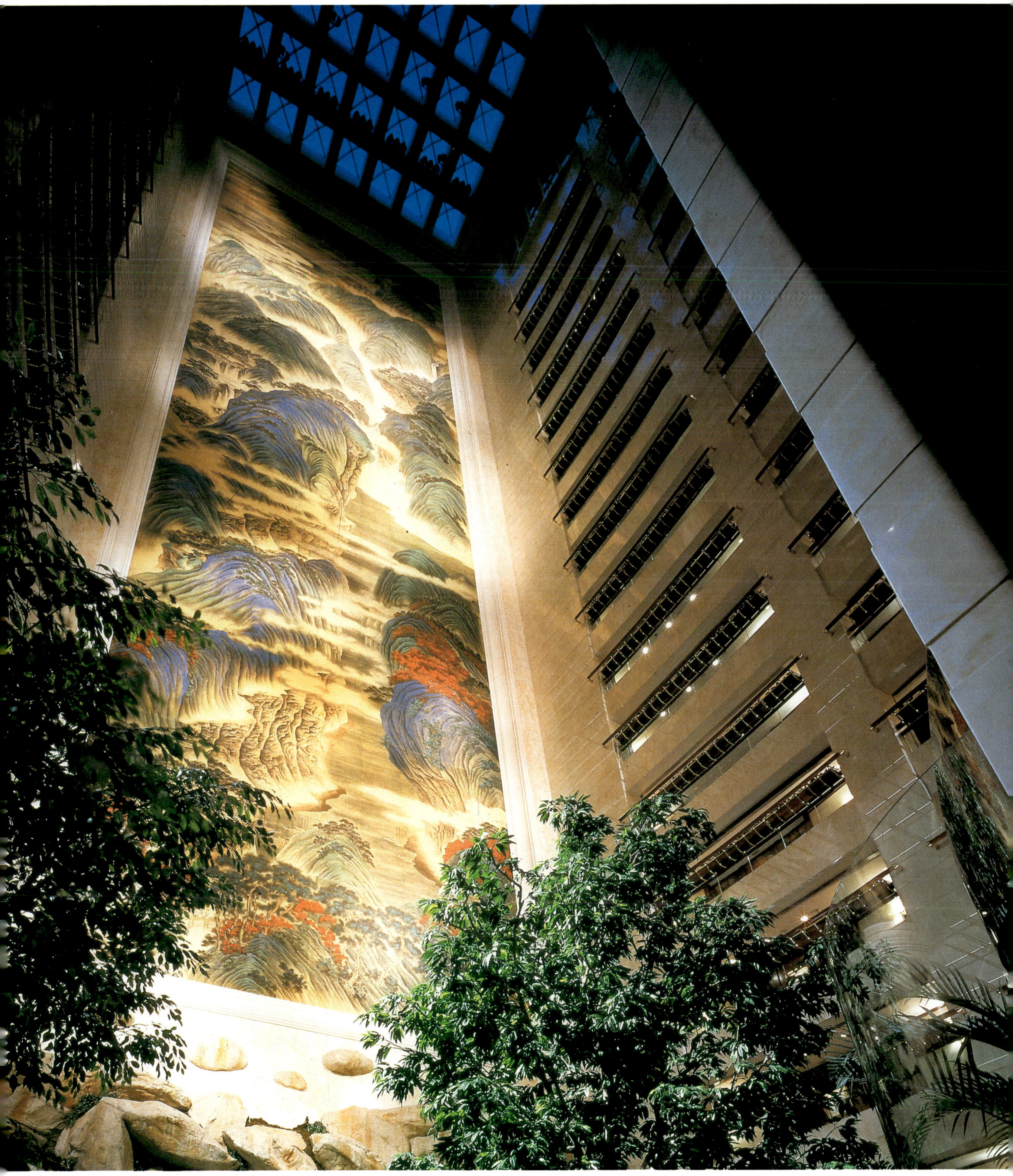

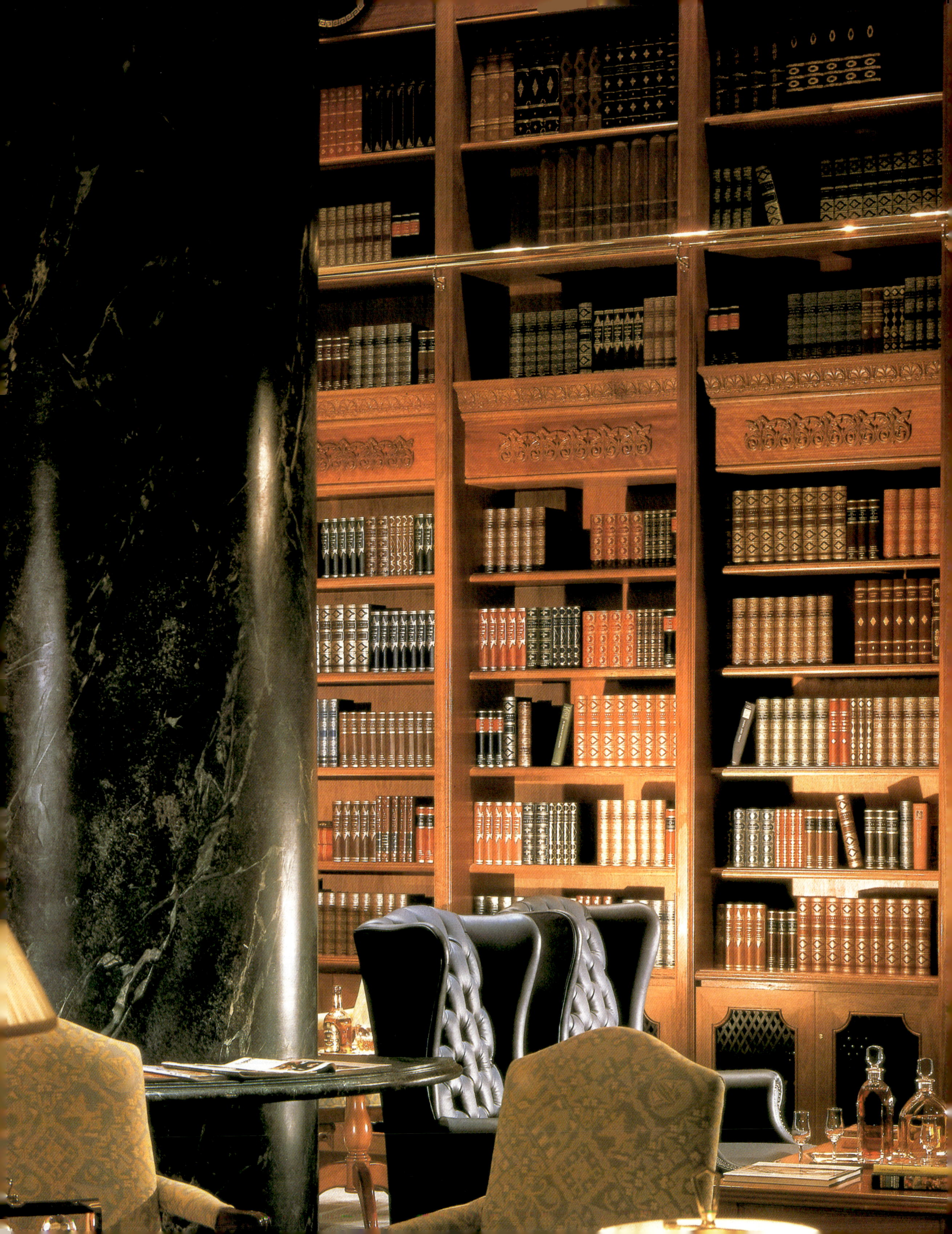

Left: On the 39th floor of this ultra-modern hotel, the library simulates the atmosphere of an English club. The interior designers were instructed to borrow features from the traditional grand hotels of Europe, and the results can be seen in all parts of the hotel. **Top:** The ballroom, furnished for banquets. **Above left:** The gourmet restaurant "Petrus". **Top:** Seating in a guest suite. **Above:** The lobby with giant chandeliers made by the Viennese firm Bakalovits.

Left: An imposing, vaulted barrel roof characterizes the 17-storey 400-room hotel in this complex inspired by ancient models.
Right: The design of the hall and guest-rooms (below right) has the classical touch of turn-of-the-century Viennese architecture.

HYATT REGENCY LA JOLLA
San Diego, USA, 1989
Architecture/Interior Design: **Michael Graves**

One of the seven hills of Rome gave its name to the Aventine, a mixed complex built on a hill beside Interstate Highway 5 in La Jolla, Southern California. This extraordinary example of commercial idealistic architecture was clearly inspired by ancient models. Imposing structures reminiscent of classical antiquity and the Renaissance combine to create an artificial urban forum. Red and yellow sandstone and sand-coloured plaster are the main materials used in this 150-million-dollar project. The individual, clearly recognizable structures consist of a seventeen-storey hotel with 400 rooms, an eleven-storey office block with a circular tower, the rotunda of the health club and four restaurants. The buildings are linked by pergolas, fountains and a series of fairly small open spaces. One of the central points of reference is the large swimming pool. Concealed within the complex is a multi-storey car park.

For the architect, Michael Graves, the project offered a chance to create postmodern narrative architecture on a large scale with much the same consistency as in his Disney projects, though not so compulsively geared to amusement. What is instructive about the backward-looking utopia that informs the complex – which in spite of its antique pretensions was bound by a limited budget – is the fact that it is possible, in this suburban no man's land, to unite work with leisure and an urban environment with a recreation area. In this Acropolis of the nineties, the banal functions of office work, overnight accommodation and physical fitness present themselves as august pursuits. At the marble entrance to the office block, employees and visitors are greeted by the more than life-size torso of a Roman senator, headless but dignified.

Graves was also responsible for the interior design. His passion for Viennese art nouveau, especially Josef Hoffmann, dictated the furnishing of the lobby and the other public areas. Here no expense was spared in providing marble for columns, floors and walls. The carpeting, too, like many other features of the décor, was designed by Graves. Compared with the spacious atrium, two storeys high and adorned with palms, to which a broad staircase leads down from the reception area, the guest-rooms are modestly proportioned. The hotel has many rooms available for functions and conferences, including a hall that can hold 1,100 people, and sixteen other conference rooms. Terraces provide access to the health club, swimming pool and squash courts.

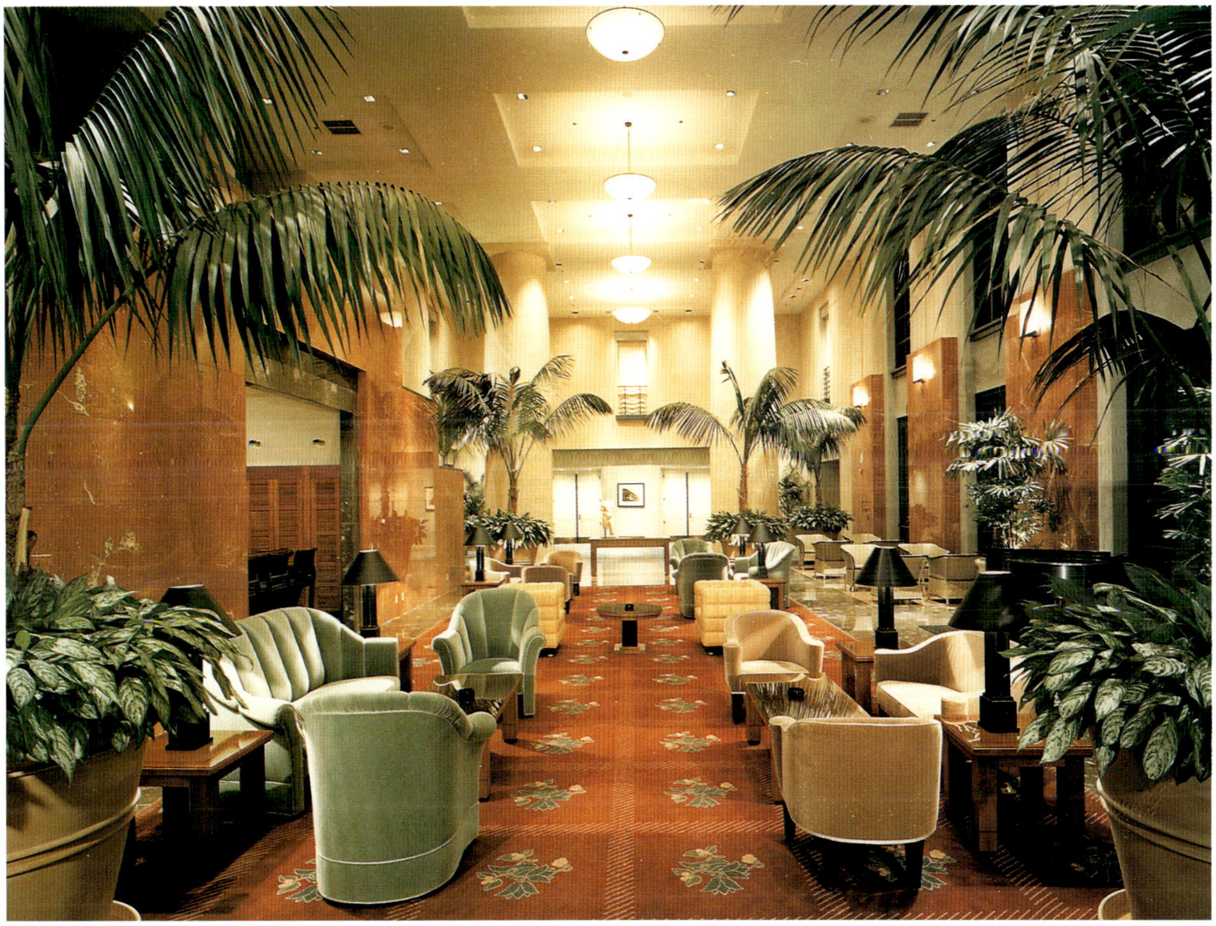

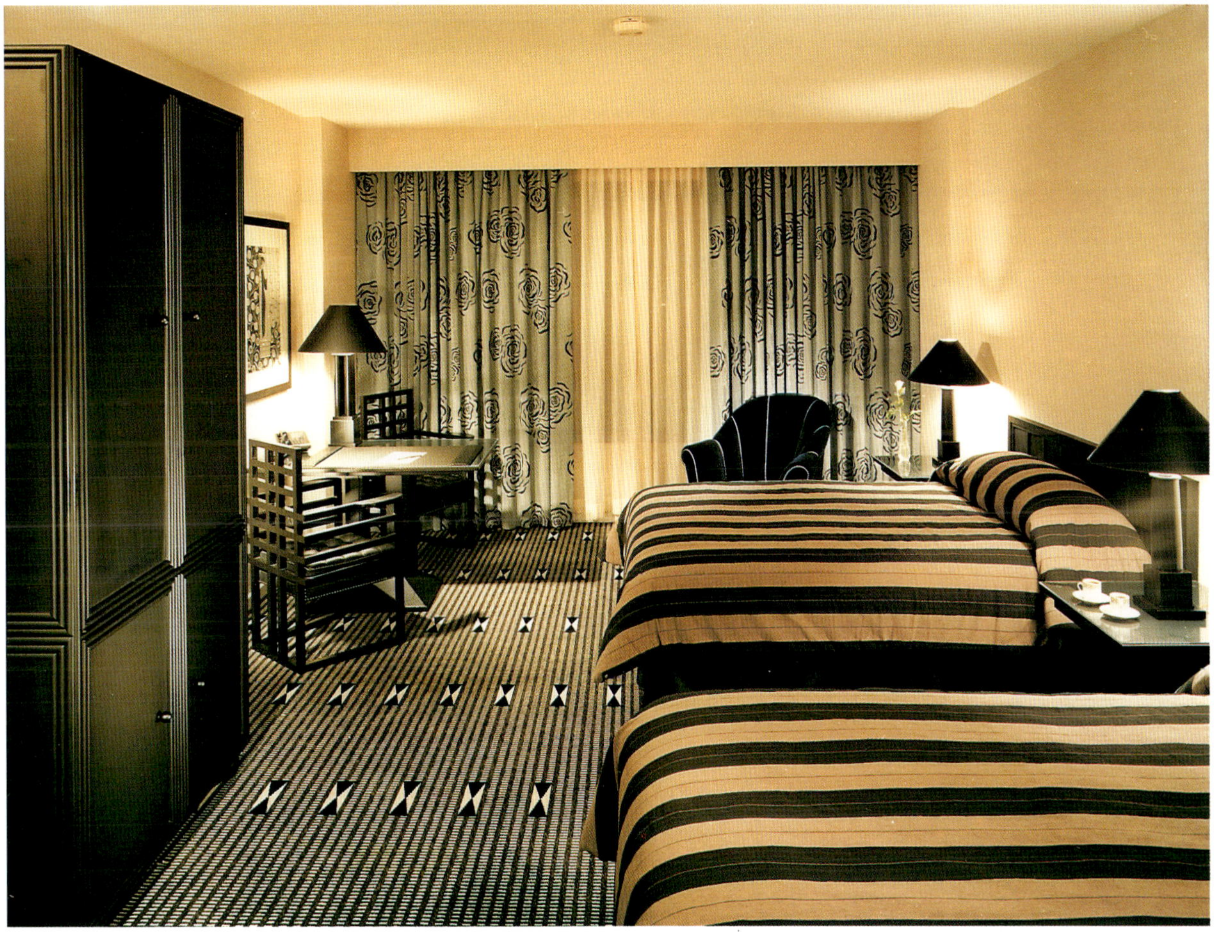

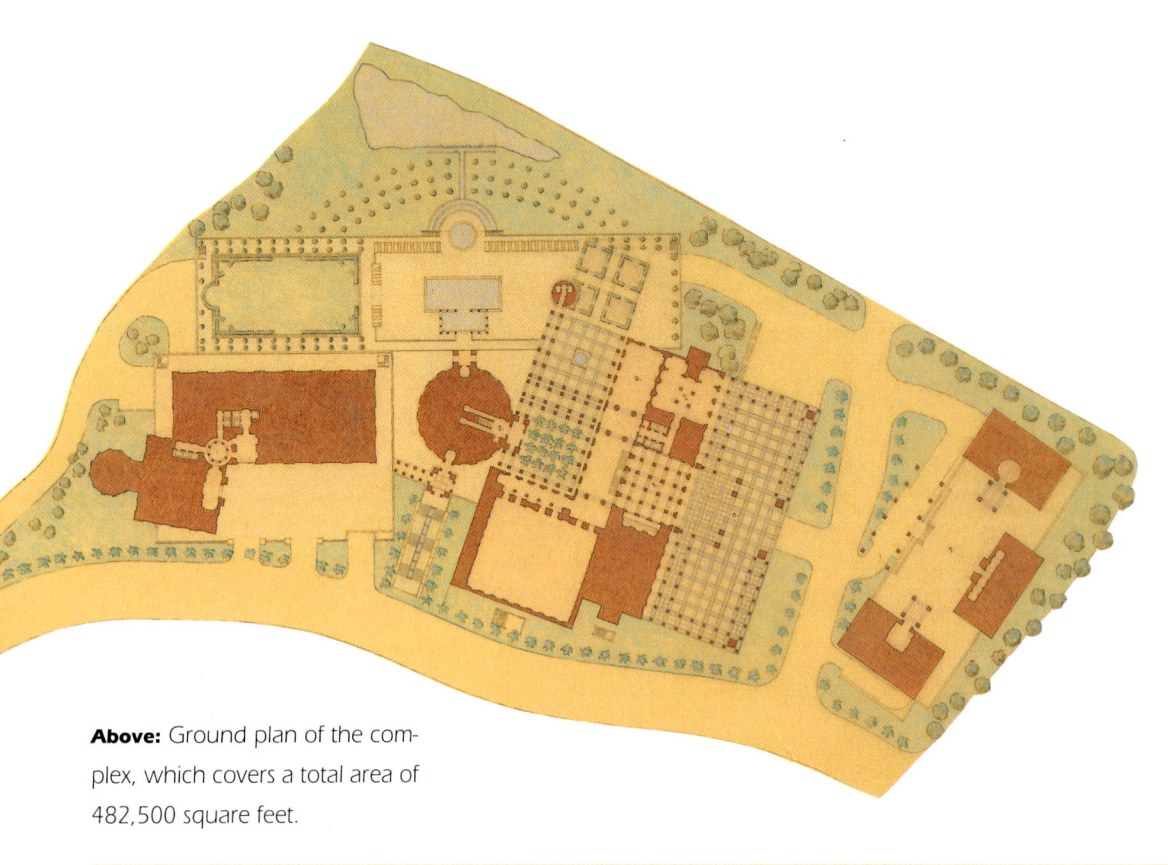

Above: Ground plan of the complex, which covers a total area of 482,500 square feet.

Below: Michael Graves conceived his master plan for the Aventine project in La Jolla, Southern California as an idealized development of one of the seven hills of Rome. It consists of a hotel (left), an office block with an additional round tower (right) and a health club in the form of a rotunda (centre). Between these clearly recognizable buildings he places pergolas, pavilions, swimming pools and arcades, as in a Roman imperial villa.

MARITIM HOTEL
Cologne, Germany, 1990

Architecture: **Gottfried Böhm, Kraemer, Sieverts & Partner, Stefan Schmitz**

Interior Design: **Reinhardt + Sander, Franjo Pooth, Elisabeth Böhm**

This new hotel was intended as an important piece of urban repair, filling in one of the last big gaps left by the war and completing Cologne's Rhine panorama at this particular point, next to a bridge that carries a large volume of traffic. Gottfried Böhm, a local architect, was commissioned to elaborate a design that had won the first prize in a competition. This proved a happy choice. In his home city, Böhm had been known almost solely for his work on church buildings, although a number of projects carried out abroad had brought him international acclaim and demonstrated the superb contextuality of his characteristic vocabulary, which continues and develops expressionist and modernist traditions.

In various ways the Maritim Hotel takes up layers of urban history. In its overall design it is a secularized three-nave ensemble in which the hotel wings represent the aisles, and the large glass hall – 100 metres long, 24 metres wide and 20 metres tall at its highest point – forms the centre. The congress hall and the conference areas towards the bridge are attached to the main structure rather like side chapels. The form of the roof copies the gables of the old city nearby, and the small-format tufa of the facing masonry is a common regional feature. The glass hall is open to passers-by and forms an attractive new public space, reminiscent not only of the building that once occupied the site – the old market hall, destroyed in a air raid – but also of an unrealized design by the architect for another site a few hundred metres down-river – the proposed Wallraff Richartz Museum/Ludwig Museum.

The accommodation in the Maritim Hotel – 454 rooms and suites, two halls for 1,600 and 500 people respectively, 25 conference and banqueting rooms, several restaurants and cafés, a fitness centre, a swimming pool and shops – is located in a structural mass that is richly articulated but never overwhelming. The generous, transparent, forum-like spine of the structure was achieved by optimal utilization of the available land. The austere architecture, which avoids any historicizing elements, is compatible with the use of nobler materials – brass and polished granite – inside the hall to provide the embellishment that is expected by visitors.

For the appointment of the rooms (except for one suite designed by Elisabeth Böhm), the restaurants and function rooms, it was decided to adhere to the code of the Maritim group. This produces nondescript interiors belonging to the mainstream of the up-market catering trade, which contrast, in their provinciality, with the spirit of the architecture.

Left and right: The Maritim Hotel consists of two hotel wings and a glass hall (100 metres long, 24 metres wide and 20 metres high at the apex) which forms a central aisle between them.

Below right: Cross-section of the building: the forum-like glass hall forms the centre, with the accommodation wings on either side of it. Adjacent to the complex is a congress hall. **Bottom:** An interior view of the congress hall.

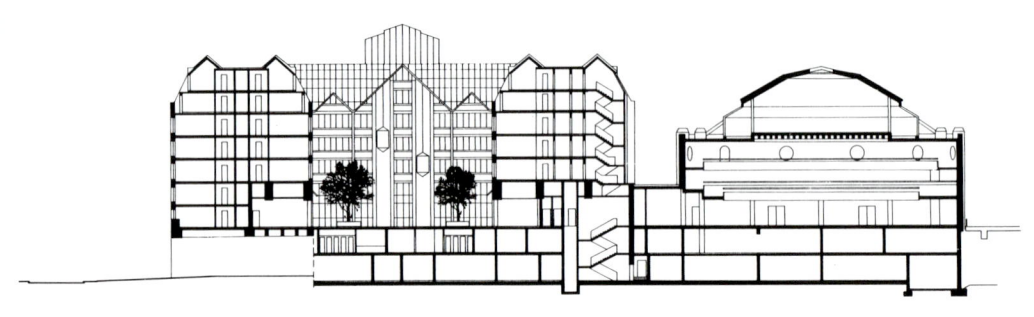

The suite designed by Elisabeth Böhm is decorated predominantly in atmospheric pastel shades.

179

Left: Helmut Jahn's Paris airport hotel. A glass hall links the two long accommodation blocks.

HYATT REGENCY ROISSY
Paris, France, 1992

Architecture: **Murphy/Jahn Architects, Jean-Marie Charpentier**

Interior Design: **Hirsch/Bedner & Associates**

Paris, one of the world's great tourist and business centres, was until recently a blank spot on the map for the almost ubiquitous Hyatt Group. Wishing to gain a foothold in Paris, the group chose not the centre of the city, but the periphery. The new hotel at Roissy, next to Charles de Gaulle Airport, resulted from a competition and was designed by the successful American architect Helmut Jahn. This architectural star, celebrated for his spectacular skyscrapers, had to make do here – given the proximity of jets and approach lanes – with a moderate five-floor building. The complex consists of two narrow, round-ended blocks, parallel but unaligned, 120 metres long, 40 metres apart, and linked by a glass hall 21 metres high. The silvery aluminium facing of the outer walls and the large serigraphed glass surfaces appear to reduce the substantial volume of the building. The high-tech touch is a homage to the world of aviation and a foretaste of Jahn's next airport hotel, now under construction at the terminal of Munich's new airport.

Hyatt's investment at Roissy was a response to the growing tendency to do business deals and hold conferences at nodal points in the transcontinental airline network. The business centre at the Hyatt Regency Roissy is well equipped for the purpose. In addition to 13 conference rooms and a hall that can hold up to 500 people and offers every audio-visual refinement, it provides office facilities, a multilingual secretariat and even an extensive business library. The main restaurant is located in the atrium under a twelve-tonne metal structure suspended from the roof; there is also a lounge bar and another bar with live music. Of the 388 rooms, all sound-insulated against the roar of the jets, 14 are suites – including the large Presidential suite, which has 160 square metres of floorspace. As usual in Hyatt hotels, the top two guest floors are reserved for the Regency Club, which has its own lounge and conference rooms, reached by separate lifts. Relaxation for business travellers and stopover guests is provided by the large fitness centre and an indoor pool; tennis courts are located in the garden surrounding the building.

Unlike most airport hotels, which usually resemble charmless batteries of sleeping units, the Hyatt Regency Roissy sets new standards of quality in both architecture and five-star comfort. The interior design – by Hirsch/Bedner & Associates, the American team responsible for many Hyatt interiors – is aimed at mitigating the cool techno-aesthetics. Fortunately this is achieved by a "soft" approach that relies partly on natural elements such as water and plants, and thus avoids the simulation of luxurious intimacy that serves as camouflage in other projects.

Above: The atrium with lounge areas and a restaurant roofed by a large steel construction.

Right: The guest-rooms, which were designed by Hirsch/Bedner, clearly contrast with the aeronautical high-tech of the architecture.

Left: The austere hotel building erected on a triangular site beside the Landwehrkanal in Berlin.
Right: Inside, artworks and light furniture soften the severity of the monumental architecture.

GRAND HOTEL ESPLANADE
Berlin, Germany, 1988
Architecture: **Jürgen J. Sawade**
Interior Design: **Johanne and Gernot Nalbach**

When Berlin investors were planning the new Grand Hotel Esplanade in the eighties, the name was all-important: the historic Esplanade in the Potsdamer Platz had been a high-class hotel, frequented by the grandees of the Wilhelminian Empire and the Weimar Republic. Though partly destroyed, it had survived the Second World War and stood isolated in the no man's land near the Berlin Wall. Five hundred metres to the west as the crow flies, the new Esplanade was to be built on a triangular site beside the Landwehrkanal. The architect, Jürgen J. Sawade, conceived the five-star hotel on two sides of the triangle; it thus filled the edges of the block. The remainder of the site was to be occupied by a glass-covered road leading down to the multi-lane highway by the canal and lined by a massive wall of polished stone. The architect's credo was: "Deliberate reduction, meaningful simplicity, extreme clarity and rigour, purity and restraint in the use of materials and colours" – a principle that ran counter to many of the postmodern projects on show at the International Exhibition then running in Berlin. Indeed, in the public areas Sawade subjects the guest to a harsh and at times dispiriting therapy that is only partly mitigated by the works of art displayed and the distinctly friendly, narrative décor of the restaurants and the bar. Architecturally well thought-out though it is, the entrance situation is psychologically misconceived. The "wall of water", by the Zero artist Heinz Mack, conjures up a permanently rainy atmosphere, and the asphalt forecourt behind it has all the allure of a tradesmen's entrance. Once in the lobby, the guest walks across an expanse of mirror-smooth granite to the seemingly endless reception desk, reminiscent of a menacing and scarcely welcoming control barrier.

Although the interior architects, Johanne and Gernot Nalbach, did not see it as their function to provide a counterpoise in the field of design, it is to their credit that the architectural severity gives way to sober comfort, especially in the 369 rooms and suites. Their own designs supplement the range of Italian seating. The upholstery fabric in the lobby and suites is by Le Corbusier.

The Grand Hotel Esplanade was commissioned by two Berlin realtors who attached great importance to their own collection of contemporary art. The "New Wild", who came to prominence in the eighties, are well represented, along with works by the Zero Group. For the guest-rooms a special edition of printed graphics was produced, with contributions by, among others, the painter Elvira Bach and her associates Helmut Middendorf, Bernd Koberling and Markus Lüpertz.

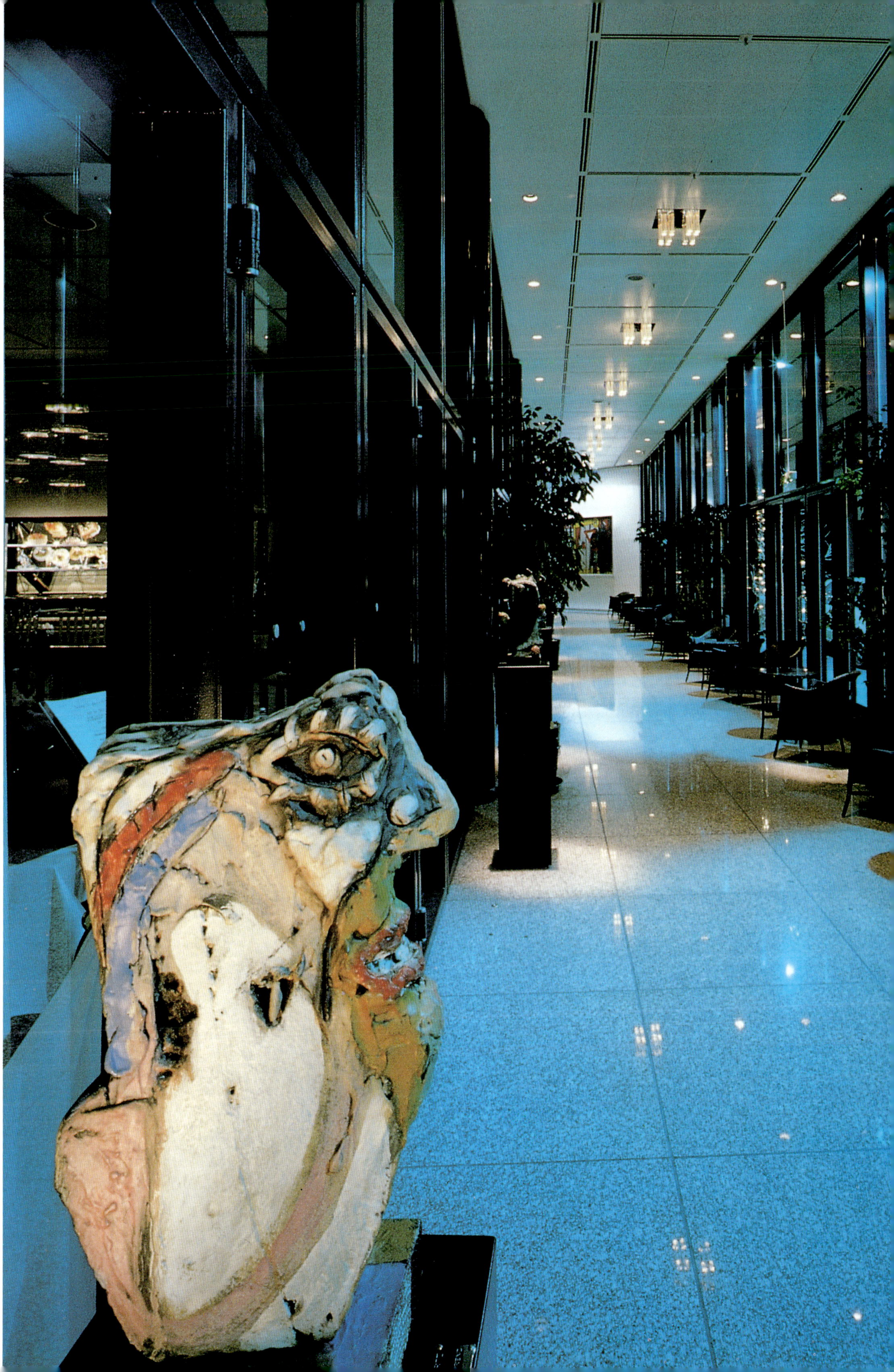

A view of the reception hall with its polished granite floor.

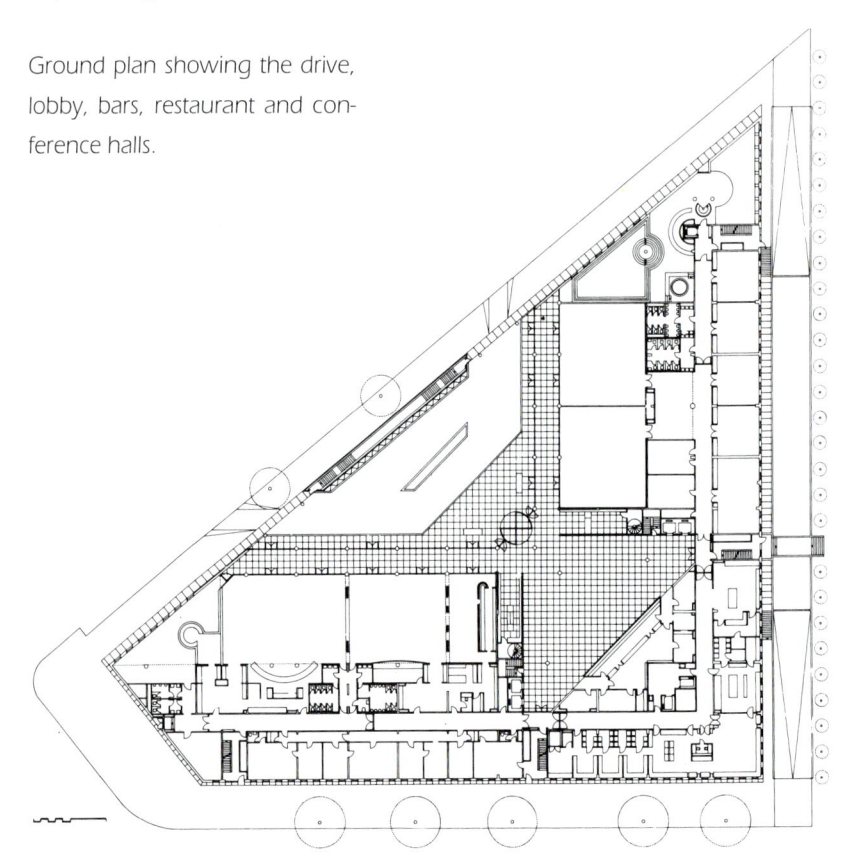

Ground plan showing the drive, lobby, bars, restaurant and conference halls.

Left: The Presidential suite aims at theatrical effects. The interior architects have created a set using a "starry sky" ceiling, curtains, elegant furniture from Italy and a lamp sculpture by Luciano Baldessari.

Right: The Comfort suite can also be used as a business lounge and is designed in classic modern style.

185

Left: On the roof of the new Convention and Exhibition Center in Hong Kong is a bathing lake shared by the luxury Grand Hyatt and New World hotels.

Right: The grandeur of art deco is revived in the entrance to the ballrooms of the Grand Hyatt, perfectly staged by hotel designers Hirsch/Bedner.

Overleaf: The foyer, with its gilded dome, granite-faced columns and wrought-iron banisters, is a spectacular, eclectic combination of European and Far Eastern styles.

GRAND HYATT HONG KONG
Hong Kong, 1989
Architecture: **Ng Chun Man & Associates**
Interior Design: **Hirsch/Bedner & Associates**

Nowhere in the world are modern five-star hotels belonging to international chains packed as closely together as they are in Hong Kong. In this Far Eastern metropolis it is hard to outdo the competition, and so a high standard had to be achieved in the new Grand Hyatt. The hotel is part of the giant Convention and Exhibition Center, on whose broad six-storey base stand two terraced, indented mirror-glass towers, one of them occupied by the New World Hotel, which is relatively moderate in its layout, the other by the Asian flagship of the Hyatt group, which rises to a height of 31 storeys. They share the bathing lake and garden landscape laid out on the roof of the Center.

"Our remit was to design a romantic, opulent hotel interior that would combine features of Eastern and Western culture and above all fit in with the tradition of the grand hotels built in Asia between the turn of the century and the thirties." This is how the interior architects Hirsch/Bedner & Associates define their task. Being experts in exclusive international hotel design, they responded to the challenge with bravura. Of all the revival feats of recent years, the Grand Hyatt Hong Kong can claim to present the most aesthetically convincing reinterpretation of the splendour of the *fin de siècle* and art deco, combined with antique elements, both Asian and Western.

The imposing elliptical lobby, flanked by two sweeping staircases, is the prelude to a feast of costly materials and ornamental forms. Black marble reflects interiors resplendent with warm, gold tones. Seven restaurants and bars, a shopping arcade, twelve halls and function rooms, a swimming pool and a health club are available at the Grand Hyatt, together with a conference and exhibition centre – in addition to the open-air leisure world, already mentioned, on the upper deck between the two hotel towers. Part of the concept is the reservation of seven floors for special suites served by separate lifts, a swimming pool and conference rooms; this is the Regency Club, an exclusive hotel within a hotel for guests who want to get away from standard five-star tourism. Yet even the normal format of the 575 rooms is impressive (the average floorspace is 44 square metres). All have marble bathrooms and every comfort. They are designed in bright colours, affording a pleasing contrast with the red and black accents of the Chinese accessories and the exotic woods used for the furniture.

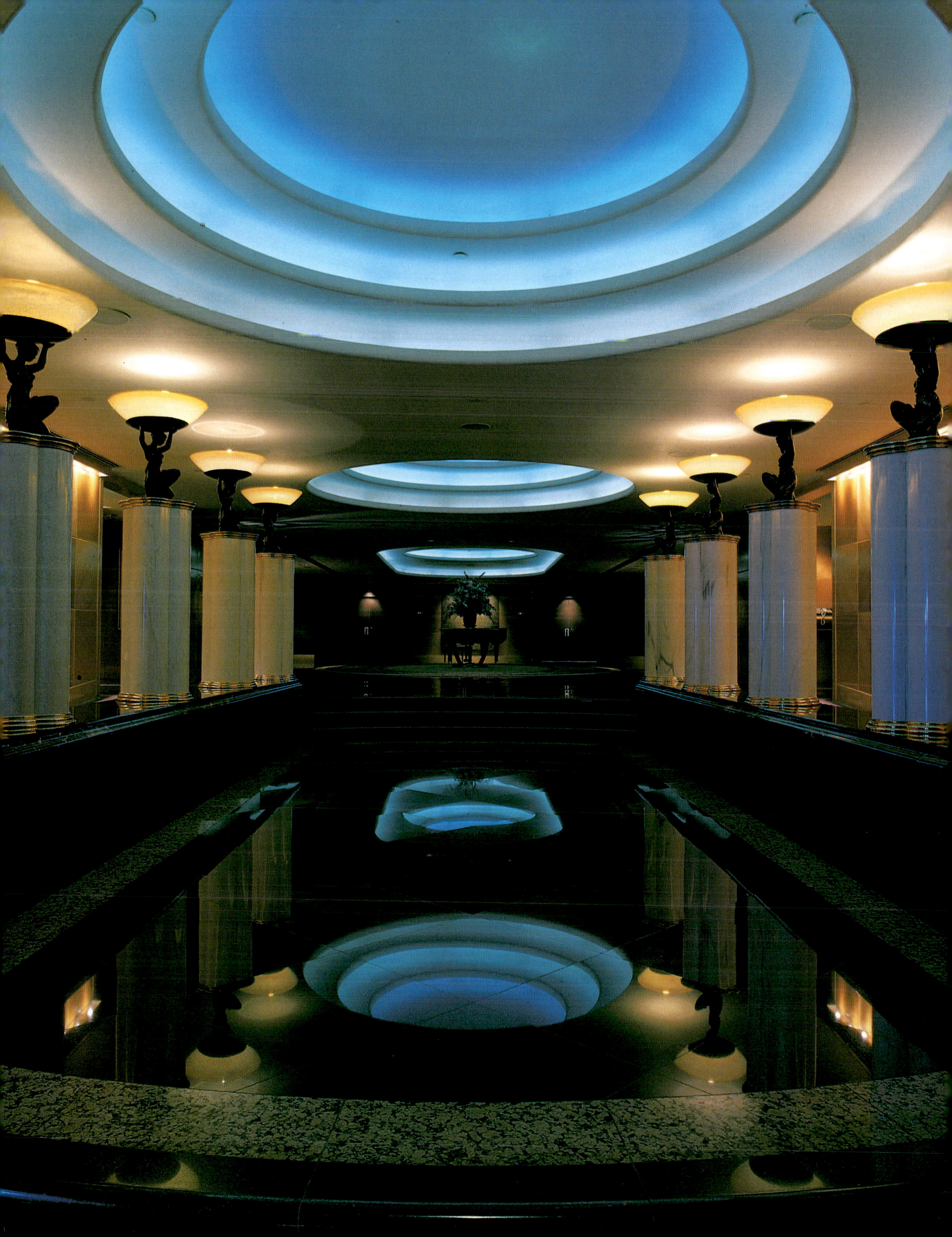

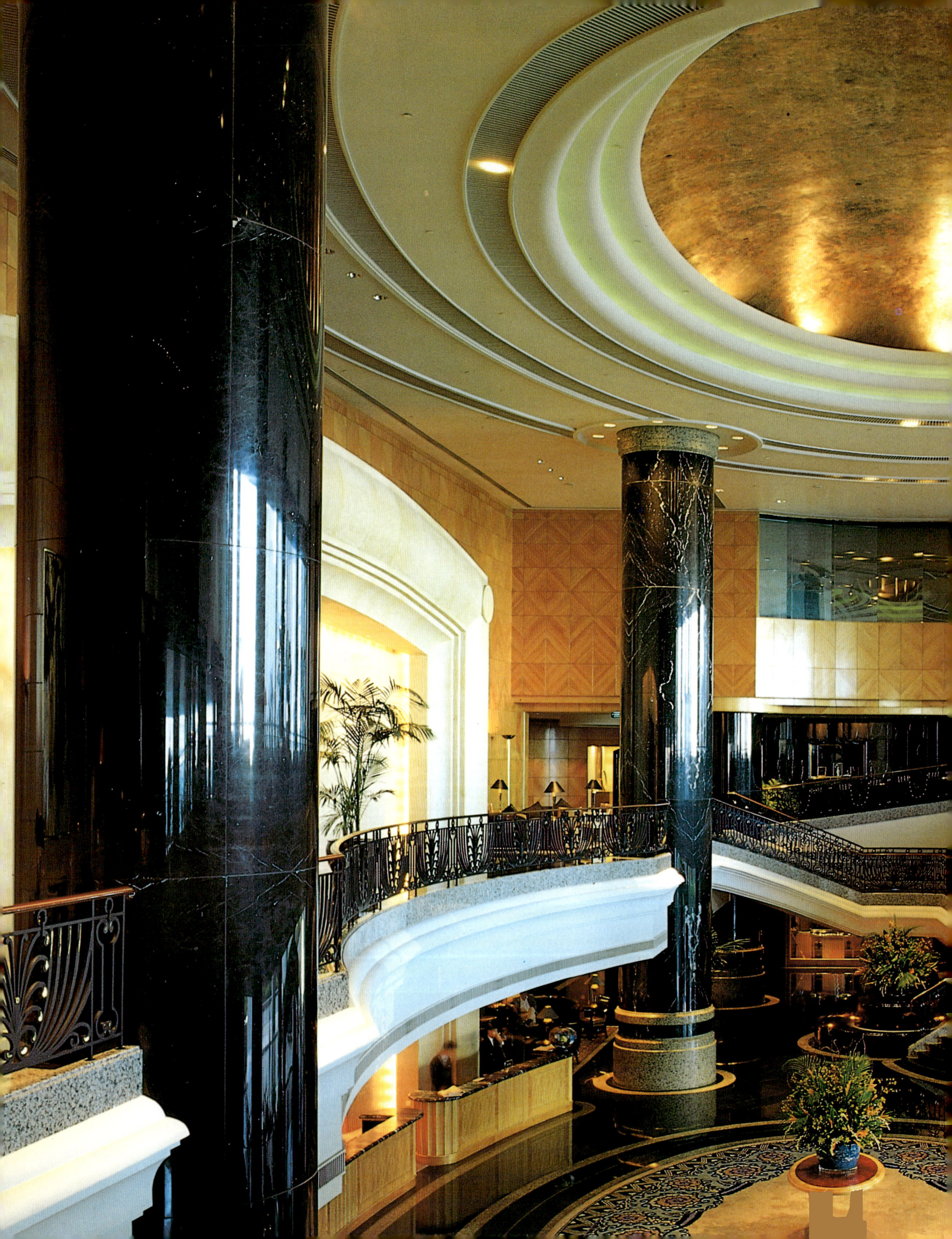

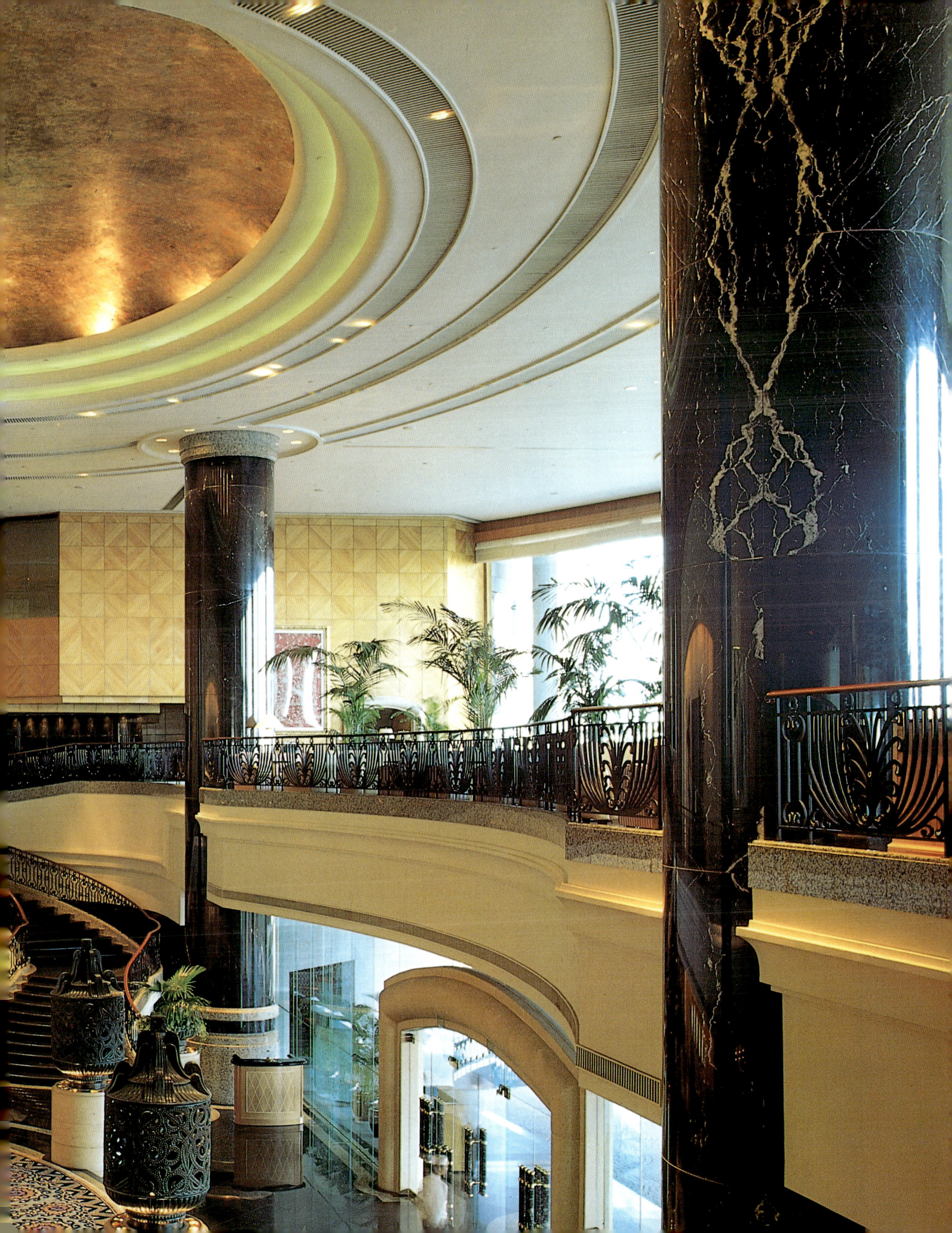

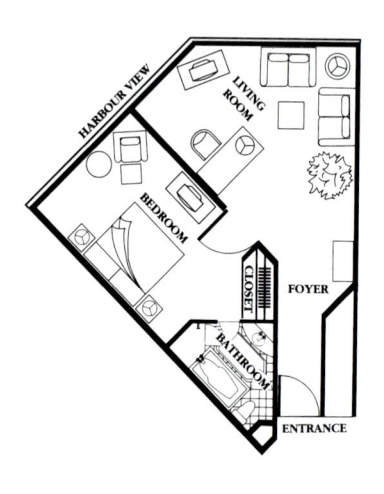

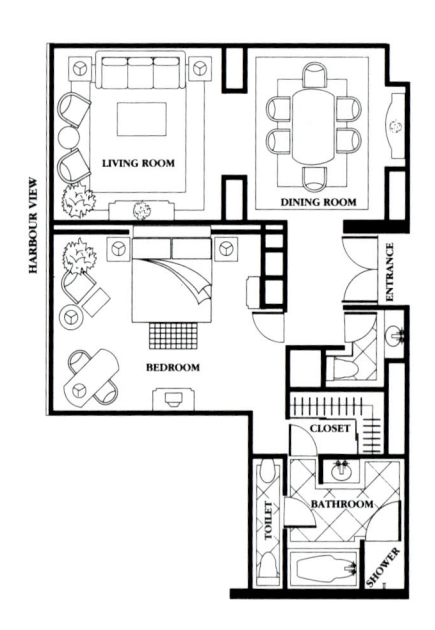

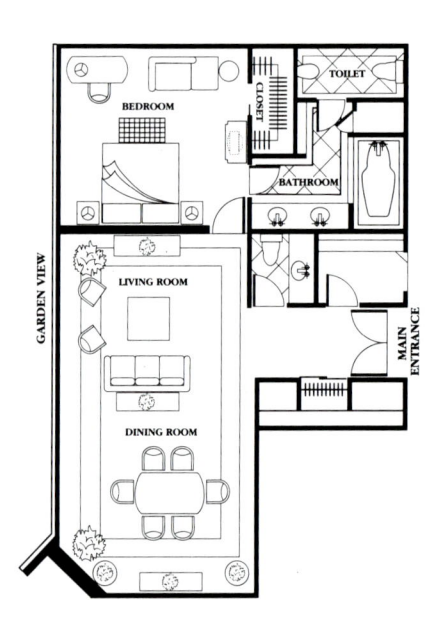

Above: The polygonal structure of the hotel means that the layout of the suites varies. **Top:** Most suites have a view of the harbour.

Right: The Cantonese restaurant "One Harbour Road" is one of the Grand Hyatt's six eating places, each of which offers a different cuisine.

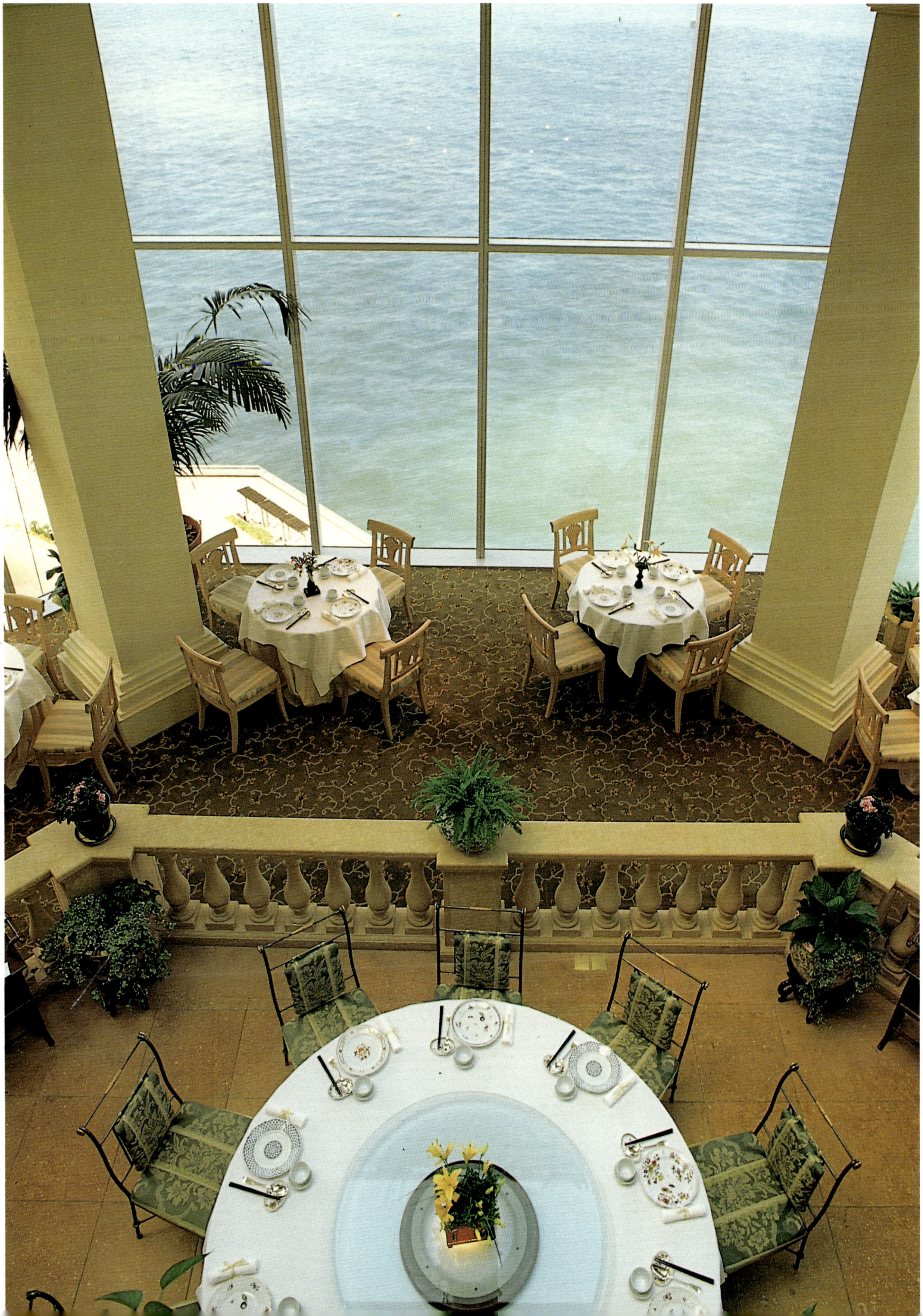

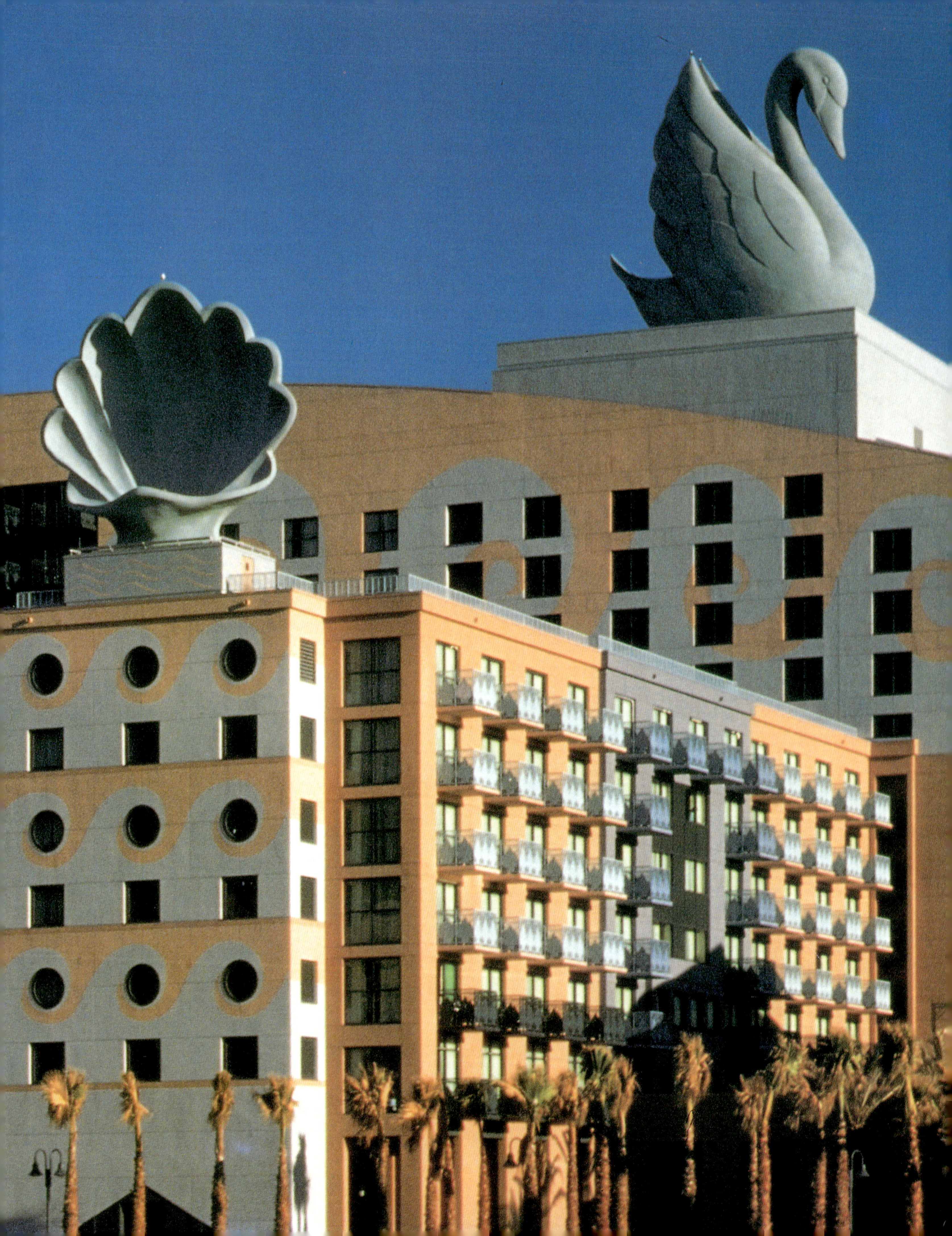

5 RESORTS AND FANTASY HOTELS

The 1980s saw the birth of giant vacation complexes – self-contained holiday worlds which, on Hawaii, in the Caribbean or on Far Eastern coasts, provided the jet-set tourist with facilities for swimming, golf and yachting, aquasports and *haute cuisine*, all concentrated on one site. Multimillion-dollar investments (verging at the upper limit on billions of dollars) spawned luxury hotels that were often quite indiscriminate in their lavish invocation of historical or folkloric building styles: Roman baths, Polynesian lagoons, Balinese temple areas – anything was possible. The economic aim was to channel all of the guests' holiday expenditure towards the hotel and to provide unmatchable entertainment and comfort. Sometimes this led to amazing feats of holiday architecture, for example such varied five-star resorts as the Hyatt Regency Waikoloa and the Sheraton Mirage, Port Douglas.

Fantasy hotels, no less lavish and even more audacious in the entertainment they offer, are the pride of Las Vegas, the Eldorado of gambling and showbusiness. The last word in excessive design and immense profit is the Mirage, home of the white tigers tamed by the celebrated duo Siegfried and Roy. This hotel is proof positive of the fact that if enough money is available, almost any fantasy can be realized in the Nevada Desert.

Rather more modest, but much more assured in their narrative strategy, are Michael Graves' two Disneyworld hotels in Florida. Here, entertainment architecture becomes a playful experience; despite the obsession with colourful detail and triviality, there remains an ironic detachment from the far more naturalistic attractions of Disneyworld proper, which are designed to promote child-like identification.

Below left: The ideal self-sufficient holiday world: the extensive grounds of the Hyatt Regency Waikoloa on the coast of Hawaii.

HYATT REGENCY WAIKOLOA
Hawaii, USA, 1988

Architecture: **Lawton & Umemura Architects**

Landscaping: **Tongg, Clarke & Mechler, Howard Fields & Associates**

Interior Design: **Hirsch/Bedner & Associates**

In the late 1970s the Hyatt group decided to supplement its range of top-class hotels with holiday resorts that would surpass anything so far available in terms of expense, size and luxury. The originally European idea of the holiday club which provides the guest with round-the-clock entertainment and so absorbs all his holiday funds, was matched with the luxury standards of American-led five-star tourism. Multi-million dollar investments generated dream worlds made up of fantasy architecture and exotic flora and fauna.

The Hyatt Regency Waikoloa in Hawaii, which opened in 1988, was a peak achievement, unsurpassed by subsequent projects. The cost of building the resort, which covers more than 250 hectares and lies beside an artificial lagoon, amounted to 360 million dollars.

The three main buildings, scarcely rising above the tops of the palm trees, contain 1,241 rooms and suites. Guests are conveyed by boat or Venetian gondola along one and a half kilometres of specially constructed waterways; on land they are carried by a futuristic tubular railway. The lava landscape has been converted into a tropical garden inhabited by parrots, swans, cranes, flamingoes, many types of fish and the endangered nene goose, the Hawaiian national bird. Half-a-dozen Atlantic dolphins play in a separate part of the saltwater lagoon. Whoever is not satisfied with the lagoon or the "Kona Pool", with its waterfalls, water chutes and grotto bar, can visit the many other swimming baths and the "Anara" fitness complex. Tennis courts and a private Par-72 golf course, complete with clubhouse, are among the other standard facilities.

The architectonic stage-set in no way conflicts with the synthetic landscape or the natural world beyond. An abstract grand gesture was evolved, blending with the water and the greenery and avoiding trite borrowings from history. The interior design was undertaken by Hirsch/Bedner & Associates. Apart from a collection of antiques – mainly of oriental and Pacific provenance and assembled at a cost of three-and-a-half million dollars – the furnishing of the lobby and restaurant areas is in tune with the generally relaxed and by no means over-ostentatious character of the resort. The rooms – most with a sea view – are decorated in pastel shades and contain no heavy furniture. Basketwork chairs and light upholstery characterize this jet-set colonial style.

Below: Imperial garden architecture: an enormous stairway leads from the lobby to the lagoon.

Overleaf: The different parts of the resort are linked by a railway. Transport is also provided by boats and gondolas.

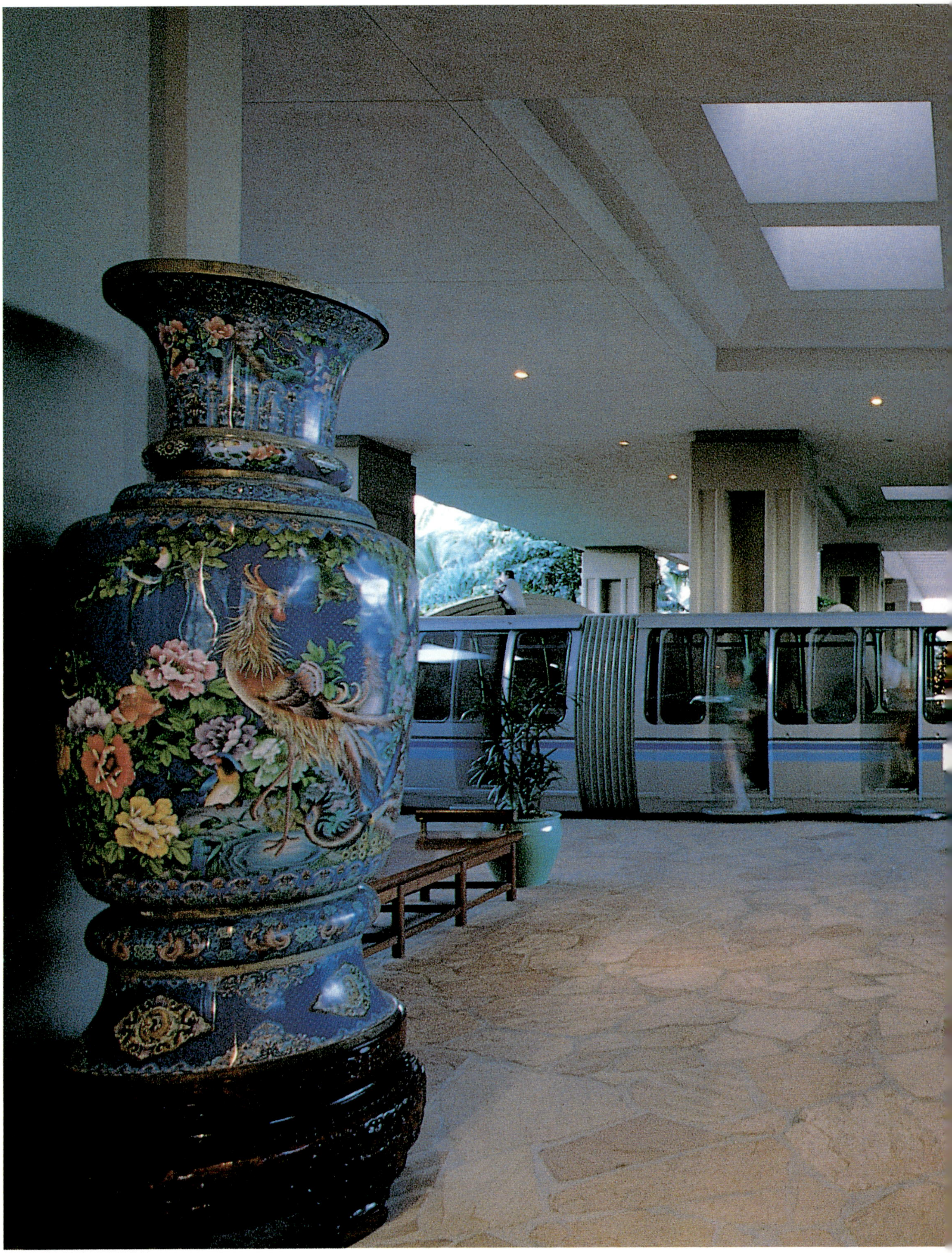

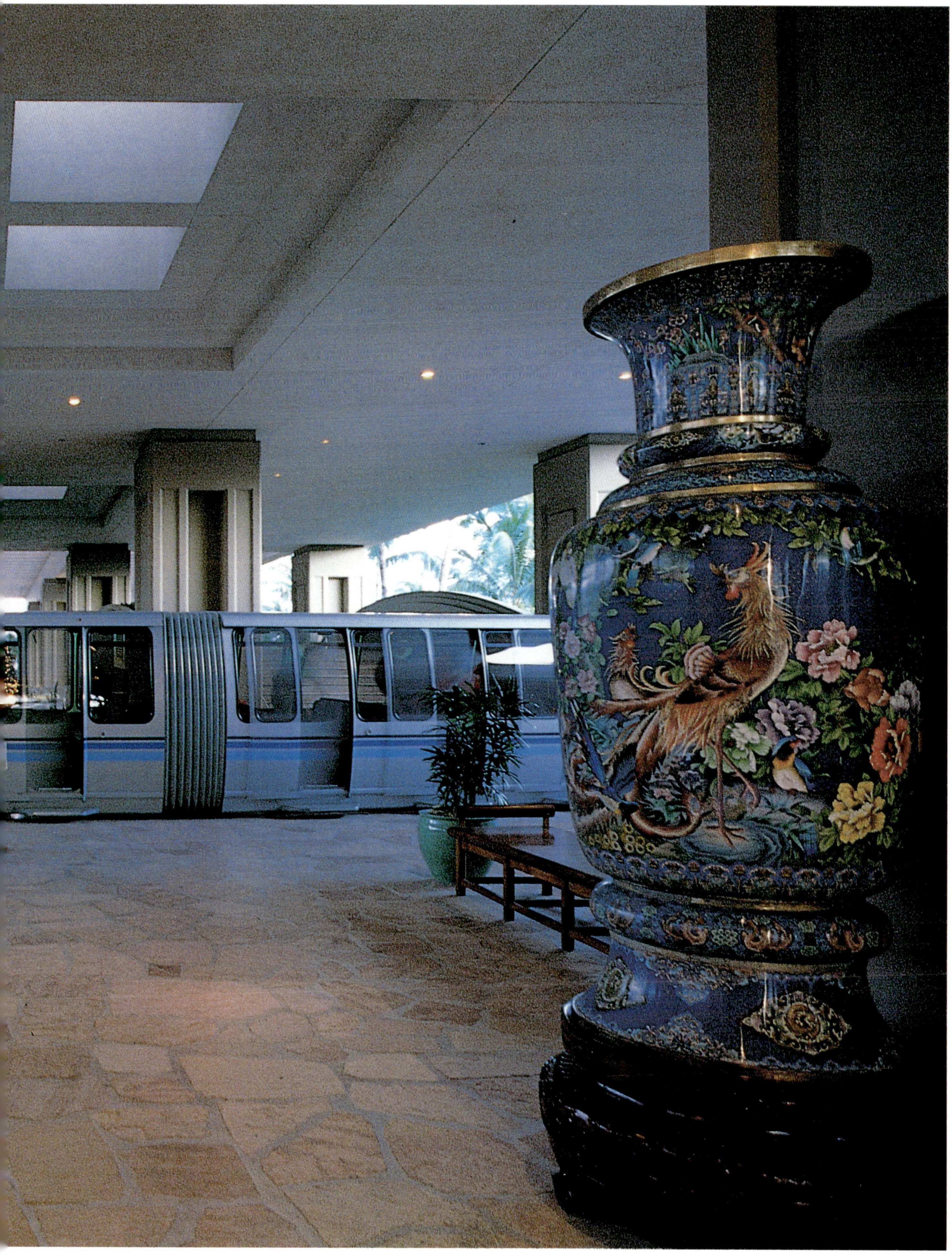

Right: A glass-roofed atrium in the shopping arcade. The public areas are open and have been designed to harmonize with the surrounding landscape.

Above left and left: Borrowing from Far Eastern lifestyles: a suite designed in the Japanese style.

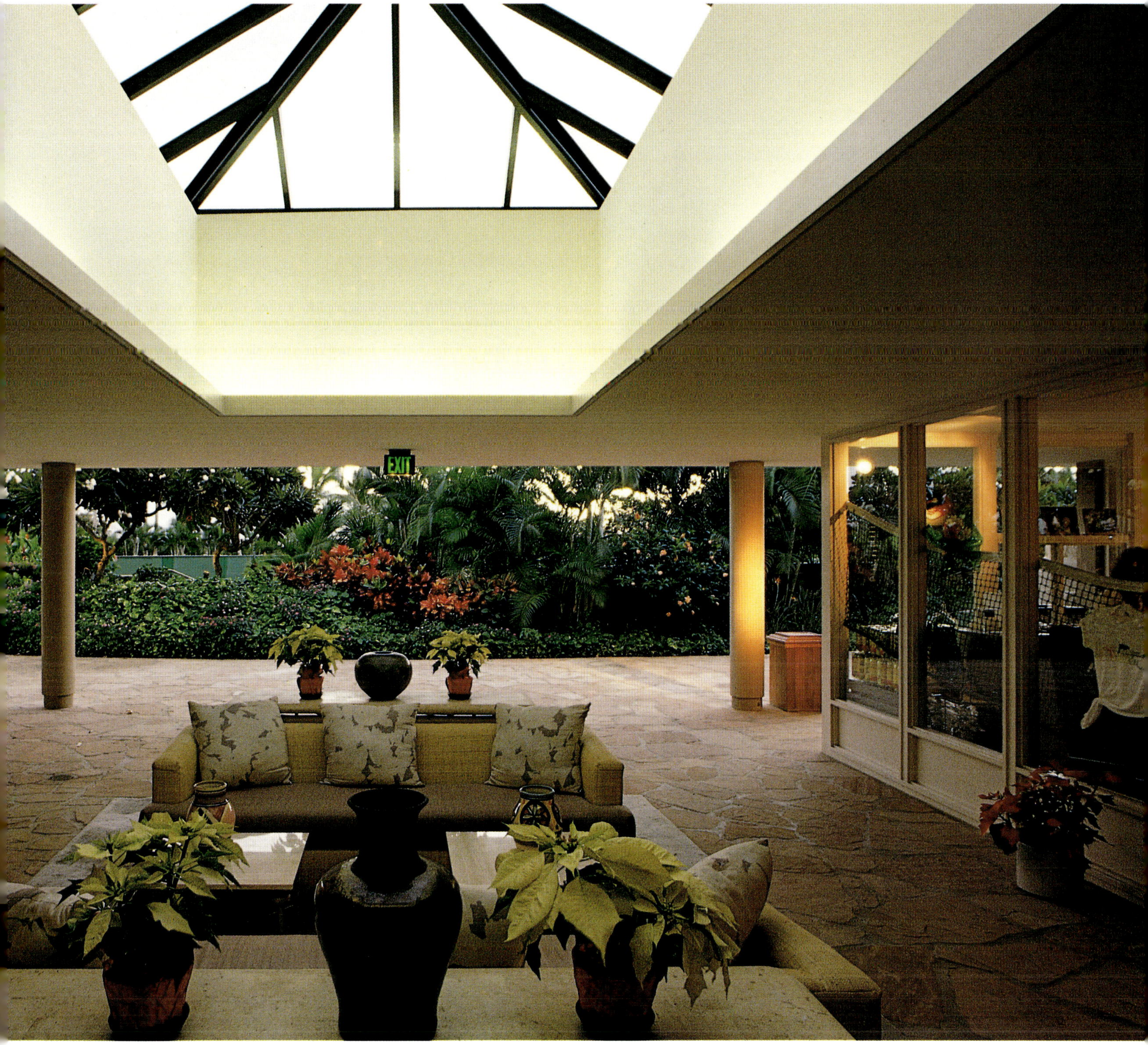
EXIT

Left: Postmodernism with features of local Queensland architecture: the central building and artificial lagoon of the Sheraton Mirage resort at Port Douglas.

Right: In the lobby of the hotel complex, the rather light colonial style of northern Australia is combined with items of luxury such as polished granite, heavy, period furniture and antiques.

SHERATON MIRAGE
Port Douglas, Australia, 1987

Architecture: **Desmond Brooks International, Media Five**

Interior Design: **Barry Peters**

In the tropical north of Australia, where the unspoilt wilderness of the Cape York peninsula begins, the Sheraton Mirage Port Douglas is the last bastion of five-star civilization. Only 20 kilometres separate the vast, untouched tropical rainforests from the luxury site beside the white Pacific beach. It is to this contrast that the project of Christopher Skase (an Australian entrepreneur who has since gone bankrupt) owes part of its charm. Yet the architecture and the landscaping show proper respect for the exposed site. The planners of Media Five, who originally operated in Hawaii, have created a successful synthetic dream world: small, unadorned, pastel-coloured blocks with roofs of corrugated iron – postmodern, with a nod in the direction of the regional colonial style of Queensland – are surrounded by an artificial saltwater lagoon whose turquoise expanse covers two hectares.

The whole project stretches out unobtrusively along four miles of formerly virgin beach near Port Douglas. It was stipulated that none of the hotel buildings and chalets lining the golf course on the seaside should rise above the tallest treetops. About 250 million Australian dollars were sunk in the sandy soil. The hotel complex is surrounded by a two-part Par-72 golf course, each part with nine holes, and a gleaming white country club was specially built, overlooking the green. This is a regular venue for international competitions such as the annual contest between Great Britain and Australia or the "Super Skins Game". Next to the clubhouse are nine floodlit tennis courts. A short distance away, in the small town of Port Douglas, an annexe was built – the Marina Mirage, which has a shopping centre, restaurants and a harbour for yachts. This is the starting point for diving and fishing trips to the Great Barrier Reef, which lies not far offshore.

The interior architecture of the hotel's main building matches the airiness of colonial architecture with the international glamour look. The match is no misalliance, however, despite the gleaming marble and the usual pot-pourri of antiques and reproductions from every age and continent. The décor, by the Melbourne interior designer Barry Peters, is as lavish as necessary and as well-mannered as possible – compared with other phantasmagorias in the five-star cosmos. The 300 rooms and suites, all ranged along open staircases, corridors and pergolas, are comfortable and luxurious without being extravagant. More individual and expensive, and in some cases furnished with flawless modern Italian elegance, are the two dozen guest-houses in the grounds of the resort, some of them privately owned. Serviced by Sheraton, they are let out throughout the year.

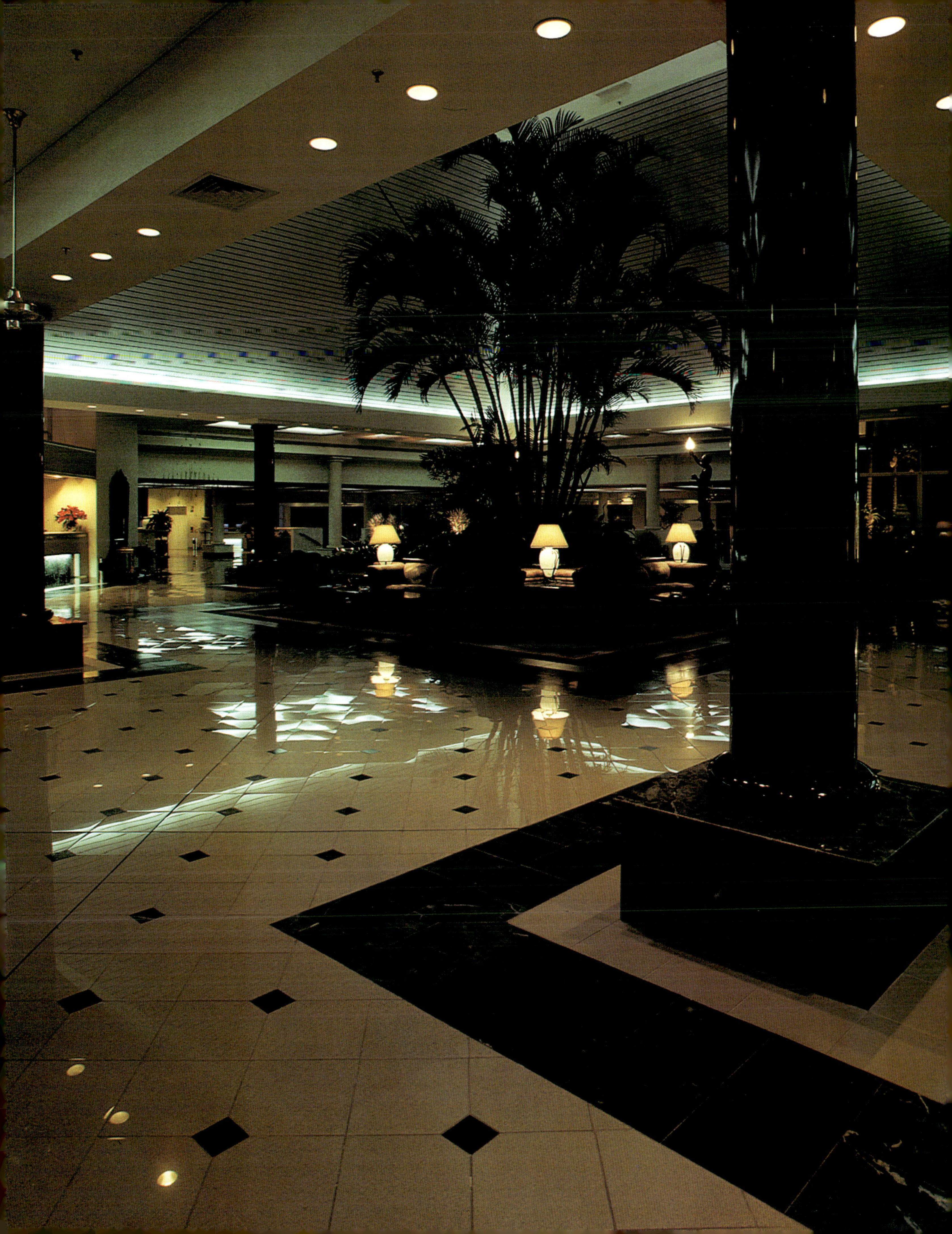

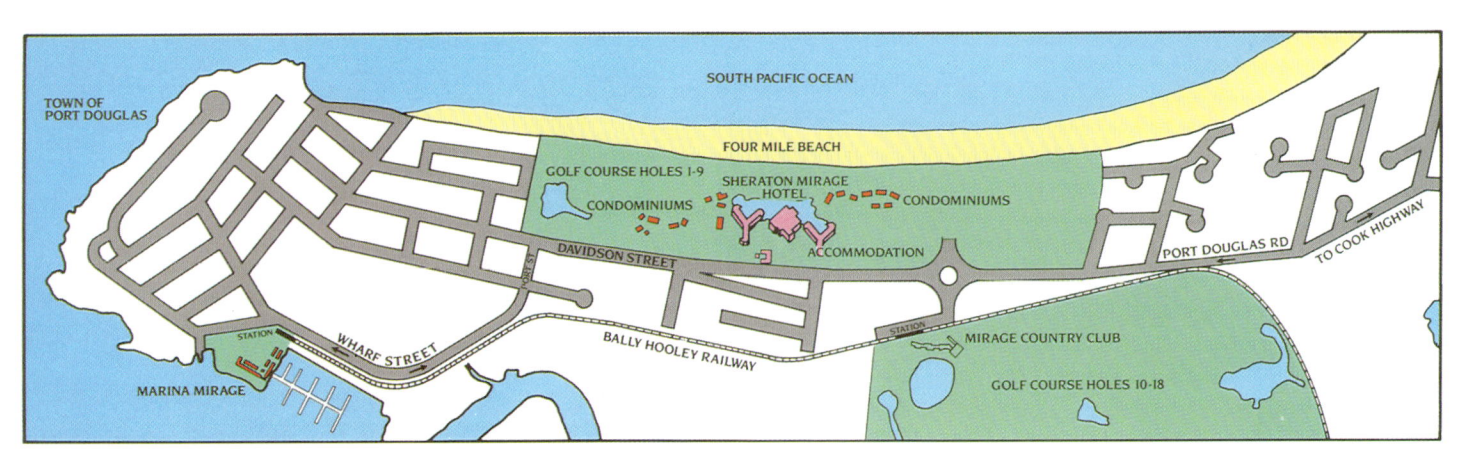

Above: A bathroom in the Presidential suite. **Right:** A bedroom in one of the guest villas. The combination of a natural, tropical setting with extreme five-star luxury is the hallmark of the resort.

Left: The three compounds of the Sheraton Mirage surround the little town of Port Douglas: the hotel grounds and golf course, the Mirage Country Club and golf course, and the Marina Mirage with its marina and shopping centre, the starting point for excursions to the Great Barrier Reef.

Below: Along the golf course lying between the hotel and the beach stand detached guest villas with individual top-quality furnishings. Some are privately owned, but are managed and looked after by the hotel.

THE MIRAGE
Las Vegas, USA, 1989

Architecture: **Joel David Bergman/Atlandia Design**

Interior Design: **Roger P. Thomas/Atlandia Design**

The gambling and showbusiness Eldorado set in the Nevada Desert entered architectural history when the American architect Robert Venturi wrote a controversial essay urging his fellow professionals to learn from Las Vegas. The vibrant, glitzy world of the Strip, the neon-lit main artery of the city, which only comes alive at night, became a metaphor for the switch to postmodernism. That even Las Vegas still has something to learn when it comes to illusionist attractions, luxury, entertainment and glamour was demonstrated by the casino owner Stephen A. Wynn when he opened the Mirage in 1989.

Next door to the legendary Caesar's Palace, this newcomer to the Strip speaks only in superlatives. The immense, Y-shaped 30-storey complex contains 3,054 rooms, including suites, villa apartments and Lanai bungalows with private pools. In front of the entrance stretches a lagoon complete with cascades, grottos and a mini-volcano that erupts every few minutes. The economic heart of the complex, the casino, evokes a vision of South Sea romance. Behind the reception, real sharks and stingrays swim in a 75,000-litre room-high aquarium. The statutory dolphinarium is there too, and for good measure there is also a well-tempered tropical rainforest. To crown it all, the world-famous tiger-taming duo, Siegfried and Roy, put on a regular performance showing off their white tigers to the guests, and the habitat of the big cats is part of the Mirage's adventure land.

The investment costs, including the price of the land, amounted to 610 million dollars. They were soon recouped, for the takings from the casino and the hotel have set new records, even by Las Vegas standards. Even without the profits from gambling, the Mirage comes out on top financially as the most successful new foundation in hotel history.

The entertainment machine is perfectly organized, both for the mass of visitors and for the better-off clientele intent on exclusivity and more discreet pleasures. The large show theatre accommodates an audience of 1,500, and other halls are designed for 5,000. One can dine in French style in an ambience of extreme art nouveau kitsch, or enjoy exotic dishes seated on a bamboo chair under hanging orchids in front of a foaming waterfall. The shopping arcade offers all the best makes of goods. The top five floors are reserved for penthouse suites, with private lifts and butlers.

In view of this profitable "gigantomania", there can be no disputing about style. Las Vegas, a place in the middle of nowhere, takes its identity from luck, and when luck strikes, anything is possible. The Mirage is thus an example of experience architecture, authentic because it is unprecedented.

Left: The Mirage on the Strip in Las Vegas. Behind the gleaming façade of this three-wing hotel complex are 3,054 rooms and suites.

Below: Among the artificial paradises the Mirage has to offer is a tropical rainforest with waterfalls and computer-regulated haze. Everything is under glass in an atrium almost 30 metres high.

Behind the seemingly endless reception desk in the lobby is a gleaming 75,000-litre aquarium populated by sharks and stingrays.

The furnishing of the rooms is geared to a wide public rather than being limited to big spenders, and combines features of bourgeois and tropical styles.

Left: The layout of the double project, with the Dolphin on the right and the Swan on the left. Situated at the edge of Disney World, this is the largest hotel and congress complex in the south-east of the United States.

Right: Monuments of postmodern entertainment architecture: The Disney World Dolphin, with 1,510 rooms (top) and the Disney World Swan, with 758 rooms (bottom).

THE DISNEY WORLD SWAN/ THE DISNEY WORLD DOLPHIN
Orlando, Florida, USA, 1989/1990
Architecture/Interior Design: **Michael Graves**

The Walt Disney concern, wishing to launch a new and ambitious type of entertainment architecture, decided on this huge twin-project on the edge of Disney World in Florida. Michael Graves, a professor of architecture at Princeton who had initially been inspired by the Bauhaus but had long since converted to the colourful neo-classicist style of postmodernism, proved the ideal partner. His cheerful monumentalism was transformed here into a lively theatrical show. Just as Disney's theme parks are fantasy worlds combining fairytale with sci-fi, historical folklore with film legends, so the Disney World Swan and the Disney World Dolphin playfully exploit an allegorical repertoire. The pharaohs turn up in Comicland; art deco is paired with tropical flora, beach romance, marquees and sunny Matisse motifs. Everything is kept within the one-dimensionality of the cartoon, and artificiality is emphasized. The amusement to be derived from the transparency of the illusion is what distinguishes Graves's hotels from the strategy of the rest of Disney World, which aims rather at identification and naturalistic imitation tailored to the level of the child. Graves's achievement is notable for its insistence on a special quality of experience and a degree of detachment, but it cannot be repeated ad lib, as is demonstrated by the distinctly inferior standard of the architect's Hotel New York, conceived for the new Eurodisney Park near Paris. Here the inadequate simulation of a metropolitan myth turned out to be merely a poor copy of an original that remains alive both in memory and in reality.

The huge Florida complex, with over 2,200 rooms, is the largest hotel and congress centre in the south-eastern USA. While creating inventions for the guests' delight, the architect still had to satisfy the rigorous requirements of international hotel chains as regards function and expense. The Swan, which cost 120 million dollars to build, contains 758 rooms and suites, a ballroom and more than 30 conference rooms. It is part of the Westin Group. The larger Dolphin cost 250 million dollars and has a rather higher standard of comfort; it has 1,510 rooms and suites, eleven restaurants and bars, a congress hall, an exhibition hall, and again more than 30 conference rooms. It forms part of the ITT Sheraton empire. Guests at either hotel can use all the gastronomic and service facilities available within the complex, and the hotels share the same pool and beach landscape. To see the attractions of Disney World, guests are transported by a regular boat service on artificial lakes and canals. The whole complex, from the huge roof sculptures of the swan and the dolphin down to the smallest details of the room furnishings, was designed by the architect. The furniture, décor and accessories are the products of an ingenious naïvety.

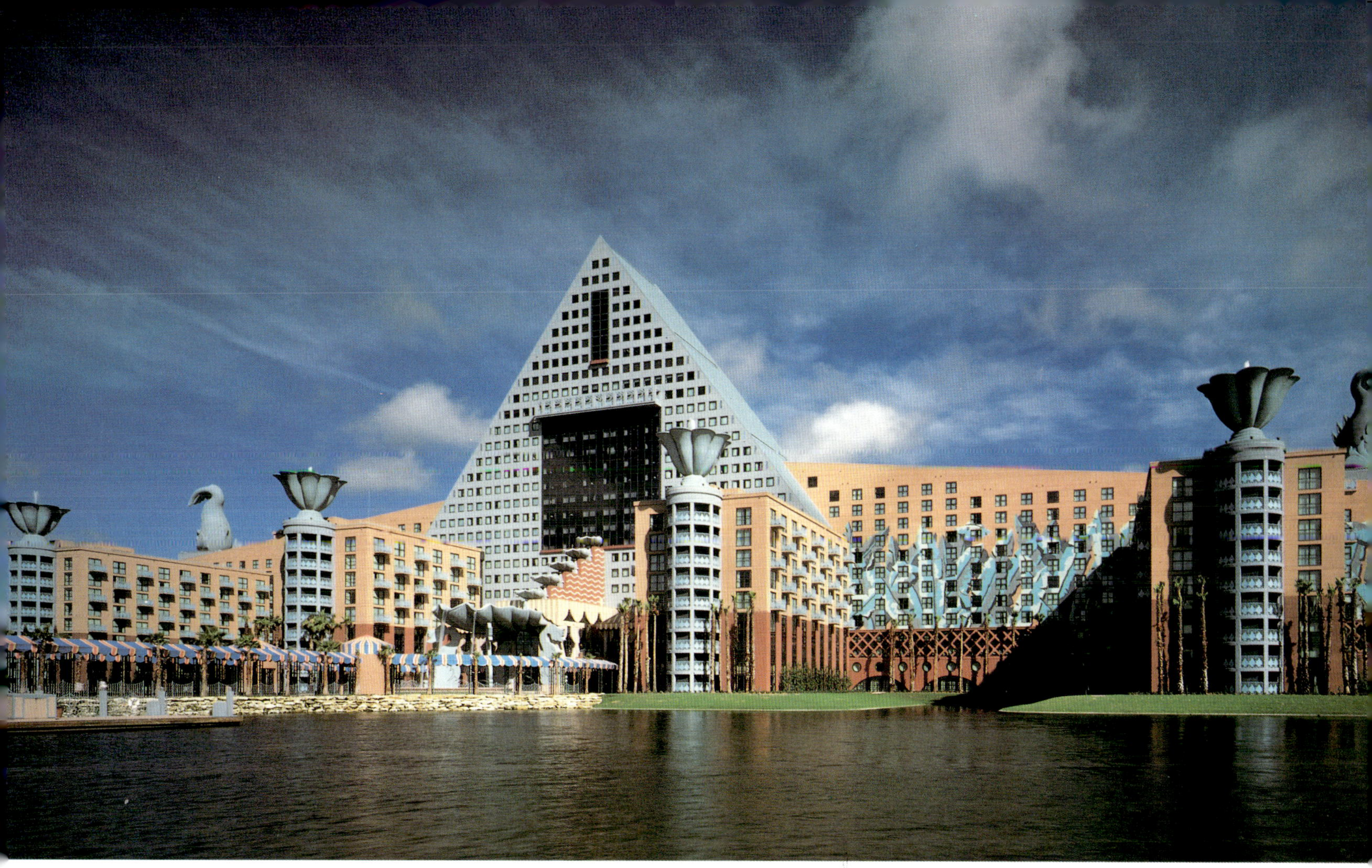

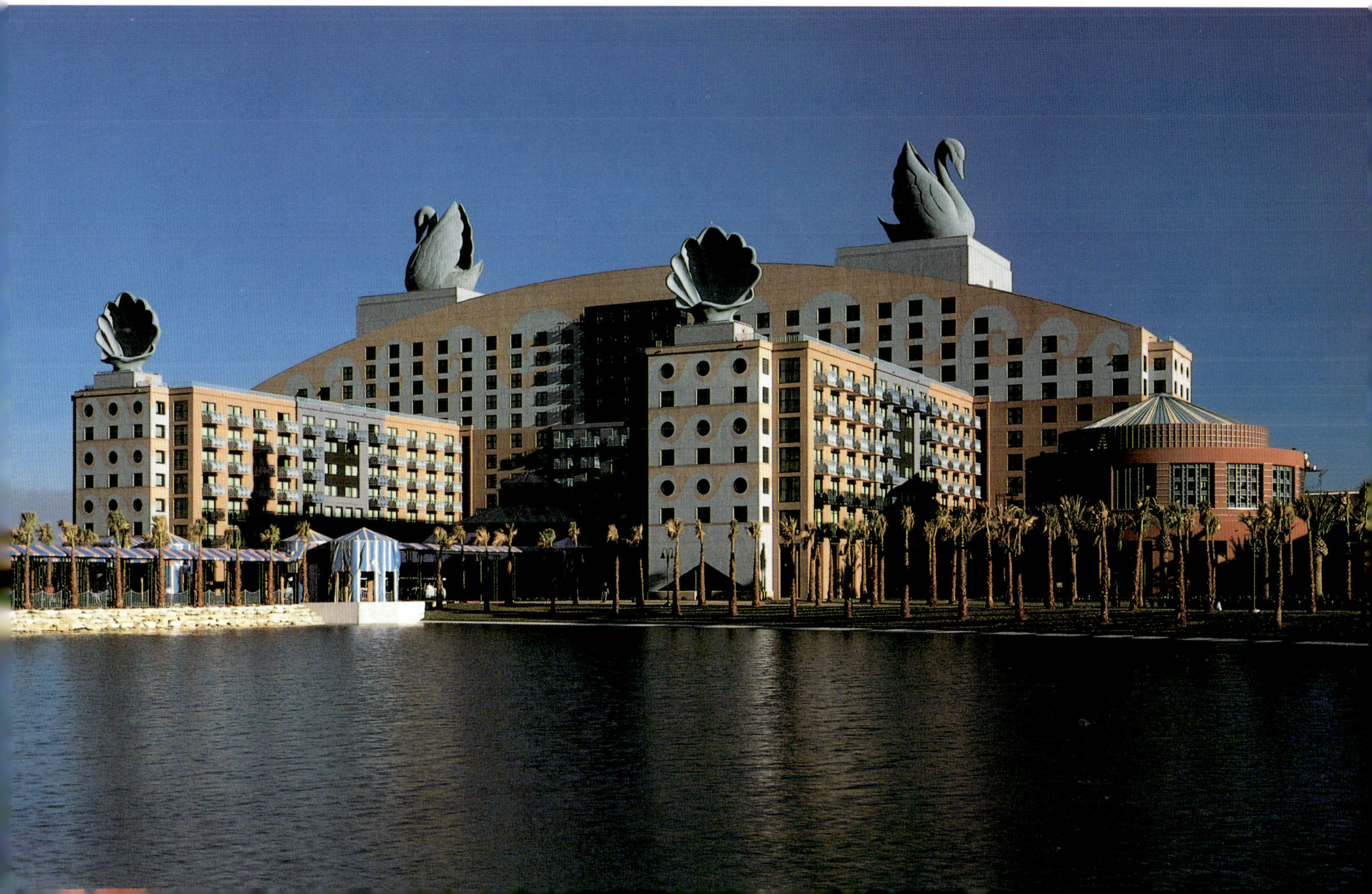

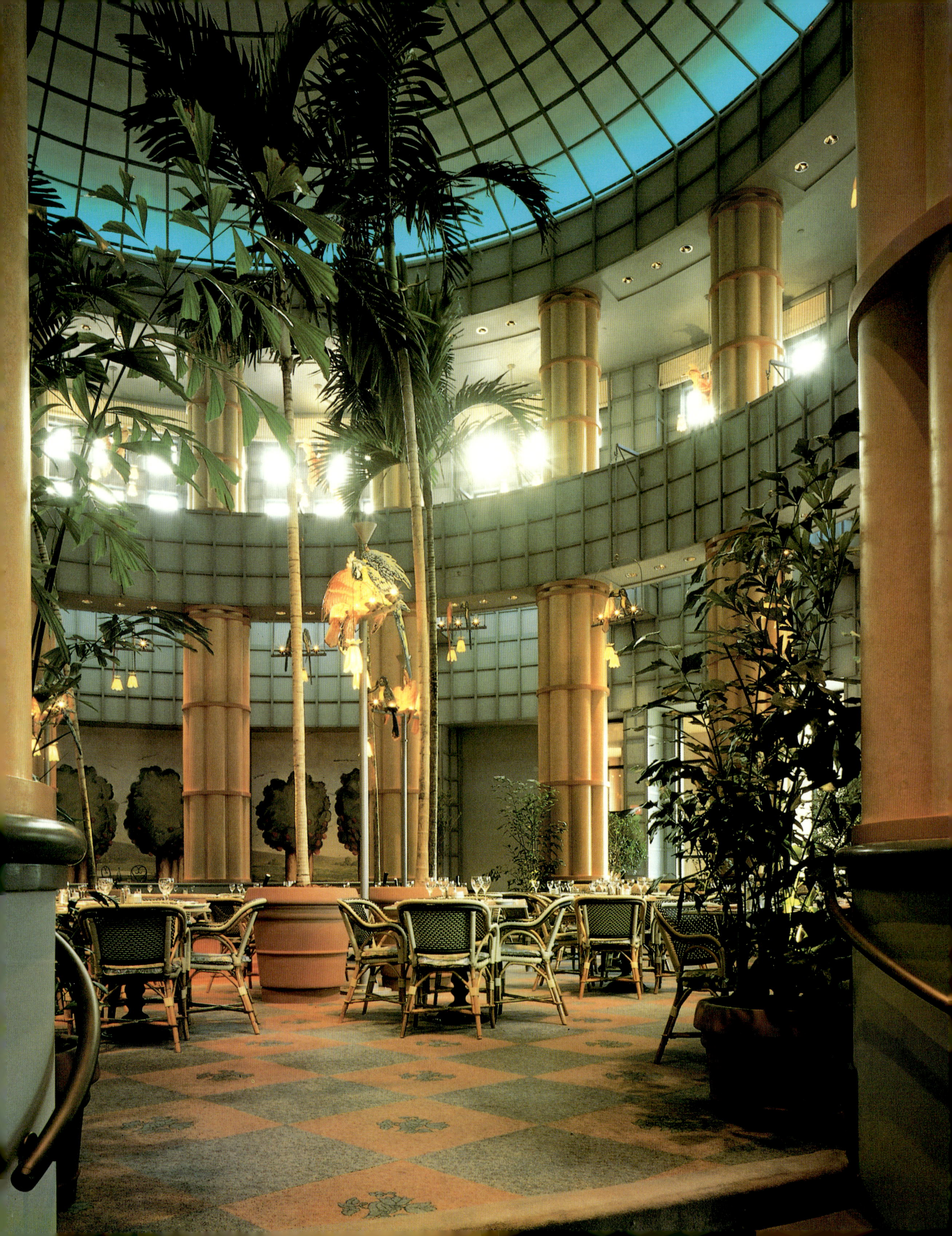

Left: The Garden Grove Café in the Swan, like the whole of the hotel's interior, is designed in the fanciful narrative style developed by Michael Graves specifically for these buildings.

Above: The décor of the Copa Cabana Lounge at the Dolphin complements the Disney Park's world of childish illusion.

211

Left: The dining room on one of the floors of the Royal Beach Club at the Swan. In some suites the architect offers alternatives to the "pop festival" of images and colours.

Left: Typical guest-rooms turn grown-ups into children. Various fruit motifs, like the pineapple here at the Swan, pervade the design of the whole complex.

Right: The central corridor at lobby level in the Swan with a fountain dedicated to the eponymous bird.

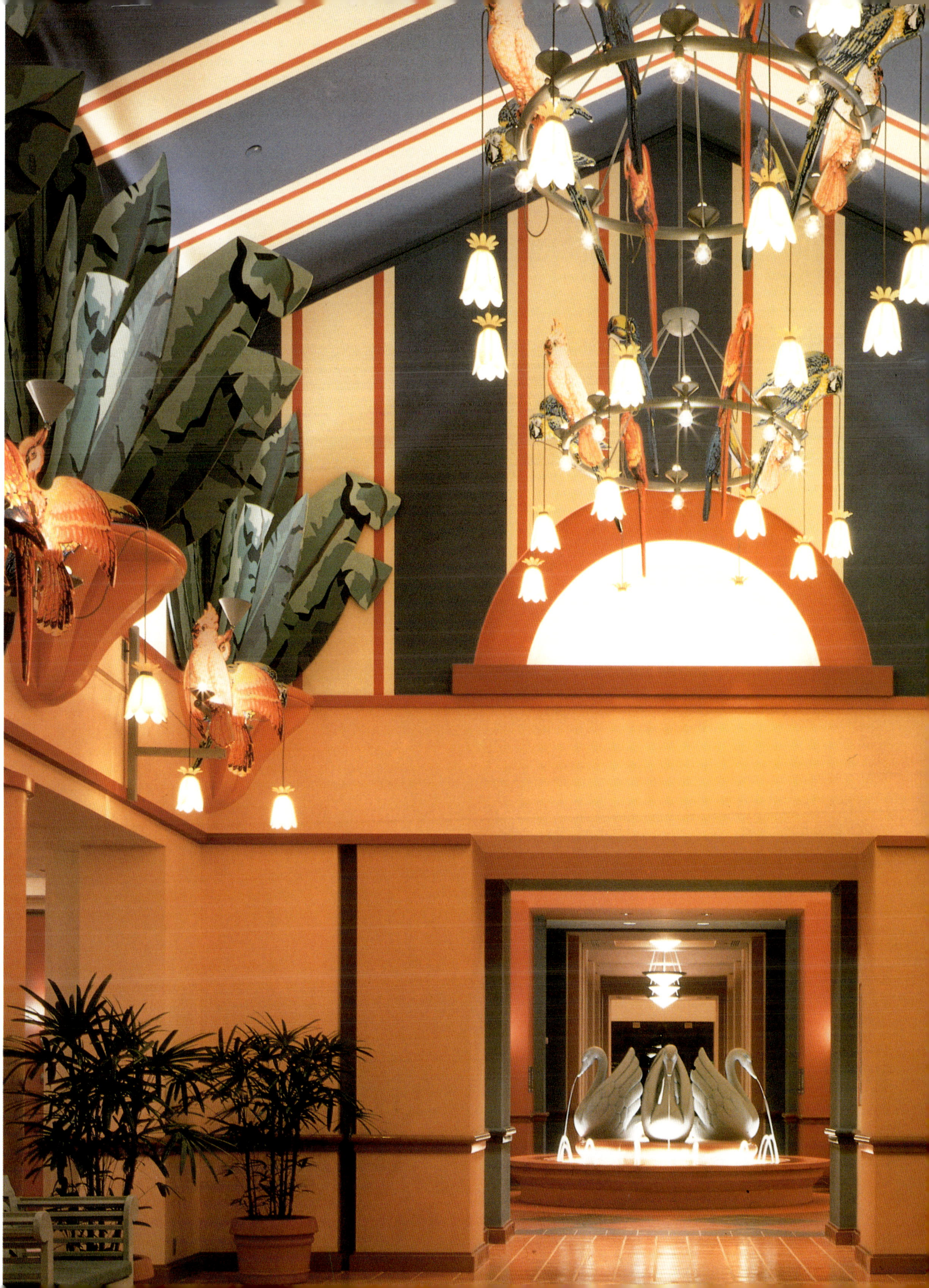

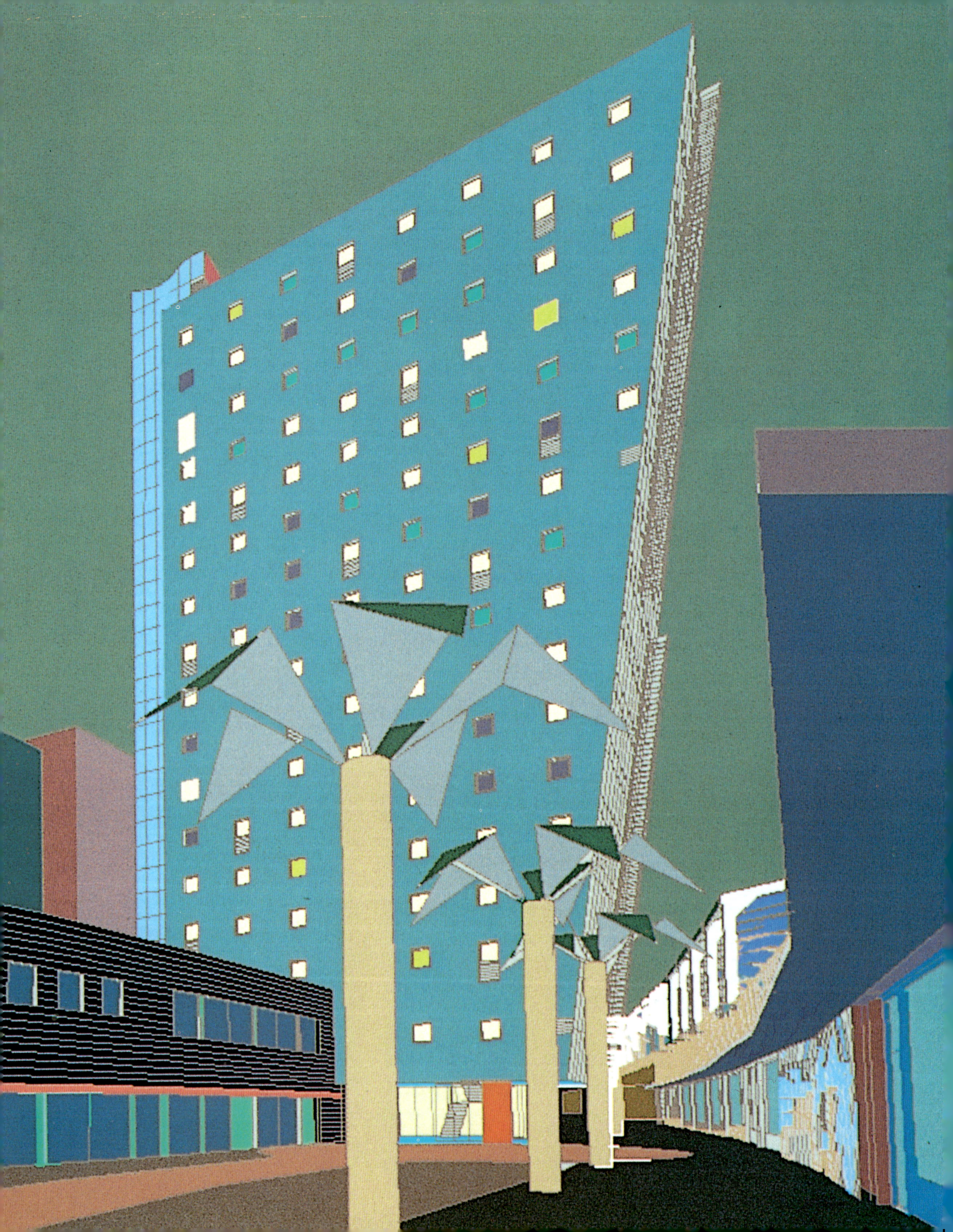

6
VISIONS AND PROJECTS

No BOOK ABOUT NEW HOTEL design would be complete unless it took account of architectural visions yet to be realized and projects in the course of construction. The hotel's suitability as a theme for modern architecture and a modern lifestyle was discovered long ago by the pioneering architect Adolf Loos. His metamorphosis of a grand hotel into a Babylonian structure has literary forebears. He presented his ideal hotel at the Salon d'Automne in Paris in 1923, naming his design after Arnold Bennett's novel "The Grand Babylon Hotel". His plan envisaged a terraced Babylon with over a thousand beds.

The earliest project in this chapter – no less enormous and no less visionary – was conceived by Arquitectonica, a group of architects based in Florida. Their monumental Helmsley Center, with a hotel wing, shops and offices, was to become a landmark on the promenade in Miami. Zaha Hadid's Club Hotel was to be built in a similarly exposed position, on the top of a hill overlooking Hong Kong. Her Billie Strauss hotel, a more distant and modest variant of neoconstructivist architecture, is now planned as a campanile between two old houses in Kirchheim, South Germany.

Among the unbuilt landmarks of modern architecture are the cantilever arm designed by the Viennese firm Coop Himmelblau for the Gartenhotel Altmannsdorf in Vienna, and Rem Koolhaas's visionary project for a congress hotel in Agadir, designed like an oriental town. Another town-like conglomerate has been devised by the Italian Ettore Sottsass for the centre of Kuala Lumpur. Here too hotel architecture is planned as part of an imaginary, multicultural setting. Realistic projects already under construction include Georg Ritschl's Intercity Hotel in Berlin and the airport hotel near Munich, designed by Helmut Jahn and Jan Wichers.

It is nevertheless impossible to dismiss a suspicion that the flowering of contemporary style, combining avant-garde, luxury and fantasy, is coming to an end. The hotel business has become tougher, and experiments now have to justify themselves. When a large hotel group like Marriott has closed almost the whole of its architectural division, when international enterprises are drastically cutting back on expenses and restricting business travel, and bookings in top-class hotels are shrinking dramatically, when the Italian Ciga chain is being forced by excessive debt to dispose of many of its palace hotels – including Les Bains on the Lido, immortalized in Thomas Mann's *Death in Venice* – and when new projects at the lower end of the market (one-star to three-star hotels) are running into thousands, it is clear that individuality in architecture and interior design no longer enjoys the priority shown in the examples assembled here.

Left: The Helmsley Center on Biscayne Bay, a new landmark for Miami which has not yet been realized. A hotel was to occupy the high-rise building on the left.

Right: This early model shows the sea front of the Helmsley Center with marina. The gatehouse and the oval tower were intended for apartments, and a shopping centre was to be built in the basement.

THE HELMSLEY CENTER
Miami, USA, 1981
Architecture: **Arquitectonica**

In Miami, along Biscayne Bay, are ranged the much acclaimed high-rise buildings of the Arquitectonica duo Bernardo Fort-Brescia and Laurinda Spear. These two local architects – married with six children – have demonstrated their own colourful and extravagantly modernist style with such landmarks as the Palace, the Atlantis and the Imperial – all large apartment complexes and flamboyant monuments of the booming eighties, when Miami was a financial haven for international funds, partly from the drug trade.

The Helmsley Center was to have been the crowning glory of the Arquitectonica projects. With floorspace of over 140,000 square metres it was to include housing units, offices, shops and a hotel. The design combines three tower buildings with a common five-storey base that accommodates town houses, shops and a car park. The central tower, 36 storeys high, is a gatehouse with a square façade, and with a pool and jogging track on the roof. This tower is flanked by an oval skyscraper with 55 floors and another with 65 floors, terraced towards the top and with curving façades.

The lower part of this building, the tallest in the Helmsley Center, was intended to be used for offices and a hotel. The whole complex was to have its own marina, and on the roof of the basic structure there was to be a large pool landscape. The idea of the high-rise building as an urban portal was again taken up by Arquitectonica in its proposal for a large project in San Antonio, Texas, where the Horizon Center was planned as an administrative and hotel project, but it too, like its predecessor in Miami, was halted at an early stage.

Both projects are interesting in that they represent a possible vision of large-scale American building. The vertical dimension, far from paying a postmodernist tribute to history, becomes an autonomous architectonic sculpture. The concentrated exploitation of ground space, necessitated by economic considerations, produces a lively and varied configuration that is reminiscent – and not just coincidentally – of fictive CAD-generated architectural structures. At all events, the Helmsley Center illustrates Philip Johnson's comment on the work of Spear and Fort-Brescia: "... Arquitectonica ... is the gutsiest team in the business."

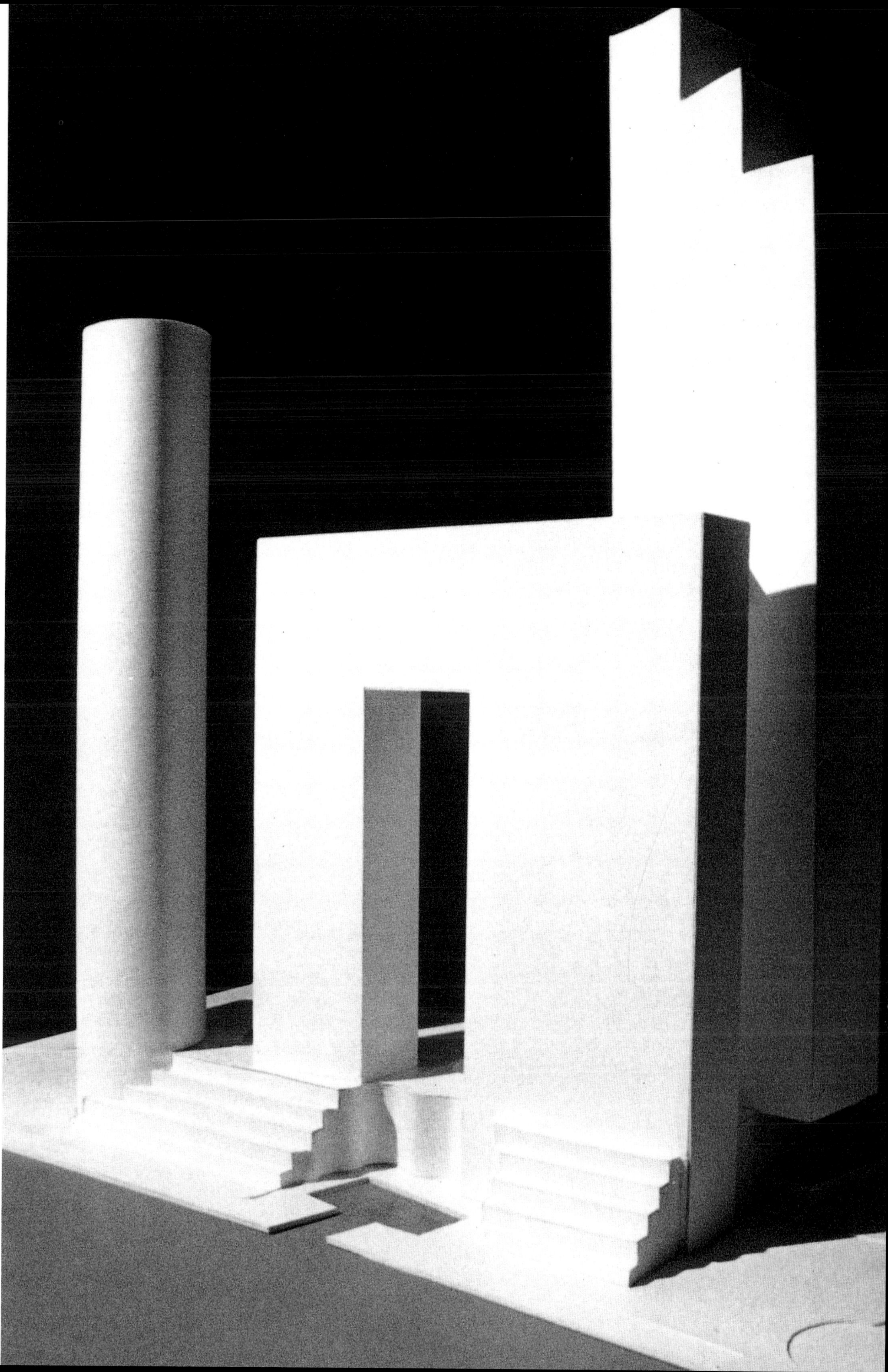

Left: As envisaged by Rem Koolhaas, the hotel was to be integrated into the roof zone.
Right: The ground plans are reminiscent of the patterns on a modern oriental carpet.

CONGRESS HOTEL
Agadir, Morocco, 1990
Architecture: **Rem Koolhaas/O.M.A.**

As a participant in a competition, the avant-garde architect Rem Koolhaas planned a congress centre, linked with a hotel, for the Moroccan town of Agadir. The particular climate prevailing on the Atlantic coast of south-western Morocco led to a functional scheme so far unknown in any hotel in this climatic zone. The structure consists of three areas stacked on top of one another. The lowest of these in Rem Koolhaas's large, square-shaped design comprises congress halls, auditoria and exhibition galleries dug into the ground. The different volumes and contours of the three components enable him to realize an overall architectural structure that resembles the landscape, its curving forms a continuation of the surrounding dunes. Koolhaas intersperses these imaginatively constructed hills and valleys with connecting paths, roads and flights of steps.

Growing out of the organic hill landscape and the ground-level zone are the supports and irregularly shaped pillars that hold a monumental square roof slab. Along with the irregular forms of the auditoria, foyers, assembly rooms and approaches, they suggest a varied architectural landscape. The hotel proper is built on the roof slab, hovering over the forest of columns with auditoria and walkways between them. The space underneath it is shielded from sun and rain and acquires a special aura deriving from its architectural forms and the natural light entering through domes; it thus contributes to the unique quality of the whole. This intermediate zone is neither an interior nor an exterior space. During the day it is lit by irregularly arranged skylights that produce an atmosphere reminiscent of a mosque. The natural daylight becomes a theatrical device, replaced at night by artificial light from the ceiling.

One of the main attractions of the building is its roof extension as a hotel. The base slab of the roof and the one forming the ceiling are of cast concrete. This autonomous square zone makes it possible to create a structure resembling an Arab settlement. On this isolated level Koolhaas takes the opportunity to draw exhaustively on the wealth of regional building forms. To crown the roof landscape – literally – he plans a royal suite with a golden, dome-shaped roof, set upon a round conference hall and visible for miles around. The adjacent accommodation area in the suite, like the other apartments, is designed in the form of an Arab house. Like the cubic buildings of an Arab settlement, the guest-rooms are arranged around open courtyards cut into the second roof shell. This level is connected by escalators with the public zone below, from which the individual meeting rooms, exhibition foyers and auditoria are reached.

The rigorous division of the centre into roof zone, communication landscape and congress area makes for easy orientation and presents the architect with an unsuspected wealth of interesting design possibilities. Koolhaas envisages his Agadir congress centre as an architectural landscape. He sees the world that arises dynamically, now broad, now narrow, between the modelled ground architecture and the ceiling slab as a contemporary interpretation of an Islamic space. This zone between heaven and earth will honour Islamic building traditions by employing coloured tiles, polished concrete and mosaics.

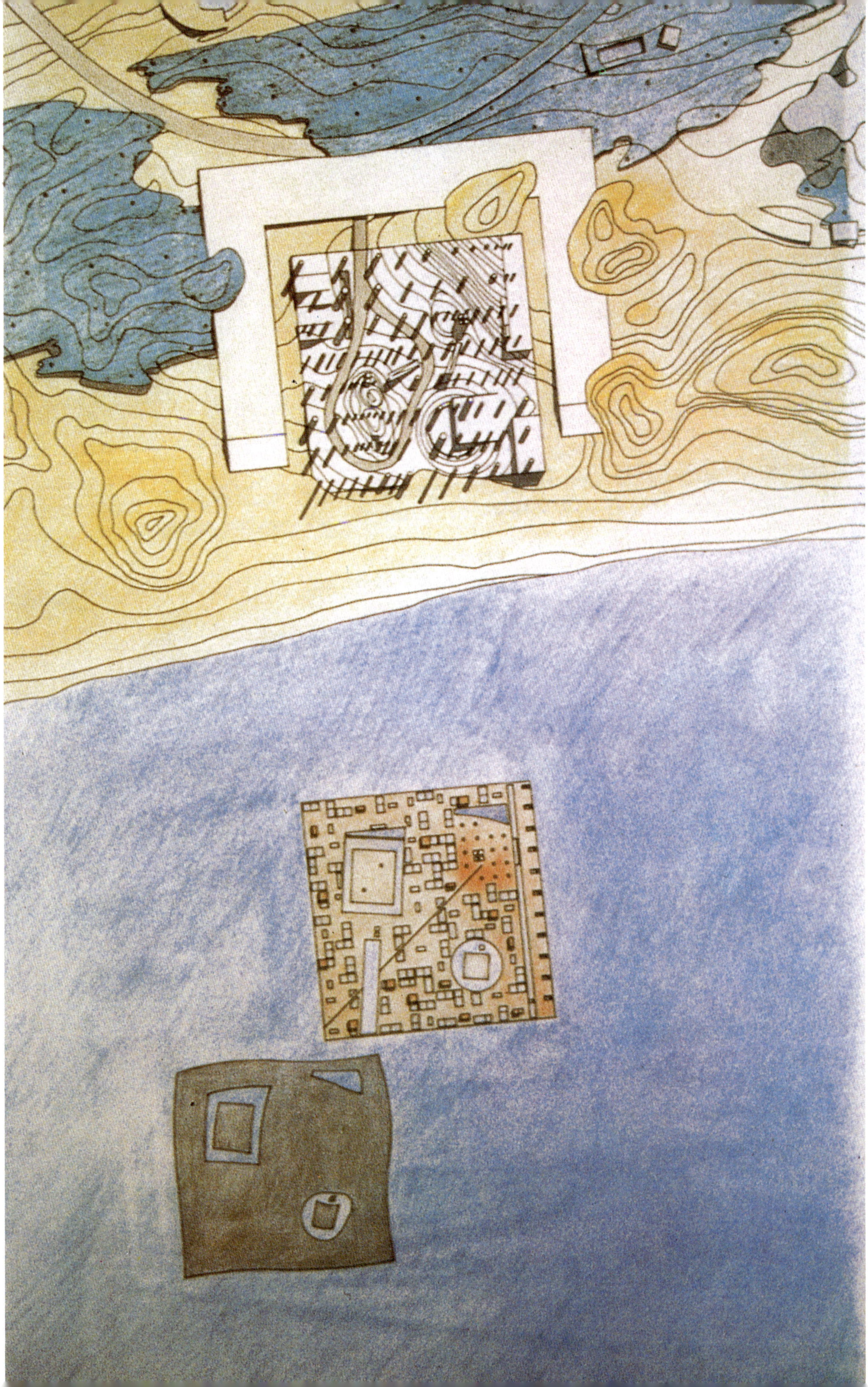

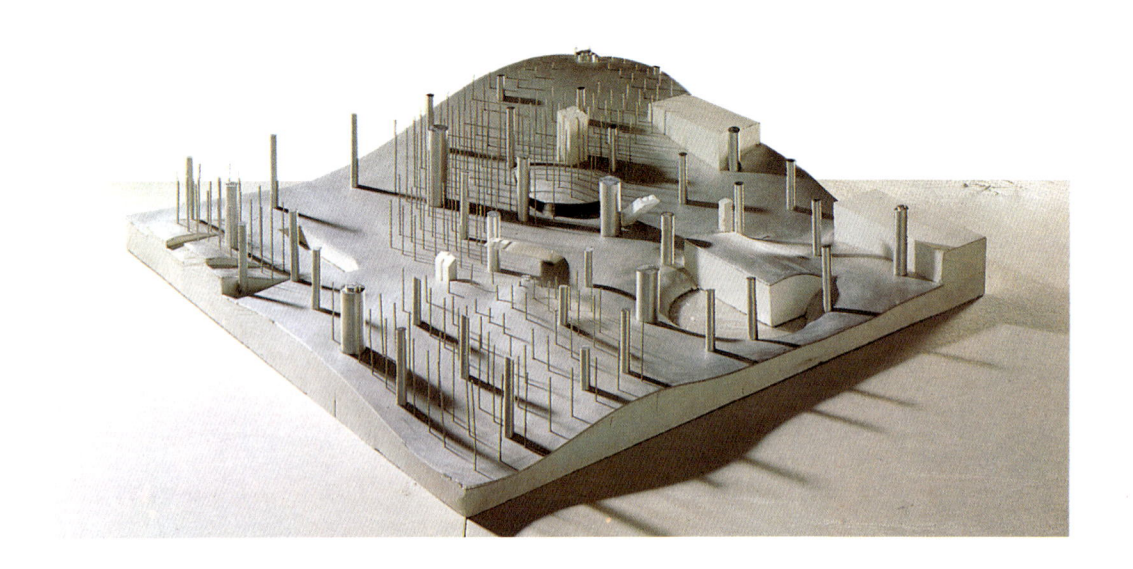

Above: Supports of the most varied shapes rhythmically articulate the busy lower zone, containing open areas, foyers and auditoria.

Right: The royal suite is designed as a round structure with a golden dome visible from the distance.

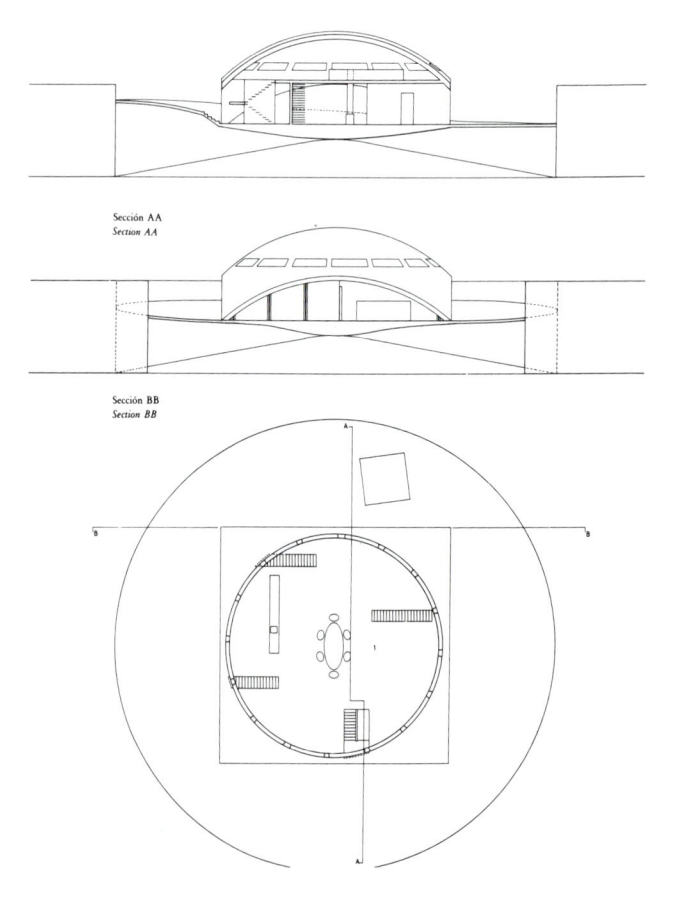

Sección AA
Section AA

Sección BB
Section BB

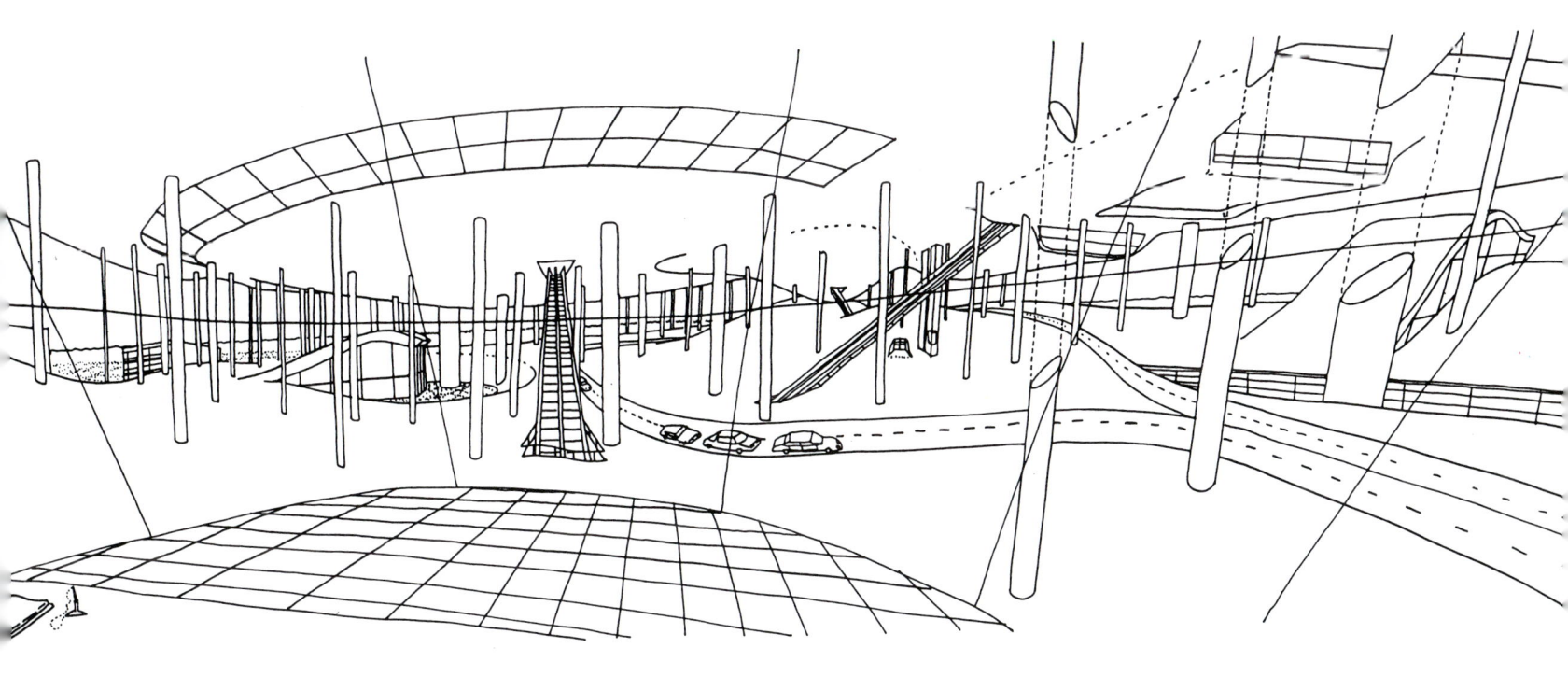

Above and top: Under the hotel in the roof zone is a foyer with an urban flavour that takes up the gentle undulations of the surrounding dune landscape. With its forest of columns it offers a modern interpretation of Islamic space.

221

Left: This hotel, due to be built next to Berlin's Zoo Station, consists of a tower structure slanting towards the tracks and a row of shops running parallel to the railway embankment.

Right: Ground plans of the two-storey row of shops (centre and bottom) and of some accommodation floors and the roof garden in the hotel tower (top).

INTERCITY HOTEL
Berlin, Germany, 1988/90
Architecture: **Georg Ritschl**

This project is part of the German Federal Railway's strategy for moving up-market, not only by improving the intercity rail network, but by raising the dreary image of the average railway hotel to the standard of modern three-star comfort. In 1988 the young Berlin architect Georg Ritschl won a civic competition for a project intended to fill an empty site next to the Zoo Station in West Berlin. At that time, with the capital still divided, the plan to build on land owned by the Reichsbahn, which belonged to the German Democratic Republic, was still an aim for the future; in the wake of German unification, it became a matter of urgency.

The extremely narrow site, which is hemmed in on one side by the slightly curving rail viaduct, and on the other by the backs of several existing buildings, and must leave room for the future rehearsal stage of the neighbouring Theatre of the West, called for a kind of architecture that evinced a clear creative will, rather than a readiness to compromise. In its surface aesthetic Ritschl's design stages a pop-revival of the fifties, but it is eminently rational in terms of city planning and brings a new urbanity to a forgotten backyard. The spearhead of the flat, two-storey shop and service complex at track level points towards the Kantstrasse, a major traffic artery. The silhouette of the 17-storey hotel tower shoots up between the station and the neighbouring buildings as an expressive visual barrier, broadening out towards the top on the side of the tracks. Its blue surface with square windows is intriguingly framed by the mirror façade on the narrow side of the structure.

The lobby and the office quarters are located on the ground floor; on the first floor are the restaurant, approached by a separate staircase, and several conference rooms. The bedroom floors are arranged in a parallel ground plan, their furnishing and dimensions (18.2 square metres) conforming with the prescribed standard of the Intercity Hotel Company. The extra-large floors resulting from the sloping glass façade are used for specially furnished suites with panoramic views. Altogether there are 305 rooms. A roof terrace can be used as a sun deck with a café. The correspondence between the station and the new station hotel is created by the high, silvery glass façade that slants towards the tracks and mirrors the arriving and departing trains.

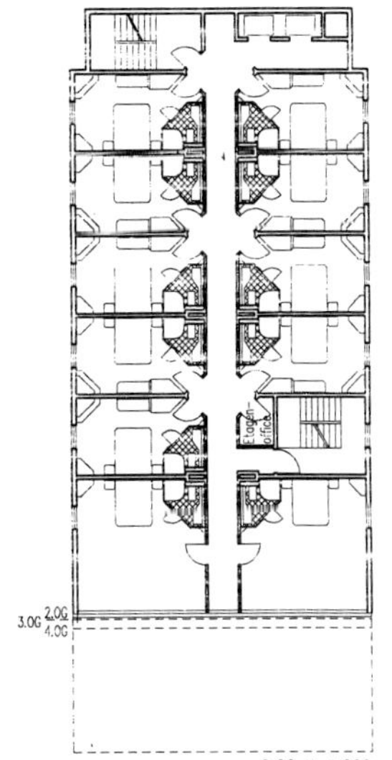

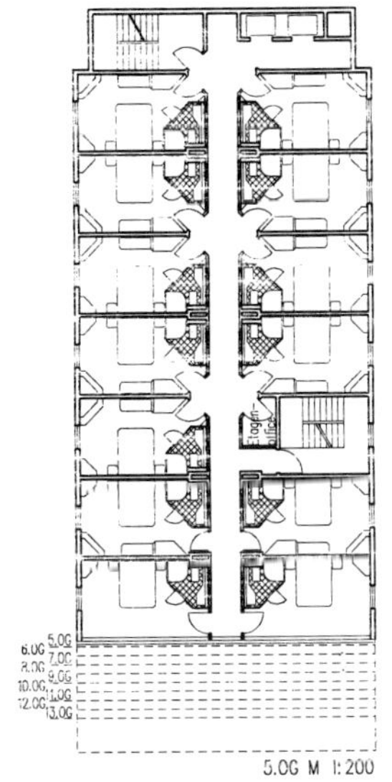

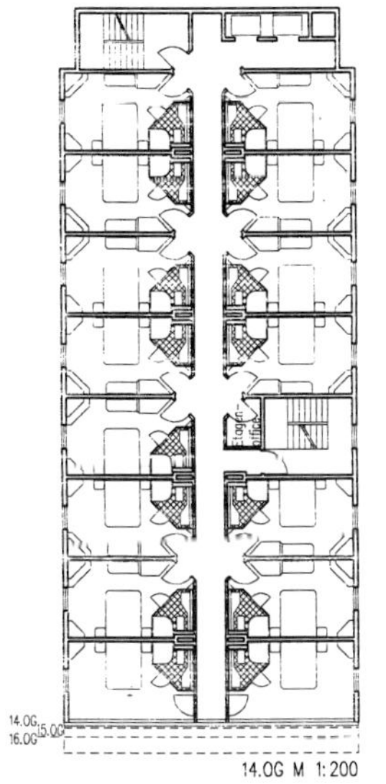

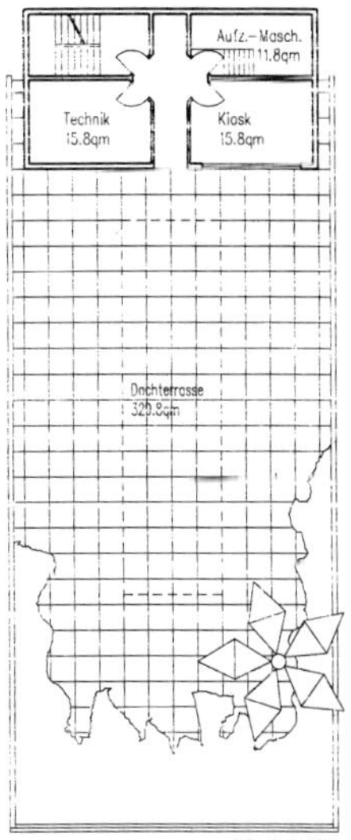

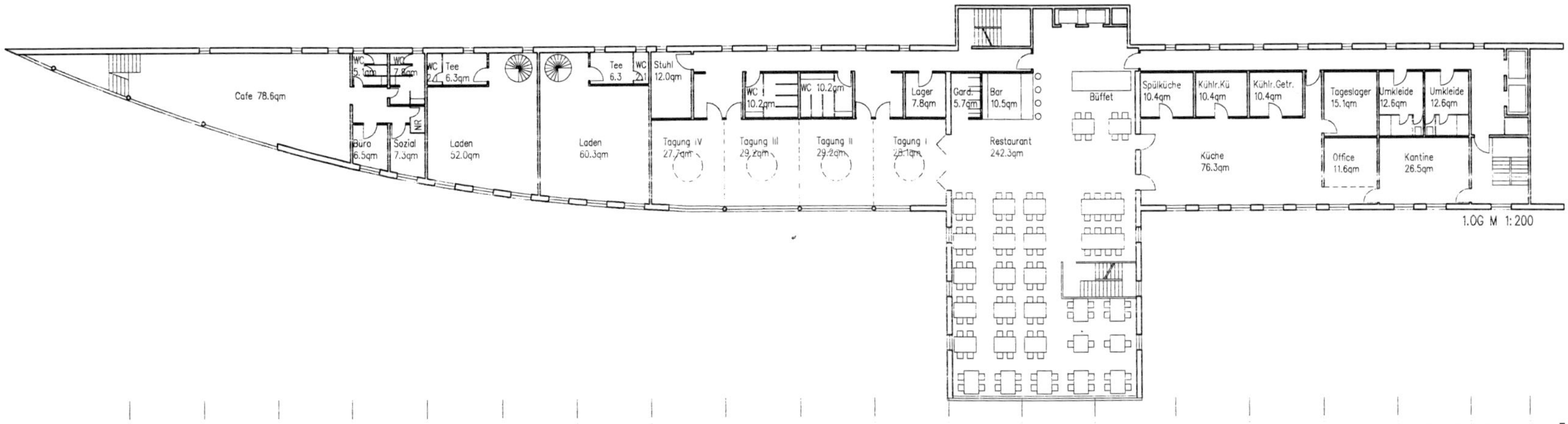

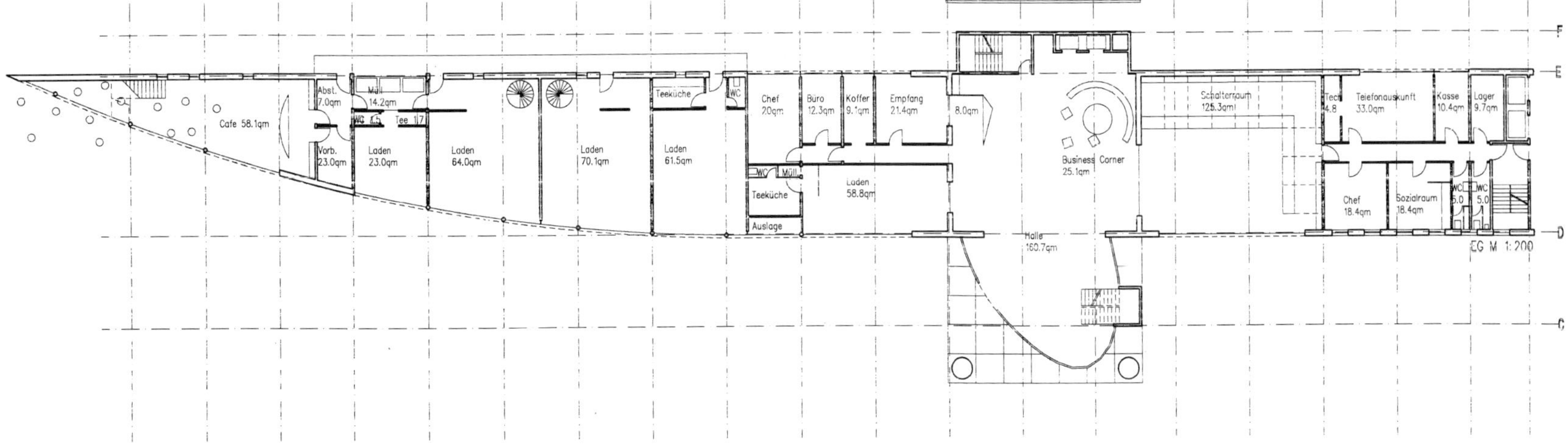

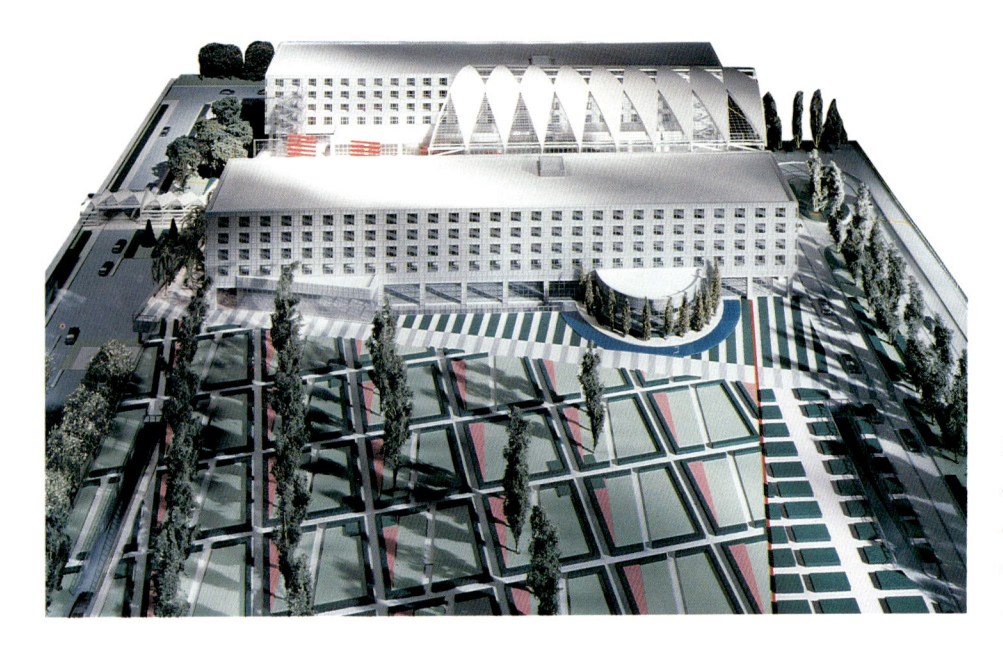

Left: At Munich's new airport the architect Helmut Jahn conceived an atrium hotel with a geometric garden. Underneath the garden is a car park.

KEMPINSKI AIRPORT HOTEL
Munich, Germany, 1991
Architecture: **Murphy/Jahn**

Interior Design: **Jan Wichers**

Right from the beginning the new airport Munich II, occupying a green-field site near the little town of Erding, 50 kilometres from the city, pursued high architectural objectives. Not only the long, white terminal building, crouched in what was once marshland, but the service buildings, freight halls and hangars were to live up to the standards of the modernist revival. Not surprisingly, when Helmut Jahn, a German-born American, was engaged to draw up a general plan for a hotel and congress complex, he started from a position oriented towards a technical aesthetic.

The first phase in the building of the Munich Airport Center (MAC) – planned for completion in 1994 – is a 389-room hotel, not unlike its immediate forerunner, the Hyatt Regency Roissy, which opened in 1992 (see page 180). Here, too, two long accommodation blocks (measuring 115 x 20 metres) are linked by a construction of glass and steel that spans more than 40 metres, creating a light-flooded plaza. Unlike the Paris building, however, the new Munich hotel is not set in a no man's land disfigured by a miscellany of dreary commercial buildings, but matched by architecture of at least equal worth – hence the greater importance attached to landscaping. The hotel compound includes geometrically arranged gardens above an underground car park.

The interior design is in the hands of Jan Wichers, who intervened sensitively in earlier five-star hotels built by the Kempinski group. Here, too, he departs from the usual routine. In the restaurant areas he adapts aeronautical motifs as elements in his room design, but alienates them through a discerning choice of materials. He furnishes the lobby in the modern Italian style, and in the appointment of the rooms he strikes a balance between an imaginative and functional use of space and a display of unobtrusive but obvious elegance.

The two four-storey accommodation blocks can be reached from the atrium lobby. One floor below is the recreation area, with swimming pool, sauna and fitness centre. Pedestrian walkways link the hotel with the airport terminal. Other additions to the Munich Airport Centre will be architecturally integrated with the hotel complex, and this will be underlined by the extension of the atrium roof to adjacent buildings.

Left: Model for a room in the Kempinski Airport Hotel. The interior architect Jan Wichers is intent on achieving objective elegance.

Below: The modular architectural plan requires an economical use of space. Ranged along the wall opposite the bed are the suitcase stand, wardrobe, TV shelf and seating corner.

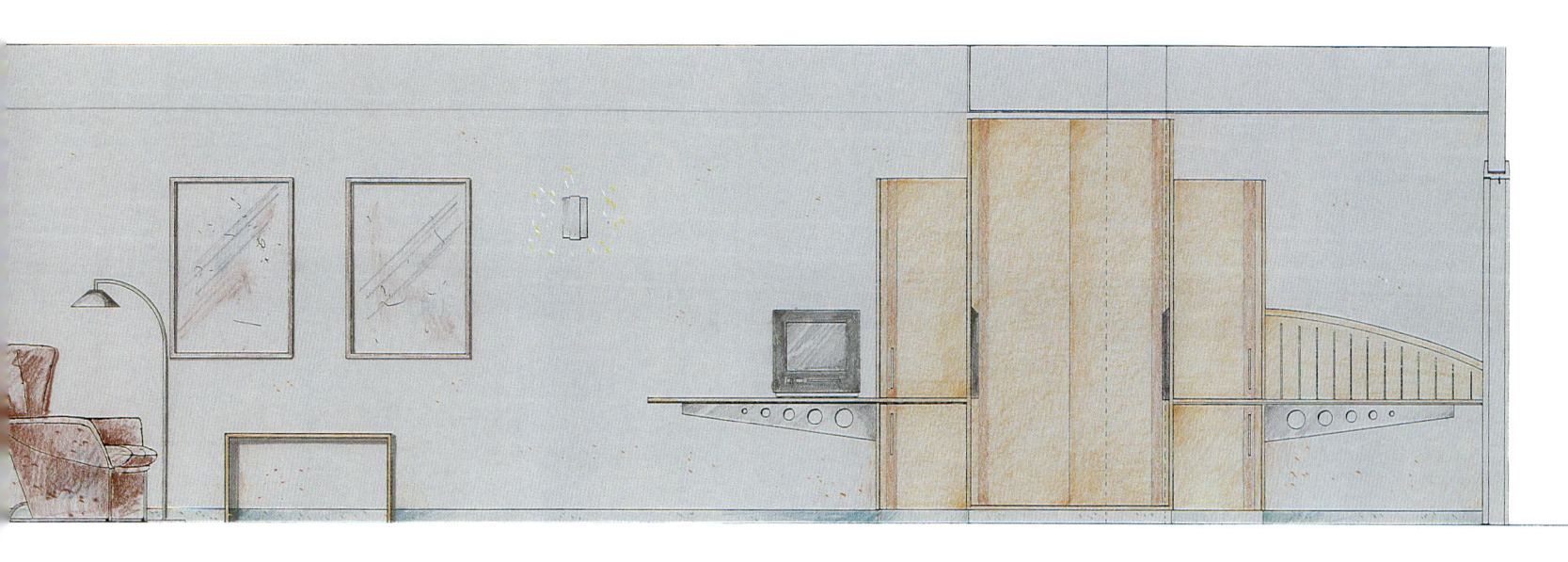

Left: Comfort in a limited space and a careful choice of materials are the chief characteristics of a model bathroom for the hotel.

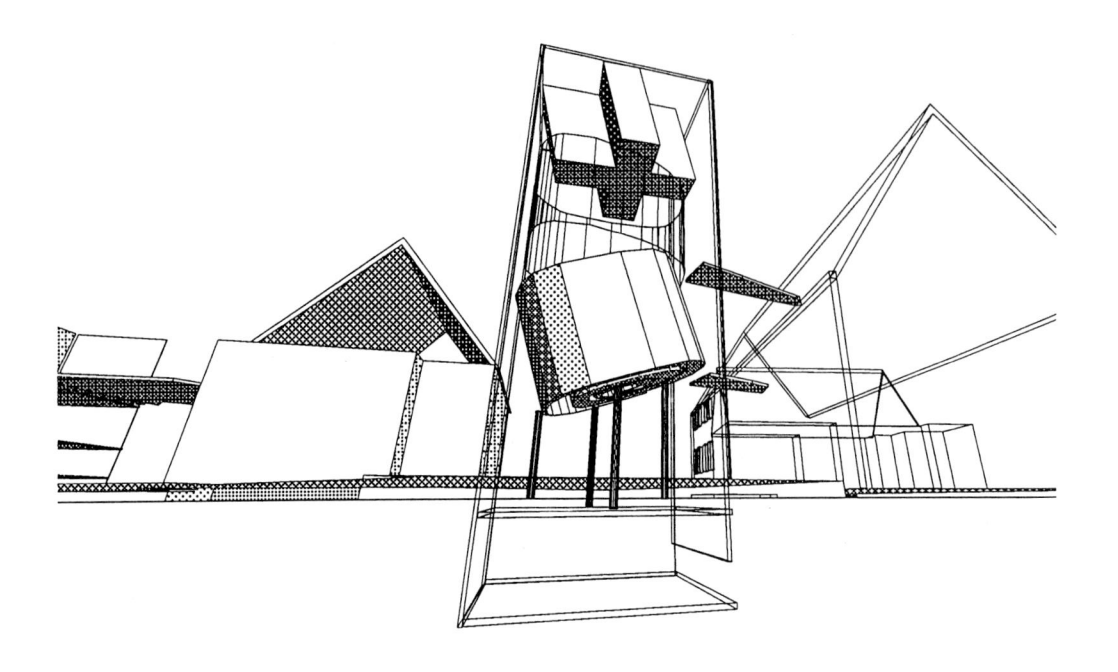

BILLIE STRAUSS
Kirchheim, Germany, 1992
Architecture/Interior Design: **Zaha Hadid**

Above: A campanile in Zaha Hadid's daring design is intended to become an inhabitable work of art.

Right: Architectural studies for the hotel project planned in South Germany.

Extreme hotel architecture will shortly be on view at the foot of the Schwäbische Alb, a range of hills in South Germany. There, for the past decade, the gallery owner Billie Strauss has run a wine cellar in a half-timbered house that is over 300 years old and was once the municipal hall of the Swabian village of Nabern. This successful businesswoman now plans to break out of pure half-timbered romanticism by having the adjacent building – which is also of historic interest – expanded into a small, exclusive hotel (rather than restored as an antique) by Zaha Hadid, an Iraqi-British avant-garde architect. In the architect's plans the rooms are laid out as models of her dynamic modern interior design. The ground plans are distorted and the internal walls skewed. On the outside, too, the London-based designer draws attention to the bold combination of avant-garde architecture and historic fabric by placing a glass campanile between the two old buildings, though this will not rise above the roof-ridge of the original farm. Here her architectural vocabulary, insisting on elementary forms, is to be celebrated as a work of art.

Within the steel scaffold of the glazed tower, four room-shaped structures are stacked one upon another, displaying Hadid's architectural language – her hallmark – to the outside world. The floor plans of these small guest-rooms are as varied as the forms they represent – cross, spiral, star and ellipse. A bridge links the tower to the original barn, which is also extended.

That there is a demand for such eccentric hotel concepts even in the provinces has been demonstrated by some projects already realized, such as Pflaums Posthotel in Pegnitz, Germany, where modern design, contrasting with another half-timbered house which is also over three centuries old, has proved wholly successful (see page 38).

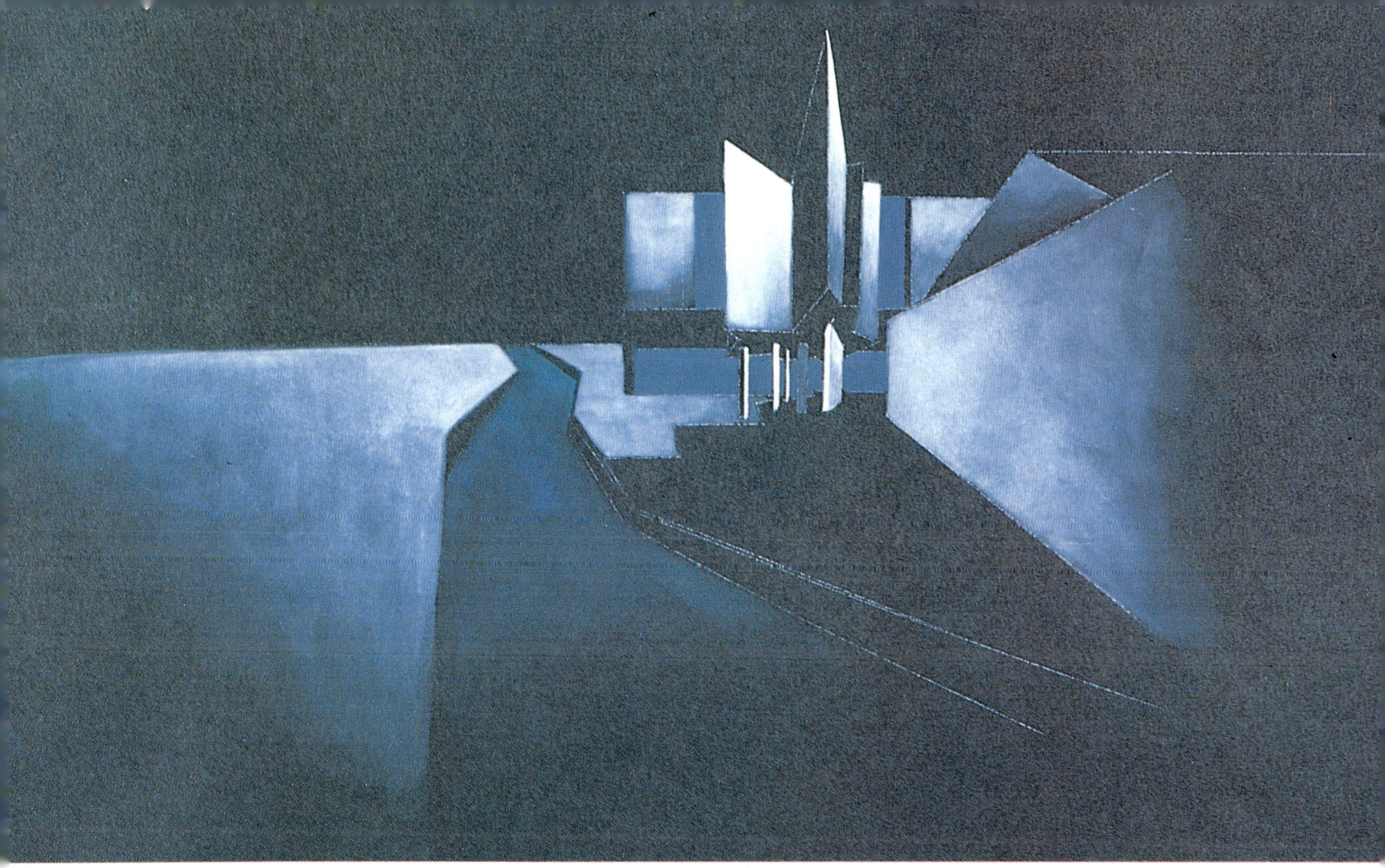
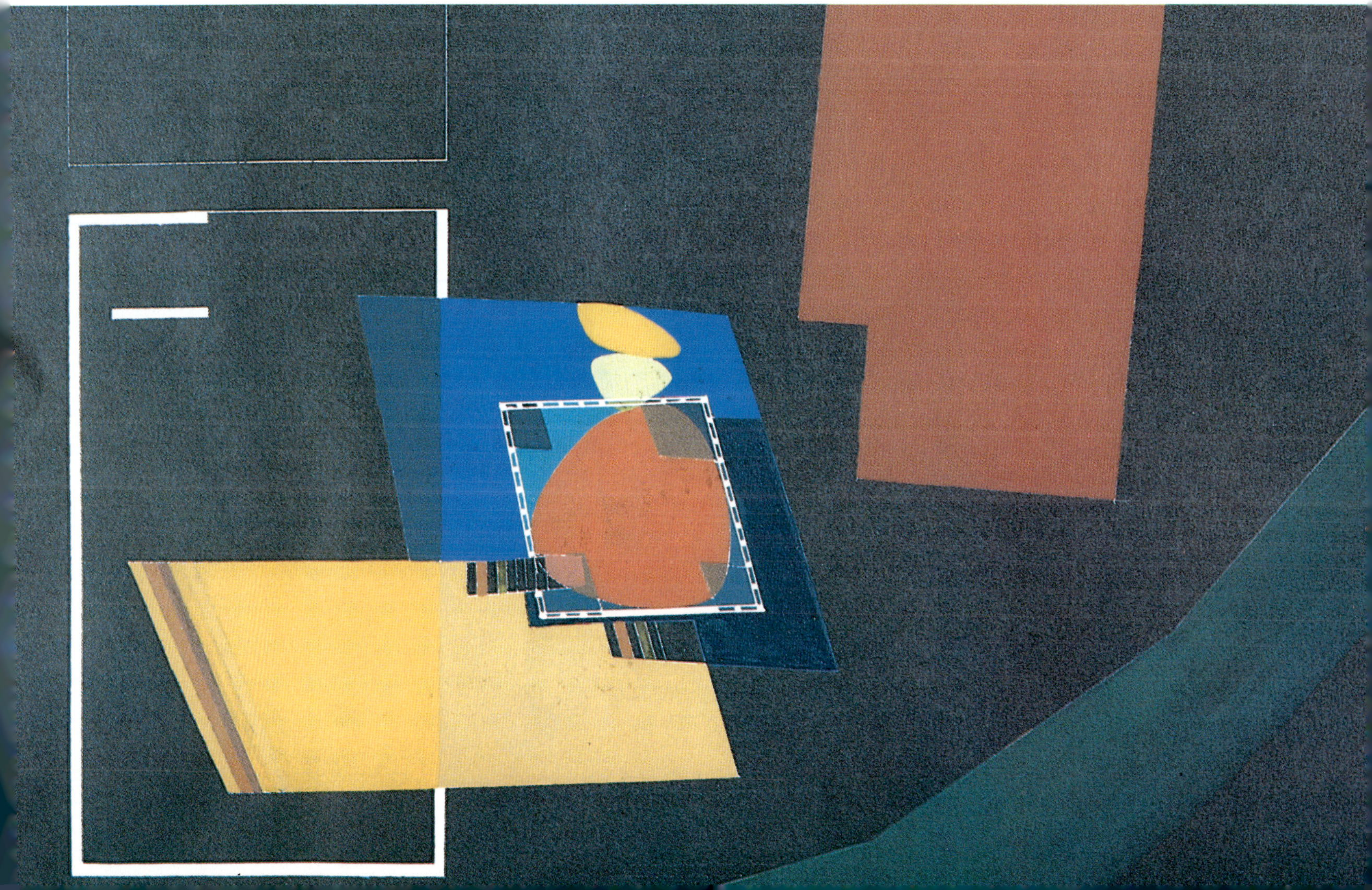

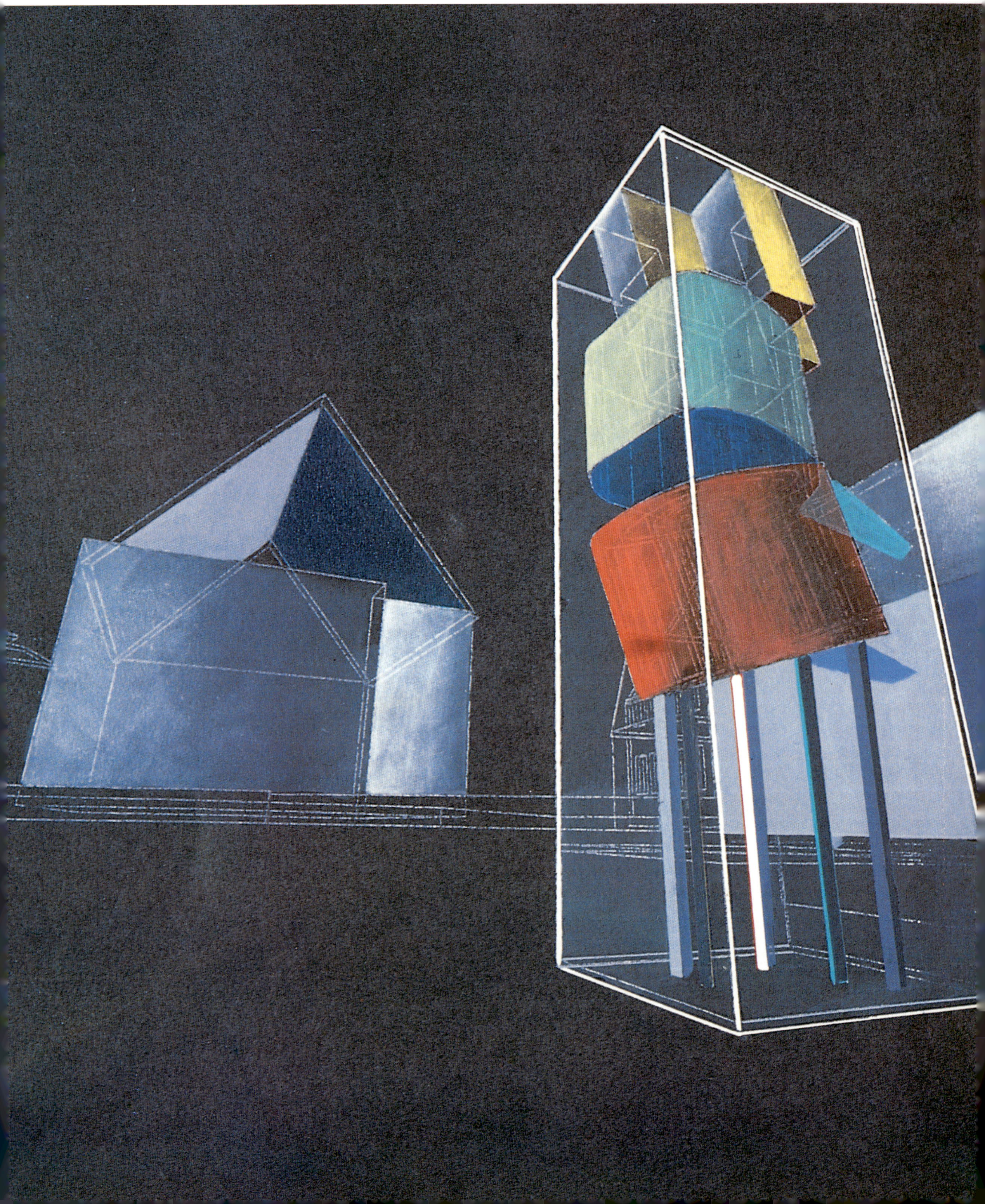

Left: To signal the bold combination of avant-garde architecture and historic fabric, Zaha Hadid has placed a campanile between the two old buildings; it will not rise above the roof-ridge of the old farmhouse.

Below right: A side view of the campanile.

Below and bottom: Ground plans of the star-shaped and cross-shaped hotel apartments.

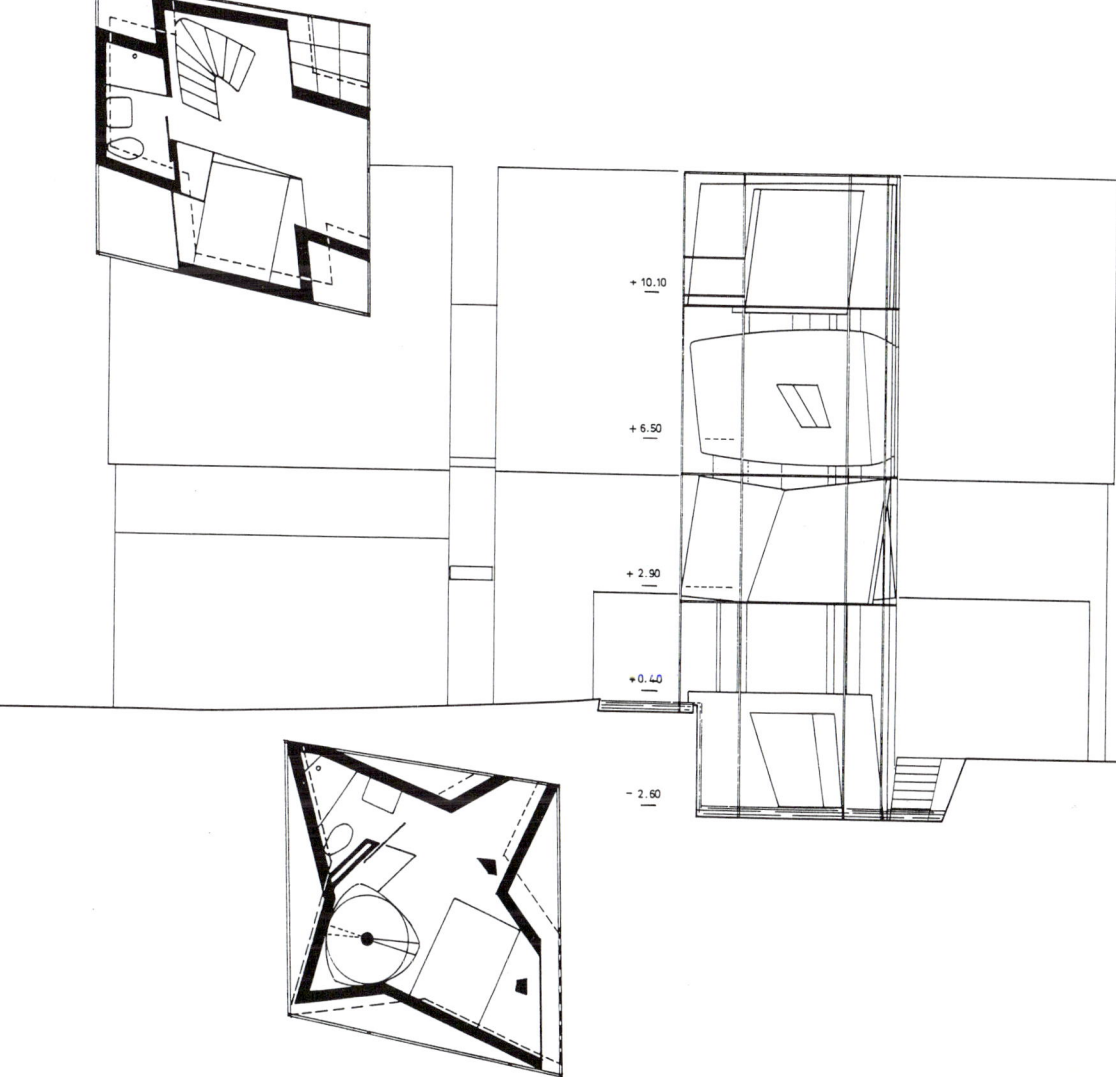

SPREEHOTEL TREPTOW
Berlin, Germany, 1990
Architecture: **Gottfried Böhm**

Above: When planning a hotel complex in a recreation area on the outskirts of what was once East Berlin, the architect tried to achieve a harmonious blending of nature and architecture.

Right: The architect's drawing provides for a rotunda-shaped central building with eight others, also circular, housing the guest-rooms.

Among the foremost building tasks in Berlin, now that the city has once more become a focus of economic activity in the wake of German unification, are hotel projects, which have to cater to a growing stream of business visitors. In what was formerly the eastern sector of the metropolis there is also a need for urban revival and for the regrading and upgrading of sites. It is in this context that one should view the commission, given by a West German investor to the office of Gottfried Böhm, to design a new hotel in the traditional recreation area of East Berlin beside the River Spree, between Treptower Park and the Plänterwald. The site has a stock of old trees that merit preservation, and it was stipulated that any building erected on it must be confined roughly to the proportions of an earlier restaurant that was much frequented by city-dwellers out for the day. The intention was to preserve the site's traditional role as a popular gastronomic resort, even within the context of a rather more upmarket hotel complex.

Böhm's architectural design, with its round pavilion form, resembles a solitaire that blends with the tall treetops in which it is set. The complex, approximately 18 metres in height, comprises a small round hall and eight guest-houses, also circular and grouped freely around the main building. Walkways link each floor to the hall, which forms a generous, transparent centre, measuring 500 square metres, and is used as a foyer and a venue for functions. The restaurants and conference rooms are on the ground floor. The predominantly glass façades of the buildings form a chameleon-like skin that takes on the varying colours of nature. The roof landscape exploits the interplay of trees and architecture and the formal affinity between them. Shell-like constructions overarch the hall and the guest towers. Views between the buildings, mirror images and intermediate spaces can be seen through the glass shell of the hall.

On each of the four upper floors of the guest accommodation, eight rooms are grouped around a central access area. The Spreehotel Treptow has 256 double rooms, each with 35 square metres of floorspace. The flower-shaped plan of the floors produces unexpectedly satisfying room shapes and actually facilitates their functional arrangement. The standardization of the architecture, which was achieved despite the apparently loose layout of the hotel, and its expressive, organic, sculptural quality allows for the use of prefabricated elements and thus contributes significantly to the economics of the project.

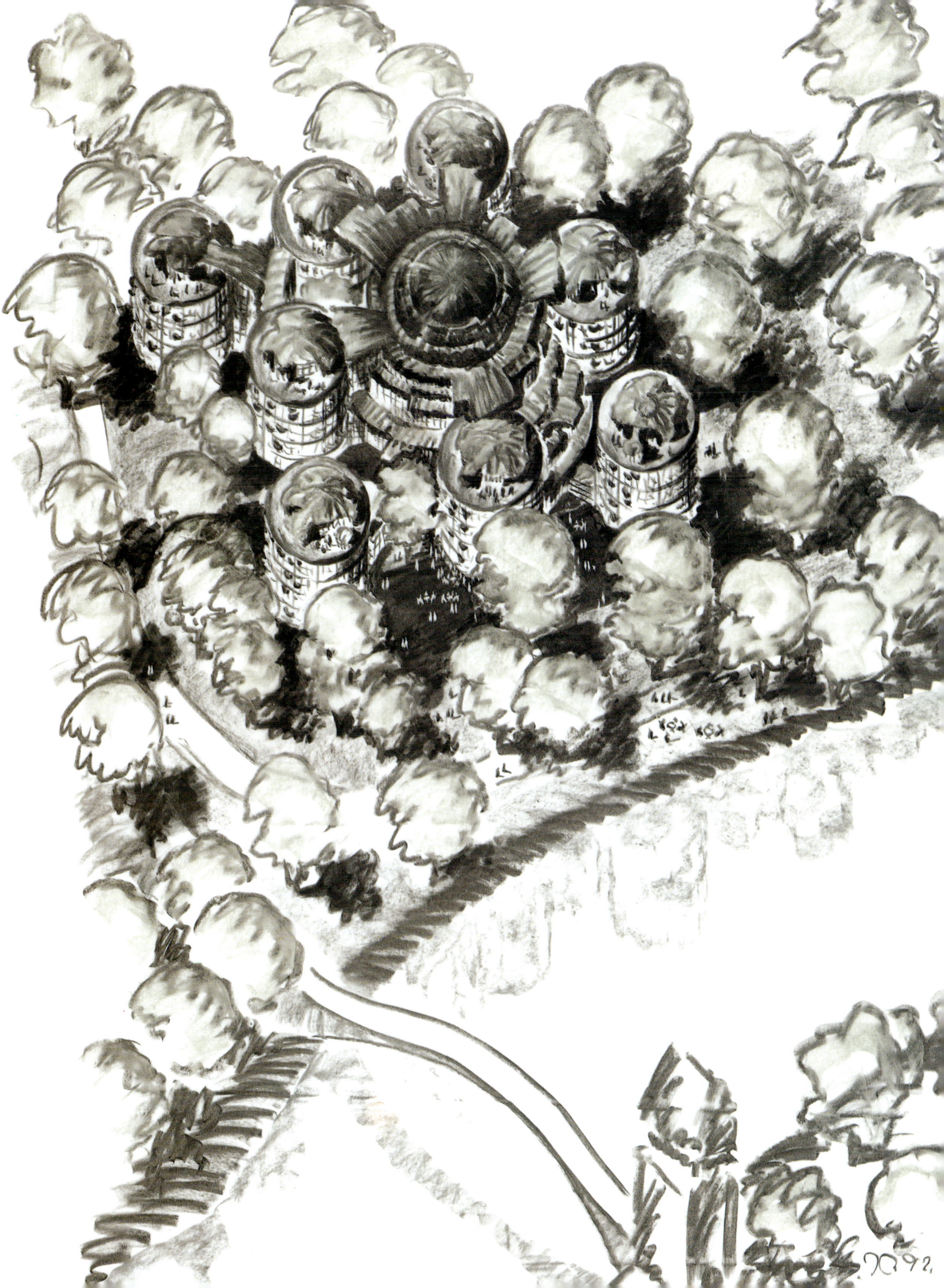

Left: Lido architecture for the Japanese Pacific coast: sketches for the Ocean hotel by Aldo Rossi.

THE OCEAN
Chikura, Japan, 1990
Architecture: **Aldo Rossi/Morris Adjmi**

One has the feeling of being transported to the Italian coast. It is the thirties, war is a long way off, and the Duce is still powerful. Aldo Rossi's design for the Ocean hotel exudes the spirit of Mediterranean modernism – holiday architecture from the days when mass tourism was in its infancy. But the invocation of a past era is intended for the Japanese present. There is a plan to build a bridge across the bay of Tokyo, linking the metropolis with the prefecture of Chiba, and a large number of new building projects are emerging on the coast, which will then be more accessible.

Among these is Rossi's project in the little fishing town of Chikura. The wedge-shaped building, occupying a long, narrow strip of land by the sea, is 100 metres in length, and the floors have a maximum width of 13 metres. The repetitive rows of windows in the yellow façade are interrupted on the landward side by a huge, white, central structure and two vertical sections, also white, which house the lifts. Access to the building is through the main entrance in the middle. The building, which is crowned by two golden balls, gives the future lido of Chikura a landmark that will generate many postcards. Towards the beach, along the sloping edge of the site, the base of the building becomes visible. Here the central structure has the green cross-girders that are typical of Rossi (and have already been overdone in his design for the façade of the Duca di Milano hotel in Milan). The architect's signature is also unmistakable at the narrow end of the building, where a spiral fire escape is concealed in a voluminous white column.

Each floor has fourteen rooms. The middle section is occupied by maisonette suites. The seaview is reserved for the residents; corridors run along the landward side. On the ground floor there are to be places for eating and drinking including a restaurant, a bar, a coffee shop and a beach terrace. As the sea is polluted, the roof with its pergola and swimming pool offers a sensible alternative to guests who are keen on bathing.

Whether this hotel will ever be built is in the lap of the gods, as is the fate of many other prestige projects by European architects in the wake of the crisis in the Japanese property market. It is therefore not certain whether Rossi's promise to arriving guests, which he wanted to inscribe on a bronze tablet, will ever reach them. The inscription was to read: "Whoever enters this house will be happy forever."

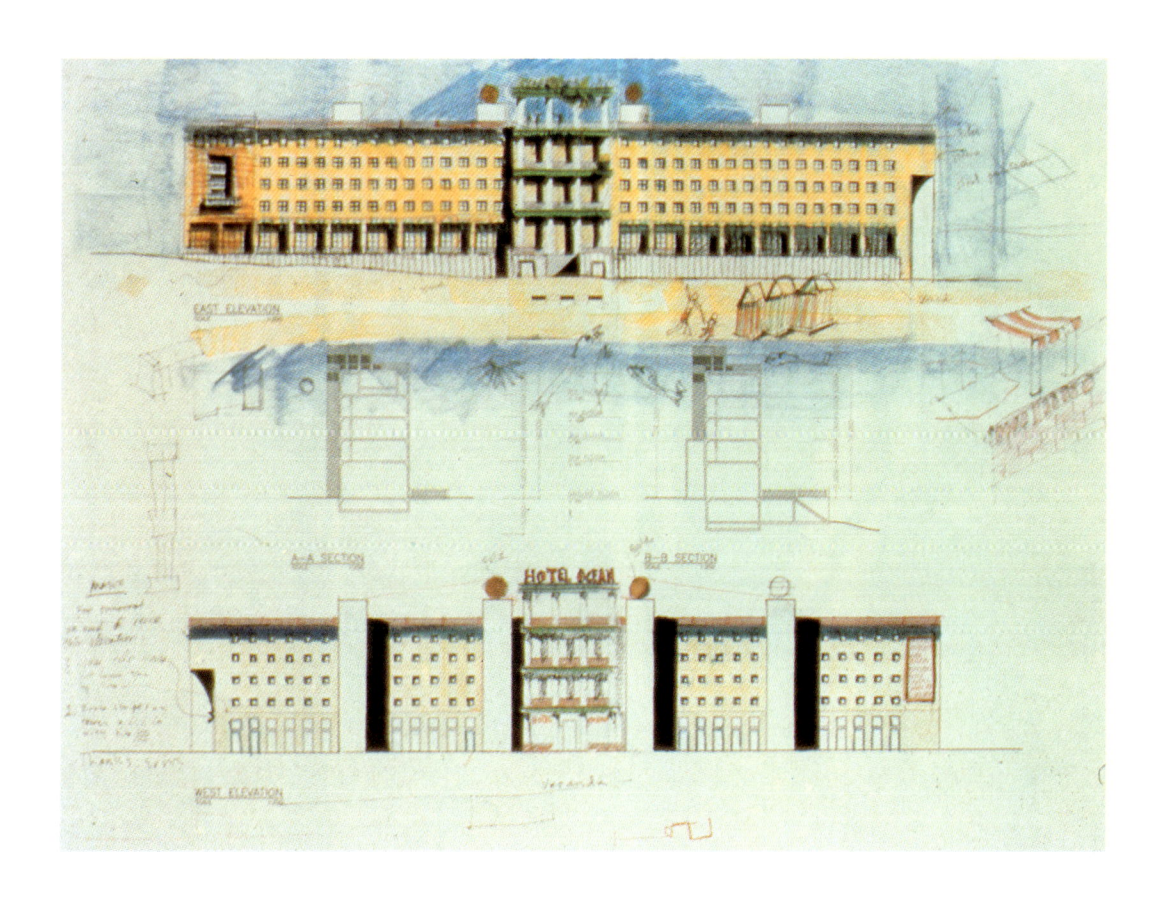

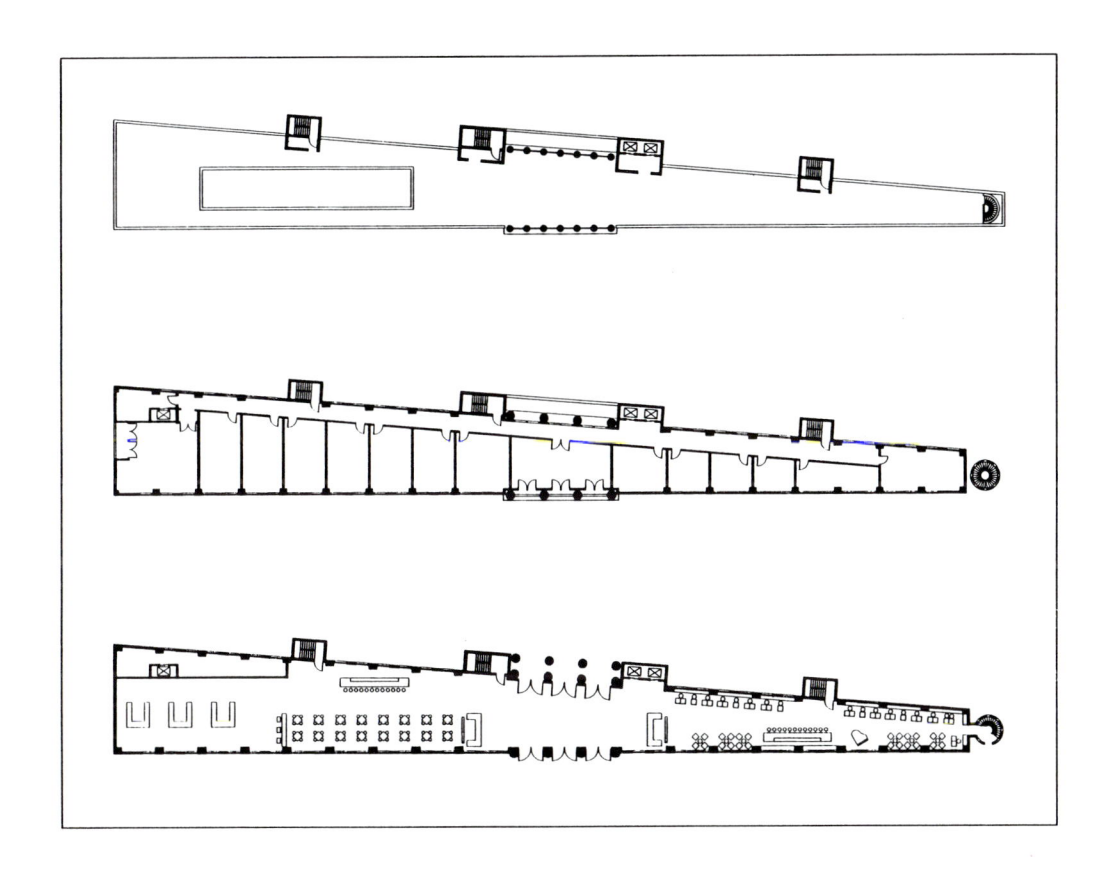

Above: The 100-metre yellow façade with its white, gold-crowned central structure rises to a roof garden. Behind the red balustrade there is a swimming pool.

Left: The wedge-shaped ground plan leaves space for 14 rooms on each floor and for two-floor suites in the middle section. The ground floor is reserved for restaurants.

233

Left: The inner courtyard of the new complex in the centre of Kuala Lumpur is roofed by glass domes (not seen in the model).

CENTRAL COURT
Kuala Lumpur, Malaysia, 1992
Architecture: **Ettore Sottsass, Johanna Grawunder**

On a dreary car park between the Chinese market and the busy embankment in the Malaysian capital Kuala Lumpur, private investors are planning a new popular quarter. Many old Chinese houses having been pulled down and new buildings hastily erected, a new kind of thinking is beginning to take root among town planners and investors in south-east Asia. The Malaysian Central Market Development Corporation has therefore engaged the Milanese architect Ettore Sottsass to explore new kinds of land use that will take the former character of the quarter into account.

Sottsass's imaginative design pays due heed to Asian tradition, envisaging a complex that will amount to a collage of popular architectural forms entered through a "Gate of Welcome". The whole area will be utilized in the manner of an old business quarter and will contain shops, a supermarket, restaurants, bars and a three-star hotel with 70 rooms and two large suites on the roof of the complex.

Since the triangular site has one side facing the river and another bordering on the Chinese market, where there was once a hotchpotch of Chinese shop buildings, the Milanese architects took their inspiration from the local tradition of building with small components. In keeping with this local style they evolved an intricate conglomeration of houses on supports, open verandahs, narrow passages, flights of steps and houses piled one on top of another. In terms of town planning, this modern jumble, reminiscent of a small town, will be held together by a triangular piazza. In conformity with the Mahommedan influence in the country, it will be covered by a mosque-like roof structure, involving numerous domes, to protect it from the monsoon and the heat.

The hotel is entered at ground level and the accommodation floors reached by lift. Its design is deliberately simple and in tune with national traditions. Hence, apart from the obligatory TV and video room, no areas are reserved solely for hotel guests. Restaurants and bars are open to the public, so that the guests do not find themselves in a ghetto situation, as they can in big western-style hotels. It was stipulated that the simple structural forms should be such as could be handled without difficulty by local craftsmen. In keeping with the national religion the architecture took on a Moorish-Mahommedan aspect in forms and materials. The piazza is laid out with coloured tiles like the courtyard of a mosque.

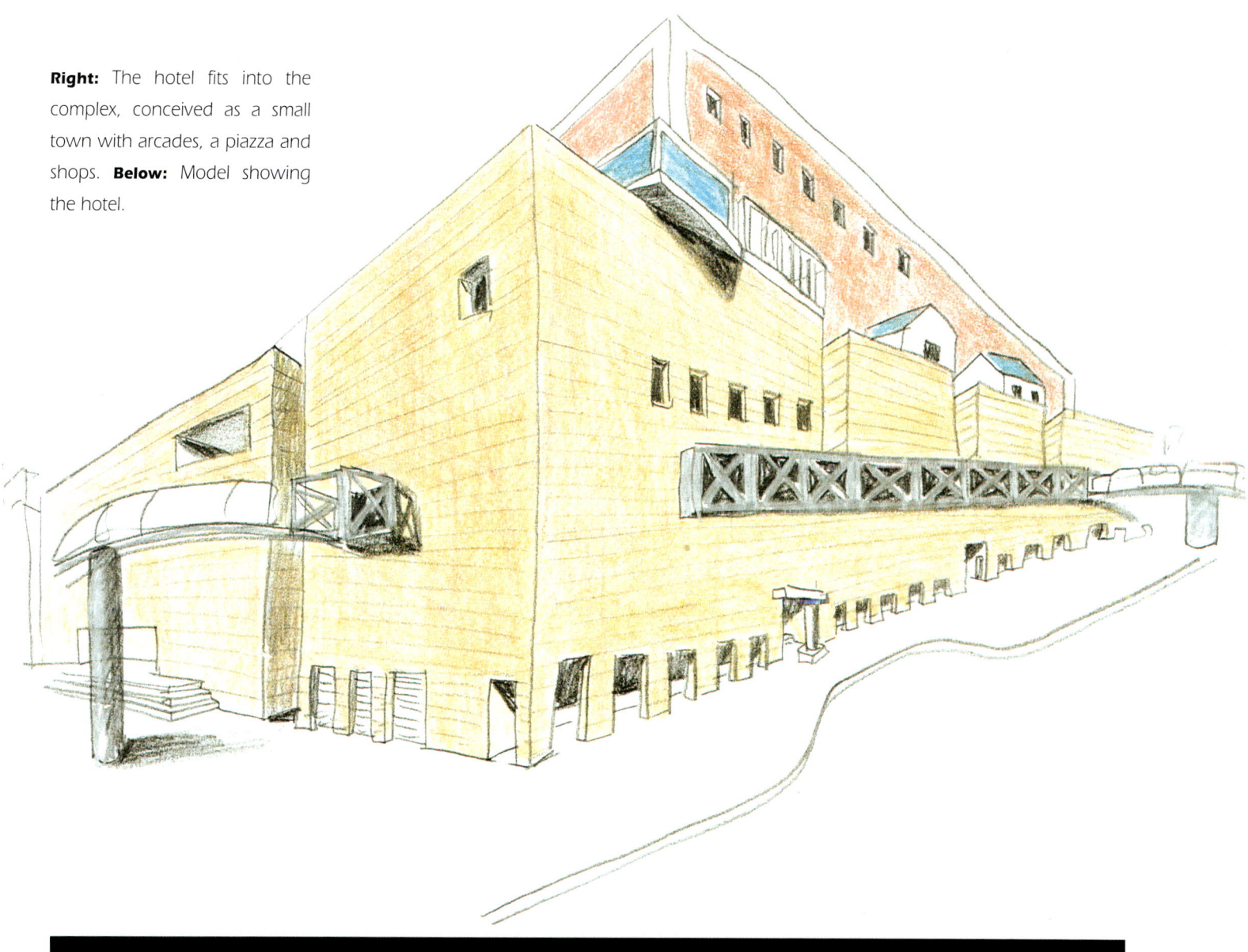

Right: The hotel fits into the complex, conceived as a small town with arcades, a piazza and shops. **Below:** Model showing the hotel.

235

Below right: The hotel rooms occupy the upper floors of one wing of the three-sided block. Bars and restaurants are located outside it, to encourage the guest to join in the public life of the quarter.

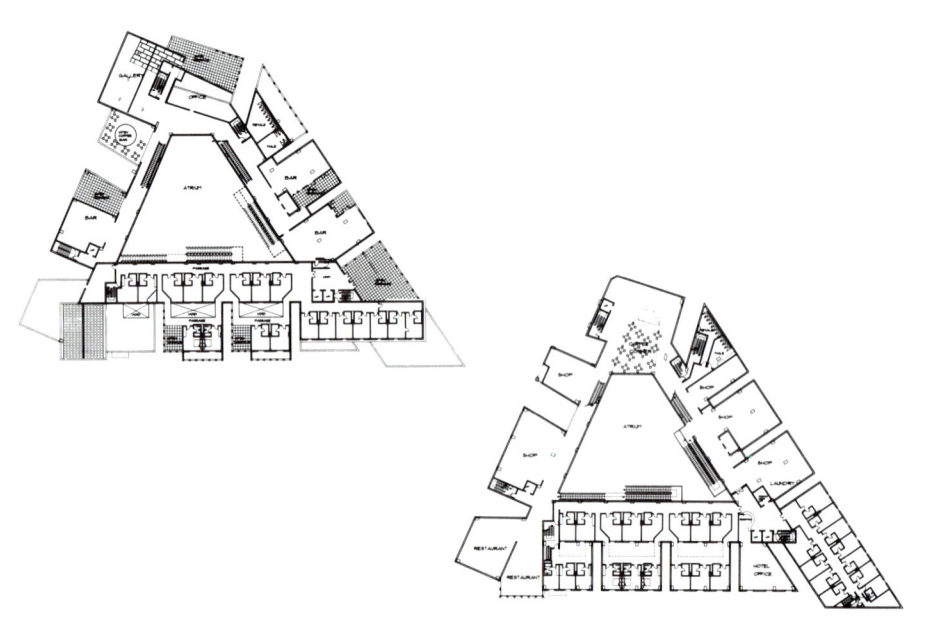

Right and below: Façade designs by Johanna Grawunder for the inner walls of the piazza. The Moorish influence is clear and accords with the Muslim tradition of Malaysia.

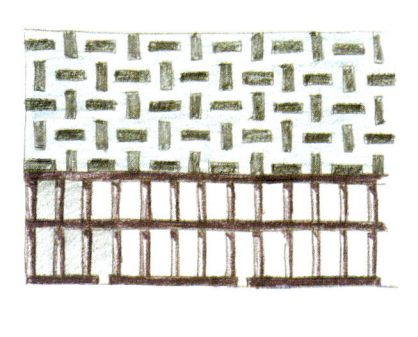

237

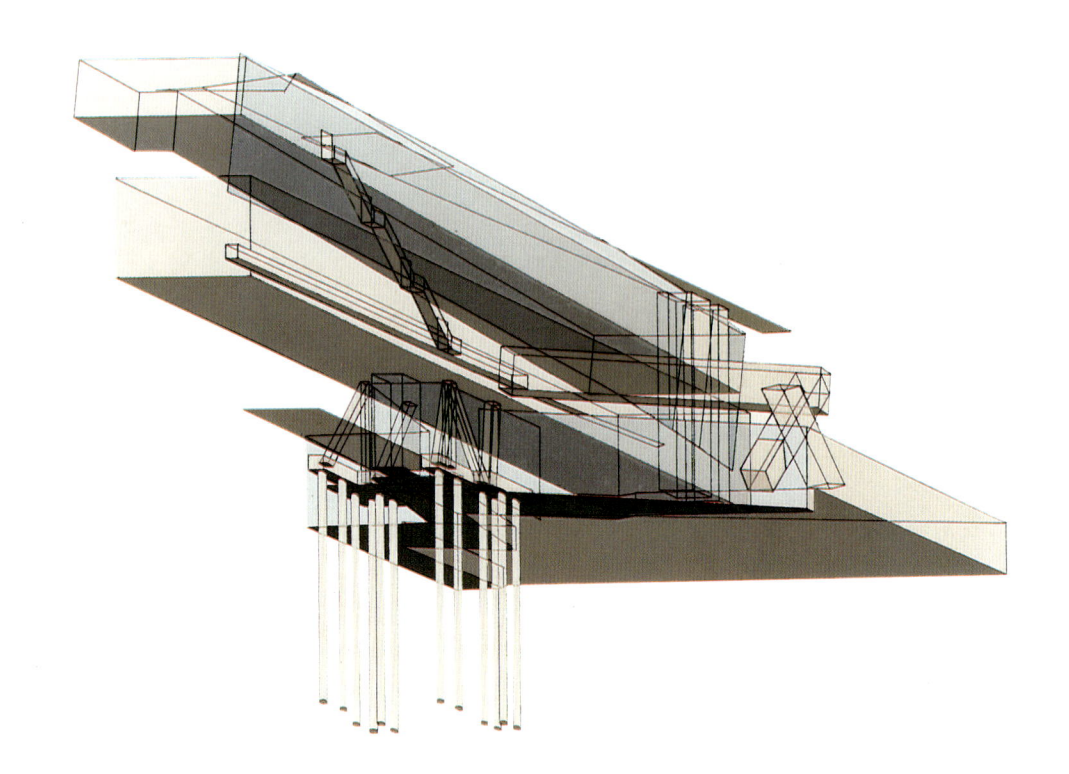

Above: Model of the hotel near Vienna planned by Coop Himmelblau. The project is to be built on the cantilever principle, arching over a lake.

GARTENHOTEL ALTMANNSDORF
Vienna, Austria, 1988/90
Architecture: **Coop Himmelblau**

It seems to be the fate of Austrian leaders of the architectural avant-garde that whatever they design for Vienna is seldom realized. Hence Coop Himmelblau, in spite of their international reputation, have to resign themselves to the role of mythical outsiders, though one of the partners, Wolf D. Prix, has for a long time held master classes at Vienna University. Even the project for extending and redesigning the existing Gartenhotel Altmannsdorf is still at the planning stage, and there is no knowing when work will begin.

When a competition was held for the project, Coop Himmelblau's design won first prize. It involves using the cantilever principle to build a 30-metre-long steel construction that will contain several floors and project over the lake in front of the site. This deconstructivist form, which combines different interpenetrating levels and lines of force, is intended to house 50 guest-rooms, a restaurant, a conservatory, a fitness centre and conference rooms. The total floorspace will amount to 3,225 square metres. The structure will be carried by three foundation supports of considerable depth, and the result will be a building that appears to defy the laws of gravity, a configuration that frees itself from the shore and lifts itself, as it were, over the water – more a technological construct than a haven of hospitality.

The commission includes the interior architecture and even the furnishing. Coop Himmelblau took advantage of this rare chance to design a total work of art in order to produce simple interiors that are nonetheless surprising in their spatial effects and demonstrate the innovatory qualities of the team of Prix and Helmut Swiczinsky – qualities that are at present little known because they are generally not much in demand. The completion of this project – which is of fairly marginal importance for the career of the Viennese architects – would be significant as a testimony to the times, if only because it offers the first opportunity to realize an architectural and furnishing design by Coop Himmelblau that is specified down to the smallest detail. The client, a local hotel company, would of course have to show more courage than other Viennese clients to date. For the architects, who suffered a painful setback when the city authorities reneged on a firm commission for a spectacular redesigning of the Ronacher Theatre, the daring little hotel by the lake at Altmannsdorf might be some slight compensation.

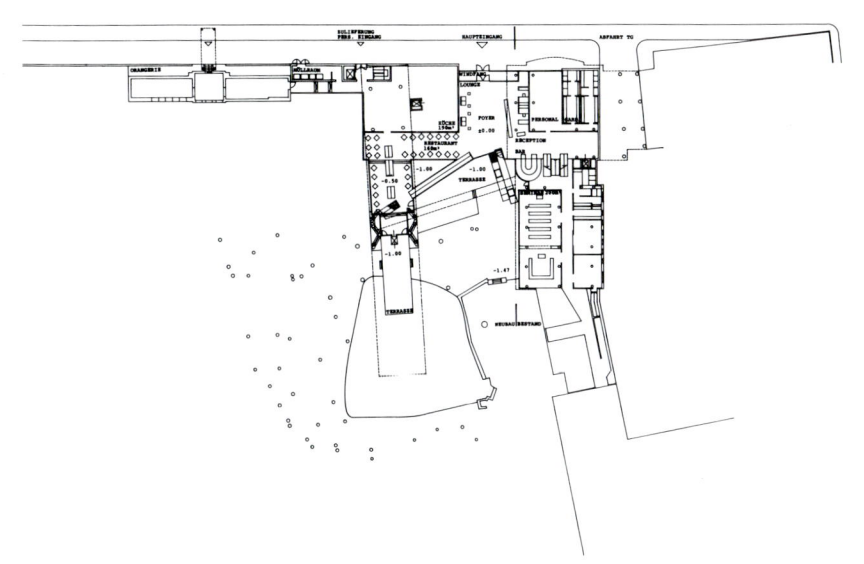

Above: Model of a hotel room. The architects had the rare opportunity also to determine the design of the furniture.

Above: The ground plan of the whole hotel. **Right:** A section drawing of the new building and the existing structure.

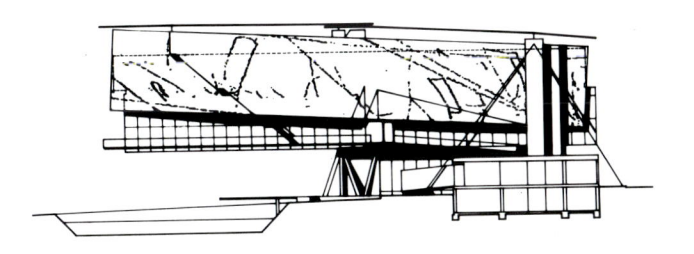

239

ARCHITECTS AND DESIGNERS

ADIEU NEW YORK DESIGN,
KAISER-FRIEDRICH-RING 3,
6200 WIESBADEN,
GERMANY.
Adieu New York Design was founded in Wiesbaden in 1986 by the interior architect Dieter Brell and the artist Leif Trenkler (both born in 1960) as a planning office. After an apprenticeship as a cabinet-maker Brell qualified at the technical college in Wiesbaden. Trenkler studied at the art academies in Düsseldorf and Frankfurt, and after initial furniture collections in his own right, was commissioned to design fair stands and hotels. The company's interior design projects include Kelly's Hotel in Bensheim, Germany (1992).

ARC+,
18 RUE LIONEL TERRAY,
74000 ANNECY,
FRANCE.
ARC+ was founded in Annecy by the architect and hotel specialist Michel Couasnon (born in 1937). With the Geneva planning firm SISS, which has existed since 1980 and is also managed by him, he carried out the revitalization of the lake hotel The Imperial Palace at Annecy. Born in Paris, Couasnon graduated in 1956 from the hotel college of Thonon, then studied at the school of tourism in Nice. He studied business management at Heidelberg and from 1960 to 1971 ran restaurants and hotels in Germany and Spain. At the same time he studied building, and as a government adviser was later responsible for the building of new hotels in Senegal. With SISS Couasnon has realized projects in the Middle East and Europe. Apart from restaurants and hotels he has also worked on bank, office and housing projects.

ARQUITECTONICA,
2151 LEJEUNE ROAD, SUITE 300,
CORAL GABLES, FLORIDA 33134,
USA.
Arquitectonica is an architect's office founded in Miami in 1977 by Laurinda Spear and her husband Bernardo Fort-Brescia. Fort-Brescia was born in Lima, studied at Princeton and Harvard until 1975, and then taught at the University of Miami. Spear is from Miami and studied at Brown University and Columbia. She was awarded the Rome Prize for architecture in 1978. Arquitectonica has become internationally known for its striking projects which, while adhering to the modernist canon, are unprecedented in their colourfulness and the surreal combination of structural volumes and subtle alienation effects. Important buildings include housing complexes such as The Palace, The Imperial and The Atlantis, the North Dade court building in Miami, the head office of the Banco del Credito del Peru in Lima, the Rio shopping centre in Atlanta and the Center for Innovative Technology near Washington.

ALFREDO ARRIBAS ARQUITECTOS,
BALMES 345, 1–2A,
08006 BARCELONA,
SPAIN.
Alfredo Arribas was born in Barcelona in 1954 and studied at the Escuela Tecnica Superior Arquitectura, where he is now professor. Since 1982 he has been president of the Spanish interior design organization (INFAD). Important projects are the night clubs Velvet Bar (with Miguel Morte) and Torres de Avila (with Javier Mariscal) in Barcelona and the disco/restaurant complex Barna Crossing in the Il Palazzo hotel, Japan. For the 1991 Frankfurt Book Fair Arribas designed the presentation of the Spanish publishing houses. In 1992 he undertook the artistic design for the opening ceremonies of the Olympic Games in Barcelona.

ATLANDIA DESIGN,
3260 SOUTH INDUSTRIAL ROAD,
LAS VEGAS, NEVADA 89109,
USA.
Atlandia Design is the name of the planning section of the hotel firm Mirage Resorts in Las Vegas. The chief architect Joel Bergman (born in 1936) realized among other projects the Golden Nugget casino hotels in Atlantic City, Las Vegas and Laughlin (rebuilt or extended), and The Mirage in Las Vegas. The latest project is the hotel-casino Treasure Island, due to open in Las Vegas in 1993. The chief interior architect with Atlandia is Roger P. Thomas, who was responsible for the design and furnishing of all the above-mentioned buildings.

GOTTFRIED BÖHM,
AUF DEM RÖMERBERG 25,
D-5000 COLOGNE 51,
GERMANY.
Gottfried Böhm, son of the architect Dominikus Böhm (known for expressionist church buildings), was born at Offenbach in 1920. He spent his school years in Cologne, then studied architecture and sculpture in Munich. In 1948 he married the architect Elisabeth Böhm. In 1955 he took over the management of his father's architectural practice in Cologne, where he now works with his three sons Stephan, Peter and Markus. He was appointed Professor of Urban Planning at Aachen University in 1963. In 1986 he won the Pritzker Prize. Böhm's sensitive architectural language, developing the expressive origins of modernism, and the superb contextuality of his designs brought him early international recognition. Important buildings include the Pilgrimage Church at Neviges, the head office of Züblin in Stuttgart, Saarbrücken Castle (restoration), the head offices of the Deutsche Bank and Arbed in Luxembourg, the Maritim Hotel in Cologne (with Kraemer Sieverts & Partner and Stefan Schmitz), the library in Mannheim and the University of Bremerhaven.

YVES BOUCHARLAT,
2 PLACE DU PETIT COLLÈGE,
69245 LYON,
FRANCE.
Yves Boucharlat was born in 1950 in Lyon, where he took his architect's diploma in 1974. From 1976 he worked in partnership with Pierre Vurpas and Claude Vigan, and in 1987 set up his own office. He works mainly on hotel and restaurant projects. After the Cour des Loges in Lyon he worked on the Parc des Loges in Mégève, L'Aubergade in Puymirol, the Hotel des Berges in Illhäusern, the Prunier, Le Taillevent and Paul Bocuse restaurants in Paris and other projects. The special quality of Boucharlat's interior design lies in the surprising sensitivity with which he harmonizes contemporary stylistic elements with historic structural fabrics.

BRANSON COATES ARCHITECTURE,
23 OLD STREET,
LONDON EC1V 9HL,
UK.
Branson Coates Architecture was founded in 1985 by Nigel Coates, who studied at Nottingham University and the Architectural Association (AA), and Doug Branson, who graduated from the AA in 1975. Nigel Coates was born in Malvern, England, in 1949. He has scored his greatest successes in Japan with his narrative architecture (Narrative Architecture Today – NATO). In the Far East this "architectural narrator" is regarded as a leading representative of European architecture. As well as working on architectural projects with Branson Coates Architecture, Coates creates furniture designs for Poltronova and SCP. During the great Japanese property boom, Branson Coates Architecture won numerous commissions to design bars, restaurants and shops. Their projects include: a house (1985) and shop (1986) for Jasper Conran, Silver jewellery shop in London (1987) and shops for Katharine Hamnett and Jigsaw. Projects in Japan include: the Metropole restaurant (1985), Bohemia Jazz Club (1986) and Caffe Bongo (1987) in Tokyo, Noah's Ark restaurant in Sapporo (1988), the Marittimo hotel in Otaru (1989), the Nishi-Azabu Building in Tokyo (1990), the Taxim restaurant bar/club, Istanbul (1991), a tower for the Nishi-Azabu Building and a restaurant and cardroom at the Mayflower Golf Club, Tokyo.

COOP HIMMELBLAU,
SEILERSTÄTTE 16/11A,
1010 VIENNA,
AUSTRIA.
Coop Himmelblau was founded in Vienna in 1968 by the architects Wolf Dieter Prix (born in 1942) and Helmut Swiczinsky (born in 1944). Their attempts to enlarge the concept of architecture through numerous visionary projects quickly secured them a place in the international avant-garde. They are among the protagonists of deconstructivism and were represented in the "Deconstructivism" exhibition at the New York Museum of Modern Art in 1988. In 1993 a large exhibition was devoted to their works at the Pompidou Centre in Paris. As well as their Vienna office they have another studio in Los Angeles. Prix is Professor of Architecture in Vienna, where he holds master classes. The practice's projects include: Funder Factory 1&3, St. Veit/Glan, Carinthia, the Ronacher Theatre, Vienna, an administrative and shopping complex in St. Pölten and Open House, Malibu.

DESMOND BROOKS INTERNATIONAL,
P.O. BOX 888,
SOUTHPORT, QUEENSLAND 4215,
AUSTRALIA.
Desmond Brooks International has operated since 1982 as an architectural firm on the Gold Coast of Queensland, Australia. For 25 years its founder Desmond Brooks was the head of Media Five Group in the United States, working mainly in Hawaii. An Australian by birth, he now runs one of the largest and most diversified planning offices in the country, with branches in Brisbane, Sydney and Melbourne. The Mirage resorts at Port Douglas and on the Gold Coast, realized for the media and tourist concern Quintex (which went into liquidation in 1989), are the outstanding examples of Brooks' concept of architecture, which relates contextually to landscape and regional building styles.

WOLFGANG DÖRING,
DÜSSELDORFER STR. 155,
D-4000 DÜSSELDORF 11,
GERMANY.
Wolfgang Döring was born in Berlin in 1934 and was educated in Düsseldorf until 1954. He studied at the Technical University of Munich and graduated from the Technical University of Karlsruhe. He worked with Max Bill, Egon Eiermann and Paul Schneider-Esleben before setting up his own office in Düsseldorf in 1964. Since 1973 he has held a chair in design and building construction at Aachen University. An early champion of industrialized construction procedures, he wrote a book on the subject, *Perspektiven einer Architektur* (1970). He later rejected standardized modern building and its destructive effects on towns, and cultivated an architecture committed to classical proportions and contextuality. He has realized projects in Germany, France, Saudi Arabia, Italy and Spain, including not only commercial buildings, but villas, apartment blocks and the Rolandsburg hotel in Düsseldorf. His first high-rise building, the Eurocenter in Neuss, is at present being planned.

MARIE-CHRISTINE DORNER,
16 RUE NOTRE DAME DE LORETTE,
75009 PARIS,
FRANCE.
Marie-Christine Dorner was born in Strasbourg in 1960 and belongs to the younger generation of French furniture and interior designers. She first worked in Japan, where she designed the La Bohème bar in Yokohama and furniture for Edition Idée. She then made a career for herself as an interior architect and furniture designer in France and Spain. Her conversion of the Paris hotel D'Isly brought her international fame. In 1989 she was commissioned to design the interior of La Comédie Française restaurant in the Palais Royal, Paris. She has designed furniture and objects for Casas, Scarabat, Baccarat and Artelano.

RENA DUMAS ARCHITECTURE INTÉRIEURE,
5 RUE DU MAIL,
75002 PARIS,
FRANCE.
Rena Dumas studied at the École National Supérieure des Métiers d'Art in Paris, graduating in 1961. As an interior architect she worked until 1964 in various teams on the Athens Hilton and other projects. From 1965 she began to work independently on designs for apartments and shops. Between 1968 and 1970, as the manager of Robert Anxionnat, a firm of interior architects, she worked on the Paris office of Time-Life. In 1971 she founded her own firm, RDAI. She is responsible for the interior design of Hermès boutiques throughout the world (her husband is the head of the Hermès empire). Her other projects include offices and banks in Paris and London, the public areas of exclusive residential developments, restaurants and two hotels – La Pergolese in Paris and the Seiyo Ginza in Tokyo. She is also involved in furniture and product design for Ercuis, Galerie Agora, Hermès, Fourniture and other companies.

PETER GLYNN-SMITH ASSOCIATES,
32 DUNCAN TERRACE,
LONDON N1 8BS,
UK.
Peter Glynn-Smith, born in 1932, studied art at the art college in Stoke-on-Trent and design at the Bartlett School of Architecture in London. He designed furniture and interiors for Laszlo Hoenig and Halliday's in Oxford and London until 1960, then spent three years in Los Angeles at the office of Welton Beckett, collaborating on hotel and airport projects. Charles Eames enrolled him in his team for the IBM pavilion at the New York World Exhibition. Since 1964 he has had his own design studio in London. He has been responsible for the interior architecture of numerous restaurants and hotels, including the Tower Hotel, the Embassy Hotel and the Sterling Heathrow in London, the Commodore in Paris, the Maritim in Gelsenkirchen, Germany and the Babylon in Amsterdam, and has designed furniture in collaboration with Rodney Kinsman.

MICHAEL GRAVES,
341 NASSAU STREET,
PRINCETON, NEW JERSEY 08540,
USA.
Michael Graves was born in Indianapolis in 1934, and studied at the universities of Cincinnatti and Harvard and at the American Academy in Rome. Since 1962 he has been a professor at Princeton, where he opened his own office in 1964. At first Graves was one of the "New York Five", along with Richard Meier, Charles Gwathmey, Peter Eisenman and John Hejduk – a group engaged in continuing the traditions of the Bauhaus and White Modernism. Switching abruptly to a classical repertoire, Graves became a protagonist of American postmodernism. Typical buildings are the Humana office building in Louisville and the Clos Pegase winery in the Napa Valley. His treatment of his themes became even more playful in the projects he undertook for the Disney concern: the head office in Burbank, the Dolphin and Swan hotels in Disneyworld, Florida and the New York hotel in Eurodisney near Paris. Graves is also a furniture and product designer, and has produced designs for Alessi, Vorwerk, Swid Powell, Arkitektura, WMF and others.

JOHANNA GRAWUNDER,
C/O SOTTSASS ASSOCIATI,
VIA BORGONUOVO 9,
20121 MILAN,
ITALY.
Johanna Grawunder was born in San Diego, California, in 1961 and graduated in architecture at California Polytechnic State University in 1984. In the same year she became assistant professor at California State University in Florence, where she has held a visiting professorship since 1985. In 1991 she was guest professor at the College of Arts in Berlin. She has worked with Sottsass Associati since 1985, and in 1989 became a partner. Exhibitions include "Nove" ceramic lamps (1987), "Memphis Luce" (1988), "Abet-Material Lights" (1988), "Marmorea" by Ultima Edizione (1988), Salviati (1989), "Sedia" by Promosedia (1989), "Cleto Munari Collection" (1991), "Woman in Design" (1991).

ZAHA M. HADID,
10 BOWLING GREEN LANE,
LONDON EC1,
UK.
Zaha M. Hadid was born in Baghdad in 1950. She rapidly became probably the best-known woman architect in the world, although she had realized hardly any

buildings. Her design drawings in the deconstructivist mode are among the boldest and most fascinating in contemporary architecture. She caused a furore with her generous, dynamic designs for Edra and Vorwerk. She studied at the Architectural Association in London under Rem Koolhaas and Elia Zenghelis and then worked at the Office for Metropolitan Architecture (OMA). Her designs became known partly through the Philip Johnson exhibition "Deconstructivist Architecture" (1988) in the Museum of Modern Art. Important designs include the "Wavy Back Sofa" (1988) for Edra and a fire station for Vitra (1991) in Weil am Rhein.

KONRAD L. HEINRICH,
ÄNNE-SCHULTE-STR. 22,
D-5000 COLOGNE 91,
GERMANY.
Konrad L. Heinrich was born in Berlin in 1937. From 1961 to 1964 he studied architecture at the Werkkunstschule, Cologne, and the Art College in Düsseldorf. Since 1984 he has had his own office in Cologne. His work chiefly involves the restoration of ancient monuments, including churches and secular buildings. In 1991 his exemplary planning of the Wasserturm Hotel in Cologne won him first prize in the competition for the decoration "Europa Nostra".

HIRSCH/BEDNER & ASSOCIATES,
909 WEST PEACHTREE STREET,
ATLANTA, GEORGIA 30309,
USA.
Hirsch/Bedner & Associates was founded by Howard Hirsch in 1964. It is now the world's biggest hotel design firm, with offices in Los Angeles, Atlanta, Hong Kong, Singapore and London, and numbers the Hyatt Group and many other top-category hotel chains among its clients. The firm offers a comprehensive range of services, from interior architecture and artistic consultancy to the sale and maintenance of projects. Altogether it has been responsible for over 300 hotels, including the Grand Hyatt in Hong Kong, the Conrad Hilton in Chicago, The White Swan in Canton and The Churchill in London.

STEVEN HOLL ARCHITECTS,
435 HUDSON STREET, 4TH FLOOR,
NEW YORK, NY 10014,
USA.
Steven Holl was born in 1947 and studied architecture in Seattle and Rome. After graduating from the University of Washington, he worked at the Architectural Association in London. In 1976 he set up his own practice in New York and soon attracted world-wide attention with his projects. Since 1981 he has been professor in the Department of Architecture at Columbia University, New York, and has taught at the universities of Syracuse, Seattle, Philadelphia and elsewhere. His buildings include a commercial and residential complex in Fukuoka, Japan, and the Dreamland Heights hotel in Seaside, Florida. In 1988 he won the competition for the American Memorial Library in Berlin. Holl's architecture, which develops the progressive modernist canon, has been the theme of exhibitions at the Walker Art Center, Minneapolis, and in Seattle and Japan.

REM KOOLHAAS,
OFFICE FOR METROPOLITAN ARCHITECTURE,
BOOMPJES 55,
3011 XB ROTTERDAM,
THE NETHERLANDS.
Rem Koolhaas was born in Rotterdam in 1944. Before studying architecture at the Architectural Association (AA) in London, he worked as a journalist and screen writer. He studied at Cornell University on a Harkness Scholarship between 1972 and 1973, and then at the Institute of Architecture and Urban Studies, New York. In 1974 he received the Progressive Award for a house designed jointly with Lucinda Spear. In 1978 he published a study of the effects of mass culture on architecture and city planning entitled *Delirious New York, a Retrospective Manifesto for Manhattan*. In London in 1975 he joined with Elia and Zoe Zenghelis and Madelon Vriesendorp in founding the *Office of Metropolitan Architecture (O.M.A.)*, which is concerned with both practical and theoretical problems of architecture and culture. As most of their commissions came from Holland – among them the extension of the parliament building in The Hague – O.M.A. moved to Rotterdam. Projects include a prison in Arnhem (1980-88), the city hall, The Hague (1987), The Netherlands Dance Theatre, The Hague (1987) and apartment blocks in Paris and Berlin. Works by Koolhaas were shown at the "Deconstructivism" exhibition at the Museum of Modern Art, New York, in 1988.

KRAEMER SIEVERTS & PARTNER,
WOLFENBÜTTELER STR. 45,
D-3300 BRAUNSCHWEIG,
GERMANY.
Kraemer Sieverts & Partner was originally founded in 1935 by the architect Friedrich Wilhelm Kraemer and has operated under its present name since 1975. In the context of post-war West German reconstruction the office soon became highly successful at planning large-scale projects in the field of school and government buildings. Kraemer Sieverts & Partner now has offices in Braunschweig, Cologne, Frankfurt and Magdeburg and is one of the largest and most competent architectural firms in Germany. Its speciality remains in the commercial and public sector. Important buildings include the DKV headquarters in Cologne, VEW headquarters in Dortmund, the Deutsche Bank in Düsseldorf, a ministry in Riyadh and the Maritim hotel in Cologne (with Gottfried Böhm).

LABORATORIO ASSOCIATI,
VIA VINCENZO MONTI 25,
20123 MILAN,
ITALY.
Laboratorio Associati is an architectural practice in Milan, founded in 1978 by Lorenzo Carmellini (born in 1940) and Rocco Magnoli (born in 1949). The practice, made up of architects and town planners, began to concentrate increasingly on interior design. Thanks to a style that relied on craftsman-like precision and perfectionist planning, Laboratorio Associati soon became the house architects of the fashion designer Gianni Versace, for whom they have designed more than 150 shops in the past 12 years. Adhering to the old architectural ideal of designing everything from the building to individual items of furniture, they have realized the following international projects: a winter resort village for 2,500 people in Japan, holiday villages for the Club Méditerrané in Italy and The Halkin hotel in London.

LAWTON & UMEMURA
Lawton & Umemura was a firm of architects working on commercial and hotel projects in Hawaii, its most notable project being the Hyatt Regency Waikoloa. It is no longer in business.

LEESE ROBERTSON FREEMAN DESIGNERS,
UNITS 1-4, FIRST FLOOR, ABERDEEN MARINA TOWERS,
8 SHUM WAN ROAD,
ABERDEEN, HONG KONG.
Leese Robertson Freeman Designers was originally founded in London by the architect Paul Leese and the interior architect George Freeman. They have now been joined by a third partner, Charles Robertson. Since 1980 another office has operated in Hong Kong under Leese's direction, designing interiors for a number of large hotel projects in the Far East, including the Shangri-La hotels in Peking, Bangkok, Penang and Jakarta. From the point of view of cost and opulence, their stylistic combination of traditional European hotel luxury and Asian features is best represented by the Island Shangri-La, Hong Kong.

CHRISTIAN LIAIGRE,
122 RUE DE GRENELLE,
75007 PARIS,
FRANCE.
Christian Liaigre is an interior architect and furniture designer born in Niort, Deux-Sèvres in 1943. Among the commissions undertaken by his Paris office are the design of boutiques, hotel layouts and museums, and the development of furniture collections. Large interior projects have included offices and a private residence for Kenzo, Paris, the Guanahani Hotel, Saint Barthelemy (French Antilles) and the renovation of the Villa Mallet Stevens, Paris. Current projects include the Lalique Museum in Kamakura, Japan, holiday villages for the Club Méditerranée in Africa, Greece and Bora Bora, the head office of Crédit Mutuel in Paris, and a housing project with 200 houses in Japan.

MANSER ASSOCIATES,
BRIDGE STUDIOS,
HAMMERSMITH BRIDGE,
LONDON W6 9DA,
UK.
Manser Associates was founded by the architect Michael Manser in 1961 as a planning office. Since 1983 Manser has been in partnership with Andrew Rogers, and in 1988 his son Jonathan became co-director of the firm. Manser was president of the Royal Institute of British Architects (RIBA) from 1983 to 1985. Working on the pragmatic principle that the client should be offered good modern architecture at a reasonable price, Manser Associates took on a large number of buildings and conversions – office projects, industrial projects, churches, schools and social housing. At the same time they have advised on the restoration and re-utilization of listed buildings. Important projects include the head office of London Regional Transport, a housing complex and marina in Sussex and the Sterling Hotel at Heathrow Airport.

MBM ARQUITECTES S.A.,
PLACA REIAL 18, PRAL
08002 BARCELONA,
SPAIN.
MBM Arquitectes – Josep Martorell (born in Barcelona in 1925), Oriol Bohigas (born in Barcelona in 1925), David Mackay (born in Eastbourne, Sussex, in 1933) and Albert Puigdomenech (born in Barcelona in 1944) – are important representatives of the "Escuela de Barcelona", who insist on constructive logic and lay stress on craftsmanship and traditional materials such as brick. Apart from historically significant residential buildings, the group was commissioned in 1986 to design the Olympic village, a task of great importance in terms of urban planning.

JOSEP JUANPERE MIRET AND ANTONIO PUIG GUASCH,
GCA
PASEO DE GRACIA 90,
08008 BARCELONA,
SPAIN.
Josep Juanpere Miret and Antonio Puig Guasch were born in 1952 and 1958 respectively in Barcelona and founded the architectural studio GCA there in 1986. Juanpere Miret studied architecture at the college in Barcelona, Puig Guasch at the technical college in Vallés. One of the successful teams during the construction and designer boom preceding the Olympics, they distinguished themselves in numerous projects that were related stylistically to the contemporary avant-garde, but made concessions to a broader taste through their pragmatic elegance. Buildings and extensions include the Condes de Barcelona hotel, the Havana Palace and the Calderón in Barcelona, housing projects in Barcelona and Bilbao, the Halley and Maresme Boulevard shopping arcades in Barcelona, and shops for Trau, Pedro Morago, Oro Vivo, Bonit and Polo Sur in various Spanish cities.

MICHAEL MOORE DESIGN,
2100 JACKSON STREET,
SAN FRANCISCO,
CALIFORNIA 94115,
USA.
Michael Moore was born in 1960. He studied at the University of California and Westmont College, Santa Barbara, then worked first for Bryars Interior in Montecito and later for Macys. He subsequently became an independent interior designer in the private and commercial fields and was nominated one of "the country's top five innovative designers" by Meredith Publications (*Traditional Home* and *Metropolitan Home* magazines).

MURPHY/JAHN ARCHITECTS,
35 EAST WACKER DRIVE,
CHICAGO, ILLINOIS 60601,
USA.
Murphy/Jahn Architects in Chicago is one of the most successful architectural practices in the USA. Helmut Jahn was born in Germany in 1940. He used show effects long before postmodernism became fashionable, and his spectacular skyscrapers and building complexes radiate a special glamour. In 1966, having studied architecture in Munich, Jahn won a Rotary Scholarship to the Illinois Institute of Technology, Chicago, where he worked under Gene Summers. In 1967 he and Summers joined Charles F. Murphy Associates, a firm employing a team of several hundreds. In 1981, after years as chief designer and partner, Jahn became head of the firm, which now operates as Murphy/Jahn Architects. The practice's most important buildings include the Illinois State Center, Chicago, O'Hare Airport Terminal, Chicago, One Liberty Place, Philadelphia, the Messeturm, Frankfurt and the hotel projects Hyatt Regency Roissy near Paris and Kempinski Airport Hotel, Munich. Murphy/Jahn also won the competition for the German Sony Center on the Potsdamer Platz, Berlin.

NALBACH & NALBACH,
WEIMARER STR. 3-4,
1000 BERLIN 12,
GERMANY.
Johanne and Gernot Nalbach (born in 1943 and 1942 respectively) have shared an office in Berlin since 1975. Both are Austrians and studied at the Technical University in Vienna. After graduating in 1969 Johanne began work as an architect. Gernot, having become an assistant at the Technical University, moved in 1970 to the Berlin College of Arts and became Professor of Industrial Design in 1975. In 1985 he was elected to the Chair of Design at the University of Dortmund. The same year saw the foundation of Nalbach Design GmbH in Berlin, with a branch office in Dortmund and another in San Francisco. The practice's architectural projects include work for the International Building Exhibition (IBA) in Berlin and housing projects in Vienna. Interior design projects include the Grand Hotel Esplanade and the Art Hotel Sorat in Berlin. The practice has also been involved in product design for Vorwerk, Eggers, Semperlux and Flachglas AG, and exhibition architecture for the IBA Berlin, "Berlin – modern architecture", "Berliner Wege" and "Raymond Loewy".

JEAN NOUVEL, EMMANÜEL CATTANI ET ASSOCIÉS,
4 CITÉ GRISET,
75011 PARIS,
FRANCE.
Jean Nouvel, Emmanüel Cattani et Associés is a Paris office run by Jean Nouvel and the Swiss architect Emmanüel Cattani. Nouvel was born at Fume, Lot-et-Garonne, in 1945, and studied at the École Nationale Supérieure des Beaux Arts, qualifying as an architect in 1971. Among his office's most important projects are the housing complex Nemausus in Nîmes, the congress hall in Tours, a new watch factory for Cartier and the Institut du Monde Arabe (1987) in Paris, a building which placed Nouvel in the front rank of his generation of architects. In Paris he is planning the high-rise Tour sans fins in La Défense, and in Cologne he won the competition for the largest building in the Media Park. Nouvel's way of working, oriented towards technical innovation and a modern formal vocabulary, also finds expression in furniture design and he has designed for Ligne Roset, Ecart International and others. He was responsible for both the exterior and interior design of the Hauterive and Les Thermes hotels.

DIRK OBLIERS DESIGN,
FRIEDRICH-EBERT-STR. 27,
8672 SELB,
GERMANY.
Dirk Obliers was born in 1949 in Bochum, Germany. He studied visual communication at the Folkwang School in Essen until 1973. In 1980, after various jobs in advertising and design firms, he became head of creative design in the architectural division of Rosenthal AG in Selb, and also set up his own practice in Selb. His main activities are hotel/interior design, product design and corporate design. His most important interior design projects are the artists' room in the Rosenthal Casino, Selb, Pflaums Posthotel, Pegnitz and the Hansa Hotel, Kulmbach, and development work for the hotel group Steigenberger. At the 75th Hotel, Motel and Restaurant Show in New York in 1990 Obliers won the first two places in the category Hotel Design/Luxury Suites (for Pflaums Posthotel).

O.M.A. (OFFICE OF METROPOLITAN ARCHITECTURE) – see **REM KOOLHAAS.**

JORGE PENA MARTIN,
ESTUDIO RIOJA ARQUITECTOS,
CALLE RIOJA 11,
41001 SEVILLA,
SPAIN.

Jorge Pena Martin studied architecture in Seville. After graduating in 1975 he taught at the same college and won numerous prizes for apartment blocks, urban planning projects and public buildings. In 1990 he converted the monastery of San Juan de Aznalfarache into the Betania Hotel, and in 1991 rebuilt a courtyard of the archbishop's palace as the Los Seises Hotel.

GAETANO PESCE,
67 BOULEVARD BRUNE,
75014 PARIS,
FRANCE.

Gaetano Pesce was born in 1939 in La Spezia, Italy, and studied architecture at the University of Venice, where he graduated in 1963. He now lives in Paris and New York. His work as a designer follows an experimental art-related concept that employs new materials and technology but often expresses itself in bizarre, amorphous forms. He has designed furniture for Cassina, B&B Italia, Vitra and others, and exhibition architecture for Italian design shows in New York and Tokyo. Interior designs include the "El Liston" bar in the hotel Il Palazzo, Fukuoka, Japan.

BARRY PETERS

Barry Peters worked as a design consultant for the Australian media and tourist concern Quintex, which went into liquidation in 1989, and was responsible for the interior design of the Mirage resorts in Port Douglas and on the Gold Coast. He was self-taught and began his career as a shop-window decorator in Melbourne. He then worked for a number of interior architecture firms. In the late 1970s he designed shops for the Australian jewellery chain Hardy Brothers, which had been taken over by Quintex. He then devoted himself to Quintex's two hotel projects, which were completed in 1987 and 1988. Peters has since left Australia.

URBANO PIERINI,
VIA RUFFINI 7,
20123 MILANO,
ITALY.

Urbano Pierini was born in Milan in 1939. Having qualified at the Milan Polytechnic, he joined the office of the architect Giovanni Muzio in 1960. As well as specializing in regional planning, he has realized numerous residential and commercial buildings in and around Milan.

UGO LA PIETRA,
CORSO GARIBALDI 50,
20121 MILAN,
ITALY.

Ugo La Pietra, born in Bussi in 1938, is one of the Italian designers who, through numerous exhibition projects, have helped to establish the importance of design world-wide. He completed his studies at the Milan Polytechnic in 1964, and in 1973 became one of the founders of Global Tools and the design editor of *Domus*. He also worked as a designer and art director for Busnelli. His most important designs include the "Pretenziosa" chair (1984) for Busnelli and a marble table (1988) for Up & Up. In 1979 he received the Compasso d'Oro. His large exhibition projects include "Cronomatica" (1980) at the Venice Biennale and "Casa Telematica" (1983), a futurist project for the total provision of TV and radio around the home which was presented at the Milan furniture fair. He is Professor of Architecture in Turin and Palermo and Professor of Design at the Instituto Statale d'Arte in Monza.

JOHN PORTMAN & ASSOCIATES,
225 PEACHTREE STREET NE, SUITE 201,
ATLANTA, GEORGIA 30303,
USA.

John C. Portman Jr was born in 1924 and studied at the Georgia Institute of Technology in Atlanta, where he graduated in 1950. In 1953 he opened his own office in Atlanta and in 1956 went into partnership with the architect H. Griffith Edwards. Since Edwards' retirement in 1968 the firm has operated as John Portman & Associates. Numerous large hotel, commercial and administrative complexes in the big cities of America and Asia mark Portman out as one of the most significant architects of recent decades. Apart from their highly commercial functionality, his buildings are characterized by an unfailing elegance and sense of form; only marginal concessions are made to postmodernism. Important projects include the Peachtree Center, Atlanta, the Embarcadero Center, San Francisco, the Shanghai Center, Shanghai, the Hyatt hotels in Atlanta and San Francisco, the Westin hotels in Atlanta and Los Angeles, the Marriott Marquis hotels in New York and Atlanta, the Regent Hotel in Singapore and the Portman Hotel in San Francisco.

ANDRÉE PUTMAN,
C/O ECART INTERNATIONAL,
111 RUE SAINT-ANTOINE,
75004 PARIS,
FRANCE.

Andrée Putman first studied music at the Paris Conservatoire under François Poulenc. Having worked for several years as a stylist and journalist, she founded the design firm Créateurs et Industriels, teaming up with fashion designers including Issey Miyake and Jean Charles de Castelbajac. Her own enterprise, Ecart International, now concentrates on producing new designs and re-editions of classic modernist designs. Interior design projects include the Museum of Modern Art in Bordeaux, the Palladium night club (with Arata Isozaki), a villa and shops for the watch firm Ebel and a restaurant in the French Expo pavilion in Seville. Putman's hotel projects (the St James's Club in Paris, Morgans Hotel in New York, the Wasserturm Hotel in Cologne and Le Lac in Japan), reveal her mastery of a genuine French tradition and forge a link with the golden age of the 1920s and 1930s.

GEORG RITSCHL,
ALT-MOABIT 73,
1000 BERLIN 21,
GERMANY.

Georg Ritschl was born in 1959 in Berlin and studied there. Having completed his studies, he worked for Kollhoff and Ovaska, Berlin (1984–5), O.M.A., Rotterdam (until 1986) and von Gerkan, Marg & Partner, Hamburg (until 1988). In 1988 he founded his own studio in Berlin. Current projects include the Weberpark, Babelsberg, and the Intercity Hotel at the Zoo Station in Berlin.

ALDO ROSSI,
VIA MADDELENA 1,
20121 MILAN,
ITALY.

Aldo Rossi was born in 1931 in Milan, where he studied architecture at the Polytechnic. He set up his own practice in 1961. In 1965 he became a professor in Milan and has since held chairs at the universities of Venice, Zurich, Harvard and Yale. He wrote an influential book entitled *The Architecture of the City*, and his opinions and projects made him the most important representative of rationalism. His buildings include the Gallaratese housing project in Milan, the San Cataldo cemetery in Modena, an administrative centre in Perugia, the San Felice opera house in Genoa, the faculty of architecture in Miami and the Il Palazzo hotel in Fukuoka, Japan. He won the competition for the unrealized German Historical Museum in Berlin and was the winner of the 1990 Pritzker Prize. He has also worked on product designs for Alessi, Molteni and other companies.

JÜRGEN SAWADE,
KURFÜRSTENDAMM 212,
1000 BERLIN 15,
GERMANY.

Jürgen Josef Sawade was born in 1937 in Kassel, Germany. Until 1966 he studied architecture at the Technical University of Berlin, where he then worked as assistant to Oswald Mathias Ungers. Since 1970 he has had his own planning office in Berlin. After various visiting professorships (at UCLA, Cornell, Cooper Union, Vienna and elsewhere), he was appointed to a chair at the University of Dortmund. Sawade's rigorous style, schooled in rationalism but not bound to the dogmatism of his teacher Ungers, is documented by numerous housing projects in Berlin. Other projects (all in Berlin) include the IBM office building, the rebuilding of the theatre on the Leniner Platz and the Grand Hotel Esplanade.

ETTORE SOTTSASS,
VIA BORGONUOVO 9,
20121 MILAN,
ITALY.
Ettore Sottsass was born in Innsbruck in 1917 and graduated from the University of Turin in 1939. Since 1947 he has worked in Milan as a designer. From 1958 he was chief design consultant for Olivetti and was responsible for numerous innovative design concepts in information electronics. In 1980 he set up Sottsass Associati. In parallel with his consultancy practice, Sottsass became involved in experimental projects, beginning with the "radical architecture" of the 1960s which was continued by the "Memphis" group (with Matteo Thun, Aldo Cibic, Marco Zanini, Peter Shire and others), whose works initiated the "new design" of the 1980s. Sottsass's work has been exhibited in numerous galleries and museums in New York, Tokyo, Paris, Milan and elsewhere, and has been much discussed in the press and in books. Since 1990 Johanna Grawunder, Mike Ryan and Marco Susani have been junior partners of Sottsass Associati. The firm has been involved in furniture, product and graphic design for Abet, Alessi, Cassina, Esprit, Knoll International, ERG Petroli, Mitsubishi, NTT, Olivetti, Philips Consumer Electronics, Seiko, Takenaka, Zanotta, Zumtobel and others. Architectural projects of recent years include interior designs for Esprit and Alessi, the Zibibbo bar at the Il Palazzo hotel in Fukuoka, Japan, a house for Daniel Wolf in Colorado, USA and a hotel and shopping mall in Kuala Lumpur, Malaysia.

PHILIPPE STARCK,
3 RUE DE LA ROQUETTE,
75011 PARIS,
FRANCE.
Philippe Starck was born in 1949 in Paris. The son of an aircraft constructor and inventor, he attended the École Camondo, but left without qualifying. He began his design career with an "inflatable house" for the actor Lino Ventura's charitable organization Perce-Neige. From 1971 he spent two years working as "art decorator" for Pierre Cardin. The early eighties saw his meteoric rise to fame, though he sees himself not so much as a designer, but rather as an artist in show business. Interior design projects include an office at the Elysée Palace for President Mitterrand, the Bain-Douches night club and Café Costes in Paris, the Royalton and the Paramount Hotel in New York and the Teatriz restaurant/bar in Madrid. His first big architectural projects were Nani-Nana and La Flamme d'Or in Tokyo. He has also designed furniture for Driade, Baleri, Kartell, Vitra and other manufacturers.

KIYOSHI SEY TAKEYAMA
Kiyoshi Sey Takeyama, who heads Amorphe Architects & Associates, was born in Osaka, Japan, in 1954. He studied architecture at the universities of Kyoto and Tokyo, and obtained his doctor's degree in 1984. Important buildings include dental clinics and residences in Takao (1982) and Koga (1983), the OXY building in Nogizaka (1987) and a villa in Karuizawa (1988). In 1986 he won second prize for his design of the Shonandai Civic Centre, received commendations for his new National Theatre, and won the competition for the Aicha Prefectural Centre.

TONGG, CLARKE & MECHLER,
615 PIIKOI STREET, SUITE 1501,
HONOLULU, HAWAII,
USA.
Tongg, Clarke & Mechler is the oldest firm of landscape architects in Hawaii and one of the largest. The firm's chief planner is Steve Mechler, and the managing director is Alan B. Clarke. The firm specializes in tropical parks and gardens and has achieved world-wide success, having designed some of the most spectacular resorts on the Hawaiian islands, for instance the Hyatt Regency hotels in Kauai and Waikoloa and the Westin hotels in Kauai and Maui. Further afield, it has built resorts in Australia, Guam, India, Indonesia, Japan, Korea, Malaysia, Saudi Arabia, Singapore and Taiwan.

SHIGERU UCHIDA,
STUDIO 80,
1-17-14 MINAMI-AOYAMA,
MINATO-KU, TOKYO 107,
JAPAN.
Shigeru Uchida was born in 1943 in Yokohama, Japan, and studied at the Kuwazawa Design School until 1966. In 1981 he founded Studio 80 with Ikuyo Mitsuhashi and Toru Nishioka. Among their many interior design projects are showrooms for the fashion designers Issey Miyake and Yohji Yamamoto, apartment blocks, restaurants and the hotel Il Palazzo. They have also been involved in furniture and product design. In 1988–9 Uchida organized the Designers' Week in Tokyo and in 1989 was responsible for the presentation of Japanese design at the Europalia in Belgium.

PIERRE VURPAS & ASS.,
29-31 RUE SAINT GEORGES,
69005 LYON,
FRANCE.
Pierre Vurpas was born in 1949 and received his architect's diploma in Lyon in 1974. He then worked as a graduate student with the commission for the care of monuments at Chaillot in Paris. From 1976 to 1987 he worked in partnership with Yves Boucharlat and Claude Vigan in Lyon, then set up his own office. Buildings and interior extensions include three hotels – the Cour des Loges and La Tour Rose in Lyon and the Château de Lacoix Laval at Charbonnières – and the Pierre Brossolette school at Ouillin. Vurpas is a representative of the Lyon school of younger architects who, when addressing the problem of the long-neglected historic centre of Lyon, arrived at a nostalgia-free approach that enabled them to combine conservation with innovation.

STUDIO JAN WICHERS,
MITTELWEG 162,
2000 HAMBURG 13,
GERMANY.
Jan Wichers was born in 1944 and has run his studio for design and interior architecture in Hamburg for 25 years. Apart from product designs for many international firms, including B & B Italia, De Padova, Rosenthal, Up & Up and Villeroy & Boch, he has worked on numerous projects in Europe and overseas, especially hotels. Among these are the Schlosshotel Bühlerhöhe, the Vier Jahreszeiten in Munich, the Atlantic in Hamburg, Schloss Fuschl near Salzburg, the Ciragan Palace in Istanbul, the Grand Hotel in Washington and the Libertador in Buenos Aires. The Kempinski Airport Hotel at the new Munich airport (architects: Murphy/Jahn) is currently under construction.

JEAN-MICHEL WILMOTTE,
ARCHITECTURE INTÉRIEURE,
4 QUAI DES CÉLESTINS,
75004 PARIS,
FRANCE.
Jean-Michel Wilmotte was born in 1948 and studied at the École Camondo. He founded his practice, Governor, in Paris in 1975, followed by other offices in Nîmes and Tokyo (1986). In addition to architecture, Wilmotte has designed furniture, lamps and complete interiors. Large projects include the redesigning of the town hall and the museum in Nîmes, galleries and a bookshop in the Grand Louvre, office accommodation for Canal, Technal showroom in Toulouse, salerooms for Grenier à Sel in Avignon, the Espace Kronenbourg in Paris and the Bunkamura Cultural Centre in Tokyo. At present Wilmotte is working on galleries in the Richelieu wing of the Louvre and for the museum of art in Lyon. Work at the planning stage includes housing projects in France and a golf club near Osaka, Japan. Wilmotte has won many prizes for design and has been awarded the title of Chevalier des Arts et Lettres.

WONG & OUYANG,
3/F, 250 KING'S ROAD,
HONG KONG.
Wong & Ouyang has existed since 1972 as a large architectural, engineering and design firm with a staff which currently numbers over 350. In addition to the head office in Hong Kong, it has branches in Singapore and Malaysia. It specializes in large projects in the field of office and hotel building, schools and housing, and has carried out projects in China, Singapore, Malaysia, Korea, India, Australia and Canada. Among the company's numerous projects in Hong Kong is the Island Shangri-La hotel.

PROJECT INFORMATION

NAME Morgans Hotel

ADDRESS 237 Madison Avenue, New York City, NY 10016, USA.
Tel. (212) 686 0300
Fax (212) 779 8352

ROOMS/FACILITIES 66 single rooms, 18 double rooms, 28 suites including penthouse, breakfast room

COMPLETION 1984

CLIENT Morgans Hotel Group, 140 East 63rd Street, New York, NY 10021, USA.

INTERIOR DESIGN Andrée Putman

SUB-CONTRACTORS/ SUPPLIERS Carpets and furniture: Ecart and custom built

MANAGEMENT Morgans Hotel Group, New York

NAME Wasserturm Hotel

ADDRESS Kaygasse 2, 5000 Cologne 1, Germany.
Tel. 221 20080
Fax 221 2008888

ROOMS/FACILITIES 10 single rooms, 38 double rooms, 42 suites, Restaurant im Wasserturm with roof terrace, Bar im Wasserturm, conference and banqueting rooms for up to 60 people, sauna, solarium, underground car park

COMPLETION 1990

CLIENT Hopf-Wasserturm-Grundstücksgesellschaft

ARCHITECTURE Konrad L. Heinrich

INTERIOR DESIGN Andrée Putman, Ecart International

SUB-CONTRACTORS/ SUPPLIERS Structural engineering: Krings; technical engineering: Kalinowski + Kappe, Fernbach; sanitation: Radiator/n; electrics: Rhein Elektra; furniture/fittings: Ecart International, Dennery; upholstery: Soutumier; floor coverings: Anker-Teppichfabrik, Tekima, Jules Flipo; bath: Ahlmann Maschinenbau; tiles: Dehnke; painting: Peiniger

OPERATOR Hopf Holding

NAME Le Lac

ADDRESS 1219 Kodachi, Kawaguchiko-Cho, Minamitsuru-Gun, Yamanashi, Japan.
Tel. 0555 73 3309

ROOMS/FACILITIES 8 rooms, restaurant for 46 people, bar

COMPLETION 1990

CLIENT Maruko Inc.

INTERIOR DESIGN Andrée Putman, Ecart, with collaborators Bruno Moinard and Flavie Austruit

SUB-CONTRACTORS/ SUPPLIERS Furniture: Ecart, Paris

NAME La Villa

ADDRESS 29 rue Jacob 75006, Paris, France.
Tel. 4326 6000
Fax 4634 6363

ROOMS/FACILITIES 32 rooms, bar, jazz club

COMPLETION 1988

CLIENT Vincent Darnaud

ARCHITECTURE J. A. Dorel, Paris

INTERIOR DESIGN Marie-Christine Dorner

SUB-CONTRACTORS/ SUPPLIERS Furniture: L.C.S.D., Godefroy; sanitation: Ballas et Matey; lighting: Blautany; mirrors and glazing: Saalburg; carpets: Taiping

OPERATOR Vincent Darnaud

NAME Art Hotel Sorat

ADDRESS Joachimsthaler Str. 28-19, 1000 Berlin 15, Germany.
Tel. 30 884470
Fax 30 88447700

ROOMS/FACILITIES 75 rooms, breakfast restaurant, conference room

COMPLETION 1990

CLIENTS Silvia and Gerd Gädeke

ARCHITECTURE Klaus Effenberger; Johanne and Gernot Nalbach

INTERIOR DESIGN Johanne and Gernot Nalbach

SUB-CONTRACTORS/ SUPPLIERS Fitted furniture: Eggers; furniture: Dey, Kartell, Hansen, bd Disegno, Palucco, ClassiCon, Casigliani; floor coverings: Vorwerk, Betonsteinwerk Otze; wall lighting: Brendel; door handles: Vieler

OPERATOR Sorat Hotel Verwaltungsgesellschaft

NAME Pflaums Posthotel

ADDRESS Nürnberger Str. 14, 8570 Pegnitz, Germany.

ROOMS/FACILITIES 75 rooms, 25 suites, 2 restaurants (Rotisserie Pflaumengarten, Posthalter Stube), bar Zum Säbel Napoleons, 5 conference rooms, swimming pool, sauna, fitness room, indoor golf course, 5 garden areas as terraces

COMPLETION 1989–1992

CLIENT Andreas and Hermann Pflaum

ARCHITECTURE Dirk Obliers, Heinrich Pflaum

INTERIOR DESIGN Dirk Obliers

SUB-CONTRACTORS/ SUPPLIERS Fittings: Friedhelm Hübner; furniture: Friedhelm Hübner, Cassina, Vitra, deSede, WK; floor coverings: Vorwerk, Zimmer, Anker Teppichfabrik; wallpapers: Tescoha; wall material: Abet Laminati; ceilings: Barrisol, Dekorplattenwerk; light-conducting fibres: Eugen Reissinger, Kotzolt; wall lights: Art-Line; table lamps: Artemide; fabrics: JAB Anstoetz; sanitary fittings: Hartkopf, Hoesch, High-Tech, Matteo Thun by Keramag; bathroom furniture: Keuco; entertainment electronics: Philips Consumer Electronics, Bang & Olufsen;

OPERATOR Andreas and Hermann Pflaum

NAME	Hauterive
ADDRESS	3 Place Camille Hosteins, 33270 Bouliac, France. Tel. 5620 5219 Fax 5620 9258
ROOMS/FACILITIES	16 rooms, 2 suites, 2 restaurants (Saint James, Opera Planete Bouffe), Bistroy brasserie, bar, 2 conference rooms, wine shop
COMPLETION	1989
CLIENT	Jean-Marie Amat, SCI Les Jardins de Haute-Rive
ARCHITECTURE	Jean Nouvel, Emmanüel Cattani et Associés
INTERIOR DESIGN	Jean Nouvel
SUB-CONTRACTORS/ SUPPLIERS	Construction: Tiliet; structural engineering: Treffel, L. Fruitet; landscaping: Yves Brunier; lighting: Luceplan; furniture: Jean Nouvel/Eric Pouget/Ligne Roset; bathrooms: Sopha Vola; woodwork: Trad. Bois, Chabosseau; painting: Mare; plasterwork: Musset-Eutrope
OPERATOR	Jean-Marie Amat

NAME	Les Thermes
ADDRESS	Cours de Verdun, 40100 Dax, France. Tel. 5856 4242 Fax 5856 4810
ROOMS/FACILITIES	90 rooms, restaurant, bar with terrace, conference room, thermal bath with therapeutic facilities
COMPLETION	1992
CLIENT	Compagnie Thermale de Dax
ARCHITECTURE	Jean Nouvel, Emmanüel Cattani et Associés
INTERIOR DESIGN	Jean Nouvel
SUB-CONTRACTORS/ SUPPLIERS	Construction work: Kephren Ingenierie; technical engineering: Veritas Agence Landes; air-conditioning: Courtois; security system: Casso Gaudin; landscaping: Yves Brunier & Lauricoste
OPERATOR	Compagnie Thermale de Dax

NAME	Le Cheval Blanc
ADDRESS	Place des Arènes, 3000 Nîmes, France. Tel. 6676 3232 Fax 6676 3233
ROOMS/FACILITIES	19 rooms, 7 suites, gourmet restaurant, American bar, wine bar, 2 conference rooms
COMPLETION	1991
CLIENT	SENIM, Régine Choukroun and Jean Boyer-Gibaud
ARCHITECTURE	Jean-Michel Wilmotte
INTERIOR DESIGN	Jean-Michel Wilmotte with Sabine Boyer-Gibaud, Claire Sentis, Claude Thomas, Pascal Petit
FURNITURE DESIGN	Jean-Michel Wilmotte
OPERATOR	SENIM

NAME	D-Hotel
ADDRESS	2-5-15 Dotonbori, Chuo-ku, Osaka, Japan. Tel. 6 212 2995 Fax 6 212 7462
ROOMS/FACILITIES	12 apartments
COMPLETION	1989
CLIENT	Daitaki Co. Ltd
ARCHITECTURE	Kiyoshi Sey Takeyama/ Amorphe Architects
INTERIOR DESIGN	Kiyoshi Sey Takeyama/ Amorphe Architects
CONSTRUCTION	TIS & Partners, Soh Mechanical Engineers

NAME	Dreamland Heights
ADDRESS	Seaside, Florida 32459, USA. Tel. 800 635 0296
ROOMS/FACILITIES	8 guest apartments, lobby bar, Bud & Alley's restaurant, assembly rooms, shops
COMPLETION	1989
CLIENT	Robert S. Davis, Seaside Community Development Corporation
ARCHITECTURE	Steven Holl
INTERIOR DESIGN	Steven Holl
SUB-CONTRACTORS/ SUPPLIERS	Construction: New Creation Builders; structural engineering: Robert Lawson; technical engineering: R. B. Stotz; appointments: Feinberg Associates
OPERATOR	Seaside Cottage Rental Agency

NAME	The Royalton
ADDRESS	44 West 44th Street, New York, NY 10036, USA. Tel. 212 869 4400 Fax 212 869 8965
ROOMS/FACILITIES	167 rooms, 28 suites, restaurant with bar, Round bar, health club
COMPLETION	1988
CLIENT	Morgans Hotel Group, Philip Pilevsky, Ian Schrager, Steve Rubell, Arthur Cohen
ARCHITECTURE	Gruzen Samton Steinglass
INTERIOR DESIGN	Philippe Starck
SUB-CONTRACTORS/ SUPPLIERS	Construction: Paul Haigh; lighting design: Jules Fisher & Paul Marantz; colour consultants: Stephen Sills; wood fittings/bathroom equipment: Maville; furniture: Maville, Dacheville, Yves Halard, Vinchenard, Lelieure; floor coverings: Brigitte Starck; aluminium casting: Dacheville; plasterwork: S.O.E.; co-ordination accessories/ graphic design: Tracy Turner; painting: Donald Kaufman; uniform design: Fred Leiba
OPERATOR	Morgans Hotel Group

NAME	The Paramount
ADDRESS	235 West 46th Street, New York, NY 10036, USA. Tel. 212 764 5500 Fax 212 354 5237
ROOMS/FACILITIES	580 rooms, 12 suites, Mezzanine Restaurant & Bar, Brasserie du Theatre, The Whiykey Bar, Dean & Deluca Expresso Bar, conference room, gaming room, sports room, magazine kiosk.
COMPLETION	1990

CLIENT Morgans Hotel Group, Ian Schrager, Philip Pilevsky, Arthur Cohen
ARCHITECTURE Anda Andrei
INTERIOR DESIGN Philippe Starck
SUB-CONTRACTORS/ SUPPLIERS Lighting design: Jules Fisher & Paul Marantz; furniture: Philippe Starck, Marco Zanuso, Franco Albini, Jean-Michel Frank, Antoni Gaudí, Carlos Riart, Jasper Morrison, Marc Newson
OPERATOR Morgans Hotel Group

NAME Otaru Marittimo
ADDRESS 1-3-1, Ironai, Otaru, Japan.
Tel. 81 134 273300
Fax 81 134 292810
ROOMS/FACILITIES 25 rooms, restaurant, bar, lobby, museum
COMPLETION 1989
CLIENT Jasmac Co. Ltd, Tobishima
ARCHITECTURE Branson Coates Architecture/ Douglas Branson and Nigel Coates; contact architect: Dan Architecture
INTERIOR DESIGN Branson Coates Architecture/ Douglas Branson and Nigel Coates
ARTISTS INVOLVED Annabelle Grey (painting, textiles); ZaZa Wentworth Stanley (painting: guest-room corridor lobbies, Egyptian Mummy in Alexandria Suite); Emma Harrison (painting: Manhattan, reception); Wilma Johnson (portraits: Bombay, Alexandria, Naples); Beverley Beeland (sand-blasted windows and screens); Tobit Roche (paintings: Bombay Jungle, Bombay Palace, Bombay Market); Mark Brazier-Jones (door handles); Tom Dixon (chandelier); Karen Spurgin (embroidery); Dirk van Dooren (environmental video: fish video); Why Not Associates (logo for tableware, stationery, matches, linen); Steve Husband (painting: guest-room corridor, lobbies); Stuart Helm (special painting: main staircase); Andrew James (painting of Star bar ceiling); Oriel Harwood (ceramic plaque in "London" guest-room); Simon Moore (icebergs in restaurant, fish tanks); Kate Malone (ceramics in restaurant).
SUB-CONTRACTORS/ SUPPLIERS Furniture: SCP ("Tongue" chairs, "Tongue" sofas); hand-made carpets: V'soske Joyce; organization of antiques: Omniate

---

NAME Triton
ADDRESS 342 Grant Avenue, San Francisco, California 94108, USA.
Tel. 415 394 0500
Fax 415 394 0555
ROOMS/FACILITIES 97 single rooms, 36 double rooms, 7 suites, 2 restaurants with bar areas
COMPLETION 1991
CLIENT Bill Krimpton, General Partner, 191 Sutter Street, San Francisco, CA 94104, USA.
ARCHITECTURE Wil Wong, 2710 Webster Street, San Francisco, CA 94123, USA.
INTERIOR DESIGN Michael Moore Design
SUB-CONTRACTORS/ SUPPLIERS Lighting: Terry Ohm; furniture: Roy Thomas for Mike Furniture; carpets: Donghia; wall painting (lobby mural): Will Barker; wall paintings in the guest-rooms: One-of-a-Kind Design; gold leaf lobby walls: One-of-a-Kind Design; "Laughing Columns": Arlene Elisabeth
OPERATOR Kimco Hotel & Restaurant Management Co.

NAME Kelly's Hotel
ADDRESS Wormser Straße 14, 6140 Bensheim 1, Germany.
Tel. 06251 63087
Fax 06251 4063
ROOMS/FACILITIES 112 rooms, bistro restaurant, daylight conference room, 3 group work-rooms, sauna, solarium
COMPLETION 1992
CLIENT Darmstädter Hotel Consulting GmbH
ARCHITECTURE Zimmermann/Zimmermann, Darmstadt
INTERIOR DESIGN Adieu New York Design/ Dieter Brell/Leif Trenkler
OPERATOR Darmstädter Hotel Consulting GmbH

NAME Il Palazzo
ADDRESS 3-13-1 Haruyoshi, Chuo-ku, Fukuoka City, Fukuoka, Japan.
Tel. 92 7163333
Fax 92 7243330
ROOMS/FACILITIES 62 rooms, lobby, restaurant, 4 bars and nightclub
COMPLETION 1989
CLIENT Mitsuhiro Kuzuwa, Jasmac Co. Ltd
ARCHITECTURE Aldo Rossi, Morris Adjmi; Associate architect: Mitsuru Kaneko
INTERIOR DESIGN Hotel/restaurant: Shigeru Uchida/Ikuyo Mitsuhashi; furniture: Shigeru Uchida; lighting: Harumi Fujimoto; Barna Crossing: Alfredo Arribas, (interior), Quin Larrea, Juli Capella (creative director), Javier Mariscal (art collaborator); El Dorado bar: Aldo Rossi, Morris Adjmi; Zibibbo bar: Ettore Sottsass, Mike Ryan; El Liston bar: Gaetano Pesce with Patric Daumas, Parrish Puente, Tim Tait, Myriam Seckler; Oblomova bar: Shiro Kuramata
OPERATOR Jasmac Co. Ltd

NAME Los Seises
ADDRESS Calle Segovia, Seville, Spain.
Tel. 5 4229495
Fax 5 4224334
ROOMS/FACILITIES 43 rooms, bar, swimming pool
COMPLETION 1991
CLIENT Alberto Moreno
ARCHITECTURE Jorge Pena Martin
INTERIOR DESIGN Jorge Pena Martin
SUB-CONTRACTORS/ SUPPLIERS Alberto Dominges Abingor

OPERATOR The Los Seises does not belong to a hotel group.

NAME Hotel Montalembert

ADDRESS 3 rue de Montalembert, 75007 Paris, France.
Tel. 4548 6811
Fax 4222 5819

ROOMS/FACILITIES 56 rooms, restaurant, American bar with fireplace

COMPLETION 1991

CLIENT Groupe Stephane Andrieu, 5-7 avenue Mac-Mahon, 75017 Paris, France

ARCHITECTURE Mr. Plessier, 8 ter rue Jonquoy, 75014 Paris, France

INTERIOR DESIGN Christian Liaigre

SUB-CONTRACTORS/ SUPPLIERS Lighting: Manufactor; bronze wall lights, door handles and ashtrays: Eric Schmitt; panorama photographs in rooms: Jean-Pierre Godeaut; floor coverings: Bartholomeus; wallpapers: Designer's Guild

OPERATOR Grace Leo Associates

NAME The Halkin

ADDRESS Halkin Street, Belgravia, London SW1X 7DJ, UK.
Tel. 071 333 1000
Fax 071 333 1100

ROOMS/FACILITIES 41 rooms (including 19 de luxe, 10 suites, 12 double rooms), restaurant, meeting room

COMPLETION 1991

CLIENT Mr & Mrs Ong

ARCHITECTURE Laboratorio Associati

INTERIOR DESIGN Laboratorio Associati

SUB-CONTRACTORS/ SUPPLIERS Carpentry and furnishings made in Italy

---

NAME Cour des Loges

ADDRESS 2468 rue du Boeuf, 69005 Lyon, France.
Tel. 7842 7575
Fax 7240 9361

ROOMS/FACILITIES 63 rooms and suites, Tapas des Loges restaurant, breakfast/ tea room, library, conference rooms, wine cellar with tasting room, Athisma art gallery, LesThermes swimming pool with sauna/jacuzzi, garden terraces

COMPLETION 1987

CLIENT Jean-Luc and Hélène Mathias, SCI "L'Hotel"

ARCHITECTURE Yves Boucharlat, Pierre Vurpas

INTERIOR DESIGN Yves Boucharlat, Pierre Vurpas

SUB-CONTRACTORS/ SUPPLIERS Construction: Coquaz; joinery: Giraud-Dupont, Garnier; metalwork: Snaer; electrics: Clemessy; heating and air-conditioning: Danto Rogeat; furniture: Cassina, B & B Italia; carpets: Tisca, Toulemonde Bochart; wood flooring: Rhodanienne de Revêtement; painting: Morel; plasterwork: Peturaud, CRM; wash stands: Philippe Starck; fabrics: Etamine; entertainment electronics: Bang & Olufsen

OPERATOR Cour des Loges S.A

NAME La Pergolese

ADDRESS 3 rue Pergolese, 75116 Paris, France.
Tel. 4067 9677
Fax 4500 1211

ROOMS/FACILITIES 40 rooms, breakfast restaurant

COMPLETION 1991

CLIENT Edith Vidalenc

INTERIOR DESIGN Rena Dumas

SUB-CONTRACTORS/ SUPPLIERS Lighting: Luceplan, Artemide, Flos, FontanaArte; furniture: Cassina, B & B Italia, Kartell; floor coverings: Cogolin; wash basins: Andrée Putman

OPERATOR Edith Vidalenc

NAME The Havana Palace

ADDRESS Gran Via de los Corts Catalanes 647, 08010 Barcelona, Spain.
Tel. 93 4121115
Fax. 93 4122611

ROOMS/FACILITIES 145 rooms and suites, Grand Place restaurant, La Copula bar, Gran Via lounge, ballroom for 200 people, 2 function rooms for 130 and 70 people respectively

COMPLETION 1991

CLIENT Luis Borrell Calonge, RCM S.A.

ARCHITECTURE Josep Juanpere Miret, Antonio Puig Guasch, GCA

INTERIOR DESIGN Josep Juanpere Miret, Antonio Puig Guasch, GCA

SUB-CONTRACTORS/ SUPPLIERS Furniture: GCA; bathrooms: Grohe, Vanguardia, Inox

OPERATOR Diagonal Hotels

NAME The Imperial Palace

ADDRESS 32 avenue d'Albigny, 74000 Annecy, France
Tel. 5009 3000
Fax 5009 3333

ROOMS/FACILITIES 98 rooms and suites; 3 restaurants (La Voile, Brasserie du Parc, La Pascaline), Imperial Casino; 2 bars; congress centre with 15 conference rooms, beauty centre

COMPLETION 1988

CLIENT Hopf Holding, Ville d'Annecy

ARCHITECTURE SISS S.A.

INTERIOR DESIGN ARC+/SISS S.A., Michel Couasnon

SUB-CONTRACTORS/ SUPPLIERS Construction: Kronismus; sanitation: Sani-Lacs Porcher; lighting: Le Dauphin, NRA & JJ Amoyal, Light Cibles; furniture: Longoni; floor coverings: Alp-Sol, M. Viollet, Stoddard France, Ceramica Mirage, CS Steel, Object Carpet, Dancan; wood fittings: Dimenop; wall coverings: Placide Joilet, Baeckert, Muraspec, Nobilis Fantan, Engler; metalwork: Viglino; painting: Gauthier, Seynod

OPERATOR Hopf Holding

NAME Hotel Claris

ADDRESS Pau Claris 150, Barcelona, Spain.

	Tel. 3 487 6252
	Fax 3 215 7970
ROOMS/FACILITIES	142 rooms, 2 restaurants, private museum, lobby/bar, roof-top swimming pool
COMPLETION	1991
CLIENT	ASTIL/PAI
ARCHITECTURE AND INTERIOR DESIGN	J. Martorell, O. Bohigas, D. Mackay, A. Puigdomenech; collaborators: P. Ramis, B. Herrera
SUB-CONTRACTORS/ SUPPLIERS	Joan Sanz/Esclo S.A
OPERATOR	Derby

NAME	Rolandsburg
ADDRESS	Rennbahnstr. 2, 4000 Düsseldorf 12, Germany. Tel. 211 610090 Fax 211 6100943
ROOMS/FACILITIES	59 rooms, restaurant, bar, terrace, 3-5 conference rooms, swimming pool, sauna, fitness room
COMPLETION	1988
CLIENT	Rolandsburg Hotel Betriebsgesellschaft
ARCHITECTURE	Wolfgang Döring
INTERIOR DESIGN	Wolfgang Döring
SUB-CONTRACTORS/ SUPPLIERS	Construction: Bilfinger & Berger; interior appointment: Vedder; partition walls: Hüppe Form; furniture: Rosenthal, Cassina; marble: Schmitz & Co.; tiling: Kaiser, Contega; tableware: Rosenthal, WMF
OPERATOR	Rolandsburg Hotel Betriebsgesellschaft

NAME	The Portman (Pan Pacific Hotel)
ADDRESS	500 Post Street, San Francisco, CA 94102, USA. Tel. 415 771 8600 Fax 714 957 0803
ROOMS/FACILITIES	348 rooms, 3 suites, restaurant, lobby bar, conference centre, 2 ballrooms, conference room, 4 conference suites, gift shop
COMPLETION	1987
CLIENT	Portman Properties
ARCHITECTURE	John C. Portman & Associates
INTERIOR DESIGN	John C. Portman & Associates
SUB-CONTRACTORS/ SUPPLIERS	Acoustics: Paoletti, Lewitz; walls: D. Zelinsky, Chrisanthou, Fabri-Trak, Prisma Mirror Wall Cladding; lighting design: William Lam; lighting: Al Lighting, Artemide, A. W. Pistol, Boy, Chapman, Classic Illumination, David Thorne, Premier Chandelier, Rainbow Lamp, Sentinel, Sirmos; furniture: B & B Italia, Brayton International, Brickel, Brueton, Cedric Hartman, Dunbar, Knoll International, Larsen, Pace Collection, Thonet, Barclay, Dunhill, Kroehler Contract; floor coverings: Design Wave/Tuftex, Harbinger, Hollytex, Knoll International, Milliken, Pacific Crest Mills, Soraya; fabrics: Ametex Contract, Architex International, Award, Blau, Boris Kroll, Brayton Textile Collection, Chestnut Fields, Design Tex, Harrington, Jack Lenor Larsen, Knoll Textiles, Pacific Hide & Leather, Payne, Scalamandre, Shelby Williams, Unika Vaev, Valley Forge; painting: Devoe; garden layout: Elliots, Architectural Supplements, Barclay, Finealum, International Terra Cotta; entertainment electronics: Quasar/Maco Associates, RCA
OPERATOR	San Francisco 109 Inc

NAME	Furkablick Hotel
ADDRESS	(in summer) 6491 Furkapasshöhe, Switzerland. Tel. 044 67297 (in winter) Rue des Moulins 29, 2000 Neuchâtel, Switzerland. Tel. 38 245323
ROOMS/FACILITIES	8 single rooms, 11 double rooms, 2 restaurants
COMPLETION	1988-91
CLIENT	Marc Hostettler
ARCHITECTURE	O.M.A. and Rem Koolhaas
SUB-CONTRACTORS/ SUPPLIERS	Wood and sanitation: local craftsmen; stairs: Scorpio; robot: Thierry Petre
OPERATOR	Marc Hostettler

NAME	Der Teufelhof Basel
ADDRESS	Leonhardsgraben 47, 4051 Basel, Switzerland.
ROOMS/FACILITIES	8 rooms, gourmet restaurant, wine bar, bar, two theatres
COMPLETION	1988
CLIENT	Monica and Dominique Thommy-Kneschaurek
ARCHITECTURE	Hans Pösinger/Basler Baugesellschaft
INTERIOR DESIGN	Monica and Dominique Thommy-Kneschaurek
ARTISTS INVOLVED	Rooms are redesigned every two years. First phase: Anna Oppermann, Petr Hrbek, Flavio Paolucci, Ueli Berger, Francis Limérat, Hubertus Gojowczyk, Moel Cuin, Joos Hutter. Second phase: Marie Bourget, Hubertus von der Goltz, Werner Buser, Klaus Schmidt, Guido Nussbaum, Felice Varini, René Straub.
SUB-CONTRACTORS/ SUPPLIERS	Furniture: Cappellini, Dux Design; lamps: Artemide
OPERATOR	Monica and Dominique Thommy-Kneschaurek

NAME	New Siru
ADDRESS	Place Rogier 1, 1000 Brussels, Belgium.
ROOMS/FACILITIES	101 rooms, Brasserie Siru restaurant, 2 meeting rooms, each for 80 people
COMPLETION	1932/1989
CLIENT	S.A. Arthotel, rue des Croisades 2, 1210 Brussels, Belgium.
ARCHITECTURE	De Simpel/Lechien Bd. Botanique, Brussels
INTERIOR DESIGN	Galila Hollander, Atelier 20
SUB-CONTRACTORS/ SUPPLIERS	Floors: BIC Kortrijk; sanitation: Grohe/ Washmobile Italien; lighting: Espace et Lumière; furniture: CDD Antwerpen
OPERATOR	Hôtel Siru S.A

NAME	Spadari al duomo
ADDRESS	Via Spadari 11, 20123 Milan, Italy. Tel. 2 72002371 Fax 2 861184
ROOMS/FACILITIES	40 rooms, American bar
COMPLETION	1991
CLIENT	Marida Martegani
ARCHITECTURE	Urbano Pierini
INTERIOR DESIGN	Ugo La Pietra
ARTISTS INVOLVED	Gio Pomodoro (open fireplace in the vestibule); Valentino Vago (frescoes in the breakfast room); Ugo La Pietra (wooden furniture)
OPERATOR	Marida Martegani

NAME	L'Atelier sul Mare
ADDRESS	Via Cesare Battisti, Castel di Tusa, Sicily. Tel. 0921 34295
ROOMS/FACILITIES	40 rooms, 2 restaurants, 2 bars
COMPLETION	1982
CLIENT	Antonio Presti
ARCHITECTURE	Michelle Cancella
INTERIOR DESIGN	Hidetoshi Nagasawa, Fabrizio Plessi, Paolo Icaro, Michele Canzoneri and others
SUB-CONTRACTORS/ SUPPLIERS	Corridors with objects by Bobo Otera and pictures by Elisabeth Frolet and other young artists. Furniture by Mario Ceroli and others
OPERATOR	Antonio Presti

NAME	Atlanta Marriott Marquis
ADDRESS	265 Peachtree Center Avenue, Atlanta, Georgia 30303, USA. Tel. 404 521 0000
ROOMS/FACILITIES	1,674 rooms, 80 suites, 5 restaurants, 5 lounges, 2 ballrooms, 44 conference rooms, exhibition area, indoor and outdoor swimming pools, sun terrace, fitness centre with sauna, gaming room, shopping centre
COMPLETION	1985
CLIENT	Portman Developers, Ivy Street Hotel Ltd
ARCHITECTURE	John C. Portman & Associates
INTERIOR DESIGN	John C. Portman & Associates, Marriott Interior Design
SUB-CONTRACTORS/ SUPPLIERS	Construction: J. A. Jones Construction Company; structural engineering: John C. Portman & Associates, Weems-Doar Engineers; electrical engineering: Newcomb & Boyd; art consultancy: ConsultArt; acoustics: J. R. Ballentine Associates; audio-visual planning: Bolt Beranek & Newman; graphics consultants: Muhlhausen Design & Ass.; lighting design: William Lam; floor coverings: US Mosaic Co., Williams Tile & Terrazzo, G. F. Richardson, Stonhard, Develo; painting: Fasher Painting & Decorating; lifts: Otis
OPERATOR	Marriott Corporation

NAME	Sterling Hotel Heathrow (The Heathrow Hilton)
ADDRESS	Terminal 4, Heathrow Airport, Hounslow, Middlesex TW6 3AF, UK. Tel. 081 759 7755 Fax 081 759 7579
ROOMS/FACILITIES	397 rooms, 3 restaurants, atrium bar, conference hall, 12 conference rooms, business centre, health club, swimming pool, 3 shops
COMPLETION	1990
CLIENT	BAA Hotels
ARCHITECTURE	Manser Associates, Jonathan Manser
INTERIOR DESIGN	Manser Associates, Peter Glynn-Smith Associates
SUB-CONTRACTORS/ SUPPLIERS	Construction: Higgs & Hill; steel construction: Worldwork, Surrey Steel Buildings; structural engineering: YRM Anthony Hunt Associates; technical engineering: F. C. Foreman & Partners; kitchen planning: CDS Associates; acoustics: Hann Tucker Associates; landscaping: John Brooks; lighting: DPA Lighting Consultants; glazing: Exterior Profiles, Straeker, Casealey; roof: Robseal Roofing; lifts: Fujitec; electrics: N. G. Bailey & Co.; bathrooms: Hosby; furniture: Atrium Ramm Contract Furniture, Cadsana; wall and floor tiling: Tiling Co.; floor coverings: Quickwood, Tyndale Carpets; wall coverings: Helen Sheane Wallcoverings; painting: Wakes Decorating; swimming pool: Penguin
OPERATOR	BAA Hotels

NAME	The Island Shangri-La
ADDRESS	Pacific Place, Supreme Court Road, Central, Hong Kong. Tel. 877 3838 Fax 521 8742
ROOMS/FACILITIES	531 rooms, 34 suites, 5 restaurants (Petrus, Nadaman, Summer Palace, Island Café, Lobster Bar), Cyrano bar, 2 lounges, ballroom, 9 conference rooms, swimming pool with cocktail bar, health club, sauna with steam bath, shopping mall
COMPLETION	1991
CLIENT	Swire Properties
ARCHITECTURE	Wong & Ouyang
INTERIOR DESIGN	Leese Robertson Freeman Designers
SUB-CONTRACTORS/ SUPPLIERS	Lighting design: Corbett Design; art consultancy: Sandra Walter; sanitation: Toto Kiki, BSC; lighting: Hop Shing Loong Lamps, Ricardo Lighting, E. Bakalovits Söhne; wall coverings/fitted furniture: Entasis, Cetec, St John Bosco Trust, Decca Ltd, Hong Kong Teakwood Works, Kuen Lee Interior Decoration, Kangotic Decoration; floor coverings: Taiping, Waly Decorative Products, Perfect Marble Company, Aconci & Sons; fabrics: Markasia, T Adair & Sons
OPERATOR	Shangri-La International

NAME Hyatt Regency La Jolla

ADDRESS 3777 La Jolla Village Drive, San Diego, CA 92122, USA.
Tel. 619 552 1234
Fax 619 552 6066

ROOMS/FACILITIES 400 rooms and suites, Barcino restaurant, Café Japenco, lobby bar, Michael's Lounge, ballroom, 16 conference rooms, 12 meeting rooms, swimming pool, health club with spa, badminton, squash

COMPLETION Hotel: 1989; the whole Aventine complex: 1990

CLIENT Jack Naiman, The Naiman Company, Aventine Partners

ARCHITECTURE Michael Graves; Langdon Wilson Mumper Architects

INTERIOR DESIGN Michael Graves; Wilson & Associates

SUB-CONTRACTORS/ SUPPLIERS General contractor: Neilson Construction Company; art: Gavin Hamilton, Bertel Alberto Thorwaldsen; decorative painting: Ora B. Hopper and Son; lighting design: Wheel Gersztoff Friedman Associates, Focus Lighting; furniture: Stuart-Clark; floor coverings: Couristan Carpets

OPERATOR Hyatt Hotels & Resorts

NAME Maritim Hotel

ADDRESS Heumarkt 20, 5000 Cologne 1, Germany.
Tel. 221 20270
Fax 221 2027826

ROOMS/FACILITIES 454 rooms and suites, 4 restaurants, piano bar, 2 function rooms, 23 conference rooms, swimming pool, steam bath and sauna, shops

COMPLETION 1990

CLIENT Maritim Hotelgesellschaft

ARCHITECTURE Gottfried Böhm; Kraemer Sieverts & Partner; Stefan Schmitz

INTERIOR DESIGN Reinhardt & Sander; Franjo Pooth; Elisabeth Böhm

SUB-CONTRACTORS/ SUPPLIERS Décor: Bolko; sanitation: Hüppe, Villeroy & Boch; lighting: Erco, Staff; furniture: Wollenweber, Lauser; floor coverings: Desso; carpets: Tescoa; lifts: Otis; garden layout: Forster

OPERATOR Maritim Hotelgesellschaft

NAME Hyatt Regency Roissy

ADDRESS Avenue du Bois de la Pie, F-95913 Roissy Charles de Gaulle, Paris, France.
Tel. 1 4817 1234
Fax 1 4863 0081

ROOMS/FACILITIES 388 rooms and suites, restaurant, lounge bar, entertainment centre, ballroom, conference hall, 9 conference rooms, business centre, swimming pool with bar, fitness centre, sauna

COMPLETION 1992

CLIENT Foncière Hôtelière de Roissy

ARCHITECTURE Murphy/Jahn Architects; Jean-Marie Charpentier

INTERIOR DESIGN Hirsch Bedner & Associates

SUB-CONTRACTORS/ SUPPLIERS Construction: Société Auxiliaire d'Entreprises de la Région Parisienne; steel construction: Les Charpentiers de Paris; roof: Hoogovens Aluminium, Kal Zip; façade: Alucobond, AMCC; glass constructions: Verrières Zénith, Super Sky; landscaping: Peter Walker & Partners; lighting design: PHA Lighting Design; lifts: KONE

OPERATOR Hyatt International Hotels

NAME Grand Hotel Esplanade

ADDRESS Lützowufer 15, 1000 Berlin 30, Germany.
Tel. 30 261011
Fax 30 2629121

ROOMS/FACILITIES 369 rooms, 16 penthouse rooms, 10 suites, 5 business suites, presidential suite, Harlekin and Orangerie restaurants, 2 bars, ballroom, 5 conference rooms, swimming pool with bar, whirlpool, 3 saunas, shops

COMPLETION 1988

CLIENT Grundstücksgesellschaft am Lützowufer & Co. Hotel KG, Dieter Hauert/Dietmar Otremba

ARCHITECTURE Jürgen J. Sawade

INTERIOR DESIGN Johanne and Gernot Nalbach

SUB-CONTRACTORS/ SUPPLIERS Lighting design: Christian Bartenbach

OPERATOR Grand Hotel Esplanade GmbH & Co. Betriebs KG

NAME Grand Hyatt Hong Kong

ADDRESS 1 Harbour Road, Wanchai, Hong Kong.
Tel. 588 1234
Fax 802 0677

ROOMS/FACILITIES 540 rooms, 22 exclusive suites, 11 speciality suites, 2 presidential suites, 6 restaurants (One Harbour Road, Grissini, Tiffin, Grand Café, Cascades, JJ's), Champagne bar, entertainment centre, ballroom, 4 function rooms, 7 conference rooms, business centre, bathing landscape, separate "Regency Club" pool, tennis courts, golf driving range and putting green, fitness centre, sauna, shops

COMPLETION 1989

CLIENT Polytown Co., New World Development Co.

ARCHITECTURE Ng Chun Man & Associates

INTERIOR DESIGN Hirsch/Bedner & Associates

SUB-CONTRACTORS/ SUPPLIERS Construction: Hip Hing Construction; steel construction: Chung Wah; façade technique: Builder's Federal/URC; technical engineering: Honeywell; technical planning: Parsons Brinkerhoff; landscaping: Belt. Collins & Associates; acoustics: Arup Acoustics; art consultancy: Art Guild International; lighting: Lightsource; electrical engineering: Trident Engineering; fitted furniture: HK Teakwood; furniture: William Switzer Donghia, Kentfull; interior fittings/decoration elements/bathrooms: BSC, ANOK; bathroom fittings: Dornbracht; wall coverings: Chunwall International; granite: Marmi Formigari; floor coverings: Tsen Wui,

Taiping; iron goods: Dorma; swimming pool: P & A Engineering; lifts: Schindler

OPERATOR Hyatt International Hotels

NAME Hyatt Regency Waikoloa

ADDRESS One Waikoloa Beach Resort, Big Island of Hawaii 96743, USA.
Tel. 808 885 1234
Fax 808 885 7592

ROOMS/FACILITIES 1,741 rooms and suites in three building complexes, 6 restaurants (Cascades, Donatoni's, Imari, Water's Edge, Orchid Café, Kona Provision Co), 6 snack and cocktail bars, disco, ballroom, 18 function rooms, several swimming pools with cascades and chutes, Anara health club with saunas and steam baths, 8 tennis courts, golf course, shops, tropical landscape garden with exotic fauna, museum trail, artificial lagoon, tubular tram system, passenger boats

COMPLETION 1988

CLIENT Transcontinental Development Company; the Bass Family of Fort Worth Texas, Hyatt Corporation, KG Hawaii Corp., TSA International Limited, Hemmeter Investment Corporation

ARCHITECTURE Lawton & Umemura Architects

INTERIOR DESIGN Hirsch/Bedner & Associates

SUB-CONTRACTORS/ SUPPLIERS Landscaping: Tongg, Clarke & Mechler; water planning: Howard Fields & Associates

OPERATOR Hyatt Hotels Corporation

NAME Sheraton Mirage

ADDRESS P.O. Box 172, Port Douglas, Queensland 4871, Australia.
Tel. 070 995888
Fax 070 005885

ROOMS/FACILITIES 300 rooms and suites; guest villas with 2 to 4 bedrooms, 3 restaurants (Macrossans, The Coffee Shop, Lagoon Bar), Daintree Lounge bar, ballroom, 3 conference rooms, shopping arcade, lagoon, pools, "Mirage Country Club", fitness room, bar and restaurant, 18-hole golfcourse, 9 tennis courts, "Marina Mirage" with 40 shops, 5 restaurants and snack bars

COMPLETION 1987

CLIENT Quintex Group, Christopher Skase

ARCHITECTURE Desmond Brooks International, Media Five

INTERIOR DESIGN Barry Peters

SUB-CONTRACTORS/ SUPPLIERS Interior planning/lighting design: Desmond Brooks International

OPERATOR Sheraton ITT

NAME The Mirage

ADDRESS 3400 Las Vegas Boulevard South, Las Vegas, Nevada 89193, USA.
Tel. 702 791 7111

ROOMS/FACILITIES 3,054 rooms and suites, 8 apartments, 6 bungalows with private swimming pools, 5 restaurants, coffee shop, snack bar, ice cream parlour, casino, Theatre Mirage hall with 1,500 seats, 2 ballrooms, 12 function rooms, bathing landscape with cascades, lagoons and grottos, tennis courts, fitness centre with sauna, "The Esplanade" shopping centre, deep sea aquarium, atrium with tropical rain forest, enclosure with white tigers, dolphin pool

COMPLETION 1989

CLIENT Golden Nugget Inc.; Stephen A. Wynn

ARCHITECTURE Joel David Bergman/Atlandia Design

INTERIOR DESIGN Roger P. Thomas/Atlandia Design

SUB-CONTRACTORS/ SUPPLIERS Lighting: Primier Chandelier; Algert Lighting; interior fittings: Henry Conversano & Associates; furniture: Shelby Williams, A. Rudin, Luciano Antiques; Venaman; Nodsmiths, Gasser, floor coverings: Catello Tile & Marble, Couristan Carpets, Milliken Carpets; wall coverings: Silk Dynasty, Sellars & Josephson; Newcastle, Kneedler Fauchere, Jen Jen; fabrics: Manuel Canovas, Brunschwig & Fils; Scalamandre, Glant, Clarence House, First Editions, Design Tex, Blau, accessories: Now & Zen, Wild Card, Luciano Antiques, Golden Bo-Tree

OPERATOR Mirage Resorts Incorporated

NAME The Disney World Swan

ADDRESS 1200 Epcot Resort Boulevard, Lake Buena Vista, Florida 32830, USA.
Tel. 407 934 3000
Fax 407 934 4499

ROOMS/FACILITIES 758 rooms and suites, 5 restaurants (Palio, Garden Grove Café, Kimonos, Splash Grill, Lobby Court Lounge), ballroom, 31 function rooms, 6 business suites, conference rooms, swimming area (shared with the Dolphin Hotel), fitness centre, shops

COMPLETION 1989

CLIENT Walt Disney Productions; Tishman Realty & Construction Co.; Aoki Corporation, Metropolitan Life Insurance

ARCHITECTURE Michael Graves; Alan Lapidus

INTERIOR DESIGN Michael Graves, Patrick Burke

SUB-CONTRACTORS/ SUPPLIERS General management: Aoki Corporation; structural engineering: DeSimone, Chaplin & Associates; engineering: Lehr Associates; landscaping: Herbert Halback Inc.; lighting design: Fiorentino Associates; interior appointments: Wilson & Associates; murals: Anita Rosskam, Maer-Murphy Inc., Robert Braun; acoustics: Cerami & Associates; water planning: William Hobbs; tents: Future Tent Mintec

OPERATOR Westin Hotels & Resorts

NAME The Disney World Dolphin

ADDRESS 1500 Epcot Resort Boulevard, Lake Buena Vista,

Florida 32830, USA.
Tel. 407 934 4000
Fax 407 934 4099

ROOMS/FACILITIES 1,510 rooms and suites, 7 restaurants (Sum Chows, Harry's Safari Bar & Grill, Coral Café, Tubbi Checkers, Carnevale, Dolphin Fountain, Cabana Grille), 4 bars, ballroom, 29 function rooms, conference hall, exhibition hall, business centre, "Camp Dolphin" children's day centre, swimming area and lagoon (shared with the Swan Hotel), fitness centre, 8 tennis courts, shops

COMPLETION 1990

CLIENT Walt Disney Productions; Tishman Realty and Construction Co.; Aoki Corporation, Metropolitan Life Insurance

ARCHITECTURE Michael Graves; Alan Lapidus

INTERIOR DESIGN Michael Graves, Patrick Burke

SUB-CONTRACTORS/ SUPPLIERS General management: Aoki Corporation; structural engineering: DeSimone, Chaplin & Associates; technical engineering: Lehr Associates; landscaping: Herbert Halback Inc.; interior appointments: Wilson & Associates; furniture: Heritage, Adelta; floor coverings: Brintons

OPERATOR ITT Sheraton

NAME The Helmsley Centre

ADDRESS Miami, Florida, USA.

ROOMS/FACILITIES Apartment, shopping and hotel complex with marina, various pools

PLANNING PERIOD 1981

ARCHITECTURE Arquitectonica

NAME Congress Hotel

ADDRESS Agadir, Morocco.

ROOMS/FACILITIES Royal suite, auditoria, galleries and restaurants

COMPLETION Project

ARCHITECTURE Rem Koolhaas/O.M.A. (Office for Metropolitan Architecture)

254

NAME Intercity Hotel

ADDRESS Kantstr. 8–11, 1000 Berlin 12, Germany.

ROOMS/FACILITIES 305 rooms, restaurant, bar, 4 conference rooms, row of shops with café, customer centre of German Federal Railway

PLANNING PERIOD 1988–1993

CLIENT Intercity Hotel GmbH; VdeR;

ARCHITECTURE Georg Ritschl

OPERATOR Intercity Hotel GmbH

NAME Kempinski Airport Hotel

ADDRESS Flughafen München II, Erding, Germany.

ROOMS/FACILITIES 389 rooms and suites, bistro, gourmet restaurant, 2 bars, ballroom, 10 conference rooms, business centre, swimming pool, fitness centre

COMPLETION 1994

CLIENT Flughafen München GmbH

ARCHITECTURE Murphy/Jahn Architects

INTERIOR DESIGN Jan Wichers

SUB-CONTRACTORS/ SUPPLIERS Structural engineering: Cronauer, Schlaich Bergermann & Partner; engineering: Kühn Lehr; landscaping: Peter Walker, Gottfried Hansjakob; lighting design: Francis Krahe; furniture: Cassina

OPERATOR Kempinski AG

NAME Billie Strauss

ADDRESS Project c/o Galerie Billie Strauss, Werfmershalde 16, 7000 Stuttgart, Germany. Tel. 711 283808

ROOMS/FACILITIES 20 rooms, hotel bar, lobby

COMPLETION Project scheduled for 1993

CLIENT Bachofer-Strauss-Strauss GBR

ARCHITECTURE Zaha M. Hadid with Patrik Schumacher; overall planning: Manfred Strauss

INTERIOR DESIGN Zaha M. Hadid

NAME Spreehotel Treptow

ADDRESS D-1000 Berlin, Germany.

ROOMS/FACILITIES 256 rooms, restaurant, function hall, conference rooms

PLANNING PERIOD 1990–

CLIENT Erbengemeinschaft Gadegast

ARCHITECTURE Gottfried Böhm, Jürgen von Kietzell

NAME The Ocean

ADDRESS Chikura, Chiba, Japan.

ROOMS/FACILITIES 48 rooms and suites, restaurant, bar, coffee shop, function rooms, beach terrace, fitness centre, roof terrace with pool

PLANNING PERIOD 1990–1992

ARCHITECTURE Aldo Rossi, Morris Adjmi

NAME Central Court

ADDRESS Centre of Kuala Lumpur, Malaysia.

ROOMS/FACILITIES Hotel with 70 rooms, shopping centre, restaurants, piazza

COMPLETION Project

CLIENT Central Court Development Corporation, Kuala Lumpur

ARCHITECTURE Sottsass Associati/Ettore Sottsass with Johanna Grawunder; contact architect: Zainal Teh

---

NAME Gartenhotel Altmannsdorf

ADDRESS Hoffingergasse 26-28, 1030 Vienna, Austria.

ROOMS/FACILITIES 50 rooms, restaurant, conservatory, conference rooms, fitness centre, sauna

PLANNING PERIOD 1988–1990

CLIENT Merkur Hotel Gesellschaft

ARCHITECTURE Coop Himmelblau

INTERIOR DESIGN Coop Himmelblau

SUB-CONTRACTORS/ SUPPLIERS Construction: Uniprojekt

PHOTOGRAPHIC CREDITS

The authors and publishers wish to thank the following photographers for the illustrations they made available:

Ardiles-Arce, Jaime (Atlanta Marriott Marquis, the Portman); Boissière, Olivier (Hauterive); Brooke, Steven (Swan/Dolphin); Brunetti, Federico (Spadari); Bryant, Richard/Arcaid (the Royalton, Sterling Heathrow); César, Robert/Archipress (Le Cheval Blanc); Couturier, S./Archipress (Hauterive, Les Thermes); Ferrer, Emilio Rodriguez (Havana); Frahm, Klaus (Grand Hotel Esplanade, Art Hotel Sorat); Gaertner, Rainer (Wasserturm); Giger, Claude (Teufelhof); Hahne, Eberhard (L'Atelier sul Mare); Hewitt, David/Anne Garrison (Grand Hyatt La Jolla); Leistner, Dieter (Maritim); Limberger, Bernd (Grand Hyatt Hong Kong); Meyer, Peter Moody (Cour des Loges, Hyatt Regency Waikoloa); Nacása and Partners (Il Palazzo); Neumann, Horst (Claris); Obliers, Dirk (Pflaums Posthotel); Prandini, Ezio (The Halkin); Raebiger, Harald (Los Seises); Renson (Kelly's); Riehle, Tomas (Rolandsburg); Schaewen, Deidi von (La Villa, Le Lac, Morgans, Wasserturm, Montalembert, The Royalton); Schott, Franziska & Marco Schibig (Furkablick); Schwager, Wolfgang (Wasserturm, New Siru); Siegelmann, Lisa (Sheraton Mirage); Vack, Tom (The Paramount); Valentine-Hames, E. (Marittimo); Warchol, Paul (Dreamland Heights)

Thanks are also due to the following hotels for providing pictorial material:

D-Hotel, Osaka; The Halkin, London; L'Imperial, Annecy; The Paramount, New York; La Pergolese, Paris; The Portman, San Francisco; Rolandsburg, Düsseldorf; The Royalton, New York; Spadari, Milan; Teufelhof, Basel; Triton, San Francisco